GOOD GOVERNANCE

Good Governance

Concept and Context

HENK ADDINK

OXFORD
UNIVERSITY PRESS

OXFORD
UNIVERSITY PRESS

Great Clarendon Street, Oxford, OX2 6DP,
United Kingdom

Oxford University Press is a department of the University of Oxford.
It furthers the University's objective of excellence in research, scholarship,
and education by publishing worldwide. Oxford is a registered trade mark of
Oxford University Press in the UK and in certain other countries

First Edition published in 2019

Impression: 2

Published in the United States of America by Oxford University Press
198 Madison Avenue, New York, NY 10016, United States of America

British Library Cataloguing in Publication Data
Data available

Library of Congress Control Number: 2018967700

ISBN 978–0–19–884115–9

Printed and bound by
CPI Group (UK) Ltd, Croydon, CR0 4YY

This book is for Julia

Preface

This book deals with good governance, and more specifically with its concept and context. The last decades have witnessed the emergence of many principles of good governance. These principles function in different contexts and their manifestations are often as different as the contexts themselves. To comprehend this hotchpotch of principles, the overarching idea of good governance is explained in this book. What is good governance as a concept and how does it relate to the rule of law and democracy? Thereby, six particular principles are articulated as the core principles of good governance: properness, transparency, participation, effectiveness, accountability, and human rights. These six principles are understood as the substantive core of good governance, although different jurisdictions can assign different formal names to these principles.

In this book, it is argued that good governance has risen as a third dominant concept in the modern state. Alongside the rule of law and democracy, good governance is becoming increasingly important for the legitimacy of state authorities, as the former predominant function of the nation state gradually declines. However, good governance is also used in nongovernmental contexts, and this is briefly mentioned over the course of the eighteen chapters. This book remains primarily concerned with the state and its relationship with the citizens, but also its relevance for good governance on a regional and international level.

The book consists of three parts. The first part explores good governance from a rather abstract perspective in which general aspects of good governance are elaborated upon, such as the concept of good governance, the multilevel developments (national, regional, and international), and the conceptual links between good governance and the rule of law and democracy. The second part is focused on an in-depth analysis of the six individual principles of good governance, based on four criteria: the developments, the concept, the institutions involved, and the sources. The third part deals with the application of the principles of good governance on the national level. In this part, we give a description of their application in each region, as well as country by country, using the same structure and with a strong focus on the countries of the European Union. Similarly, we also look at three countries in other regions of the world: Australia, Canada, and South Africa. It is my hope and expectation that professionals and students will profit from the work presented here, so that good governance becomes properly consolidated in law and governance.

In preparing this book I have benefited from the support of many colleagues and friends, too numerous to mention here. My thanks go to Paul Craig who stimulated my interest in this area and has been a steadfast supporter of this project and a constant source of inspiration. I am grateful to (former) Dean Timothy Endicott and the Faculty of Law of Oxford University for hosting me and giving me the opportunity to spend long hours in the library and have discussions with several staff members. Special thanks also go to my colleagues, including (former) (vice)deans Henk Kummeling and Ige Dekker, here at the Faculty of Law, Economics and Governance of Utrecht University, who made this study possible and with many of whom I have had interesting discussions.

I also want to thank the members of the 'good governance research group' for their inspiring discussions on the topic. PhD studies by members of this group have been published or are on the way to publication: 'Good Governance and Enforcement, the Principle of Transparency', 'Good Governance and Public Contracts, the Principle of

Effectiveness', 'Ombudsman and Good Governance, the Principle of Participation', 'Principles of Good Governance and Public Procurement', 'Good Governance and Integrity and Principles of Good Supervision'.

I am very grateful for the help from several students of the course Principles of Good Governance and student assistants and especially from Ms Mariette van der Tol and Mr George Necsa-Damacus. Many thanks also to Julia for being there and bearing with me when writing this book.

Henk Addink
October 2018

Contents

Table of Cases

UNITED KINGDOM

EUROPEAN UNION

European Court of Justice

Court of First Instance

INTERNATIONAL

Australia

Canada

East African Court of Justice

Tables of Legislation, Treaties, and Conventions

UK STATUTES

OTHER NATIONAL LEGISLATION

Australia

Austria

Canada

Finland

Germany

Greece

EUROPEAN LEGISLATION

European Directives

European Regulations

European Decisions

INTERNATIONAL INSTRUMENTS

List of Abbreviations

AAR	Annual Activity Report
ACER	Agency for Cooperation of Energy Regulations
ACP	African, Caribbean, and Pacific
ACT	advance corporation tax
ADR	alternative dispute resolution
AMPs	annual management plans
APS	Annual Policy Strategy
art	article
arts	articles
CAP	Common Agricultural Policy
CCP	Common Commercial Policy
CEEP	European Centre of Enterprises with Public Participation and of Enterprises of General Economic Interest
CEN	European Committee for Standardization
CF	Cohesion Fund
CFSP	Common Foreign and Security Policy
CHR	European Commission on Human Rights
CLWP	Commission's Legislative and Work Programme
CRD	comment response document
CSDP	Common Security and Defence Policy
CT	Constitutional Treaty
DAC	OECD's Development Assistance Committee
DCFR	Draft Common Frame of Reference
DG	directorate-general
EACI	Executive Agency for Competitiveness and Innovation
EBA	European Banking Authority
EC	European Community
ECB	European Central Bank
ECHR	European Convention on Human Rights
ECJ	European Court of Justice
ECSC	European Coal and Steel Community
ECtHR	European Court of Human Rights
EDA	European Defence Agency
EEAS	European External Action Service
EPC	European Political Community
ESC	European Social Charter
EU	European Union
Europol	European Police Office
FAC	Foreign Affairs Council
FRA	Fundamental Rights Agency
Frontex	European Agency for Management of Operational Cooperation at External Borders
GAC	General Affairs Council
GAERC	General Affairs and External Relations Council
GALA	General Administrative Law Act (the Netherlands)
GDP	gross domestic product
IACHR	Inter American Court on Human Rights
ICCPR	International Covenant on Civil and Political Rights

ICESCR	International Covenant on Economic, Social and Cultural Rights
IGC	Intergovernmental conference
IMF	International Monetary Fund
IPM	Interactive Policy Making
LGAC	Legislative and General Affairs Council
MEP	Member of the European Parliament
NAPs	national action plans
NCAs	national competition authorities
NGO	non-governmental organization
NSRF	National Strategic Reference Framework
OECD	Organisation for Economic Co-operation and Development
OEEC	Organisation for European Economic Co-operation
OLAF	European Anti-Fraud Office
OMC	Open Method of Co-ordination
PECL	Principles of European Contract Law
PSC	Political and Security Committee
QMV	qualified majority voting
SEA	Single European Act 1986
TEU	Treaty on European Union
TFEU	Treaty on the Functioning of the European Union
TFRA	Task Force for Administrative Reform
UDHR	Universal Declaration of Human Rights
UNDP	United Nations Development Programme
WTO	World Trade Organization

PART I

DEVELOPING THE CONCEPT OF GOOD GOVERNANCE

1

Good Governance

An Introduction

Good governance is a concept used not only by lawyers but also by politicians and, more generally, the public at large. Theologians, philosophers, social scientists, economists, and lawyers all have different perspectives on good governance. For example, a lawyer may naturally be led to describe it as part of a legal system, usually used to construct a legal rule of a given wish or aspiration. A legal principle makes sense only if a connection can be established with such a system and an adequate concept of law.[1] In that concept, each discipline has its own dimension to contribute, and if different dimensions are brought together, they might create a complete approach to good governance, bringing the greatest possible benefits to society. In a more interdisciplinary approach with a legal, social science, and economic perspective, there are common questions about the functioning of the government and citizens' protection against abuse by the government. The questions are related to the type, distribution, and application of policy instruments, and to the supervision, control, and legal protection in relation to this application.[2] This entire approach of good governance can improve the quality of the government, since the government should prevent maladministration and minimize corruption.

Governance concerns a state's ability to serve its citizens. It involves the rules, processes, and behaviours whereby interests are articulated, resources are managed, and power is exercised in society. Despite its open and broad character, governance relates to the very basic aspects of the functioning of society and its political and social systems. It is described as a basic measure of a society's stability and performance. As this society develops a more sophisticated political system, governance evolves into the notion of good governance.[3]

1. Good Governance: A Cornerstone of the Modern State

The concepts of the rule of law, democracy, and good governance are the cornerstones of the modern state. These cornerstones make up the structure of the state and its institutions, the position of the governmental institutions and the citizens, and the norms for the relationship between the government and the citizens. These are partly overlapping concepts but the distinctive elements can be identified. The rule of law starts with the idea of the legal base of government actions and the need for protection of citizens' fundamental rights. Democracy gives the rule of law depth and especially concerns transparency and participation of the citizens. Good governance is not only about the further development of the rule of law and democracy but it also includes

[1] Hart 1997. [2] Addink 2010a, ch 5; Addink 2013.

[3] European Commission, *Communication on Governance and Development*, October 2003, COM (2003) 615; Boustra 2010.

the elements of accountability and efficiency of the government. These elements are sometimes qualified as elements of the social 'rechtsstaat', but then the conceptual legal character is underestimated.[4] Good governance is significant because it is both a norm for the government and a citizen's right. This justifies good governance as a genuine third cornerstone.

The development of these notions started at different moments in history and has often been linked to a state's level of development. The first principle was the rule of law and the second was democracy. Both were to become major elements of the liberal state. Intertwined with them, aspects of good governance developed into the third vital dimension of the state. Rather than developing separately, good governance thus developed in a process of mutual influence. This process is still evolving.

The modern state thus has three pillars: the rule of law, democracy, and good governance. The three concepts—sometimes qualified as abstract principles—are all fundamental notions that have been accepted in most of the world's modern states. Although their interpretations may differ from one country to another—often due to differences in economic and cultural factors—there is a national core in each state from which the principles evolved.

The rule of law holds that law conditions a government's exercise of power only, and that the state's subjects shall not be exposed to any arbitrary will of the rulers. Furthermore, rights are protected by law. Two major traditions exist in the Western world, which can be distinguished as the common law traditions on the one hand and the civil law traditions on the other. They are attached to different interpretations of the rule of law. The common law countries usually adhere to a narrow or thin conception of the rule of law, known simply as the rule of law. In the civil law traditions, a broader or thicker conception is upheld, known as *rechtsstaat, l'Etat de droit*, and *Stato del diritto.*[5] The 'thin' conception is mainly concerned with principles of procedural fairness, whereas the 'thick' conception embraces substantive criteria and universal principles or values in which there is a need for a calculable, norm-based state action.[6] Elements of the *rechtsstaat* are first, legality; second, division, separation, and balance of powers; third, protection of fundamental rights; and finally judicial control.[7] In addition to the three classical powers (the legislator, the executive, and the judiciary), there is growing attention towards the controlling 'fourth power', such as the Ombudsman or the Court of Audit.[8] In spite of these different conceptions, a strong consensus however exists on the rule of law as a fundamental concept.

Democracy is about the influence of the people on the policies and the activities of the government. A distinction could be made between direct and representative democracy. In a direct democracy, the people can influence politics directly. In a representative democracy, the people regularly elect representatives who represent the people's interest and defend the citizen's rights. In the literature, a study has been made about unitary, self-correcting democracy, as developed by Dicey concerning pluralist democracy.[9] The role of the government in a pluralist democracy is to protect and promote diversity. This theory deems human nature selfish and acquisitive, and can be traced back to the United States. Based on this, new ideas have been developed and critical remarks have been made on constitutional reform and democracy in the United Kingdom and on participatory democracy.[10] The following components are seen as the

4 Schlössels and Zijlstra 2017, 25.
5 Urbina 2002, ch 4, 225–43. Note: the Rule of Law cannot aptly be translated into French.
6 Neumann 2002, 6–20.
7 Burkens and others 2017, ch 3.
8 Addink 2005a, 251–73.
9 Dicey 1959, 339–40.
10 Craig 1990, chs 2–4, 7, and 11.

most important elements of democracy: legislation by parliament, ministerial accountability to the parliament, transparency of administration, participation for interested parties, and protection of minorities.[11] Although there is not yet a specific, universally accepted, definition of democracy, equality and fundamental freedoms are at least identified as important characteristics of it. All citizens should be equal before the law, and all should have equal access to power. In a representative democracy, every vote has equal weight. In principle, no restrictions may apply to anyone who aspires to become a representative. Legitimized rights and liberties legally guarantee the freedom of citizens. The notion of representative democracy has arisen largely from ideas and institutions that developed during the European Middle Ages, the Age of Enlightenment, and in the American and French revolutions. Democracy has been called 'the last form of government' and has spread across the globe in the last century.

Good governance is a norm for the government and a citizen's right. Within the concept of good governance, more specific conditions have been formulated. These norms are sometimes linked to the norms of rule of law and democracy, but mostly they have their own contents. Aspects of good governance are properness, transparency, participation, effectiveness, accountability, and economic, social, and cultural human rights. These elements have developed into universal elements of good governance, although other norms or differing terminology might be found in practice as well, but these are accepted across cultures or are applicable across the board. These six basic elements of good governance have been found to be the hard core of the concept. An example could be the specification or restriction of the application of the principles of good governance to the field of administration. In the broader perception, the principles of good governance apply to all the powers of the state. Later in this book, a distinction will be made between principles of good governance and principles of good administration. In short, the broad conception of good governance can be specified according to the three types of state powers. It is about principles of good legislation for the legislator; principles of good administration for the administration; and principles of good judicial procedures for the judiciary.[12] In the context of administration, two groups of principles have been joined: the principles of good regulation and the principles of better regulation. Some of the principles are also being used in the field of corporate and private law. Here we prefer to use principles of good governance in the context of the government, and principles of corporate governance in the context of companies.

2. Good Governance and Law

Good governance has to be described as part of the legal system to label the principles of good governance as legal principles. In the context of the more extensive juridification of society, the legal appearance of the principles is becoming more and more important. Therefore, it is interesting to make this connection between good governance and law and to formulate an adequate concept of good governance law. However, this makes sense only if a connection can be made between such a system and an adequate concept of law, because then we can speak about principles of good governance as legal principles.

The concept of a legal system requires a further specification, which contains norms and enforcement. The perspective chosen here primarily focuses on good governance

[11] Van Wijk, Konijnenbelt, and Van Male 2005, 42; Konijnenbelt and Van Male 2014, 42.

[12] Addink 2005.

as a part of different legal orders, like domestic, regional, and the international legal order. The European order receives special attention. It should be realized that any legal regime has its own intellectual and ideological foundations, and good governance is no different. The ideas behind good governance must be made concrete as elements of a legal system according to the applicable secondary rules so that they can be recognized as legal principles of good governance. There is usually a close relationship between political ideas and their translation into legal substance. There are many bridges between law, ethics, and morality, and therefore it remains important to distinguish the philosophical ideal from the legal thought. At the same time, it is important not to lose sight of the ideological foundations of good governance. The very idea of good governance presupposes a certain concept of government and its relations with individual citizens. Naturally, it includes the evolvement of thinking from government to governance.

Three steps have to be taken from the legal concept to the legal positivism of good governance: identification of the principles, their development as legal norms, and enforcement of those norms.[13]

The first step—identification—can be done by either a top-down or a bottom-up approach. First, the top-down approach concerns the international and regional (ie European) levels. Those who can legitimately initiate a process of norm creation at the international and the regional (eg European) level must agree on the operationalized aspects of good governance. In that context, it is relevant to realize that there may exist limitations and restrictions on the national level. From the bottom-up approach, there are inherently existing limitations to state power. State entities have been charged with a certain mandate: to shield the human being from the threats of daily existence. Naturally, that is not the same as the state being an almighty machine, tyrannically controlling everyone under its jurisdiction. As a matter of principle, the state has to limit its actions according to, at least, civil rights, for example, the right to privacy. Responsibilities in the sphere of social and economic rights follow.

The second step concerns the internalization of the thus-defined legal norms in terms of legal commitment. It is about the implementation of international and regional legal norms by developing policy rules and other types of regulations at national level and the process of positivism of the legal norms on good governance. This process of positivism can be achieved in different legal forms and by different governmental institutions. Under the bottom-up approach, on the national level, different aspects of the principles of good governance have to be codified. We can think of codification of the different principles of good governance in general norms but also as the specification of these general principles in other government documents. These norms of good governance should be internalized in governmental actions.

The third step contains the enforcement of legally binding norms, to be guaranteed at the abovementioned levels: international, regional, and national. Choosing which of these levels is appropriate will depend on the contents of the norms and the legal framework. If we take the principles of good governance to be rights, the question consequently and necessarily arises whether these principles should be *enforceable as rights*. This is known as the positivistic approach of good governance.

[13] Tomuchat 2003; Van der Jagt 2006.

3. Good Governance and Human Rights

The implementation of good governance and human rights in general, and economic, social, and cultural rights, to a great extent depends on the substantive principles of good governance. Human rights (and especially the legal provisions protecting these rights at all levels) correspond to or include different principles of good governance.[14] So, in essence, we find the principles of good governance in the discussions about human rights, but often these principles are only recognized as human rights and not as principles of good governance. The topic of the principles of good governance cannot easily be pointed to in the field of human rights, but nevertheless there are strong links. Good governance principles have also been developed by specific human rights, but the underpinning dimension here is that of good governance.

The direct link between good governance and human rights can be illustrated in Table 1.1, which gives an overview of articles in human rights treaties where principles of good governance have been described.

Table 1.1 Articles in human rights treaties where principles of good governance have been described

Treaty	UDHR	ICCPR	ICESCR	ECHR	ESC
Due care		(13)		6(1) (due care)	
Legal certainty			4, 8(1d,2)		
Equality	1, 2	3, 14(1)	Preamble par. 2, 2(2), 3, 7bis	14	20, 27
Public participation	6, 8, 14(1), 21(1,2), 29(1)	6, 9(4,5), 13, 16, 25		5(4), 6(3b-e), 13, EP3	15, 22
Transparency		8, 40			21, 29
Accountability	30	1, 5, 40		19	
Effectiveness	22, 25(1)	2, 3, 17(2), 22(3), 23(4)		5(2,3), 13, 17	
General			Preamble par. 2, 2(3)	1 (shall secure), 2(1) (protected by law)	Part I

A second, relatively new, development in the strong relation between human rights and good governance is the emergence of the subjective right to good administration. Such a right to good administration emerged as a new fundamental right, and it applies to every person coming into contact with governmental institutions and bodies. The right to good administration is included in European Union law. It was already recognized in the Charter of Fundamental Rights of the European Union adopted in 2000 (Nice Charter)[15] and further confirmed in article 6-1 of the Lisbon Charter and is nowadays qualified as the Charter of Fundamental Rights of the European Union.[16]

Article 41 of the Charter states the following with respect to good governance:

[14] Addink 2010a, ch 1.
[15] Kańska 2004, 296–326; Pfeffer 2006; Wakefield 2007; and Classen 2008.
[16] Addink 2012a, 11.

1. Every person has the right to have his or her affairs handled impartially, fairly and within a reasonable time by the institutions and bodies of the Union.
2. This right includes:
   - the right of every person to be heard, before any individual measure which would affect him or her adversely is taken;
   - the right of every person to have access to his or her file, while respecting the legitimate interests of confidentiality and of professional and business secrecy;
   - the obligation of the administration to give reasons for its decisions.
3. Every person has the right to have the Community make good any damage caused by its institutions or by its servants in the performance of their duties, in accordance with the general principles common to the laws of the Member States.
4. Every person may write to the institutions of the Union in one of the languages of the Treaties and must have an answer in the same language.

These provisions show that there is not (yet) a general right to good governance but there is a subjective right to good administration which covers several aspects of good governance. It is probably best to say that some aspects of the principles of good governance have been codified in article 41 of the Charter.[17] The focus is on procedural rights, but there still may be some problems with regard to adopting a more substantive right to good governance, such as the fear of administrative rigidity.

The first paragraph of article 41 formulates a kind of umbrella right, which is given more substance by the requirements regarding the way citizens of the European Union should be treated by the institutions and bodies of the Union. These requirements refer to impartiality, fairness, and decision-making within a reasonable time. Paragraph 2 of the article specifies the obligation to hear an individual citizen when his interest is concerned directly. Such an individual should have access to one's own file and the competent authority is obligated to give sufficient reasons for the decision. Furthermore, under specific circumstances, a right to compensation is granted to individuals who suffer damage because of the European Union's actions. This right is stated in article 340 of the Treaty on the Functioning of the European Union (hereafter TFEU). The article is applicable only in the case of unlawful acts of EU institutions or by the wrongful conduct of EU servants.[18] And finally, everyone has the right to be answered in his or her own language. Interestingly, particularly formal and procedural elements have been laid down in these rules. That is understandable as case law on these procedural issues is relatively well-developed, but the substantive elements of good governance are not to be neglected.[19]

The discussion on the scope of application of article 41 of the Charter epitomizes the more general discussion regarding the interrelation between general principles and Charter rights but also the (problematic) protection of the right to good administration in the EU integrated administrative law system with various input from the national and EU levels.[20] Precisely because article 41 of the Charter defines its scope of application by reference to the *direct* administration of the European Union, its relationship with the principles of good administration and the rights of the defence remains a rather controversial topic.[21] Relevant also is the case law related to article 41, summarized as follows:[22]

[17] Addink 2008. [18] Widdershoven 2007, 319–24. [19] Wakefield 2007.

[20] Mihaescu Evans 2015.

[21] Opinion AG Bobek, 7 September 2017, ECLI:EU:C:2017:650. Case C-298/16 *T and A Ispas v Direcţia Generală a Finanţelor Publice Cluj*.

[22] Ibid.

It is clear that a number of the different 'operative' components placed under the umbrella of the 'right to good administration' by the second paragraph of Article 41 also reflect specific general principles of EU law. Of particular importance in this regard is the general principles of respect for the rights of the defence, including the right to be heard, or the duty to state reasons.

88. It is equally clear that the principle of the protection of the rights of the defence, which is pertinent to the circumstances of the present case, is applicable to Member States when they are acting within the scope of EU law, if national authorities are contemplating the adoption of a measure which will adversely affect the person in question.

89. On the other hand, it is doubtful whether such general principles, such as the rights of the defence in the present case, have exactly the same content as Article 41 of the Charter. For one thing, the explicit limitation in the wording of Article 41 of the Charter impedes, as Advocate General Kokott puts it, its content from simply being 'transposed without more ado to bodies of the Member States, even when they are implementing [EU] law'. On a more conceptual level, doing so would come dangerously close to the circumvention of the explicit provision of Article 41 of the Charter.

90. In the light of this important remark, each of the components of Article 41 has to be carefully and independently considered. This is particularly the case for the right of access to the file, which found its way into the wording of Article 41 as a result of a jurisprudential evolution that itself had its origins in the assessment of the practice of EU institutions in the specific field of competition law.

91. In short, the applicable general principle is the respect for the rights of the defence. Its content with regard to the Member States' application of EU law may differ from the (specific and autonomous) guarantees provided for in Article 41 of the Charter, which are applicable to the direct administration of the EU.

4. Good Governance and the Main Developments

The history of good governance as a phenomenon can be divided roughly into four phases. In the first phase, the focus is on the national level. In the second phase, we see activities of international organizations in relation to the development of the concept of good governance. On the European level this can be distinguished between the contribution of the Council of Europe (the third phase) and the contribution of the European Union (the fourth phase).

In the Netherlands, the first phase started in the 1930s with the development of unwritten principles of law by the judiciary. These principles were focused on the work of the administration and principles of proper administration. That was and still is a rather narrow approach of good governance, especially since to date this concept has been approached from a more formal perspective. Initially, these principles of proper administration were developed for more extreme situations and unacceptable acts by the administration. In following years, these principles were elaborated. In the 1990s, we can find in some countries a process of codification of these norms in general administrative acts. In other countries, for example France, the judiciary developed these principles in the first phase. In countries like Germany,[23] the very general principles have been written down in the constitution.

The international and European developments start at the end of the twentieth century. In the beginning of the 1990s, international organizations in the field of development aid and finance started to develop good governance norms to make sure that financial assistance is properly directed. The IMF, the World Bank, the WTO, the

[23] Schröder 2007.

UNDP, and the OECD were quite active in these fields. Not all international organizations have started with the same topics; global financial organizations have been more focused on macro-economic reform whereas political organizations sought a connection with human rights and the rule of law. It seems like there is now a growing consensus on the specification of good governance norms. Even the international organizations themselves have been reformed because of the need to abide by standards of good governance.

In relation to the developments in Europe, we have to make a distinction between the system of the European Union and the system of the Council of Europe. There are remarkable differences in the field of competences, objectives, and the structure of these organizations.

The Council of Europe was founded after the Second World War to ensure peace in Europe. Originally, it started with ten members and now that number has increased to forty-seven. Its basic aim is to achieve a greater unity between the member states, especially by promoting human rights, parliamentary democracy, and the rule of law. The European Court of Human Rights, the Commissioner for Human Rights, and the European Commission for Democracy through Law (Venice Commission) play important roles independent from but in connection with the Council of Europe. The Council makes recommendations that are not legally binding but in effect are often followed by the member states. In 1996 and in 2018 updated, the Council developed the Handbook 'Administration and You', which gives an overview of basic principles as formally respected in the member states. In 2007, they published the recommendation on Good Administration and a Code in which these principles were codified. The Council of Europe stated:

Recommends that the governments of member states:

- promote good administration within the framework of the principles of the rule of law and democracy;
- promote good administration through the organisation and functioning of public authorities ensuring efficiency, effectiveness and value for money. These principles require that member states:
  - ensure that objectives are set and performance indicators are devised in order to monitor and measure, on a regular basis, the achievement of these objectives by the administration and its public officials;
  - compel public authorities to regularly check, within the remit of the law, whether their services are provided at an appropriate cost and whether they shall be replaced or withdrawn;
  - compel the administration to seek the best means to obtain the best results;
  - conduct appropriate internal and external monitoring of the administration and the action of its public officials;
- promote the right to good administration in the interests of all, by adopting, as appropriate, the standards set out in the model code appended to this recommendation, assuring their effective implementation by the officials of member states and doing whatever may be permissible within the constitutional and legal structure of the state to ensure that regional and local governments adopt the same standards.

The report analyses all the recommendations of the Council of Europe from the perspective of good administration to date. Finally, they have systemized the different standards of good administration in concrete articles.

The European Union (as it is now known) was founded in 1951 with the Treaty of Paris. In this treaty, a European Coals and Steel Community was established by six founding countries: Belgium, the Federal Republic of Germany, France, Italy,

Luxembourg, and the Netherlands. The aim of this treaty was to secure peace between Europe's victorious and vanquished nations and bring them together as equals, cooperating within shared institutions. This aim should be considered in the light of post-war Europe. Some years later, in March 1957, the six countries agreed on the Treaty of Rome. In this second treaty, they decided to constitute a European Economic Community. Custom duties between the six countries were completely abolished in July 1968. Common policies, notably on trade and agriculture, were put in practice during the 1960s. In 1973, 1981, and 1986, many other European countries became members. After the worldwide economic recession in the early 1980s, a wave of 'euro-pessimism' swept through Europe.

The political map of Europe was dramatically changed when the Berlin Wall fell. After the fall, the unification of Germany took place in October 1990. Democracy and the rule of law were introduced in the countries of Central and Eastern Europe as they broke away from the Soviet Union. It must be said that this development was not completely new for all countries. As the Tsarist Empire broke down, some countries (like the Baltic states) tried to build up their independent countries after the model of the Weimar Republic. The Soviet Union itself ceased to exist in December 1991. At that time, the member states were negotiating on the new Treaty of the European Union. This treaty was adopted by the European Council, which is composed of presidents and prime ministers. This landmark event took place in Maastricht in December 1991. The treaty came into force on 1 November 1993. Some areas of intergovernmental cooperation have been added to existing Community structures, which were already integrated.

By then, the EU was on course for its most spectacular ambition yet: creating one single currency, the euro, which was introduced for financial non-cash transactions in 1999. Notes and coins were issued three years later in the twelve countries of the euro area. This area is commonly known as the euro zone. The euro has become a major world currency for payments and reserves alongside the US dollar.

In the meantime, increasing globalization provided Europe with new challenges, although Europeans have profited from globalization as well. New technologies and the increasing use of the internet have transformed economies and have brought social and cultural challenges. In March 2000, the EU adopted the Lisbon strategy. By this strategy, the Union aspires to modernize the European economy and enable it to compete on the world market with other major players, such as the United States and the newly industrializing countries. The Lisbon strategy encourages innovation and business investments and adapts Europe's education systems to meet the needs of the information society. At the same time, unemployment and the rising cost of pensions are putting pressure on national economies, making reform all the more necessary. Voters are increasingly calling on their governments to find practical solutions to these problems.

In the mid-1990s and in 2004, more countries became members of the European Union. In 2009, the Treaty of Lisbon was adopted to make the EU more democratic, more efficient, and increasingly able to address global problems such as climate change with one voice. The European Parliament was provided with more competences, the voting procedures in the Council were changed, and the possibility for a citizens' initiative was created. As to the structure of the EU, a permanent president of the European Council and a new High Representative for Foreign Affairs would be appointed. Further, a new EU diplomatic service was established.

In 1991, the EU Council of Ministers provided a brief description of the contents and the importance of good governance in a resolution on Human Rights, Democracy and Development. The European Court of Justice had already been using the principles of good administration. In July 2001, the Commission published a White Paper on European Governance in which some principles of good administration were further elaborated.[24] In September 2001, the European Parliament adopted a resolution containing the 'Code of Good Administration' in which European Union institutions and bodies, their administrations, and their officials should respect in their relations with the public. This Code was developed by the European Ombudsman, who based the Code on his experiences in relation to cases of bad administration. In December 2000 there was already a Charter of Fundamental Rights of Citizenship—including rights on relations with the administration—proclaimed in Nice. In chapter V on citizens' rights of the Charter, article 41 includes the right to good administration. In 2010, a link between the Lisbon Treaty and the Charter was made, so that it now has a strong legal base which will be further explained in Chapter 3, 'Good Governance and Human Rights'.

Based on these national, European, and international developments on good administration, we can see three general trends. The first trend is that in many countries most of the norms of good governance have been developed by the judiciary first. These controlling institutions are the discoverers and developers of the principles of good governance. But in several fields, these norms have been developed by the legislator, sometimes based on an initiative of the parliament. Finally, some norms were already worked out in the law and have been further developed by the Ombudsman and the Court of Audit. The second trend is that, in most situations, the principles of good governance were first developed as norms for the administration. Later, these norms have been codified as subjective rights for the citizens. The third trend is that these principles of good governance were developed in several groups. The first group is the principles of properness, the second group constitutes the principles of transparency and participation, the third group constitutes the principles of accountability and effectiveness, and the fourth and last group concentrates on human rights. There is an active interaction between these groups. Each group of principles will be elaborated in a separate chapter.

5. Structure of the Three Parts of this Book

The book consists of three parts. Part I deals with general conceptual aspects of good governance, Part II pays attention to the specification by the principles of good governance, and Part III is about the application of the principles of good governance on a national level in the different regions in the world.

In the first part we start—after the introduction—by presenting an overview of the principles of good governance on the three main levels of the legal system: the national, the regional, and the international level. Then we will focus on the national level. In two chapters, the relationship between the rule of law and good governance and between democracy and good governance will be made clear. The conclusion of these chapters is that good governance constitutes the third cornerstone of a modern democratic state. In the following chapter, the question of whether good governance is simply a norm for the administration or whether it also implies a fundamental right

[24] European Commission, *White Paper on European Governance*, July 2001, COM (2001) 428.

for citizens is discussed. The last chapter of Part I concerns the theoretical position of good governance as a principle, a fundamental right, or a value.

The second part of the book further examines the individual elements of good governance, the principles of good governance. The six principles are discussed: properness, transparency, participation, effectiveness, accountability, and human rights. On a very abstract level these principles can be seen as six individual elements of the same general and abstract principle, on a more concrete level there are six distinct principles of law. In this second part, each chapter on good governance follows a comparable structure. This structure facilitates the comparison between the different principles and contributes to a better insight. The first point of interest is why a certain principle has been developed and what the underlying concept of the principle is. Then we look at the way each principle has taken on different forms in different countries. Then which institutions are involved in the development of the principles is outlined. The different sources of the principles are described as well. Whenever possible, concrete legislation and policy rules are brought into the discussion. Finally, how the controlling institution contributes to the further development of the principles of good governance is elaborated upon.

The third part deals with the application of the principles of good governance on a national level in the member states of the European Union but also in states of other continents in the world. In this part we give a description of the application region wise and country by country and according to the same structure. We start with Europe with a strong focus on the countries of the European Union. We give an explanation on the research questions, the normative framework, and the used methodology. Then we will give an overview of the results of the study by distinguishing the following regions of Europe: Northern, Western, Southern, Central, and the United Kingdom and Ireland. Similarly, we are doing it for three countries in other regions of the world: Australia, Canada, and South Africa.

6. Conclusions

In this introduction chapter, we started to position the concept of good governance in relation to the developments of a modern state. In the first phase of the development, the rule of law concept has been developed, in the second phase this concept has been deepened in relation to the concept of democracy. The third phase shows a deepening of the concepts of the rule of law and of democracy in relation to the concept of good governance. That process of deepening the concepts of the rule of law and of democracy takes place in close connection to the concept of good governance. We concluded that good governance can be seen as the third cornerstone of the modern democratic rule of law.

Principles of good governance can only be legal principles when they have been integrated in the legal system and there is legal effect of the application of these principles. That process takes place in three phases of the legal process: in the process of making regulation, the process of implementing regulation, and in the process of controlling and enforcing the regulation by the different controlling institutions. In each of these phases we see the legal consequences of the principles of good governance. These principles are norms which are used by the legislator, the administration, and the controlling institutions like the judiciary. The principles sometimes function as norms for the administration and in other situations as protecting norms for the citizens.

The protection of good governance principles has, in effect, already taken place in the context of human rights. These were mostly not recognized as principles of good governance but as the implementation of social, cultural, and political rights of citizens. We find these principles of good governance in different international human rights treaties and regulations. The conclusion is that the field of human rights already has operationalized the principles of good governance in regulations and in the human rights case law.

In a short description of the main developments of principles of good governance, we see already a broad scale of national, European, and international principles of good governance. In constitutions, laws, regulations, and policy rules we find these principles already specified. Also, from the European level there is a strong influence on the national level for the development of the principles of good governance. We concluded with the importance of the recommendations of the Council of Europe and the specification of principles of good governance on the European Union level. Finally, the international level is also an important source of principles of good governance.

2

An Overview of Good Governance

In this chapter, an overview of the different aspects of good governance is presented. The need for good governance is explained and the specific concept and development of good governance is elaborated upon. Subsequently, the relevant institutions and the different sources of good governance are discussed.

1. Need for Good Governance

The concept and the specification of the principles of good governance have been developed at the national, regional, and international levels, according to the different problems in the relations within governmental institutions and in the relations between the government and society. Some of the principles emerged at the national level as the judiciary developed several principles to fill legislative gaps. These principles then moved on to the international or regional level where they were elaborated upon and then they return, somewhat changed, to the national jurisdiction.

On the international level, problems originally arose in the context of the financial circumstances of states. International financial institutions were the first to regulate these situations. The norms used in this context have further been elaborated upon in the field of development aid. Financial and economic issues in a number of countries have thus contributed in an important way to the development of good governance norms.

On the regional level, for example in the European Union, different aspects relating to the quality of the administration gave rise to both preventive and repressive solutions for maladministration. The judiciary and the ombudsman developed these norms of good governance partly by themselves and partly by the implementation of these codes.

Nowadays, the most urgent problems in relation to the administration can be found at the national level. Situations of bad governance still exist, such as corruption, maladministration, and mismanagement. Again, problems are tackled both in repressive ways (eg through criminal and administrative sanctions) and in preventive ways (through administrative law instruments).[1] It has to be noted that problems might be perceived as worsening because of the distance between a private actor and the administration.

A separate problem, especially at the national level, is the fragmentation of good governance norms for institutions of the state. However, this is also a growing problem at the regional and especially at the European level. In the Netherlands, such norms had been proscribed in specific administrative law acts and therefore a need for the integration of norms was created. The General Administrative Law Act (GALA) hopes to provide this integration. GALA has several advantages: the norms to be observed are clearer, which is in the interest of both citizens and the government, and it makes

[1] Addink and Ten Berge 2006, 379–419.

the norms more accessible to citizens. In addition to GALA, a Code for Good Public Governance has been published by the Netherlands Minister of Interior Affairs. The executive bodies of all public authorities adhere to this Code. The Code prescribes, for instance, how executive bodies and public servants should behave in their dealings with private citizens, businesses, and other public authorities.[2] This is important because it increases trust in public authorities among the general public and private institutions, self-awareness and integrity within the authorities themselves, the professionalism and *l'esprit de corps* within the authorities, and transparency regarding the core duties. But this is not the only Code of Good Governance; each policy (sub) sector in the Netherlands has its own Code, so that today about twenty Codes of Good Governance can be found in the Netherlands. Here we begin to see the problem of the fragmentation of the norms of good governance.

2. Concept of Good Governance

Good governance is not only about the proper use of the government's powers in a transparent and participative way, it also requires a good and faithful exercise of power. In essence, it concerns the fulfilment of the three elementary tasks of government: to guarantee the security of persons and society; to manage an effective and accountable framework for the public sector; and to promote the economic and social aims of the country in accordance with the wishes of the population. A distinction is drawn between an institutional and a functional approach in the achievement of good governance.

The institutional approach of good governance is related to, for example, a minister or a civil servant, administrative authorities, or the public prosecutor, each competent to fulfil a specific function. In the functional approach, the focus is on the fulfilment of a specific function. These functions depend on the tasks endowed to a specific institution. Within the functional approach, the licensing function and the supervision function are distinct from each other. The licensing function refers to legitimacy *ex ante*, whereas the supervision function refers to legitimacy *ex post*.

The functional content can be split into good governance as part of public law and corporate governance as part of private law. Although these are not entirely separate, public law[3] and private law have different tasks and functions and also different processes of legitimization. Whereas public competences must have a legal basis in constitutional law and should be legitimately exercised, the legitimacy of private actors' exercising of authority is still somewhat diffuse. In the literature, attention is paid to the legitimacy of transnational private regulation, in which principles of good governance are recognizable.[4] It should also be noted that the public and private use of principles of good governance mutually influence each other, and this contributes to the development of the substance of the principles of good governance.

[2] Ministry of the Interior and Kingdom Relations. Department of Public Administration and Democracy, The Netherlands Code for Good Public Governance, July 2009, 20522 | 3273–GMD32, available in English: <https://www.integriteitoverheid.nl/fileadmin/BIOS/data/Internationaal/Netherlands_Code_for_Good_Public_Governance.pdf>.

[3] Elliott and Feldman 2015, ch 1.

[4] Curtin and Senden 2011, pp. 163–88; Kingsbury, Krisch, and Stewart 2005, pp. 15–62. In this article, attention is paid to procedural standards like participation and transparency and substantive standards such as proportionality, means-ends rationality, avoidance of unnecessarily restrictive means, and legitimate expectation. (pp. 37–41).

A second point concerns the meaning of the principles of good governance: first, governance: an extensive interpretation of governance may fit the best, since both public and private actors can profit from these norms, albeit in different ways; second, principles: it is with good reason that we refer to these norms as principles. It underlines the fundamental nature of these notions and links these with other existing principles of law. Principles have a legal character so they can be invoked before the competent authority and the judiciary. Inherent to principles is that they are more flexible than regulations. To conclude, the terminology of principles of good governance is already accepted in literature, case law, and in legislation. The question may arise whether principles of good governance are mainly legal principles or policy guidelines. The answer is both: although they can serve as policy guidelines, the legal character of these norms is of striking importance. It makes the principles far less informal and more obligatory.

Some further remarks now follow concerning important terminology in the context of good governance.[5] These include governance and administration, good governance and principles of good governance, and principles of good governance and principles of proper administration.

(a) Governance and administration

First, we must note that, in some countries, no difference is made between governance and administration. In other countries, governance is related to the three or four powers in a state. Administration refers, then, to one of those powers, based on the separation or balance of powers in the modern state. The word administration has a double meaning: it is not only related to the institution but also to the activities performed by the administration. In the *Walker Oxford Companion to Law*, the following definition is provided for governance: exercise of authority, control; government, and arrangement. Two other brief descriptions of governance are: the act, process, or power of governing; the state of being governed. Two additional descriptions are: the persons or the institutions who make up a governing body (government) and who administer something; the act of governing, exercising authority (governance).

For administration, the following definitions are provided: the act or process of administering, management of a government, the activity of a government in the exercise of its powers and duties, the executive branch of a government, office of an executive officer or body, law management and disposal of a trust or estate, dispensing, applying, or tendering of something such as an oath. Also, this term is formerly used for the body of persons appointed to carry the government of the country, now usually called the government.[6]

Different definitions already exist in the field of law and many more exist in other sciences. Different meanings of the word 'governance' have been found, especially in political science. The political scientist Robert Rhodes found at least six uses for the term 'governance'.[7] He primarily refers to the methodology of government in the post-modern, minimal state, which is comparable with notions of good governance. The other sets of meanings are concerned with systems analysis, socio-cybernetic systems, and self-organizing networks. Most of these definitions are, not surprisingly, related to the political science approach.

At the same time, both the legal and political scientists agree in essence with the critics of the London School of Economics Study Group on European Administrative

[5] Addink 2005. [6] Walker 1980. [7] Rhodes 1996, pp. 652–67.

Law. They encourage the European Commission to clarify in detail the definitions in the White Paper. An institutional and instrumental perspective should be accompanied by a normative approach. In the case law of the Court of Justice of the European Union and the European Ombudsman, we often find mention of the terms 'maladministration' or 'principles of good administration'.

Both governance and administration could be used in accordance with an administrative law perspective. They imply activities promoting the general interest by the fulfilment of a public task. Therefore, here we could have used the terms 'public governance' or 'public administration' as well. However, the exercise of a public responsibility may not be fulfilled by the traditional administration on a central or decentralized level only. In some countries, several of these responsibilities are entrusted to independent administrative bodies and private institutions which carry out these activities in the general interest and which have no hierarchical relation to the other parts of the government. Norms of good governance are relevant for these institutions too. As stated above, we uphold a broad perspective on governance, although a narrow one can prevail in some countries, at least in the field of public administration.[8] This piece does not make a systematical distinction between good administration and good governance because the separation of state powers is not entirely the same in all Western countries. For example, the United States adheres to a strict separation, whereas Australia has a milder separation between the legislature and the executive.

Moreover, similar types of governance norms develop in the private sector, for example the emergence of the principles of corporate governance and the topic of corporate social responsibility in which we also recognize similar private governance norms. Governance in the public administration context refers to the principles of good governance or good administration, which often connote the development of different examples of social networks. Using principles of good governance in the process of developing networks can be seen as the secondary function of these principles. These networks can be seen as new arrangements of governance. One of the crucial features of these developments is that they concern a diversity of sectors.[9] Therefore, we have found two different functions for the development of the principles of good governance.

(b) Good governance and principles of good governance

The focus here is not on different, individual acts of governance (governance), but rather on the different principles as the overarching steering mechanisms for these activities (the principles of good governance). As we look for parameters of good governance, the focus in the discussion should be on the principles of good governance. In the literature, this is also referred to as governance, including the methodology of government in the post-modern, minimal state, which deals with the concept of good governance (but mainly the efficiency targets of new public management). These norms of effectiveness and efficiency are actually included in the principles of good governance, albeit as part of a broader norm setting. This gives nuance to a mainly economic perspective on governance.[10]

The term 'governance' has a non-normative content and therefore there is a preference to use the term 'good governance' in the legal and normative non-legal discussion. In these discussions on good governance, we refer not only to orders and decisions by

[8] Chiti 1995, pp. 241–58; Nehl 1999, p. 17.

[9] Van Kersbergen and Van Waarden 2004, pp. 143–71.

[10] IMF 2018.

the administration but also to other activities, such as private activities and factual acts. All these forms of governmental behaviour are linked with the principles of good governance and therefore the focus is on the broader perspective of governance.

(c) Principles of good governance and principles of proper administration

The literature sometimes refers to the concept of good governance as principles of good governance or principles of proper administration, but sometimes also as principles of fair administration. As already explained, the distinction between governance and administration is not that explicit in all modern states. Therefore, some scholars prefer to make a distinction between corresponding sets of principles: principles of good governance or principles of proper administration. In that case, it is better to refer to principles of good administration rather than only 'proper' or 'fair' administration, so it would express—in a modern state—the necessary deeper and broader demands of good administration over the minimum standards of proper administration. Interestingly, the European Ombudsman uses the terminology of good administration (former article 138e/article 195 EC Treaty; now article 228 TFEU).

Chapter 7 elaborates upon the details of the distinction and the relationship between the broader principles of good administration and the narrower principles of proper administration. For now, it is important to recognize the principles of proper administration as minimum standards and to regard the principles of good governance as having a higher level of ambition. Concretely, good governance is mainly about the six specified principles. Further, it is relevant to understand that a violation of the principles of proper administration is always contrary to the law, whereas a violation of the principles of good governance is often illegitimate and could be merely subsequently unlawful. Since good governance is concerned with more than the legal aspects of accountability and effectiveness, good governance essentially means more than only the traditional legal aspects. The extent to which principles of good governance are actually codified is decisive for the justifiability of alleged violations of those principles.[11]

3. Specification of the Principles of Good Governance

The concept of good governance is a meta-concept, which means that good governance is built on other concepts. These specific principles of good governance are: properness, transparency, participation, effectiveness, accountability, and human rights. These specific principles are relevant on the national, the regional, and the international level. These levels partly interact in the development and implementation of the principles. Chapter 3 elaborates upon this interaction.

[11] Two aspects are relevant in this context, a formal and a substantive one. The formal aspect is that the law prescribes what degree of attention should be given to the principles of accountability and effectiveness. The Dutch Court of Audit focuses mainly on these two principles, as elaborated in the Dutch Court of Audit Strategy 2010–12.

The substantive aspect is that, in relation to accountability and effectiveness, in practice it is more of a process than an action. Such a process can be controlled by the judiciary. These aspects are different from questions related to the civil or criminal liability of the administration as a part of the legal entity—the state. However, there are some links.

Furthermore, the principles could be interpreted differently depending on the characteristics of a specific competence and whether they fall within the scope of the executive, the legislative, or the judicial competences, or a combination of them all.

In the context of legislation and regulation, the principles are specified in proper, participative, transparent, accountable, and effective regulation which respects human rights. In the context of the administration, the principles are explained as requirements of proper, participative, transparent, accountable, and effective administration, which is not contrary to human rights. In the context of judicial procedures, we can distinguish between the above principles and effective judicial procedures which are in harmony with human rights. It can be concluded that the specification of the principles largely depends on the position of the governmental institutions involved, within the constitutional context.

When the different positions of the institutions involved are understood, it is useful to divide the six principles into sub-principles within the administrative institution. These sub-principles are interpreted differently according to the (classical) three branches of the state. In the following chapter, some examples clarify both the principles and sub-principles.

The principle of properness consists of eight subprinciples (illustrated in Figure 2.1): the requirement of formal carefulness (hearing as part of natural justice), the prohibition of the abuse of power or more specifically discretionary power, the norm of material carefulness or rationality, proportionality, legal certainty, legitimate expectations, equality, and reasoning.[12] The principle of participation is specified in relation to the scope of the principle and can be related to persons, objects, and to the stage of the decision-making process. The principle of transparency applies in relation to meetings, acts, and governmental information. The principle of accountability is divided into political accountability, judicial accountability, and financial accountability. The principle of effective administration applies in relation to a governmental act, the aim of the specific public power, and the effect of regional or international law. Finally, the principle of human rights is applies in relation to the right of good administration, classical human rights, and social human rights.

4. Institutions Involved within a Framework of Checks and Balances

As addressed previously, the three governmental institutions need different interpretations of the principles of good governance with regard to their different competences: the legislative, the executive, and the judicial power. These traditional institutions can be found at the central, the regional, and the local level, albeit they are sometimes intertwined. Therefore, it is important to realize that each of these powers could take different shapes.

In the context of good governance, growing attention is given to the influence of the so-called 'fourth power'. This fourth power is mainly understood as the influence of institutions like the Ombudsman and the Court of Audit. The fourth power term is also recognized with regard to civil servants. The scholar Crince Le Roy opens his lecture with a concise overview of several instances of fourth powers in addition to the public service, such as the existence of independent administrative bodies in the

[12] Craig 2008; Craig 2016; Harlow and Rawlings 2009.

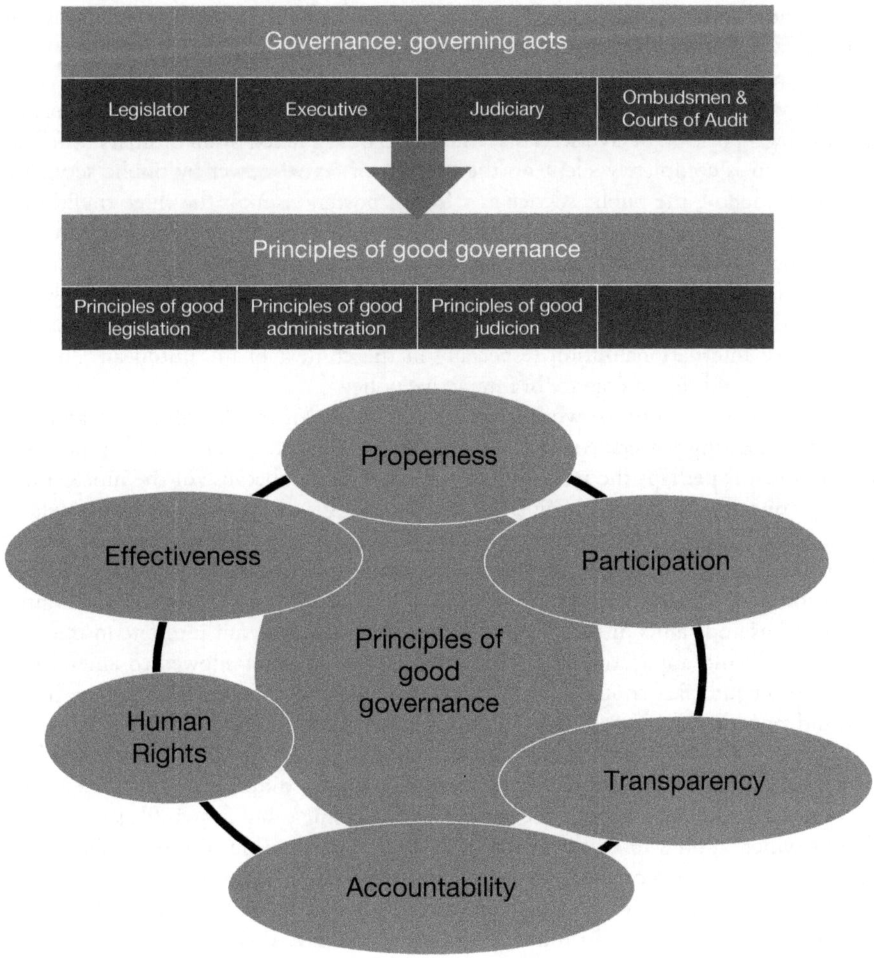

Figure 2.1 Principles of good governance

United States, the National Audit Office, and the Ministry of Foreign Affairs. [13] In the Netherlands, the National Ombudsman, the National Audit Office,[14] and the Council of State (to the extent of its advisory capacity on draft legislation) are perceived as being included in the fourth power. Not without reason, these institutions are given an independent position in the constitutional system by the Dutch Constitution itself. Since they have an important power by exercising their constitutional duties, they are distinguished as the fourth power next to the three traditional state powers or institutions. As these institutions have a mainly advisory task and are not competent to constitute legally binding rules, their actual power is often regarded as an indirect power.

[13] Crince Le Roy 1969, p. 5.

[14] The National Audit Office scrutinizes national expenditure (art 76–78 Netherlands Constitution) and the National Ombudsman examines the conduct of administrative authorities (art 78a Netherlands Constitution).

For instance, about 95 per cent of the National Ombudsman's recommendations are adopted, which is a sign of the institution's significant influence.

The concept of the fourth power as propagated by Crince Le Roy includes public servants, who have actual rather than legal power. The Dutch Constitution addresses only the legal position of civil servants, who are to be regulated by an ordinary law. The Constitution is completely silent on the exercise of actual power by public servants. In sum, to denote the public service as a fourth power, vis-à-vis the three traditional state powers—the legislature, the executive, and the judiciary—is unfortunate from a strictly legal perspective, because the power wielded by the public service is of a different, non-legal order. In 2000, Bovens made a link in his inaugural oration between the power of the civil service and public accountancy because of three important developments: internationalization (especially in the context of the European Union), privatization, and the emergence of interactive policy.[15]

A subsequent question is: what is the relation between this fourth power and the other three existing powers? And what are the relationships between these four powers? Montesquieu is perhaps the most misquoted author, both because of the nineteenth-century context of his essays on justice and law and his impenetrable writing style.[16] Quite often, Montesquieu is alleged to have discussed the English Constitution in *L'Esprit des Lois* from the perspective of a separation of powers. The purpose of this separation is to prevent the state from exceeding the limits of its powers or infringing the freedoms and rights of its citizens. The legislature should not interfere in the implementation and application of its laws; the executive is not allowed to amend the laws; and the judiciary should not (tacitly or not) introduce laws. Montesquieu, however, did not refer to a separation. He did refer to a distribution of powers, which is slightly different from separation. Distribution is about freedom and security, which is only feasible within a moderate constitution allowing for different points of view and forms of action. In such a moderate constitution, no single and indivisible sovereignty obtains which applies to all three powers.[17] As the distribution of powers shifts, the National Ombudsman can recover the balance between the state powers.

The idea of a balance of state powers was already developed by Aristotle, who saw such a balance in relation to different classes or estates. This explanation has been elaborated in the doctrine of the mixed state: a mix of monarchy, aristocracy, and democracy. In contrast, the old idea of the indivisible sovereignty of one sovereign has been fully abandoned in the doctrine of separation of powers. Another nuance is that the English discussion distinguished between separation and balance of powers. From the seventeenth century onwards in England, clear statements are found concerning the separation of powers by the likes of Bolingbroke, Harrington, and Locke. Apart from the civil tradition of the European continent, English political thought has been the most important source for Montesquieu's conception of the separation of powers. This means that Montesquieu should be regarded as belonging to those arguing for a balance of powers, which leaves room for differing interpretations. As to the National Ombudsman in the United Kingdom, this institution is closely related to Parliament, but is still an independent institution. This can be seen as reflecting the notion of a fusion of powers. In sum, various countries have chosen different interpretations of the balance of powers.

[15] Bovens 2000. [16] Foqué 1999.

[17] In fact, the assumption of state sovereignty is not correct, because the traditional focus on the modern state is being replaced by a focus on individuals. Rousseau already recognized the sovereignty of the citizens. Alleged sovereignty of the state can then only contain a kind of delegated sovereignty.

Therefore, we have institutions performing the three traditional state tasks and which should be abiding by good governance norms, encouraged by advisory councils, auditors, and ombudsmen on both the central level and decentralized levels.

In addition, some international and regional institutions apply principles of good governance, such as the International Monetary Fund (IMF), the World Bank, the United Nations, the World Trade Organization (WTO), and the institutions of the European Union.

5. Relevant Sources of Good Governance

Norms of good governance are found in the constitutions of countries and in legislation at the national, regional, and international level as well as in other documents such as decrees and regulations. Different parts of the administration have developed norms of good governance and these norms can be found in internal directives and in policy plans and policy rules. Case law from the judiciary also includes norms of good governance increasingly often. This case law is not only from national institutions but also the regional institutions and especially the European institutions like the European Court of Justice in Luxembourg and the Human Rights Court in Strasbourg. In different publications, attention has been given to these new sources of good governance. Rather recently (October 2012), the European Court of Human Rights (ECHR) explicitly referred to the importance of good governance.[18]

Additional sources are the reports of Ombudsmen, Courts of Audit, and advisory committees. In the reports of the Ombudsmen, we not only find aspects of good governance in the context of complaints handling, but also in reports containing results of research which are related to more frequent aspects in these complaints, on topics like transparency and public participation. We also see that Ombudsman institutions have developed Codes of Good Administration which have a preventive function but which are also used in the complaint-handling process. In a similar way, good governance documents are developed by the different Courts of Audit in which not only the regularity audits are relevant but also the policy audits.

6. Enforcement of Good Governance

Enforcement of principles of good governance can be carried out by way of the traditional modes of enforcement in public or private law and depending on the form of legal specification, but also by using mechanisms pertaining to international public and private law. These forms can be codified in the Constitution, General or specific Acts, Administrative Regulations as norms for the government, but these can also be review norms used by the judiciary, the ombudsman or other fourth power institutions in their enforcing and controlling activities. And finally, we see aspects of principles of good administration codified as fundamental rights for citizens.

The most traditional way of public enforcement is by way of a criminal procedure, which results in a decision of the criminal court finding that a person committed a criminal offence. Good governance principles can be found in the criminal procedure

[18] ECHR 2 October 2012, 5744/05 (*Czaja v Poland*) §70.

as such, but also in the normative framework itself, which is used by the criminal court especially when an offender is part of or concerned with the government.

More recently, we see a strong development of administrative enforcement, partially using (administrative) courts. This applies in situations where administrative authorities have the power to use administrative sanctions—like withdrawal of a decision or a decision related to an administrative fine—and in the process of applying these sanctions the administrative authorities must consider the written and unwritten legal principles of good administration. These principles play a preventive role here, but it is also possible that in the frame of administrative review by the (administrative) court these principles are also used, but in this case as review norms. The institution of the ombudsman is also using and developing these principles of good governance in a similar way, and the Court of Audit institutions are using these norms—as principles of good governance or principles of good auditing—when fulfilling their enforcement tasks.

In situations where the enforcement is done by the civil court and it is related to persons or institutions connected with the government, including the administration, the civil court will also use the principles of good governance or administration as review norms.

In addition to the national level, we see a development of enforcement on the international level, in the form of supervision or by way of sanction. International public or private institutions use such enforcement, and in some cases under the control of international courts.

Finally, there are also non-traditional enforcement modes in situations where the traditional enforcement mechanisms are not adequate. Some examples are negotiating between the offender and the enforcing authority, naming and shaming by the enforcing authority, and excluding of parties (from participating in a body or barring them from exercising their profession).

7. Conclusions

Good governance norms are necessary to prevent maladministration and corruption. We have made good governance more concrete by enumerating six groups of principles (properness, transparency, participation, effectiveness, accountability, and human rights). Their content may be tailored for each of the three branches: the legislator, the administration, and the judiciary.

We conclude that the balance of powers may be interpreted and applied differently in different constitutional systems. In the Netherlands, the fourth power is of increasing importance in strengthening the system of checks and balances.

The principles can be found in many documents of national, regional, and international context. The principles are formulated as fundamental legal principles, concrete legal norms, and policy guidelines. In the next chapter, good governance is discussed from a multi-level perspective.

3

Good Governance on Multiple Levels

Chapters 1 and 2 have explained some of the background to the concepts and the principles of good governance. Different reasons exist for the emergence of these principles, and distinct principles were identified: properness, transparency, participation, effectiveness, accountability, and human rights.

This chapter pays attention to the different levels where these concepts and principles have been developed: the national, the regional, and the international level—a multilevel perspective is then derived from those. From this perspective, we want to catch the plurality of sources of law and levels of government and show that principles travel from the national level to the European[1] or the international level and, after becoming general principles, they travel back to the national level as part of the process of internationalization, including the Europeanization of national law. In Part III of the book, the implementation of principles of good governance on the national level inside and outside of Europe is explained more thoroughly. This chapter uses the Netherlands as an introductory illustration and subsequently extends to other European countries. Special attention is drawn to processes of internationalization including the Europeanization of national level governance. From these national perspectives, we go a step further to the regional and the international levels. It is important to recognize the multiple ways in which we can implement the principles on these different levels.[2]

1. Good Governance on the National Level: The Netherlands

The origins of the principles of good governance on the national level in the Netherlands are similar to other European countries. In the Netherlands—as in most of the European countries—theories on statehood adhere to the classic concept of the rule of law, which consists of—as already explained—four aspects: the principle of legality, the balance of powers, the protection of fundamental rights, and independent judicial control. In the development of the democratic rule of law, the notion of democracy makes demands on the way the administration is organized, the procedure of decision-making, and the content of the decisions. The combination of the rule of law and the democracy concepts already creates several norms of good administration, such as properness, transparency, participation, and human rights.

Two new principles have emerged as parts of the principles of good administration: *accountability and effectiveness.*[3] Principles of accountable administration come into play in the process of ensuring that public service activities and, in particular, the exercise of decision-making powers—whether discretionary or otherwise—are carried

[1] The multilevel perspective can also be seen from the EU perspective: Hofmann and Türk 2006.
[2] Koopmans 2000, 25–34; Craig 2015.
[3] See on the principle of effectiveness: Van der Heijden 2001, 274; Préchal and Widdershoven 2017, 49–54 (effective judicial protection) and 74–91 (direct effect).

out legally, properly, and consistently with demands of fairness and good administrative practice.[4] The Dutch Court of Audit has made clear that its work will be focused on principles of good governance and, in particular, on accountability.[5]

The effectiveness principle has developed as legal scholars felt a need to know if a certain regulation produces the aimed-for result. This question has often been qualified as a factual rather than a legal question. Still, it is legally relevant and also because the principle of effectiveness is a citizen's right. The principle has normative consequences not only for the administration but also—especially on an EU-level—in the legal protection of citizens: the principle of effective judicial protection. Besides this, all decisions of the administration should be effective and timely, based on clear objectives, meet specified needs, implement policy proportionately, and be taken at the most appropriate level. So, we see that this effectiveness requirement also has consequences for new regulations.[6]

The following paragraphs elaborate upon these elements of good administration in relation to good governance, the rule of law, and democracy. It has to be stated that sometimes the evolution of an aspect of good governance will turn out not to be strictly legal in nature, but rather it will encompass morals, ethics, and policies. One has to realize that some of these moral or ethical norms have been adopted as legal norms (for instance, the principle of integrity).[7]

These factors are characteristic of specific societies in particular times, but are still sources of the principles of good governance. A strict separation between these factors and purely legal sources does not exist; there is a fluid line between them and some elements are in fact part of the positive law. In general, it is not always possible to draw a sharp line between the legal and the non-legal sources and some elements are still in the process of development from a moral norm into a legal rule.

(a) Good administration and the democratic rule of law

The principle of legality implies that all activities of the administration must be based on a law and, in the end, a formal law. On the one hand, these laws limit the scope of an institution's authority but, on the other hand, they often provide the administration with discretionary power. The discretionary power should always be carried out in accordance with written and unwritten legal norms and, in particular, the principles of proper administration, which is part of good governance. Written norms usually originate from the legislator, whereas unwritten principles originate from the judiciary.

In the Netherlands, as in most European countries, no strict separation of powers exists, and indeed not in the same sense as in the United States.[8] In the Netherlands, the balance of powers has a horizontal and vertical connotation within a system of checks and balances. The three traditional state tasks—legislation, execution, and judicial control—are not assigned to separate institutions. For example, legislation is a joined project of the government and the two Houses of Parliament. Furthermore, Supreme Offices of State (the Council of State, the National Court of Audit, and the National Ombudsman) play a role in the system of checks and balances.[9] In the

[4] See also Brophy 2002, 9. [5] Stuiveling 2003.

[6] Addink 2010c, 6–19; van den Broek 2015. [7] Addink 2012a, 103–25.

[8] This statement suggests indirectly that the United States does not have a system of checks and balances, which is not true. While the separation of powers in the United States is indeed divided, there exists a similar 'checks and balances' system that exists in the Netherlands. For example, the President can start military action, but only Congress can declare war. Or, Congress can pass a bill, but the President has the power of veto. Having these checks ensures that no power becomes too strong.

[9] Crince Le Roy 1976, 45 ff; Kummeling and Minderman 2002, 4 and 10.

literature, some suggest that the notion of checks and balances facilitates different interpretations as to different concrete policies[10] and that the demands of practice require such interpretations as long as any possible concentration of power is avoided.[11]

The Supreme Offices of State—the fourth power—function as a kind of guardian of the traditional state powers and they promote good administration.[12] This can be inferred from the opinions of the Council of State which are aimed at effectiveness and principles of proper regulation,[13] and from the activities by the National Audit Office, which also focuses on good administration.[14] With regard to the National Ombudsman, the current debate concerns the question of whether the criterion of properness implies or should imply the principles of good governance, as we see in the recommendations of the European Ombudsman.[15]

This interaction between the different institutions has more or less changed their original functions and might seem positive from the perspective of good administration. The standard has shifted to more of a perspective of good administration or broader good governance principles. The dogma of separation of powers thus fluidly shifts to a balance between the distinct powers. Their different functions still require their own perspectives upon the principles and they are responsible for the development of the individual principles. The legislator should contribute to this development by harmonizing and codifying the principles, the administration should steer the uses of available instruments, and the judiciary should develop and explain the principles by means of judicial review.[16]

As to the fundamental classical rights—civil and political rights—these have to be protected, but they largely concern the restrictions placed on the administrative power. In relation to the social rights—the socioeconomic and cultural rights—the administration is entrusted with a positive obligation. Of course, international conventions and declarations are important as sources and for the development of these rights. The Human Rights Reference Handbook states:

> Good governance and human rights are closely related. They can mutually reinforce each other in important ways. They are both concerned with the rule of law and with equity in the outcomes of government policies. And they overlap in specific areas. Their central aims remain distinct, however. Good governance is about providing society with a framework for the effective and equitable generation and division of wealth. Human rights seek to protect the inherent dignity of each and every individual.[17]

Next to these international sources, several positive obligations are codified in the Dutch Constitution. Some examples of these articles in the Constitution are as follows:

> Article 19: it shall be the concern of the authorities to promote the provision of sufficient employment

[10] Witteveen 1991, 47.

[11] Prakke, De Reede, and Van Wissen 2001, 536.

[12] As to the Netherlands, the complicated case of the Council of State is an example how two functions, which should be separated, are entrusted to one institution. The Council of state is usually involved in the process of legislation, in which process it contributes with advice on laws and regulations. At the same time, the Council of State has the highest and sometimes even the only jurisdiction in administrative cases in the Netherlands. Although the Council of State is internally split up, the situation remains somewhat unusual.

[13] Annual Report of the Netherlands Council of State 2002.

[14] Stuiveling 2003.

[15] Annual Report of the European Ombudsman for 2002, Luxembourg 2003.

[16] Addink 1999. In Chapter 3 of Addink 1999 three different positions in legal practice are elaborated upon: the checking judiciary, instrumental administration, and the harmonizing and codifying legislator.

[17] Van Banning and Van Genugten 1999, 97; Sepulveda and others 2004.

Article 20: it shall be the concern of the authorities to secure the means of subsistence of the population and to achieve the distribution of wealth

Article 21: it shall be the concern of the authorities to keep the country habitable and to protect and improve the environment

Article 22: the authorities shall take steps to promote the health of the population

Article 23 education shall be the constant concern of the government.

That being said, social rights become increasingly important and add a new dimension to the rule of law, giving it a broader interpretation. Another interesting issue in the context of good governance is the development of the human right principle in which it is the role of the administration to create the optimal conditions for the real protection of fundamental rights. Also, the Ombudsman contributes to the development of human rights as a principle of good governance, referring to this element in his recommendations.

Legal protection by the judiciary and the use of good governance with respect to judicial control are mainly relevant in the context of administrative actions and good administration. The judiciary provides for an interpretation of the written norms in relation to the principles of good governance, but will develop the unwritten principles in case law.

The principles of participation and transparency are of vital importance to the democratic dimension of the rule of law. In order to achieve real participation, information and general transparency of administration are crucial. This enables the public to gain the knowledge they need to assess if and how to participate in the decision-making process. Publication of information and the opportunity to participate can be qualified as the formal aspects of the democracy principle. Looking towards the interests of individuals or groups by the administrative authorities is the substantive side of the democracy principle.

Transparency refers to decisions and orders, meetings, and information. These norms were consolidated first in specific laws, such as the Environmental Management Act and the Planning Act. In 1994, these regulations were harmonized within the legal framework of GALA. Next to GALA, the Information Act regulates the prior conditions of transparency.[18]

Article 2: An administrative authority shall, in the exercise of its functions, disclose information in accordance with the present Act, without prejudice to provisions laid down in other statutes.

Article 8: The administrative authority directly concerned shall provide, of its own accord, information on its policy and the preparation and implementation thereof, whenever the provision of such information is in the interest of effective, democratic governance.

Article 3 states that anyone may apply to an administrative authority for information contained in documents concerning an administrative matter. An application for information shall be granted with due regard to the provisions of articles 10 and 11, which cover exceptions and restrictions. All these elements can be seen as aspects of the principles of transparent administration.

What are the parameters of good governance that apply to administrative law? The principles of good governance are specified in concrete norms of good administration. The following norms are distinguished: principles of proper administration, principles of public participation administration, principles of transparent administration, principles of human rights administration, principles of accountable administration,

[18] Environmental Management Act and the Planning Act, in force since 1 May 1992.

and principles of effective administration. Furthermore, it should be reiterated that these norms of good administration apply to all institutions involved in any executive state task.

(b) The development of the principles of good governance in administrative law

Good governance has evolved from principles of proper administration, which have a considerable history thanks to unwritten principles discovered and applied by the judiciary in case law, and to the later codification of the main judicial decisions. Gradually, specific features associated with good governance have developed, such as the principles of public participation and transparent administration. Subsequently, the principles of human rights administration came into play. More recently, the principles of accountable administration and effective administration joined the group.

After the Second World War, the state was perceived as being responsible for many more sectors, which had immediate consequences for the administration and the law. More legislation and administrative competences in different fields led to an increasing role for the judiciary. Concurrent with this broadened perception of the role of the state, the need for civil participation has increased, especially in policy fields in which individuals have direct interests. This need was primarily articulated on behalf of the citizens, but later it became clear that civil participation would have a positive influence upon the quality of the administrative institutions. Thus, both individuals and the administration would benefit from more thorough participation. However, participation needed to be regulated by law. In the Netherlands, participation rules were included in specific administrative acts. This development took place in different legal contexts, led by different institutions and instruments.[19] Together with other aspects of good governance, these rules would be integrated into one general administrative law, which is the previously explained GALA. Other European countries, such as Germany and France, laid down the basics of administrative law in a general act of administrative law. In Germany, these principles have been codified in their Constitution as a reaction to the legal constructions which had been widely misused during the Second World War. In France, an administrative judiciary and administrative procedural act has been in existence since the French Revolution in 1789. The Dutch GALA actually came quite late, only in 1994. Furthermore, many procedural rules initially developed in the case law of the judiciary were integrated into this law. Other countries started with legislation upon which the judiciary could elaborate. In the literature, several administrative law systems in Europe and the United States have been analysed and compared substantially.[20] Thus, in most European countries the aspects of good governance are codified in the Constitution or a general act on administrative law, while the Dutch principles have eventually been codified very specifically.[21]

Until the beginning of the 1990s, the role of the principles of good governance in Dutch administrative law was rather restricted to the principles of proper administration, which had been developed by the judiciary especially. The Netherlands has

[19] Addink 1999. [20] Seerden (ed) 2012.

[21] Ibid, § 4.2, *Algemene beginselen van behoorlijk bestuur in Duitsland* (Principles of Proper Administration in Germany); § 4.3, *Algemene beginselen van behoorlijk bestuur in Frankrijk* (Principles of Proper Administration in France). The development he describes makes a lot of sense from the perspective of a Dworkin-style view on the system of administrative law (as described in § 3).

different administrative courts of law[22] so the development of unwritten norms of good administration has differed from one court to another. However, the acceptance of these norms was channelled through the notion of general principles of law. Such principles also cover equality, legal certainty, legitimate expectations, due care and motivation, which were all introduced by means of case law.[23] For example, the *Centrale Raad van Beroep* (the Central Appeals Tribunal for the public service and for social security matters) accepted the role of principles of law during the 1930s; however, this was—apart from the prohibition of *détournement de pouvoir*—not laid down in legislation.

Around 1950, formal and substantive norms of proper administration raised attention. The term 'principles of proper administration' was used for the first time. The publication by Wiarda in 1952 was essential for the theoretical aspects related to the levels in which the principles of proper administration were presented. Wiarda analysed the case law of the different courts and developed some general lines.[24] From 1954 onwards, several principles of proper administration were laid down in different specific Acts as specific grounds for appeal. After the harmonization project, this was covered in article 8:77 of the GALA.

In the Dutch academic literature, three lines of thought on the principles of proper administration can be described, all of which are related to the role of the judiciary in several stages of a process and the meaning of specific norms of good administration.[25]

The first is the attention paid in the 1970s to the ways in which the judiciary used principles to test the administration and the consequences for a potential decision. As the administration only has competence to take a decision, it would have to formally renew its decision when the Court annuls it because of a formal principle. The substance of the decision would not necessarily change. When a substantial principle comes into play, this is slightly different, as the administration has to change the substance of its decision, which entails a substantive influence of the judiciary upon the administration. However, formal and substantial principles may have very different consequences.

The second, which dates back to the 1990s, is about judicial interpretation of the principles in relation to different stages of decision making. Every phase would have its own principle. The distinguishable phases are the preparation, the decision-making procedure, the decision making, determining the contents of the decision, and the publication of the decision.

The third is the attention for the theoretical basis of individual principles from the 1990s. The need for such a theoretical basis had been most urgent as to substantive principles. This is perhaps also related to the weighty consequences of breaches of those substantial principles. In a theoretical framework, the relation between the individual principles had become somewhat clearer. The study shows that a direct link between all principles does not exist and that substantive and formal principles were considerably different. An interesting example is the fact that the principles of public participation are seen by some as a specific part of the principles of proper administration, especially of the principle of due care. At this stage, the choice for separation of the principles had already been made.

[22] In an agreement of the coalition parties of the Dutch government Rutte-Asscher, the government has clearly stated its aim to integrate these special administrative courts. The draft version of the law was not accepted by Parliament.

[23] Schlössels and Zijlstra 2017, 329.

[24] Wiarda 1952, 78.

[25] Addink 1999, 23.

Although several principles have been harmonized in GALA, some principles were covered by other acts, such as the Government Information Act which regulates the principles of transparency. Sometimes a specific regulation exists regarding specific policies. However, the idea is to incorporate the Government Information Act into GALA. The principles of respect for human rights are mainly derived from the European Convention of Human Rights (classical due process rights) and the Dutch Constitution (classical and social rights). Some special administrative acts and regulations refer to specific human rights provisions. Such acts are usually instrumental to human rights policy. The Dutch legislator has developed general aspects of human rights administration, but it is the judiciary developing and interpreting these norms. The principles of accountable administration can be found in the constitutional law of the Netherlands and in criminal and private law. The principles of effective administration are especially elaborated in the new Government Accounts Act 2001. The principle of democratic administration was primarily codified as binding rules in the specific (environmental) legislation. Since 1994, the system, in essence remaining unchanged, has been laid down in GALA.[26]

In conclusion, how have these parameters of good governance developed over the years? The first conclusion is that, in the Netherlands, the principles of proper administration have been developed primarily by the judiciary and later by the legislator. Attention was primarily paid to the effect of annulling a decision by the judiciary and especially on the difference between formal and substantive principles of good governance. Second, the contents of the principles of good governance as to several phases of the decision-making process have become clearer. Another interesting conclusion is that many norms of good administration now have a preventive character too. This proves the importance of codifying such principles. It is very useful to develop a more coherent system of principles of good governance at the national level. The best way to create such a coherent system is by enacting a general regulation, such as drafting policy rules on good governance or—as a next step—creating general binding rules in legislation.

(c) Overview of the legal dimension of the principles of good governance in administrative law

As we have already seen, there are six basic principles of good governance. These principles have a specific meaning in the context of the administration.[27]

Properness entails the prohibition on misuse of power, the prohibition on arbitrariness, the principle of legal certainty, the principle of legitimate expectations, the principle of equality, the principle of proportionality, the principle of due care, and the principle of justification and motivation. Participation includes the principle of public participation related to specific people, moments, and objects. The principle of transparency applies to decisions and orders, meetings, and information. Human rights mean both classical and social human rights. Collective rights are not yet included. Chapter 12 elaborates further on the role of different types of human rights.

It is better to distinguish between types of principles, in which each has its own legal framework. From a conceptual point of view, there are no clear differences between

[26] The principle of democratic administration is further developed in the book *Algemene beginselen van behoorlijk bestuur* (*Principles of Proper Administration*) as an aspect of the principle of due care (the sub-principle of careful hearing), Addink 1999, 194–6, 207, and 220–4.

[27] Addink 1999, 73 and 272.

these principles; it is for historical reasons that these principles have been codified and developed in separate systems of Dutch legislation. These principles can be enforced within the process of judicial review. Not only the judiciary, but other independent institutions like the Court of Audit or the Ombudsman, can use these principles. The control can be carried out by parliament within the political process.

However, there are other legal aspects of the principles of good governance which have to be discussed: which administrative authorities have to apply these principles; to which administrative activities must these principles be applied; what is the binding effect of these principles when they have been applied; how can these principles be enforced? In the context of principles of good governance, the most important question is: what is the legally binding character of the principles?

It should be kept in mind that these questions concern the Netherlands. Specific principles of good governance are elaborated upon in Part II of this book, which concerns the substance of each principle. These chapters do not focus on a particular country.

The following section deals with good governance on a national level in Europe. Do various national systems converge or diverge? Are there some common denominators?

2. Good Governance on the National Level in Europe

Koopmans starts his famous article about the interaction between the legal principles on a national and on a European level by saying:

> General principles of law are, in a certain sense, commuters. Frequently, they travel from national legal systems to European Union law, as principles common to the legal systems of the Member States. Subsequently, after having been baptized as general principles of Union law, they travel back to national systems as part of the influence of Union law on national law. On their way back, however they are not always recognized as having originated in the national legal system, they have, metaphorically speaking a new attire.[28]

Koopmans explains the different ways general principles of law are handled in the national legal systems. The same is surely true for some aspects of the principles of good governance.

In 2005, the Swedish government commissioned the Swedish Agency for Public Management to conduct a survey on current regulation on Good Administration in the Member States of the European Union.[29] The Swedish government declared that it intended to work on a law on good administration for the institutions, bodies, offices, and agencies of the European Union. Such a law would be based on Article III-398 in the original Treaty Establishing a Constitution for Europe, which was comparable to article 298 TFEU. The article was originally proposed by the Swedish government's representative to the Convention on the Future of Europe and the intention was to facilitate a legal basis in the treaty which would allow European legislation on good administration. This report mirrors the development of the principles of good administration in different European countries. The Swedish report also explains the origin of the right to good administration, which can be traced back to a number of resolutions of the Council of Europe as well as to some case law of the European Court of Justice.

[28] Koopmans 2000, 25–34.

[29] Principles of Good Administration in the Member States of the European Union, Swedish Agency for Public Management, 2005.

Before the Lisbon system, good administration was codified in two documents which were not legally binding: the Charter of Fundamental Rights of the European Union, which only has the ambiguous status of a 'solemn proclamation' by three of the Union's most important institutions; and the European Code of Good Administrative Behaviour, in which the European Ombudsman elaborates upon the meaning of good administration. The further development of principles of good administration as a right is best found in the EU Treaty.

Based on the Charter of Fundamental Rights of the Union and the European Code of Good Administrative Behaviour, the Swedish Agency for Public Administration chose a set of rights and obligations considered essential for good administration.[30] These rights and obligations were then compiled into a questionnaire consisting of twelve questions. The questionnaire was distributed to all the Swedish embassies in the European countries with a request to identify a suitable English-speaking officer in the respective member state administration that could answer the questionnaire. The purpose of the survey was to examine if and to what extent some of the core principles of good administration had been transformed into legally binding rules in the national legal systems.

The results of the survey prove that a core set of principles is widely accepted in these European countries. The survey also demonstrated that most principles had been enacted in general, and in legally binding rules in constitutional or statutory legislation. However, the substantial content of the rules may vary, sometimes significantly. Subsequently the interpretation of the principles may differ. In the following list, some fine results are shown, with special attention for the shared core of principles:[31]

1. the principles of lawfulness, non-discrimination, proportionality;
2. the right to have one's affairs handled impartially, fairly, and within reasonable time;
3. the right to be heard before any individual measure is taken that would affect the citizen adversely;
4. the right to have access to their own file regarding any individual measure that would affect the person concerned;
5. the right of access to documents;
6. the obligation to receive written justification for all decisions;
7. the obligation to give an indication of remedies available to all persons concerned;
8. the obligation to notify all persons concerned of a decision;
9. the obligation to be service-minded.

One should keep in mind that, as already addressed, at least four of these principles were part of a resolution of the Council of Europe from 1977.[32] These principles were: the right to be heard, the right to access information, the obligation for authorities to state reasons, and the obligation to indicate remedies. For this reason, the results of the Swedish report are not that surprising. Another Recommendation from the

[30] This research—Principles of Good Administration—on request of the Swedish government was published in 2005. The main conclusions of the research are cited here.

[31] These principles can also be linked with the starting points of the Convention for the Protection of Human Rights and Fundamental Freedoms.

[32] Council of Europe, On the Protection of the Individuals in Relation to the Acts of Administrative Authorities, Res 77(3 1) (28 September 1977).

Council of Europe from 1980 establishes the principles of objectivity and impartiality. This means that the signatory states should have implemented these principles in some form or another. Another relevant development in the frame of the Council of Europe is related to the local and provincial level, in the frame of the European Charter of Local Self-Government and the additional protocol related to public participation on the local level. Relevant is a study on European local level participation.[33]

The report has also shown that most principles are enacted as general and legally binding rules in constitutional or statutory legislation. Most member states, with the notable exception of the common law countries, seem to have adopted a rather detailed administrative procedure act in which most of the above-mentioned principles are included. The acts are often subsidiary to other legislation following the *lex specialis derogate lex generalis* rule. The principles of impartiality and fairness as well as the principles of lawfulness, non-discrimination, and proportionality are often constitutionally guaranteed. The right to have one's affairs handled within a reasonable time, to be heard, and to have access to one's file is often regulated in an administrative procedure act with varying degrees of specificity. The obligation for officers to state reasons, to give notification and indicate remedies, and to base their acts on service-mindedness are mostly enacted through an administrative procedure act. The right to a general access to documents is often laid down in a freedom of information act or a similar act.

Different countries have enacted their administrative procedure codes at somewhat different times. From the seventeen acts included in the report, three of them were created before 1990, nine between 1990 and 2000, and six after 2000.[34] The reasons for this vary, and there can be several reasons for some countries' delay. An argumentative basis can be founded on the intergovernmental interactions of the EU influencing the member states on the benefits of employing good governance through social learning and persuasion.[35] Another reason may be found in the development of an entire new legal system in post-Soviet Union countries, which started in most cases only after 1989.[36]

In the study 'Good Governance in the EU Member States' (July 2015),[37] we investigated the interpretations and applications of good governance in the EU member states, taking into account the different functions of government bodies. Using a set of sub-questions, we investigated the differences among member states, conflicts between principles, and influences on the attitudes of states towards European issues. Good governance as a fundamental public concept in each of the member states has roots in the different phases of European history. In these phases we found aspects of the rule of law, democracy, and institutional state development, representing common and emerging good governance dimensions. Good governance is relevant not only for preventing the malfunctioning of state institutions, but more importantly in ensuring these institutions are up to the high level of governance quality needed for a modern society in the member states. It is about integrity, honesty, objectivity, and impartiality

[33] Addink 2009 and more recently the Recommendation CM/Rec (2018) participation of citizens in local public life.

[34] Before 1990: Germany, Denmark, and Sweden. Between 1990 and 2000: Italy, Portugal, Austria, the Netherlands, Spain, Poland, the Czech Republic, and Lithuania. After 2000: Greece, Slovakia, Estonia, Slovenia, Finland, and Latvia.

[35] Schimmelfennig and Sedelmeier 2004, 669–87.

[36] It should be noted that some countries had already been developing a kind of Rule of Law in the 1920s. These countries have very different backgrounds and traditions, as far as legal traditions had been present before.

[37] Addink 2015b.

and includes the prevention of fraud and corruption in the public sector. There are more factors underlining the actual importance of good governance: the prevention of fragmentation of legal norms (which impedes legal certainty and equality), and the need for good governance norms for new and independent administrative authorities like agencies.[38] Also, the complexity of modern society calls for an effective and accountable administration, with an open view to latest societal developments related to the need for openness and involvement. Those who are applying good governance norms require better knowledge of the interaction between the good governance norms applied by review-makers like the judiciary and ombudsmen, and norms developed and applied by the legislator and administration. We conclude that good governance is at the heart of the changing state and transforming judicial review.

We found good governance norms developed in the member states sometimes in a general, abstract way—for instance, the concept of the rule of law, the notion of democracy, and the functioning of classical constitutional institutions. There is, however, a tendency to specify these general dimensions of the good governance concept by principles, in some countries more than in others. We discovered a principle-based development and implementation of policies in case law and policy reports in member states. In different legal forms—constitutions, laws, policy papers, case law, and reports of ombudsman and audit institutions—six principles of good governance were found: properness and human rights; transparency and participation; and finally, effectiveness and accountability. The principles have been developed by the classical and modern powers (independent administrative authorities like agencies) of the state, both as norms for the administration as well as rights for citizens. Research results were checked by experts and have an indicative, qualitative character.

The countries of Europe have been individually investigated, resulting in country reports that were—for cultural, social, economic, and qualitative comparative law reasons—grouped into five regions: Northern Europe (NE), Western Europe (WE), Southern Europe (SE), Central Europe (CE), and the United Kingdom and Ireland. In Northern Europe, Sweden had a very strongly developed specification of the six principles of good governance, but the other countries were not far behind. In Western Europe, the Netherlands had a strong focus on the rule of law and institutional development principles, while Austria focused on the democracy-related principles. In Southern Europe, Spain and Portugal stand out through the development of the democracy principles of transparency and public participation. In Central Europe, Poland and Slovenia have developed all the principles of good governance very substantially. The Czech Republic is close behind, while the other countries are still in a general abstract phase. Finally, in the United Kingdom and Ireland, Ireland has developed these principles just slightly better than the United Kingdom.

The general conclusion of the investigation is that in the EU member states there is unity in diversity. Coherence is found in the contents of principles, while there is variety in the factual application. Differences are found in the focus on each of the three general abstract norms (rule of law, democracy, and institutional development) and to the extent to which principles have been developed (more focus on human rights and transparency than on accountability and effectiveness). In Figure 3.1 below, we distinguish phases of a gradual development of good governance. All countries use the three general abstract norms, but differences are seen in the development of the dimensions.

[38] Busuioc 2010, ch 2.

The results in the chart should not be read as a ranking of good or bad, but as the phase of good governance specification and application characteristic of each country.

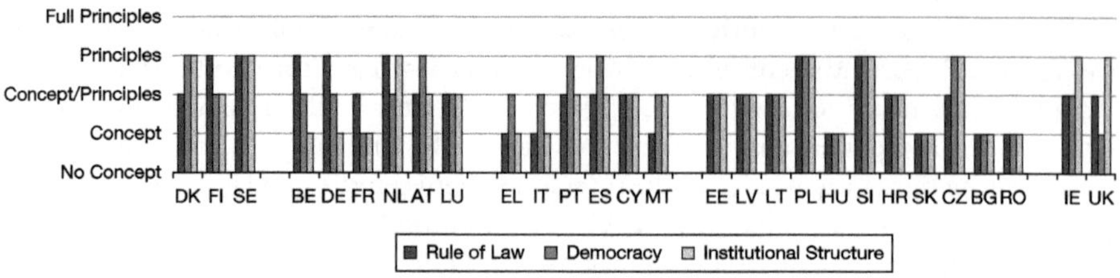

Figure 3.1 Phases of the gradual development of good governance

We investigated the application of the six principles of good governance in different policy fields: health, economy, environment, education, and social affairs. We found coherence in the principles qualification, variety in the contexts, and differences in the binding effect for governments and citizens. The specific varieties of government activities in the application of the principles in these policy fields can be found in the summary and the complete report; here, we only provide some illustrations. The principles of effectiveness and accountability are applied in an evaluative policy report in Austria describing negative effects of the differences in regulating public healthcare insurance and hospitals. The principle of a human right to a healthy environment is according to the Administrative Court in Belgium not a subjective right and only by specific legislation can this principle be realized. The principles of properness (legal certainty, carefulness), human rights (healthy environment), and effectiveness (implementation of law, achieving aims) were violated in a case concerning illegal landfills in Bulgaria because EU law was not implemented and appropriately applied.

The specific conclusions were formulated as follows. There is consensus on concepts and dimensions of good governance and we found coherence in principles qualification, variety in contexts, and differences in the binding effect. Nevertheless, there is a context variation of principles like transparency—information, publication, and manifestation—and also a different focus on three dimensions—rule of law, democracy, and institutional functioning. There is an application of principles instrumentally, protectionally, or a mix of the two and a different binding effect; there were good governance regulations in constitutions but more often in general administrative acts and by informal codes which have an indirect binding effect. We found a judicial good governance application by rule-interpretation and non-written principles and an innovative good governance application in ombudsmen and audit institutions reports. There were differences in conflict-solving good governance principles—legislator, judiciary, administration—but, nevertheless, a bottom-up good governance discussion creates trust among member states and on an EU level.

The final conclusion was that good governance is vital for further economic, social, and cultural development in the EU and that further gains can be expected from the active good governance development and application. It will create more trust among member states and citizens and will improve a bottom-up discussion within the member states regarding similarities and dissimilarities in the discussion on good governance in the EU. The ReNEUAL Model Rules can serve as a convenient framework as discussed later. Further, the development of a practical policy-related framework for the application of good governance principles is necessary, as well as working on a further codification and harmonization of good governance principles on a national level.

The specification of the results of this research and their relation to the implementation of good governance principles will be described in Part III of the book.

Even though we can discern a common core of the principles of good administration, it is equally true that the different legislators have shown great creativity in how they designed the different rules in practice. A common difference between different legislators is whether they use a *general concept* in order to let the courts specify its closer meaning afterwards, or alternatively specify *a list* that attempts to capture essential provisions beforehand. Latvia, for example, uses the term 'justified doubts' in order to capture the grounds for disqualification while Finland, among others, has a long list of possible grounds. The obvious advantage with the abstract alternative is that it does not prevent a dynamic development in the field. On the other hand, an abstract concept leaves plenty of room for administrative discretion in its application. Lists of conditions can therefore serve to minimize the scope for administrative discretion in fields where control might be more desirable than allowing for a dynamic development. For the same reason, a list of clearly articulated conditions is easier for a citizen to comprehend than a bulk of case law that uses different cases to specify the more precise meaning of a concept.

Another interesting difference is the amount of possible exceptions that are created in conjunction with a rule. Some rules are clear and foreseeable in the sense that there are a few exceptions, while others are joined by a large number of exceptions. Some areas of legislation, however, are constructed in a strikingly similar manner, with few differences in substance. The obligation to state reasons is a good example. There seems to be a general understanding between member states when it comes to stating legal and factual grounds as well as the main reasoning for a decision. The obligation to notify and the obligation to indicate remedies are two other examples. In other areas there are fewer similarities. Documentation is an example of a principle where the legal provisions differ a great deal between the European countries.

The debate on general principles of law is largely a debate on concepts, not problems of substance, as Koopmans has written.[39] Having said that, the member states indeed share many principles of good administration, although they have implemented them differently, and we must take note of the differences. As noted above, even though a rule looks the same across a number of countries, it does not mean that it is applied the same way. Principles are and will be interpreted differently and may thus refer to different things in different countries. In order to appreciate these differences, it is useful to outline four different traditions of administrative law.

(a) Four traditions of administrative law

The development of administrative law has always been deeply influenced by European history, culture, and constitutional contexts. Principles and rules of good administration may vary to reflect those different contexts. The Swedish report identifies four traditions of administrative law in Europe.

First, the *administration-centred* tradition views administrative law as an instrument for the government to run an efficient administration. As such, it is designed for the construction of efficient administration and implementation of policies. Such a view is often associated with France and countries which are heavily influenced by French legal traditions. In France, the *Conseil d'Etat* is the supreme court for administrative

[39] Koopmans 2000, 25–34.

issues and has both judicial and administrative functions. Its members are both judges of the administration and central legal advisers to the government.[40] The French tradition is governed by the notion that the most important reason for providing legal protection against the administration is not the protection of the rights of the individual, but rather to ensure that the administration adheres to law and statute.[41]

Second, the *individual-centred* tradition tends to treat administrative law as an instrument to control the government and to protect individuals against infringements of their rights. Administrative law is about the rules that keep the government within the boundaries of its competence and thus regulates the relationship between the state and the citizens. This tradition is often associated with the common law countries of the United Kingdom and Ireland, which possess a single jurisdiction for all types of cases.[42] In the United States, the well-known due process clause in the American Constitution is mainly concerned with the protection of citizens' rights. Over the past decades the courts have developed what is called the 'hard look' doctrine. This doctrine includes the duty to listen to citizens, the obligation to state reasons, and the duty to carefully study the regulation before making a decision. However, this development has created a judicial pressure on the administrative system in which a decision sometimes demands more than a hundred pages of explanation, a phenomenon that is called 'ossification'.

Third, the *legislator-centred* tradition relies on the legislator to design administrative procedures, often in the form of a very detailed administrative procedure act, or in some cases in the form of constitutional provisions. This represents the German ethos of the *rechtsstaat,* where the administration is viewed as a mere executor of the law. The result is a formalist, almost court-like, approach to administration. Germany might be seen as the typical case, but some of the newer member states also display this tradition.[43]

Fourth, the *ombudsman-centred* tradition is recognizable in the Scandinavian countries. The characteristic of this slightly more pragmatic tradition is that an independent person, who is often appointed by the parliament, works separately of the executive in order to identify problems, investigate complaints, and recommend solutions in cases of maladministration.

In reality, none of these traditions can single-handedly represent any singular state. Where one tradition may dominate, features of other traditions are often included as well.

(b) National ombudsmen and good governance

Several European states have instituted ombudsmen on the national and decentralized level. These ombudsmen assess alleged misbehaviour of state institutions. In their

[40] Its origin lies in a particular law from 16–24 August 1790, which barred the competence of the civil courts in administrative matters and came to be centred on a particular institution, Conseil d'État, which sits in the Palais-Royal in Paris, and was created in its modern form by Napoleon at the end of 1799.

[41] Schwarze 1992, 1182.

[42] Historically we find its origin in the strength of the English judiciary which was established after the Revolution of 1688.

[43] As observed earlier, some post-Soviet Union countries had already been developing a rule of law in the 1920s. Most of them took the example of the Weimar Republic, as it was the most advanced and modern system of that age. This is mainly true for the Baltic countries. No wonder, some of those countries still have German-like features in their legal systems. Some more reasons, such as the long-standing contacts between these areas are important, but that is beyond the scope of this book.

assessment, they often refer to principles of good governance, though their assessments show some variations as well.

A comparison between several countries shows difference in emphasis, as some are mainly concerned with the administration and its public servants observing legal principles in a broad sense, whereas others are focused on the protection of the rights and freedoms of citizens. These are not completely separate worlds. For example, Sweden has some of both where observance of law includes constitutional rights.

Southern-European countries, such as Spain and Portugal, emphasize foremost the protection of fundamental rights and freedoms. The Danish ombudsman sticks to the observance of the law, as he monitors whether or not a public servant pursues an illegitimate aim, takes an arbitrary decision, or otherwise commits errors or omissions in the exercise of his duties. In Great Britain, the criterion of maladministration is applied, but lacks a statutory definition, although the relevant Act expressly states that review does not extend to policy issues or purely discretionary elements of administrative decisions. The review process is only concerned with alleged injustice as a consequence of maladministration. Helder observes, referring to Stacey, that the concept of maladministration seems to invite some restraint in the process of reviewing.[44] This is not surprising, as concrete assessment criteria are not yet provided by the concept of maladministration alone. Although there has been a broadening of the scope of maladministration this has not yet resulted in an adaptation and further detailing of this assessment criterion. In short, since the limits of the concept of 'maladministration' have been reached, there is a need for new and more concrete reviewing criteria.

It turns out that the European Ombudsman has already tried to cross this bridge and offer new insights into assessment criteria, as briefly discussed below. In 1992, on the occasion of the establishment of the Maastricht Treaty, a European Ombudsman was instituted in conjunction with a right of complaint in cases of maladministration. At that time, academics have criticized the introduction of this criterion, because it was suspected to be too vague. On the other hand, this vague formulation facilitates discretion to assess different situations differently.[45] The European Ombudsman himself felt that the vagueness of the norm was precisely its strength and initially did not find it desirable to define the concept of maladministration.[46] In his first annual report, he described maladministration referring to situations in which European Union institutions failed to act in conformity with the Treaty and binding Union acts and failed to observe rules and legal principles established by the European Court of Justice and the Court of First Instance. The ombudsman also reports on situations of administrative irregularities, omissions, administrative mistakes, avoidable delays, or refusals to provide information.[47] The European Parliament, however, did not accept this interpretation and requested the Ombudsman to define the term maladministration. In his annual report of 1997, he defined maladministration as when an administrative organ omits to act in conformity with a rule or principle to which it is bound.[48]

After receiving several complaints which, in retrospect, could have been avoided if the duties of the staff of EU institutions vis-à-vis citizens were clear, in 1998 the ombudsman started an investigation to further explain maladministration. Its counterpart, good administration, was taken into consideration in this investigation. The

[44] Helder 1989, 146; Stacey 1978, 10, regards it an impediment that the British Ombudsman must limit himself to applying the criterion of 'maladministration'.

[45] Kuusikko 2001, 461. [46] Södermann 1997.

[47] Annual Report of the European Ombudsman for 1995, Luxembourg, 1996, I.3.2.

[48] Annual Report of the European Ombudsman for 1997, Luxembourg, 1998, 22f.

ombudsman researched whether he could construe a code of conduct based on rules and principles applied by European institutions. The aim of his work was to improve the relations between the European institutions and citizens.[49] In addition, he has recognized that a general tendency already existed in the member states and at international level to develop legislation governing good administration in the interests of citizens.[50] So the ombudsman indeed devised a code of good administrative conduct, 'codifying' norms or standards of good administration.[51] Subsequently, in July 1999, a draft Code of Good Administrative Behaviour was presented to the European institutions and bodies, featuring the principles already found in European case law, and which have been taken over in the member states.[52]

The code contains the principles of good administration, including the prohibition of 'détournement de pouvoir' (misuse of power) and the principles of legality, equality, proportionality, objectivity, legitimate expectations, fairness, politeness, mandatory correspondence, referral, reasonable timing, reasoned decisions and notice of decisions, the principle of openness, and so on. All these principles together exceed the scope of proper administration and go into good administration. For that reason, the ombudsman refers to them as 'principles of good administrative behaviour'. In the context of this book, we call them 'principles of good administration' or 'principles of good governance'.

Under this author's supervision, a study has been conducted on the application by the European Ombudsman of these principles after the Code. The following remarks are derived from the outcome of this study.[53] The study comprised 133 Ombudsman reports which were published between September 2001 and May 2002.[54] About twenty-five complaints referred to violations of the principles of good administrative behaviour. The Ombudsman applied two categories of principles: first, the classic substantive and procedural principles derived from administrative law; and second, the principles relating to the functioning of the administration (such as the obligation to answer letters in the language of the citizen who sent the letter, acknowledge receipt, and indicate the competent public servant, the obligation to refer the document to the competent department, and to communicate the decision to the citizen in question).

The research shows that the various principles contained in the code are effectively applied by the Ombudsman. A point of criticism is that the relationship between the principles is not always clearly represented. This is particularly true for the second category of principles, which could be readily classified as part of the principle of due care. However, substantive coherence is criticized. It would have been more satisfying if the more well-established principles were followed, as they are more expressly developed. Otherwise it soon becomes a hodgepodge of principles. Finally, a remarkable difference was observed in the way the European Ombudsman and the European Court of Justice employed the principles. The Ombudsman's purpose is protecting the individual, whereas the ECJ is more concerned with the interest of the Union and the European society.[55] Formally spoken the Court of Justice of the European Union consists of the Court of Justice and the Court of First Instance (CFI)—the latter deals with most of the cases for instance on access to information at first instance and from which there is an appeal to the ECJ. Using the terminology ECJ here, it is about the Court of Justice of the European Union.

[49] See draft recommendation of the European Ombudsman in the own initiative inquiry OI/I98/OV.
[50] Södermann 2001. [51] Södermann 1998. [52] Södermann 2001.
[53] Fennel 2002.
[54] A majority of the cases, ninety-three, concerned the European Commission, nine the European Parliament, three the European Council, and ten were about other European institutions.
[55] Fennel 2002, ch 3, Concluding Statements.

Finally, research on the same topic has been conducted, mainly concerned with the concretization of principles of good administrative behaviour by the ECJ.[56] There is a study based on the subdivision of six principles of good governance, referred to earlier.[57] The study shows that principles of responsible administration were initially applied in the context of political responsibility, although these are not given substance just through legal rules, but also through courts of audit.[58] The principles of participatory administration have been given a mainly formal, procedural content by both the courts and the European Ombudsman. The principles of transparent administration relate in particular to the accessibility of documents and the public nature of decision-making. The Court has acknowledged the principle of transparent administration as well. The Ombudsman links human rights principles relating to the administration with bad administration, whereas the Court considered these human rights principles by themselves. The principles of proper administration are afforded wider application by both bodies, although the Court is more the frontrunner and the Ombudsman the runner-up.

Is any legal tradition recognizable in this development? Not even one. The European Union has generated its own particular blend of traditions. Although the administrative system of the European Union was initially modelled on the French system, subsequent developments have led to a growing emphasis on individual rights in administrative procedures. [59]

As seen above, many actors have been involved in the development of principles of good administrative behaviour, all in their own way. These actors include the European Court of Human Rights, the Court of Justice and the Court of First Instance, the European Ombudsman, and some of the member states of the European Union. As the European Convention on Human Rights and its protocols become increasingly significant for the European Union, they may influence the further development of these principles, and even the principles of good governance in general.

3. Good Governance and the Europeanization of National Law

The developments of principles of good administration in the sphere of the European Union are not solely confined to European institutions.[60] Gradually, these developments influence the administrative law of the member states. Indeed, we are witnessing an ongoing process of Europeanization and this is not a recent development. While it is not completely new, the literature nowadays clearly recognizes that European law and administrative law are converging. That is not only in the relationship between European law and national administrative law but also in the interaction between international law and national administrative law.[61] Moreover, a stronger foundation is needed as the influence reaches beyond the traditional notion of sovereignty, especially as far as territoriality is concerned.[62]

[56] Oldenziel 2003.

[57] Participation, transparency, effectiveness, accountability, proportionality, and human rights, see Addink 2005.

[58] Oldenziel 2003, ch 10, Conclusions.

[59] For a discussion on countervailing tendencies, see Harlow 1988, 10.

[60] Prechal and Widdershoven 2017.

[61] Schmidt-Assmann 2008, 2061–79.

[62] Ibid, 2061.

(a) Two dimensions of the Europeanization of administrative law

Two dimensions are important in the Europeanization of administrative law: the instruments for the administration to act and the norms for administrative action. These dimensions are important for both the national and European levels, and also in multilevel analyses. Questions of effectiveness and accountability are also relevant in this discussion as the coherence between the national and the European level is challenged. Therefore, the development of administrative and European administrative law requires a congruent approach. Two aspects are especially important: administrative law in original national relations and the role of national administrative law in purely European relations.

(b) The challenge of designing a law on good administration for the European Union

There are several arguments in favour of adopting a law on good administration for European Union institutions.[63]

First, the current rules of EC administrative procedure have been described as a 'patchwork codification tailored to the specific requirements of sectorial policy implementation. They are barely coordinated with one another, suffer from serious gaps—in particular as regards individual protection.'[64] A standardization of otherwise scattered rules would lead to a simplification and rationalization of the administrative processes of the EU.

Second, today we see the European Union developing mainly under stimulus from the European Court of Justice and the European Court of First Instance. According to some, this is a natural and sound development. Others would consider this development more legitimate when the European legislator himself would be leading.

Third, as a consequence of the extension of the Union some practical reasons may hinder this run of things in the future. When the Court consists of a limited number of judges, it would not be unreasonably difficult to identify common legal principles. However, the Union already counted twenty-eight members in 2013, where each member delivers one judge trained in his parent legal tradition. It will become increasingly difficult to find common legal principles underlying the European administrative legal framework.

Finally, codified rules are clearer and more accessible to the average citizen than principles which are developed in case law. An administrative procedure act would not only enumerate and articulate existing principles of the Union, it would also set out clearly the principles which are relevant in the relation between the multilevel administration and the citizens.

However, while it is important to achieve sufficient protection of individual rights, it is equally important to promote efficiency and dynamism as well as to avoid—as we called it earlier—ossification by over-regulation. Too many rules incite civil servants to work out techniques for evasion or to shift their focus to compliance rather than the quality of results. This can lead to unduly cautious behaviour aimed at minimizing legal errors, thus blocking experiments and innovations.[65]

[63] Craig 2013; Hofmann and others 2014; Timmermans 2014; van Ommeren and Wolswinkel 2014; Addink 2014.

[64] Nehl 1999, 188.

[65] Harlow 1996, 11.

The European Ombudsman has stressed his role in ensuring 'good administrative practices', while reiterating the importance of avoiding negative consequences of juridification by using a considerably open definition of maladministration. 'The open character of the term is justly one of the elements which distinguish the role of ombudsman from that of the court.'[66]

The crux lies in the right balance between the citizen's legitimate rights and the public interest in the form of the administration's need for efficient procedures. A too strong emphasis on individual rights might lead to undue juridification of administrative procedures. Since specialized administrative economic law constitutes a large part of the Union's administrative law, it might even provoke the development of a strong litigation culture,[67] although the danger should not be overestimated. Many individual rights are already part of the *acquis communautaire* and at least some codes of good administrative behaviour are already adopted by the European institutions as well as published in their official journal.

These improvements might yield proper procedures, high quality decisions, and stimulate the level of rational reflection. When such a law on good governance is made subsidiary to the standing legal framework, it would not impede more detailed horizontal or vertical legislation.

The right to good administration and its legal basis in the Treaty of the European Union seems to have the potential to mature the particular blend of administrative law traditions characteristic of the European Union. Future designers of a law on good administration thus need to know of the different traditions of the member states in order to make it fit the multilevel character of administrative law. Subsequently, they need to continue complementing the original administration-centred tradition with an appropriate blend of the individual-centred, legislator-centred and ombudsman-centred tradition, in order to properly balance the rights of the individual and the European public interest.

4. Good Governance on the European Union Level

In Chapter 2, the Commission's White Paper on European Governances has been extensively addressed.[68] However, this White Paper was not the start of the discussion on good governance in the European Union because sundry publications and decisions on good governance had already been published several years before.[69]

In 1991, the EU Council of Ministers provided a brief description of the contents and the importance of good governance in a resolution on Human Rights, Democracy and Development:[70]

> The Council stresses the importance of good governance. While sovereign states have the freedom to institute their own administrative structures and establish their own constitutional arrangements, equitable development can only effectively and sustainably be achieved if a number of general principles of government are adhered to: sensible economic and social policies, democratic decision-making, adequate governmental transparency and financial accountability,

[66] Annual Report of the European Ombudsman for 1995, Luxembourg, 17.

[67] For a discussion of the litigation problem see eg Kańska 2004, 320–1.

[68] European Commission, *White Paper on European Governance*, July 2001, COM (2001) 428.

[69] Chiti 1995, 241–58; Schwarze 1995, 227–39.

[70] Resolution of the European Council of Ministers on 28 November 1991, in: Van Banning and Genugten 1999, 97 and 196–8.

creation of a market-friendly environment for development, measures to combat corruption, as well as respect for the Rule of Law, human rights and freedom of the press and expression.

In 1996, the book titled *Principes Généraux du droit en droit communautaire. Origines et concrétisation* was published. The book outlined general principles of law within European Union law and elaborated on different groups: explicit principles, implicit principles, and silent principles.[71] As to these silent principles, attention was paid in a special chapter to '*Le principe de la bonne administration*'.[72] This chapter discussed some decisions of the Court of Justice in which this principle was mentioned. The conclusion was—and this is very crucial for the further development of ideas on the principles of good governance—that the principles of good administration could be used even in situations where written rules are absent. Advocate General Van Gerven wrote in his conclusion to one of the cases:[73]

En principe, nous partageons le point de vue de la Commission. En effet, l'absence de garanties écrites n'empêche pas la Commission d'être liée, dans ses interventions, par les principes généraux du droit communautaire, qui comprennent le respect des droits de la défense (et en particulier le principe du contradictoire) et le respect du principe de bonne administration. La Cour n'a d'ailleurs jamais hésité à imposer à la Commission de respecter ces principes, même en l'absence d'un texte écrit. (. . .)

Bien que l'absence de garanties procédurales écrites ne fasse donc normalement pas obstacle au pouvoir de la Commission, nous souhaitons néanmoins souligner que, en raison de l'effet juridique, en principe immédiat, des mesures que la Commission peut prendre lorsqu'elle constate une violation d'une disposition du traité, ces mesures demeurant en tout état de cause susceptibles de recours, elle doit exercer sa compétence en s'appliquant tout spécialement à respecter les droits de la défense et le principe de bonne administration, en tout cas lorsque (comme c'est le cas en l'espèce) sa décision a également pour effet de modifier directement et individuellement la situation juridique d'entreprises (publiques).

[In principle, we share the point of view of the Commission. Indeed, the absence of written guarantees does not prevent the Commission to be bound in its interventions, by the General principles of Union law, which include the respect for the rights of defence (and in particular the principle of *audi alteram partem*) and respect for the principle of good administration. The Court has also never hesitated to impose on the Commission to respect these principles, even in the absence of a written text. (. . .)

Acknowledging that the absence of written procedural guarantees will therefore normally be no obstacle to the power of the Commission, we wish nevertheless to emphasize that, because of the judicial effect, in principle immediately, the measures that the Commission can take when it finds a violation of a provision of the Treaty remain in any case open to review. The Commission must exercise its jurisdiction in attempting to especially respect the rights of defence and the principle of good administration, in any case when (as is the case here) its decision also has the effect of altering the legal situation of (public) companies directly and individually.]

From 1998, several judgments of the European Court of Justice were published in which the Court used 'principles of good administration'.[74] In 1997, the European Ombudsman provided a definition of maladministration in his annual report. In

[71] Papadopoulou 1996. [72] Ibid, ch IV, 127–32.

[73] ECJ 12 February 1992, C-48/90 and C-66/90, *Netherlands and others v Commission*, 1992, ECR I-00565, conclusion by A-G W Van Gerven.

[74] ECJ 19 November 1998, C-252/96, *Parliament v Gutierrez de Quijano y Llorens*, ECR I-07421; ECJ 4 March 1999, C-119/97, *UFEX and others v Commission* ECR I-01341; ECJ 9 September 1999, Case T-127/98, *UPS Europe v Commission*, ECR II-02633; these terms were recently used by the ECJ in ECJ 13 February 2003, Case T-333/01, *Meyer v Commission*, ECR 2003 II-00117; the Court sometimes refers to 'maladministration', see ECJ 10 July 2003 C-472/00, *Commission v Fresh Marine Company*, ECR 2003 I-07541.

1999, he recommended a draft Code of Good Administrative Behaviour, and in the period between 6 September 2001 and 3 May 2002, in its twenty-five reports, the European Ombudsman used the terms 'principles of good administration' or 'good administrative behaviour'.[75]

In August 1999, a conference on 'General Principles of European Community Law' was held in Malmö. The fundamental purpose of the conference was to analyse the general principles, their scope in the EU legal order, and their impact at the national level—a rather top-down European law approach. Reports on general aspects, human rights, institutional principles, and some individual principles and legal systems were later published in the book *General Principles of European Community Law*.[76] During the conference, attention was paid to 'Securing the Principle of Good Administration within the Union Institutions'.[77] One of the conclusions of the conference was—with a view to the future—that the role of comparative law in the process of developing general principles should not be underestimated.[78] This should be the case not only in external relations between the European level and the national level, but also between the European institutions.[79]

It is interesting that the Commission has developed five principles of good governance in the White Paper: openness, participation, accountability, effectiveness, and coherence. In an earlier White Paper on Administrative Reform, some key principles of a European public administration were stressed: service, independence, responsibility, accountability, efficiency, and transparency.[80] These elements were elaborated rather briefly[81] in the Commission's Code of Good Administrative Behaviour.[82] So, not only the European Judiciary and the European Ombudsman, but also the European Administration (ie the European Commission and the European Council),[83] use the principles of good governance. The European Commission stated, quite restrictively, that the application of these principles reinforces the principles of proportionality and subsidiarity. In my opinion there is a broader legal effect—as illustrated here—than the reinforcement of these two principles alone.

There is criticism of this statement in the literature because the notion of good governance had not been defined.[84] However, good governance could be seen, as Curtin

[75] Fennel 2003, 5.41. [76] Bernitz and Nergelius 2000.

[77] Ragnemalm 2000, § 2.1.3 'Securing the Principle of Good Administration within the Community Institutions', 54–7.

[78] Nergelius 2000, 223–32; Koopmans 2000, 25–34.

[79] See the overview of the case law of the European Ombudsman in comparison with the European Code of Good Administrative Behaviour: Fennel 2003, 5.31–5.87. For comparison see Principles of Good Governance in case law of the European Court of Justice/Court of First Instance and European Ombudsman: Oldenziel 2003.

[80] European Commission, *White Paper on Administrative Reform*, March 2000, COM 2000 (200).

[81] See the critical remark by the European Ombudsman in his speech at the International Seminar entitled *The Ombudsmen and the European Union Law*, Bucharest, April 2001.

[82] European Commission, *Code of Good Administrative Behaviour. Relations with the Public*, 13 September 2000. This code contains norms in relation to General Principles of Good Administration (lawfulness, non-discrimination and equal treatment, proportionality, and consistency), Guidelines for Good Administrative Behaviour (objectivity and impartiality, information on administrative procedures), Information on the rights of interested parties (listening to all parties with a direct interest, duty to justify decisions, duty to state arrangements for appeals), Dealing with enquiries (requests for documents, correspondence, telephone communication, electronic mail, requests from the media), Protection of personal data and confidential information, and Complaints procedures (European Commission and European Ombudsman).

[83] Decision of the Secretary-General of the Council on a Code of Good Administrative Behaviour, 25 June 2001 (2001/C189/01).

[84] LSE Study Group on European Administrative Law, *Taking Governance Seriously*, § 1, March 2002.

and Dekker argue in their contribution to this publication, as a Dworkian 'interpretative' legal concept, structuring different conceptions around a common fundamental value.[85] In the second part of this book, we elaborate on the legal principles connected with good governance, expressing different conceptions of the principles of good governance.

In September 2001, the European Parliament adopted a resolution containing the 'Code of Good Administrative Behaviour' which European Union institutions and bodies—their administrations and their officials—should respect in their relations with the public. This Code is mainly based on the work of the European Ombudsman concerning maladministration.[86] To reiterate, maladministration occurs when a public body fails to act in accordance with a rule or principle that is binding upon it.[87] The Code specifies principles such as the absence of discrimination (article 5), proportionality (article 6), the absence of abuse of power (article 7), impartiality and independence (article 8), objectivity (article 9), legitimate expectations, consistency and advice (article 10), fairness (article 11), courtesy (article 12), the right to be heard and to make statements (article 16), a reasonable time limit for taking decisions (article 17), and the duty to state grounds for decisions (article 18). Compared to the Commission's Code of Good Administrative Behaviour, this Ombudsman's Code is clearer and more detailed.

The Ombudsman's Code contains, in essence, the classical basic substantive and procedural principles of administrative law, such as the rights of the defence, grounds for decisions, non-discrimination, impartiality, possibility of appeal, as well as some rules of good administrative functioning. Both types of norms are, because of their legal status, part and parcel of the principles of good governance.

The Code develops the fundamental rights of citizenship—including the citizens' relationship to the administration—which can also be found in the Charter of Fundamental Rights of the European Union proclaimed at the Nice Summit in December 2000.[88] The particularities of this Charter have already been described but, in general, where European law is concerned, a citizen's right to good governance exists.[89] Moreover, this Charter has inspired some of the EU's institutions and bodies to develop and adhere to these norms. This is the case for the European Parliament and the European Commission, which have both published communiqués in which they indicate that they respect the Charter in their activities. Finally, the Court of Justice and the European Ombudsman have referred to the Charter, and the Advocates-General at the Court invoke the Charter in their opinions. Eventually, good governance has been inserted in the European Union's treaty. Now, administrative regulation should follow, providing clarity and coherence.

[85] Curtin and Dekker 2005.

[86] The Annual Report of the European Ombudsman for 1995, Luxembourg, 1996, provided a non-exhaustive list of examples of maladministration; in November 1998 the Ombudsman, on his own initiative, launched an inquiry so that all Community institutions and bodies could adopt a Code of Good Administrative Behaviour.

[87] Definition in the Annual Report of the European Ombudsman for 1997, Luxembourg 1998.

[88] In the Treaty of Amsterdam in 1997 (article 6.2 of the Treaty on European Union) the EU undertook to respect the fundamental rights as guaranteed by the ECHR as general principles of Community Law.

[89] Millet 2002, 309–22.

(a) ReNEUAL Model Rules on EU administrative procedure

The project on ReNEUAL Model Rules on EU administrative procedure[90] undertaken by the Research Network on EU Administrative Law (ReNEUAL) aims to determine how constitutional values of the Union can be best translated into rules on administrative procedure covering non-legislative implementation of EU law and policies. Well-designed rules for implementation of EU law and policies could improve the quality of the EU's legal system. The ReNEUAL Model Rules are organized into six 'books'. EU law applies a mixture of tools in specific and evolving contexts of implementation of EU law and policies. Each of these tools—single case decisions, non-legislative acts of general application, agreements, and contracts—has its own specific requirements for ensuring procedural justice.

(b) Constitutional principles of ReNEUAL Model Rules on EU administrative procedure

Constitutional principles constitute decisive normative standards for the design of administrative procedures in the EU. The existence or non-existence of administrative procedural rules in the EU is not merely a 'technical' question, free of constitutional value choices. The realization of constitutional principles has a considerable potential impact on substantive outcomes. Those values and principles include the protection of the rule of law and its emanations in subprinciples such as legality, legal certainty, proportionality of public action, and the protection of legitimate expectations. Those values and principles further include the concepts of a democratic Union on the basis of a transparent system requiring not only the definition and protection of rights of participation and access to information but also, under article 9 TEU, equality of citizens in their access to Union administration. Prominently, articles 1(2) and 10(3) TEU require that, in the Union, in line with the principles of openness and of subsidiarity, 'decisions shall be taken as openly and closely as possible to the citizen'. Other individual rights and obligations underpinning the design of procedures arise from the principle of good administration as partially restated in article 41 CFR. Good administration requires that decisions be taken pursuant to procedures which guarantee fairness, impartiality, and timeliness. Good administration includes the right to be given reasons—a requirement also in the Introduction/Book I—General Provisions protected by the right to an effective remedy restated by article 47 CFR—and the possibility of claiming damages against public authorities who have caused harm in the exercise of their functions. Good administration also requires the protection of the rights of defence, language rights, and, more generally, protection of the notion of due process. In addition, good administration extends to information rights which include privacy and business secrets as well as access to information.

The preamble of the Model Rules illustrates the background and aims of the Model Rules.

> Public authorities are bound in administrative procedures by the rule of law, the right to good administration and other related principles of EU administrative law. In the interpretation and development of these model rules, regard should be had especially to equal treatment and non-discrimination, legal certainty, fairness, objectivity and impartiality, participation, proportionality, protection of legitimate expectations, transparency, and due access to effective remedies.

[90] ReNEUAL Model Rules on EU Administrative Procedure, Paul Craig, Herwig Hofmann, Jens-Peter Schneider, Jacques Ziller, Oxford 2017; Ellerbrok 2016; Ruffert 2016.

Public authorities shall have regard to efficiency, effectiveness and service orientation. Within European administrative procedures due respect must be given to the principles of subsidiarity, sincere cooperation, and clear allocation of responsibilities.

(c) ReNEUAL Model Rules on EU administrative procedure in six chapters

The ReNEUAL Model Rules of administrative procedure are organized into six 'books'. These books are designed to reinforce general principles of EU law and identify—on the basis of comparative research—best practices in different specific policies of the EU. Book I addresses the general scope of application of the model rules, their relation to sector-specific rules and the member state's law, and the definitions of wordings applied in all the summary of principles, which guide administrative behaviour, and the interpretation of all subsequent norms in Books II to VI. The latter books cover more in-depth administrative procedures in the EU that have the potential to directly affect the interests and rights of individuals. The books address non-legislative implementation of EU law and policies by means of: rulemaking (Book II), single case decision-making (Book III), contracts (Book IV), and, very important for the composite nature of EU administration, procedures of mutual assistance (Book V), and information management (Book VI).

5. Good Governance on the International Level

The issue of good governance has for a long time been an important issue in the international forum. Two policy fields form the starting point of the discussion on good governance: development aid policy and financial policy. The UN is especially involved in the development aid policy and the IMF and World Bank are the leading international institutions in relation to countries' financial policy.

National representatives negotiate agreements between countries, but it is the international organizations that have become more important. In the context of international law, we see the development of elements of international administrative law. Good governance is becoming more and more important for these international organizations. In the beginning, countries which received support from these international organizations had to fulfil these norms of good governance. Of course, it is important that these organizations also abided by the norms of good governance. Indeed, this gap was addressed.[91] In the following, the role of several international organizations in the development of good governance is explained. International organizations are, for our purposes, the UN, the IMF, the World Bank,[92] and the OECD.[93]

(a) International level, different policies

On the international level, different policies of various international institutions are concerned with good governance. First, we outline the definitions of good governance on the international level. Second, we examine the practical content of these norms

[91] Esty 2007. [92] World Bank 1997, 1–4.

[93] OECD, Development Assistance Committee, Final Report of the ad hoc working group on participatory development and good governance, Paris 1997.

for the World Bank and the OECD. Third, we compare the national and regional approaches.

The discussion on good governance is not a typical European law discussion. In international law and national law, we find similar debates, but these discussions are not always recognized as good governance discussions because the terminology varies. All the same, comparable tendencies in the discussions on good governance are recognizable in three fields of law: administrative law, European law, and international law.

(b) Relevance of different definitions on international level

In relation to the international law debate, we would like to reiterate that different definitions of good governance are used by different international institutions,[94] although all work with the notion of good governance. An elaboration on this follows in the next section. This broad international discussion on good governance started at the end of the 1980s and it is still ongoing.[95] It was—at least in the beginning—linked with development aid and the relations between more or less developed countries. Here, the principles of good governance act as *an external field of normative reference*, which is *the primary function* of these principles.

The character of the discussions often seems more political than legal, even though the legal aspect is of viable importance as to the actual activities of the administration. Further, the link with legal theory is then more easily made.[96]

So, we need to pay attention to the legal norms of good governance. The resulting question is, what is the content of the legal norms for the administration from the perspective of the legislator, the administration, the judiciary, and other controlling institutions? This is one of the central questions in administrative law. What can be found in the constitution and in other legislation, and which norms have been developed in the case law of the judiciary and other independent controlling institutions like the Ombudsman and the Court of Audit? Is the codification of such case law necessary? The developments in international law and European law and their consequences at the national level make it necessary to redefine the content of the principles of good governance, including proper administration.

(c) Definitions of good governance on the international level

Here is a brief overview of definitions of good governance. Please note that these definitions are presented not chronologically, but rather substantially.

In 1997, the IMF published a paper on the role of the IMF and the Good Governance concept.[97] It stated that good governance is important for countries at all stages of development. The IMF approach is to concentrate on those aspects of good governance that are most closely related to surveillance over macroeconomic policies—namely, transparency of government accounts, the effectiveness of public

[94] UNDP, Governance for Sustainable Human Development. A UNDP policy document, United Nations Development Programme January 1997; UNCHR Resolution 1998/72; OECD Development Assistance Committee, Part I and Part II, Paris 1997; OECD, *Governance in the 21st Century*, Paris 2001; IMF, The IMF and Good Governance, 2002; and World Bank, *Corruption and Good Governance*, 1997.

[95] Botchway 2000.

[96] Réne Foqué who used the terms 'General Principles of Good Global Governance': see Foqué 1998, 39.

[97] IMF 2018.

resource management, and the stability and transparency of the economic and regulatory environment for private sector activity.

In 1994, the UNDP gave their description of good governance.[98] They stated that good governance covers mainly participation, transparency, and accountability and that it is effective, equitable, and promotes the rule of law. It ensures that political, social, and economic priorities are based on a broad consensus in society and that the voices of the poorest and the most vulnerable are heard just as well in decision-making process on the allocation of development resources.

In 1998 and 2005, the UNCHR wrote that good governance comprises of democracy, respect for human rights and fundamental freedoms, including the right to development, transparent and accountable governance in all sectors of society, as well as active participation by the civil society, as an essential part of the necessary foundations for the realization of social and people-centred sustainable development.[99]

In 1994 and 2000, the World Bank described good governance as predictable, open, and enlightened policymaking,[100] a bureaucracy imbued with a professional ethos acting in furtherance of the public good, the rule of law, transparent processes, and a strong civil society participating in public affairs. Poor governance, on the other hand, is characterized by arbitrary policymaking, unaccountable bureaucracies, unenforced or unjust legal systems, the abuse of executive power, a civil society unengaged in public life, and widespread corruption.

The OECD's Development Assistance Committee (DAC),[101] concluded, that good governance is linked with participatory development, human rights, and democratization. They also identified the rule of law, public sector management, controlling corruption, and reducing excessive military expenditure as important dimensions of good governance.

(d) Good governance norms from international organizations to countries

International financial organizations apply requirements of good governance mainly in relation to governments of developing countries. Why was it, from a legal perspective, difficult to introduce requirements of good governance to these countries? Ryngaert and Wouters contended that this was difficult because these financial organizations had only the promotion of financial or economic purposes written down in their statutes.[102] The promotion of requirements of governance fell outside these purposes because governance is a non-economic, political element. So, the World Bank and the IMF could not put legal requirements on these countries. The solution was to define good governance in a way that it made a link with governance without being too politically outspoken: 'good order that is necessary for a positive investment climate and the efficient allocation of resources'.[103]

How did these institutions nevertheless become an example of good governance in a more political sense? The definitions of several donor states in other international organizations were more to the point. The DAC and in practice the World Bank had elaborated more political assumptions. We can conclude that financial institutions set the standard for good governance because of the need to impose borrowing conditions

[98] UNDP 1994. [99] UNHCHR 2007. [100] World Bank 1994.
[101] OECD 1995. [102] Wouters and Ryngaert 2005, 72. [103] Ibid; Binda 2015, 3.

on governments. Subsequently, these norms have been taken out of their economic origin and put into more non-economic terms.

Wouters and Ryngaert[104] conclude that the OECD is the most active organization in encouraging both member and non-member countries to implement good governance in all its aspects. The principles of good governance would transform not only the relationship between governments, citizens, and parliaments, but also the effective functioning of governments themselves. Wouters and Ryngaert listed these principles, since the OECD's expertise and guidelines are generally acknowledged as objective, reliable, and useful for member and non-member countries. The following aspects of good governance are regarded by these authors as useful: respect for the rule of law; openness, transparency, and accountability to democratic institutions; fairness and equity in dealing with citizens, including mechanisms for consultation and participation; efficient and effective services; clear, transparent, and applicable laws and regulations; consistency and coherence in policy formation; and high standards of ethical behaviour.

In their conclusions, they showed that a number of international organizations have pushed through reforms aimed at enhancing good governance standards within their own organizations over the last years, especially in light of their long-standing secrecy. A need exists for a continuous dialogue with the civil society (citizens, companies, NGOs) which still criticizes the process. But these international organizations are blind to the efforts towards participation and transparency, especially in the case of international financial institutions. Pervasive corruption and chronic mismanagement are often targets of thorough good governance reforms and UNESCO is a good example. International organizations have already come a long way in the areas of good management and public transparency. As far as participatory governance is concerned, much remains to be done.

(e) International organizations: internal effect of good governance

Apart from applying the concept of good governance to governments of countries, international organizations apply this concept to their own organizations as well. How do the World Bank and the IMF try to meet requirements of good governance in relation to their own organizations? Both have recently created agencies and procedures to enhance horizontal accountability. Accountability was formerly applied only by means of an executive board. Such a board of executive directors represent a group of countries, though the most influential have their own director. In practice, most decisions were not really made by the board, but by the staff and senior management in cooperation with the most influential countries. Nowadays, these boards frequently apply the principles of good governance.

The IMF has created an Office for Independent Evaluation, and the World Bank has constituted an Inspection Panel in order to consider complaints on alleged detriments caused by the Bank's failure to follow its own policies or procedures. They have stimulated a closer collaboration with NGOs. A considerable point of critique is that some NGOs influence the executive board more by means of lobbying than some small countries. The board should control the work of their staff more intensively by developing a transparent set of rules and an open process concerning the appointment of the head of organization.

[104] Wouters and Ryngaert 2005, 76.

(f) A modern view on principles of international law and good governance

The concept of good governance has grown into the system of international law as a consequence of developments in both international law and national legal systems.[105] This concept has clear links with the concepts of the rule of law and democracy.[106] And in these concepts links are also made with good governance.[107] At the grassroots of international law, good governance has been accepted as a principle of law in national legal systems first, and from there in regional institutions as well. Important to mention is that although the concept is not related to a few policy fields, neither is it implemented in all policy fields. Sometimes this concept is included in general regulations but most of the time only some aspects of good governance are actually included in the law and in practice these principles are developed by administrative authorities and the judiciary. So, their function as a norm for the administrative authorities and the judiciary uses elements of the principle in its review. The concept is applied as such and in different policy fields and made concrete in different types of norms. In policy papers this notion can be found, but in different types of directives and regulations the concept is worked out at the EU level. Other regional (economic) organizations are frequently working with this concept. Notably, at the EU level a right to good administration has been elaborated and concretely applied in judicial procedures. Lastly, at the EU level it is not only about one or two policy fields as it has been used in several policy fields by both administrative authorities and judiciary.

At the international level, the concept of good governance has been accepted and further developed in different treaties related to economic and environmental issues. Both courts and dispute settlement institutions have applied the principle of good governance.

The question then relates to the two approaches—narrow and broader—of principles of international law. From the narrow scope, four conditions are linked to general principles of international law: (a) the principle must be general; (b) the principle, which is a norm, can be neither a rule nor a general practice accepted as law; (c) chronologically, it must have already been recognized; and (d) this recognition is attributed to civilized nations.

In describing these conditions related to the principles of good governance, the following aspects are relevant. We speak about general principles of good governance because these principles are not restrictive to one or two policy fields; these principles are applied in the broader framework of the administrative authorities and the judiciary. These principles are norms, legal norms in the sense that although sometimes elements have indeed been codified into the law, in other situation these still represent unwritten norms. These principles are recognized in a broad sense, so that this condition has been fulfilled. Finally, these principles are accepted by civilized nations. Therefore, from the broader perspective, and keeping in mind the different functions of principles, the principles of good governance should be recognized as principles of international law.

In international law, we see a growing interaction between the sources of national and international law in both the instrumental as well as the protection aspects of international law: the principle(s) of good governance have been discovered. As a consequence of internationalization and globalization, the importance of the principles of international law has increased; the principles of international law are in transition.

[105] Addink 2015c, 288–303. [106] See Chapters 5 and 6.
[107] Zum, Nollkaemper, and Peerenboom 2014; Orellana 2009, 671–94.

In the more classical approach of the principles, in cases when no treaty provisions or clear rule of customary law exists, the additional role of principles of international law may be clearly observed. From a more modern view, these principles of international law have more than just these two functions. Therefore, it can be concluded that the concept of principles of international law is changing especially in relation to the more general principles which are accepted by many countries at the national as well as regional level. In that changing role of principles of international law, we notice that good governance principles are increasingly applied by general and specific international organizations. Some aspects of the principles of good governance are codified in international (human rights) treaties. Lastly, the principle(s) of good governance has been applied by the (inter)national courts of justice and dispute settlement bodies. The principles of good governance have a general character, as we have shown, and are not (yet) accepted either as rules or as general practice. At the same time, the concept of good governance has, chronologically, already been recognized by civilized nations as has been explained in this chapter. It is a core legal idea which is common to all civilized systems, as Schlesinger wrote in 1957, and it can be added here that the concept of good governance is more than a legal idea. Good governance is a promising principle of international law.

(g) Global governance and good governance

Global governance is governance on the international level in its broadest sense, not only by international organizations but by all actors involved, such as NGOs, states, lobbyists, and so on. Good international governance can be achieved according to the line of ownership by particular states within a multilateral organization.[108] This is not necessarily achieved through formal control of the management and the voting structure of an institution, as has been shown by the African Development Bank and Inter-American Development Bank who formally have ownership but practically do not, due to a lack of commitment by members as to the main purposes of the organization as well as due to a lack of resources.

Consensus on good governance does not necessarily foster its basic elements among states. [109] It can exclude some countries, as the process is mostly informal. For example, informal meetings are not recorded and no accountability mechanism applies to them. Due to differences in expertise, some delegations can be overwhelmed by others. Specific voting requirements could be used in order to bolster perceptions of accountability, transparency, and representation among states within an organization. For example, scholars agree that the voting structure of the UN Security Council would be perceived as more accountable if it would be more representative. Good global governance can be achieved by increasing access of non-state actors but on the condition that they themselves are bound on conditions of good governance, which means in practice that they do not cooperate with countries that are already quite influential.[110]

6. Conclusions

Good governance is a multilevel concept that includes the national, regional, European, and the international levels. The development of the concept of good governance is

[108] Wouters and Ryngaert 2005, 78. [109] Woods 2000, 61. [110] Ibid.

converging, but the more detailed specification is different as it is adapted to the specific circumstances of each level and each institution.

On the national level, the judiciary, followed by codification on the part of the legislator, have developed material norms of good governance. Subsequently, these norms are to be interpreted again by the judiciary.

The strongest developments are found in Europe. Principles of good governance have been developed in all the European countries in the context of the administration as was seen in recent research on good governance developments in the member countries of the EU, and both the European Union and the Council of Europe are active in this field, and their institutions increasingly use the terminology of good governance, although its content may still vary somewhat. Now, the European Union should strive for coherence in the hodgepodge of norms. Ongoing Europeanization and internationalization require it.

The international level is productive as well as in relation to the promotion of good governance. Different international organizations have developed these norms in their relations with countries, but the use of different definitions and specified implementation create a somewhat diffuse picture. They have also started to apply comparable norms within their own organizations. This development is applauded and supported by many NGOs and by many countries. In the literature, it has been argued that good governance is a principle of international law.

So, the multilevel aspect of good governance is explained and the final conclusion is that good governance is a multilevel concept. The next chapter elaborates on the legal theory of good governance. What is the character of these principles?

4

Principles of Good Governance

The Theoretical Perspective

This chapter elaborates upon the theoretical foundations of the principles of good governance, which can trace their roots to an area of legal research known as International and Comparative Administrative Law.[1] Research in this field is concerned with the development of administrative law in the light of globalization. This is done in a comparative way, on the one hand and, on the other hand, from a systematic-dogmatic viewpoint in which the interaction between the bodies of administrative law on the different levels and in different countries form the pivotal point of interest.

We start with an elaboration of fundamental aspects of good governance and make the link to the discussion between Dworkin and Hart about law, especially the position of the notion of principles in the concept of law. Then we examine the relationship between law and values and the link between justice and morality, especially in the context of public law. In the context of good governance, the discussion focuses on whether good governance is a norm for the administration or a citizen's right. Alexy's concept theory of constitutional rights is primarily relevant. A difference is made between Dworkin's and Alexy's approach to rules and principles. Finally, we bridge the gap between principles and values.

1. Fundamental Aspects of the Principles of Good Governance

Good governance functions as a central, organizing, and integrating point of focus for this field of law. The elaboration of the principles of good governance is very useful for the development of a normative framework concerning questions of governance in a changing and globalizing world.

Yet, within this perspective, two other strands of thought are integrated as well: first, a Dworkian style view of the system of administrative law; and second, and more specifically, Curtin and Dekker's interpretation of good governance as an interpretive concept[2] in their contribution to the book *Good Governance: The Concept and its Application by the European Union*. Werner continues this line of thought with an application of the interpretive concept but in the context of state sovereignty.[3]

Crucial to Dworkin's approach is the need to interpret law. Rules are not self-sufficient and therefore need to be interpreted.[4] He uses principles which leave a degree of discretion.[5] Thus, the link between the principles of good governance and the interpretive concept becomes clear.

[1] Janssen 2016; Scheltema 2005; Seerden (ed) 2012; Seerden (ed) 2018.
[2] Curtin and Dekker 2005, 3–20. [3] Werner 2002. [4] Dworkin 1986, ch 2.
[5] Dworkin 1977, 27 and 31.

Unfortunately, principles are not as self-evident as they may seem. Some scholars prefer to work strictly with concrete positive law while others insert somewhat abstract elements in the form of principles and individual rights and liberties. For that reason, we address this contrast, but only briefly. It should be kept in mind that these abstract elements have their own meaning in the dynamics of the judiciary, the legislator, and the executive,[6] as well as in the dynamics of national, European, and international law.[7]

The first step is Dworkin's position in his discussions with Hart. The second step is a comparison of the ideas of Dworkin and Alexy. From here, a direct link is made with the principles of good governance and the principles of proper administration. The last aspect is the double comparative approach as elaborated here: horizontal (between the countries) and vertical (between the countries and regional and international organizations).

2. Dworkin and Hart

Hart, together with Bentham and Austin, the founding fathers of the legal positivism,[8] has criticized Austin[9] for describing law solely in terms of behavioural regularity and obedience based on habits and a fear of sanctions.[10] In Hart's opinion, the positive legal framework has three defects, of which uncertainty is the first. This uncertainty is repaired by a rule of recognition. This rule of recognition refers to the acceptance of a fundamental rule by the community as a whole that assigns to particular people or groups the authority to make law. In the civil tradition, a constitution is the obvious example. What about the common law tradition, the tradition of Hart himself? In such traditions, the rule of recognition is 'a consensus among the senior officials of all branches of government'[11] and by the rule of '*stare decisis*'.[12] Van Oenen succinctly described the crucial aspects of the discussion between Hart and Austin in his summary:

> Hart improved Austin's conception by introducing the concept of a 'rule', which incorporates both an (Austinian) aspect of 'regularity' or 'measure', and a normative or 'internal aspect'. He described law as a system of (primary and secondary) rules with an internal aspect: legal subjects, or at least juridical officials, do not just 'follow' rules, they also view their rules as norms for their own and each other's behaviour.
>
> In this way, Hart added a modest 'hermeneutical' dimension to the positivist theory of law; the description of law acquires an element of interpretation, evaluation or reflection. But the moral content of legal rules or norms plays no role in this theory, the reason being the empirical fact that concrete systems of law differ strongly on this count (except for the 'minimum content of natural law', of course). Therefore, moral content cannot form part of the concept of law. Moral and legal rules are distinguished by means of secondary rules, procedural rules of recognition without a necessary moral content. [. . .]

[6] The study by Dworkin—taking the internal participant's point of view (Dworkin 1977, 14)—centres on judges, but the same remarks can be made concerning legislators and other public officials. Another argument for this choice can also be found in Dworkin 1977, at 15. But the structure of judicial argument is typically more explicit, and judicial reasoning has an influence on other forms of legal discourse that are not fully reciprocal.

[7] Dworkin especially makes the horizontal comparison: see the Elmer Case (Dworkin 1977, 15) and the McLoughlin Case (Dworkin 1977, 23); the Snail Darter Case (Dworkin 1977, 20) can be seen as an example of a vertical comparison.

[8] Hart 1961, 144.

[9] Austin 1995; Austin 2007.

[10] Hart 1961, 83–4; Soeteman 1992a; Van Oenen 1994.

[11] Edlin 2007, 235.

[12] Minns 2007.

Legal positivism does not, and indeed need not deny that legal practice has, or at last can have, a moral 'point'. What it does deny is that law cannot be described without reference to such a moral point or purpose. Dworkin however argues that the positivist framework, even when modified or 'stretched', is flawed because it cannot account for all moral principles that figure in legal practice and adjudication. The part some moral principles play in law can only be accounted for within the hermeneutical perspective that Hart's theory lacks.

Dworkin argues that Hart wrongly reduces the hermeneutical dimension of law to a sociological description of official behaviour. This does injustice to the self-image or self-conception of lawyers. Participants in a social practice, like law, always view their practice from an internal perspective.

For Dworkin, reasoning about the correct solution always involves imposing a moral 'point' on law. This 'point' functions as the focus of a construction that tries to give as much coherence as possible to applicable and related legal norms. From this perspective, moral principles that play a role in the argument for the decision should be considered as part of the law itself.[13]

(a) Hart's concept of law and the theory of Dworkin

In Hart's concept of law, two types of principles can still be found in relation to the discretion of the judiciary, principles that are part of positive law and principles as accepted by the judiciary in a plausible interpretation of a series of cases.[14] Dworkin, however, finds a third group of principles as essential, namely the principles which are part of an implicit, unconscious background latent in the legal system. His interpretive approach is built on ideals of fairness, justice, and integrity. From his perspective the model must aim at a coherent construction of the legal system. This ultimate coherence justifies the adhered principles. Ultimately, one right answer to a case can be applied throughout the whole system, if it is really a coherent system.[15] This is also applicable when competing principles are to be weighed.

(b) Linking to administrative law

The administrative law literature already links this theory of Dworkin with its perceptions on proper administration.[16] In Dworkin's work, special attention is drawn to differences between principles and rules, and principles and policies.[17] The latter may need a short explanation. Policies describe goals, whereas principles resemble rights and form 'a threshold weight against community goals'.[18]

Van der Heijden has elaborated a method to find answers to questions of administrative law.[19] He assesses about fifteen principles in a case in order to support the concept of fairness and justice. In the same case, he proves how application of the principles of fair administration is possible in combination with criteria of effectiveness and efficiency. He concludes:

> Characteristic for the found method for finding answers to questions of administrative law is that it is not only applicable in cases where judges have to rule. The method is also useful for policy analysis, ex ante and ex post, and in the situation of making and conducting policy.

[13] Van Oenen 1994, 259. [14] Hart 1961, 144. [15] Wacks 2008, 40–1.

[16] De Waard, 1987, sees a relationship between legal principles and procedural administrative law; Nicolai, 1990, makes a link between legal principles and the process of the steps of decision-making by the administration; Addink 1999, ch 2: Foundations of the Principles of Proper Administration; Van der Heijden, 2001, develops a broader theory of legal philosophy with regard to proper administrations; Popelier, 2000, makes a link with the Principles of Proper Law Making. See also Van der Vlies 1984.

[17] Wacks 2008, 45–8. [18] Ibid. [19] Van der Heijden 2001, 273.

Especially in this last situation the principles of fair administration are instrumental, because they have direct influence on changes in the real world. This instrumental character of these principles has to fit in the system of administrative law that traditionally recognizes these principles as juridical guarantees instead of instruments. This is done by defining instrumentality as a function of giving guarantees, and judicial guarantees as instruments. That results in a system that in accordance with the ideas of Dworkin can lead to answers to questions of law that are acknowledged in the concerned community as the answers that give the best possible interpretation of politics and law in this community.[20]

(c) Good governance in this system?

How does good governance function in this system? As already noted, Curtin and Dekker have found good governance[21] to be an interpretive legal concept.[22] This is in line with Dworkin[23] as well as Werner, who proposes the same in relation to the concept of state sovereignty.[24] The principles of good governance fit harmoniously within this scheme of thought. As Curtin and Dekker state:

> According to Dworkin [an 'interpretive' legal concept] plays an important role in the legal discourse in a community by structuring different *conceptions* around a common fundamental value and thus contributing to the development of the legal system of that community. These different conceptions are, to a large extent, expressed in the principles connected with the 'interpretive' legal concept.[25,26]

There are three dimensions to this. Different conceptions of good governance are expressed in different sets of principles of good governance, which in their turn form an interpretation of the relevant practices and legal materials.

As stated at the beginning of this section, good governance is perceived to be the central point of focus for both national and international administrative law.[27] This has an important consequence. It means that, since international administrative law is made up of administrative law at the different levels and areas of the global legal order, the legal materials which are relevant here comprise different parts of this whole global legal order.[28] This is in contrast with the wide range of different conceptions of good governance, as expressed by various institutions, such as the IMF and the European Commission. Besides this obvious divergence there is a range of similarities and parallels. International and comparative administrative scholarship should reveal such convergences.

The principles of good governance as presented in this book follow this paradox. Curtin and Dekker explain that concrete principles resemble different conceptions of good governance. This is perhaps a strong characteristic of good governance being an interpretative legal concept. In different circumstances, good governance may require different approaches. Convergence is then relevant, as different conceptions of good governance revolve around a common core—and there is probably considerable overlap.

[20] Ibid, 275.

[21] In the article, there is a difference in terminology: 'Governance' or 'Good Governance', but not in the method which is used. My impression is that they see these as organizational norms, however, I see them as norms for governmental actions.

[22] Curtin and Dekker 2005, 3–20. [23] Soeteman 1992b, 170ff.

[24] Werner 2002; see the article by Curtin and Dekker, 2005, and the one by Werner for a detailed exposition of this perspective.

[25] Curtin and Dekker 2005, 3–20. [26] Rawls 1999, 5.

[27] Kingsbury, Krisch, and Stewart 2005. [28] Esty 2006b.

Partly because of its dogmatic legal dimension, the principle-focused approach is sensitive to the legal aspect of those principles. Two points can be touched upon. The first is that those principles which grant the best interpretation of the relevant legal materials form part of the law. This is, of course, an idealistic description in reality; one probably recognizes a gradual evolution of different principles from a soft law character to 'harder' law. The second is that these principles are related to the legal materials, which brings its own specific normative force. In relation to this, it is useful to recall the interesting observation made by Koopmans regarding the general principles of law in European and national systems of law in general, that they

> are, in a certain sense, commuters. Frequently, they travel from national legal systems to European Union law, as principles common to the legal systems of the Member States. Subsequently, after having been baptized as general principles of Union law, they travel back to national systems as part of the influence of Union law on national law.[29]

He also concludes:

> general principles are not, or not any more, used to patch gaps left between legal provisions duly enacted by the framers of laws, constitutions or treaties. On the contrary, they are an integral part of the conceptual tools judges employ nowadays for settling conflicts.[30]

This development corresponds, in Koopmans' view, with a broader evolution in which growing reliance on general principles of law is part of the answer to the question of the increasing inadequacy of more traditional sources of law. These include the usual codes, statutes, and regulations in light of technological progress, rapid processes of social change, and the globalization of the economy.

The principles of good governance, as expressed in these several conceptions, form an interpretation of the rules expressed in the legal materials. So, as Dworkin argues, they are related to these rules in two ways. On the one hand, they fit coherently with the rules, on the other hand, the principles—as an expression of the *point* of good governance—exert an influence on these rules themselves, as Dworkin makes clear in relation to an imaginary example of the rules of courtesy:

> that the requirements of courtesy—the behaviour it calls for or judgments it warrants—are not necessarily or exclusively what they have always been taken to be but are instead sensitive to its point, so that the strict rules must be understood or applied or extended or modified or qualified or limited by that point.[31]

As a special case, we can think of the situation where a principle that has implicitly been part of the law is at a certain moment codified in a piece of legislation, as is the case with some general principles of good administration in administrative law. In this section, the principles of good governance have a function in line with the third group of principles according to Dworkin. The principles provide internal fundamental basics for the administration. Multilevel developments shape this underlying basis.

3. The Relationship between Law and Values

The literature elaborates that the relationship between law and political and moral values is often characterized as a complex topic.[32] The first is reductive, in the sense

[29] Koopmans 2000, 25. [30] Ibid, 34. [31] Dworkin 1986, 47.
[32] Cane 2002, 5.

that it adheres to positive law which is as such strictly separated from morality and allegedly free of ideology.[33] The second finds that they are inextricably connected with each other.[34]

(a) Two lines of thinking

The first positivist line of thought is interlaced with the theory of *autopoiesis*, which finds a legal system autonomous and self-referential.[35] Nevertheless, this system is cognitively open, which means that it is influenced by and may even absorb non-legal norms, making them its own.[36] From here, a link can be made with the theory between background and foreground normative theory.[37] Background theory is immanent in the law and is often stated implicitly rather than explicitly. The foreground values are found outside the law. Thus, political theories on pluralism, liberalism, or republicanism are in the foreground. The court and foreground theories use background theories; this may help lawyers by providing theoretical models which may assist the search for background values of law.

The second line of thinking is that no clear separation between rules of law and values exists or that they are even intertwined.[38] The contents of public law can only be properly understood against the background of the political theory that a society actually espouses. Such theory is part of the law. For the positivist, but not for the interpretivist, values can be immanent in the law without actually being part of it.

These two lines are also qualified as the red and the green light[39] or the line of functionalism and normativism.[40] The red light refers to positivists that believe law should be dealt with by formal, external mechanisms such as courts and tribunals. The focus is on the protection of citizens and restrictive interpretation of the scope of public power. Administrative law is then value-neutral. The green light considers law as being instrumental. The prime concern of administrative law is to facilitate the execution of public programmes and policies. Internal control and political control are preferred over a formal legal institution. For them law is value-laden and ripe for critical assessment against moral and political criteria.

(b) Values in public law

In public law, the following immanent values are recognized: representation, accountability, juridical deference, a public-private dichotomy, equality before the law, protection of the individual, access to the courts, executive authority, diffusion of public power, transparency, participation, and promotion of public interest. These values have some aspects in common. They are products of an interaction between legislative and judicial activity and are partial values latent in public law. These values are dynamic rather than static and may even outweigh each other. This should be impossible according to Dworkin, so it is here that we deviate from his theory. Practice requires it.

These values are subject to various mutual conflicts, partially due to their level of abstractness. Normative principles purport to explain and justify legal rules so that they become general. At the same time, the abstractness and immanency of these values may constitute disagreement about what concrete rules they require or justify.

[33] Kelsen 1997, 19. [34] Craig 2000, 228–30. [35] Teubner 1984, 85.
[36] Teubner 1993. [37] Harlow 2006. [38] Craig 2000, 228–30.
[39] Harlow and Rawlings 2009, 1. [40] Loughlin 1992.

Another opinion is that political theory or the theory of the state do not ignore these values and, as a result, this theory has influenced the interpretation of these values positively. Craig elaborates upon several topics which are examples of these values. These are: the nature and object of public law, three theories (red, green, and amber), the nature and object of public law, changing boundaries of state action, central concepts in public law, sovereignty, the rule of law, the separation of powers, doctrinal issues, the vertical dimension, and doctrinal issues with a horizontal dimension.

The conclusion is that law is, to a certain extent, dependent on political theory. So public law, political theory, and political science interact, which is actually accepted in the Dworkian theory of adjudication as well as in the positivistic line of, for example, Raz.[41] For Raz, legal positivism means that there is no conceptual relationship between law and morality. His theory of norms refers to rules that serve as a guide for human behaviour in a legal system. His focus is on the authority law, as well as people under a particular system and the authority that society should acknowledge as due to the law. These questions are relevant for law and society as they affect the daily lives of individuals.

4. The Nature of Principles in the Legal Theory

In the article 'Good Governance: A Norm for the Administration or a Citizen's Right?',[42] the question was whether good governance refers to principles, rights, or values in the context of the legal developments at the European level. The article showed that codes of good administration have been developed by both the European Union and the Council of Europe. Several principles of good governance have been codified and these principles are recognized in the case law of both courts. In the Lisbon Charter, good governance was established as a citizen's right. Recently, the ECtHR reiterated the importance of good governance.[43]

(a) Theory of constitutional rights

In his book, *Theory of Constitutional Rights*, Alexy develops a comprehensive conception of constitutional rights.[44] His central thesis is that constitutional rights are optimization requirements and therefore need to be balanced. He explains this as follows:[45]

> The definition of principles as optimization requirements leads straightaway to a necessary connection between principles and proportionality. The principle of proportionality (Verhältnismä ßigkeitsgrundsatz), which in the last decades has received ever greater international recognition in the theory and practice of constitutional review, consists of three sub-principles: the principles of suitability, of necessity, and of proportionality in the narrower sense. All three sub-principles express the idea of optimization. Principles qua optimization requirements require optimization relative both to what is factually possible and to what is legally possible.

What can his ideas contribute to the concept of good governance?

First, many courts are developing an enormous amount of jurisprudence engaging in constitutional rights reasoning and in some theoretical material from legal scholars. Unfortunately, not much has been written on good governance yet, but some liberal

41 Raz 2003; Raz 2009.
42 Addink 2008.
43 ECHR 2 October 2012, 5744/05 (*Czaja v Poland*).
44 Alexy 2002.
45 Alexy 2016, 65.

philosophers have actually recognized a limited number of strong rights, and constitutional courts have recognized an increasing number of relatively weak rights.[46] One core feature of constitutional rights practice is that the constitutional rights can be limited by subjecting them to a balancing exercise or an analysis concerning proportionality. This discussion is not relevant in countries where only a constitutional court exists, but each country faces tensions between fundamental rights and relative human rights.

Second, the role of good governance depends considerably on its qualification as a principle or a fundamental right. As the development of good governance is still ongoing, it is better to provide a theoretical framework in which good governance is allowed full play. Finally, we make the link—as Alexy did—between principles and values.

Alexy's theory of constitutional rights addresses the nature of and the relation between rules and principles within one legal framework. Both rules and principles are legal norms, but they have a different outlook and function. Rules refer to the aspect of positive law, while principles are optimization requirements of the legal system as a whole. This means that principles should be observed as much as possible within the given legal framework.[47] Rules are either fulfilled or not. The distinction between the two is 'a key to the resolution of central problems of constitutional rights doctrine'.[48]

(b) Principles as such and principles in the context of rules

Principles should be realized to the greatest extent legally and factually possible. Principles are therefore not definite requirements like rules are, but entail very strong claims to be fulfilled. Principles resemble certain values which are immanent to a system of law. Therefore, principles are applicable *ex systema iuridica*. The relationship between reason and counter-reason will not be decided by the principle itself.

This is quite different in the case of rules. Rules insist that one should do exactly as required, of course within the bounds of reasonableness. Alexy prefers a nuanced model as far as rules are concerned, since it is possible to incorporate an exception into a rule on the occasion of a particular case. When this occurs, the rule loses its definitive character in the particular case. The incorporation of an exception could be based on a principle. When the legal system does not prohibit the limitation of rules by incorporation of exceptions, the rules for which this prohibition applies may keep their strictly definitive character.

Principles have a certain weight, which is important in case of clashes. In general, a principle is trumped when a competing principle has a greater weight in the case to be decided. By contrast, a rule is not automatically trumped when its underlying principle is outweighed by another competing principle but rather depends on the balance of all principles involved. For example, rules passed by an authority acting within its jurisdiction are to be followed, and principles state that one should not depart from an established practice without any good reason. Such principles can be called 'formal principles'. The more weight that is given to formal principles within a legal system, the stronger the need to elaborate in concrete rules its '*prima facie*' character. When such principles are completely deprived of any weight, certain rules would no longer apply. In a situation like this, rules and principles would have the same *prima facie* character.

[46] Kumm 2007. [47] Alexy 2002, 47–8. [48] Ibid, 44.

The *prima facie* character of rules and principles has different consequences for each. The difference can also be seen in situations of burden of argumentation, which has more effect on principles than on rules. A burden of argumentation strengthens the *prima facie* character of a principle, but the *prima facie* character of a rule resting on an authoritative creation or a long-standing acceptance is something quite different and much stronger. Thus, the proposition that rules and principles differ from each other in their *prima facie* character should be maintained in spite of some necessary modifications.

(c) Radius of principles

Although it is impossible to provide an exhaustive reflection on the ideas of Dworkin concerning principles, his ideas need some explanation in addition to the section on Dworkin and Hart. We have concluded that principles are needed in addition to positive law, as positive law leaves gaps that have to be bridged.

Dworkin usually refers to principles when he talks of 'a set of standards other than rules'.[49] But he has elaborated upon the radius of principles. Dworkin leaves policies out of this radius, as policies resemble certain goals whereas principles have a dimension of weight and importance; they are requirements of justice and fairness.[50] This difference is important, as principles subsequently have a certain weight, which he calls their 'relative weight'.

Principles do not appear in an all-or-nothing fashion and do not automatically have legal consequences as rules obviously do. Principles have relative weight only until they are articulated in concrete legal rules and then they have definite reason. As long as principles have relative weight, they are to be balanced in accordance to the difference in weight; balanced but not outweighed. In this model, it is impossible to insist on a complete disregard of one principle.

(d) Differences between Dworkin and Alexy

Now we see a difference between Dworkin and Alexy. Both conclude that rules and principles are different as to their outlook and their function. Still, some differences exist between both authors. Dworkin regards rules as definite reasons whereas he regards principles as merely *prima facie* reasons which should be elaborated in concrete rules.[51] Rules automatically have legal consequences when certain conditions are met, and then in an all-or-nothing fashion.[52] To Alexy, both rules and principles are legally binding but not in the same way; they differ in character as explained above. Still, rules and principles can differ among themselves in their character. Perhaps this is more obvious for principles than for rules and therefore it is interesting to follow his way of reasoning. According to Alexy, principles already have legal consequences. Dworkin on the other hand recognizes the legal consequences after elaboration of the principles in rules.

(e) Rules and principles as reasons

Rules and principles resemble a different kind of reason. They are like *prima facie* reasons, at least as long as no exception is to be read into them. However, stating that

[49] Dworkin 1977, 22. [50] Ibid. [51] Ibid, 22–4. [52] Ibid, 22–31.

rules and principles are definitive and *prima facie* reasons does not clarify what they are reasons for.

Principles are on the whole relatively general, because they have not yet been related to the possibilities of the factual and normative world. When they are related to the boundaries of the factual and normative world, they produce a differentiated rule system. The idea of a principle-dependent differentiated rule system becomes more significant when we discuss some objections to the supposedly arbitrary nature of their balancing. The criterion of generality is only somewhat accurate, because some norms are of such a high degree of generality that they are not recognized as principles. There can be three objections to principles: the invalidity of principles, the absolute character of principles, and the breadth of principles. Invalidity of principles is concerned with extremely weak principles, that is, with principles which in no circumstances take precedent over other principles. Absolute principles are extremely strong principles, that is, principles which in no circumstances are preceded by other principles. We speak about the breadth of principles when they can be related both to individual rights and to collective interest.[53] According to Dworkin, principles are only those norms which can be offered as reasons for individual rights.[54]

(f) Principles and proportionality

The theory of principles and the principle of proportionality are related to each other. This connection is as close as it could possibly be. The nature of the principles implies the principle of proportionality and vice versa. This means that the principle of proportionality, with its three sub-principles of suitability, necessity, and proportionality in its narrow sense, logically follows from the nature of principles when principles are regarded as optimization requirements. In the theory of constitutional rights, three models have been developed: the model of pure principles, the model of pure rules, and the model of rules and principles.[55] Here the focus is on principles of good governance. The next section adds some theories of principles and values.

5. Good Governance and Integrity

In the special good governance edition of the *Netherlands Journal of Public Administration*[56] it was noticed that good governance entails, in addition to identifying principles or values, the search for principles and includes situations where principles or values are in fundamental conflict with each other. These conflicts need to be solved on a case-by-case basis, yet without arbitrariness or sole pragmatism. Furthermore, different approaches from the subjects mentioned may give rise to deeper reflections. This interrelationship between principles and the relationship between principles and values are treated in greater detail later.[57]

(a) Principles and values of public law

The concept of public values has become more visible in research and academic debates in various disciplines.[58] These values entail questions about good and evil, about

[53] Alexy 2002, 61. [54] Dworkin 1977, 82–90. [55] Alexy 2002, 69.
[56] Bestuurskunde 2011. [57] Huberts 2014. [58] De Graaf and others 2011, 8.

ethics and morality, about principles and guidelines. Honesty, transparency, efficiency, profit, and sustainability are examples of a great variety of values. These values need to be understood in dependence of the circumstances in which they have become manifest, and in relation to other values involved. Within the discipline of governance, it remains unclear how some values are positioned in relation to other values, such as private, political, and religious values. There are also values of public law, such as the value of public order, procedural order, morality, and proper administration. In the balancing exercise, three approaches can be discerned: (1) a universal approach, which means that certain values are absolute (the disadvantage of this approach is the lack of flexibility); (2) a stakeholder approach, in which values are not static and absolute, and the balancing process is dependent on the relation between political actors; (3) an institutional approach, which means that the stability of certain institutions and sets of values must be guaranteed.[59]

(b) Integrity and good governance

The term integrity often comes with good governance. Some countries give priority to integrity, maybe in part because of popular attention. In some countries, integrity is closely related to the general quality of public governance. In other countries integrity standards are enhanced in order to reduce corruption. The term integrity is used in all such circumstances, though the exact meaning of the term integrity is not always made clear. Originally, integrity entailed certain ethical or moral standards referring to individuals. Now, integrity is also often used in institutional settings where individuals are employed. Many institutions have voiced their integrity values in mission statements, internal rules or guidelines, and codes of conduct. That being so, the scope of integrity values has become much larger in comparison with its original meaning. There is yet something else, which is that principles and values are more often valued in their own right in law and in legal systems. Thus, integrity is increasingly being discussed among legal scholars, which adds a clear legal and administrative legal dimension to integrity.[60]

(c) A legal approach to integrity

This leads to new questions concerning the relation between a legal approach to integrity and the many other approaches already in place and also to questions on how governmental and extra-governmental bodies should deal with the legal dimensions of integrity. From a moral and ethical perspective, it is eventually the collective institutional integrity that counts far beyond formal codes, legislation, and other regulations. This is especially true for those representative institutions with officials that need to act exemplarily. If there is an issue with integrity, this causes a loss of confidence in the government. Unfortunately, there are already a significant number of reports on integrity issues in governmental institutions.[61] These reports furthermore show that there is a need for clarity with regards to the principle of integrity so that both officials and citizens know what they are to expect.

In the textbook *Integrity* it is explained how integrity, legitimacy, and good governance relate to each other:[62] integrity as an integral element of (principles of) good governance and the government institutions with their constant search for legitimacy

[59] Bestuurskunde 2011. [60] Van den Heuvel, Huberts, and Muller 2012.
[61] Minister Interior and Kingdom Relations 2013. [62] Addink 2012b, 102–24.

over time. It is, however, still difficult to provide for clear definitions of the separate terms. Societal changes demand flexibility of the terminology. There might also be certain differences, like a 'thick' and a 'thin' conception of these terms, potentially creating substantial differences. For example, integrity might fit into the thin conception, by meaning the absence of corruption and fraud or it might fit in the thick conception, by referring more to 'good' behaviour in general. The term 'legitimacy' might refer to that which is written in laws or to what goes beyond, such as principles or unwritten or customary law. Good governance might refer to certain standards that institutions and officials must abide by, but it might also serve as an assessment framework for 'checking' authorities, such as Chambers of Audit, ombudsman institutions, and the judiciary. The common element in integrity, legitimacy, and good governance is that these entail certain norms and standards. Although these concepts are differently used throughout academic disciplines, and must be to a certain extent, there is a need to develop a more comprehensive understanding of the concepts. Such a comprehensive understanding would enhance an interdisciplinary discussion. The main issue is to define how integrity and good governance correspond and overlap. Two other often-mentioned values—suitability and openness—are directly related to good governance, specifically to the principles of effectiveness and transparency.

(d) Integrity from the individual to the institutional domain

The principle of integrity has been expanded from the individual domain to the institutional domain. But there is something else going on. We see that these values have been increasingly frequent in the field of law: in international and European law, but also on the national level, and in the general fields of constitutional, administrative, and criminal law, but also in specific fields like municipality and civil servant law. The principle of integrity is found in the law, and this points to the link between law and good governance. There is not only a question of philosophical, ethical, or historical perspective, but also of an administrative and legal perspective on integrity. This leads to interesting questions about the content of ethical and moral values of integrity, the question of the legal dimension of integrity, the relationship between these aspects, and their evaluation by the classical administration itself and by independent external governmental agencies.

(e) Different definitions of integrity

From an ethical perspective, Huberts[63] has classified—based on the literature and research—the various definitions of integrity into the following eight visions of integrity: (1) *Integriteit als heelheid* (integrity as wholeness); (2) *Integriteit als passendheid* (integrity as appropriateness); (3) *Integriteit als professionele verantwoordelijkheid* (integrity as professional responsibility); (4) *Integriteit als bewust moreel reflecteren en handelen* (integrity as a conscious moral reflection and action); (5) *Integriteit als waarde(n) incl. onkreukbaarheid* (integrity and value(s) including integrity); (6) *Integriteit als overeenstemming met (waarden in) wet en regelgeving* (integrity and compliance with (values of) law and regulations); (7) *Integriteit als overeenstemming met geldende morele waarden en normen* (integrity and compliance with applicable standards and moral values); and (8) *Integriteit als exemplarisch ideaal gedrag* (exemplary ideal behaviour).

[63] Huberts 2012, 22; Huberts 2014.

These views are interesting because they show that the concept of integrity in the public sector can be seen from different angles. In his contribution, Huberts essentially goes to the following four distinct concepts of integrity: (a) integrity as ethical understanding; (b) integrity as a social concept; (c) integrity as a moral concept; and (d) integrity as a legal concept. These concepts could be applied either in the individual or organizational context of the public sector.

From a legal perspective the different normative frameworks for different parts of the government are relevant here.[64] When it comes to norms of integrity, because of their different constitutional position, we have to distinguish between the political heads who have an election mandate, like ministers, deputies, and councillors, the representatives of the citizens—parliamentarians—on a local, provincial, and national level, and the civil servants working on the three levels. But we also have to look at the outcome of the work done by those who are controlling these public institutions, like the court, the ombudsman, and the court of audit, by their work done for the protection of citizens.

Some remarks about the terminology of integrity, ethics, and values follow here. What is the reason that the term 'integrity' is so often used? It seems that the use of this word connotes behaviour that is appreciated. And indeed, the word integrity is linked to honesty, wholeness, and impartiality. But is it possible to be completely unbiased? In other words, when is a person prejudiced? It seems rather unlikely that there is anyone without bias. Does the concept of integrity draw the correct picture or might it have a different content?

(f) Relationship between integrity, ethics, and values

The following explanation is intended to clarify the relationship between integrity, ethics and values, and also integrity in relation to legal rules and legal principles. Ethics and morality are both related to norms and values. Norms and values are often mentioned as one entity while certain characteristics of the two concepts differ materially and therefore should be distinguished. Values are moral principles that have weight when making choices; they have experiences or characteristics which we seek to attain. Values are often formulated abstractly and positively. Standards keep more concrete rules for behaviour and are often formulated negatively. There is a distinction between moral norms, social norms, and legal standards. Values are limitless, while standards necessarily draw a line. Standards force more people to conform. Standards would have a greater objectivity because their extent is determined, while values are subjective in nature. Values are 'open' moral categories and may refer to multiple standards, and standards cannot always be traced to a specific value. Are standards indeed concrete and are values merely abstract? Are values positive and norms usually negative in nature? Are values more subjective in nature and are standards more objective? Clear answers may not be available, but an example could provide for some clarity.

An example of objectification can be found in a report of the Netherlands Academy of Science. First, some generally accepted standards for academic practice can be found and then some violations of those standards are described in the paragraph of the report entitled 'Forms of violations of academic integrity'. Scientific integrity consists of compliance with the general principles that must be adhered to in all branches of science. Some of these are: the careful execution of research and the publishing of relevant

[64] Addink 2015b.

information, scientific research results should be published in literature accessible for the public, the scientific statements should be based on objective observation and logical reasoning, and in this sense value-free, the application of the results are not value-free and possible conflicts of interest should be made known in a timely manner. In mid-June 2012, the Netherlands Association of Universities has published comprehensive policies for academic integrity on its website. This includes a code with a national model for complaints on violation of scientific integrity and one national definition of violations of academic integrity. The Code provides details on the following five principles: precision, reliability, verifiability, impartiality, and independence.

(g) Principles of integrity and good governance

Based on this example we get some idea of the answers to the questions related to the principles of integrity and good governance and law. Integrity means in this context compliance with general principles that are endorsed. In the sector of social life, it involves compliance with objective standards of integrity. And this brings us to the question of the relationship between law and integrity. Law consists not only of legal regulation but also legal principles. A question that arises is: are principles in the context of integrity consistent with the principles that we know in law? Moreover, it raises the question: are the norms and values related to integrity absorbed by the principles developed in the framework of the law or should these (partly) be distinguished? Do those requirements thus get a different content? What about the scope of the absorbed principles?

The expansion of the number of contexts in which integrity plays a role is remarkable. We find the concept in business and in government, in public but also in private life, and see a process of broadening the integrity context. The result is that the concept is less clear and has a rather abstract and ethnical connotation. The meaning given to this term comes together on an abstract level but based on its various applications. But at the application level the term will have a more concrete content, however—because of the variety of situations—this content will vary strongly from one situation to another. This is partly due to the difference in scope to be given. The concept of integrity is sometimes based on a narrow interpretation, and other times it has a much broader meaning. Besides the aspects in the narrow perspective we find also other aspects like collegiality, reliability, responsiveness, objectivity, decency, effectiveness, and efficiency. This varying scope of the concept indicates the great importance of a precise definition in connection with the discussion between different disciplines. If we do not provide such a definition, then the concept of integrity becomes an amorphous and rather meaningless umbrella term, and there is great risk of not undertaking or misunderstanding it. Moreover, there is also from a legal standpoint a need for a clear definition so that clear legal standards can be put in place.

There is a difference between good governance and integrity. Integrity has both a legal and a moral component and is focused on (but not only on) the actions and behaviour of the civil servants or public sector employees. As such, it includes some principles of good governance: properness, accountability, transparency, or sometimes human rights. But good governance is much wider, as it includes the principles of citizen participation and scrutiny and also focuses on the human rights aspects of the conduct of state bodies and employees. In most of the country reports attention has been given to the implementation of fighting and preventing corruption, also in relation to promoting integrity and good governance.

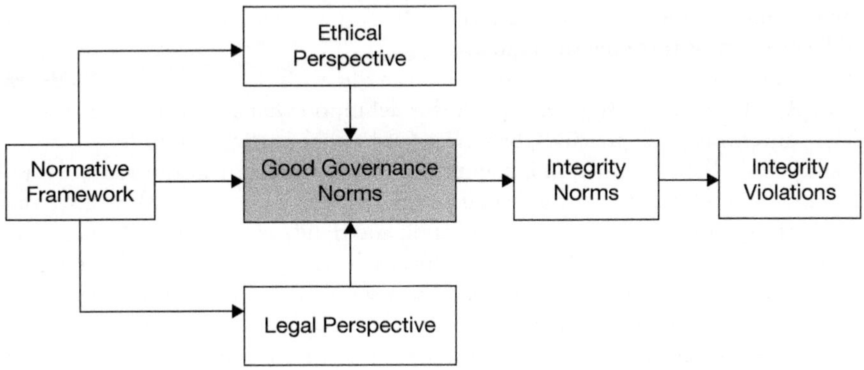

Figure 4.1 The relationship between the ethical, legal, and good governance perspectives in the public sector integrity (Dadan Anwar 2015)

So, we see that integrity norms can be part of the good governance principles. But which principles are relevant in this context? To find out, we have to start with the right side of Figure 4.1: the violation of integrity norms. There we find two approaches. In the first, more classical approach integrity violation is concerned in particular with corruption and fraud in the context of the public and private sector. These notions have a specific content in criminal law. National Penal Codes often criminalize the active and passive bribery of domestic public officials, active and passive bribery in the private sector, and active bribery during elections. Provisions on active and passive bribery sometimes also apply to national judges, former civil servants, foreign civil servants, international civil servants, foreign judges and judges of international organizations, as well as future civil servants.

Definitions of corruption and fraud are very important. In practice, the following definition of corruption in the public context has been provided: 'offering, giving, asking or receiving private gain because of the position or (non-)action of a public functionary'. Public functionaries are, in the context of penal law, civil servants as well as politicians, including governors and ministers. Elsewhere in the literature there are many other definitions of corruption.[65] The following aspects are relevant in relation to the definition of corruption.[66] First, it is important to mention that the only relevant activities are those which are carried out in relation to the function of the person. So, purely private activities are not relevant for the discussion about the content of public corruption. Second, the interpretation of persons means that functionaries are civil servants, and so are politicians; it concerns corruption in the public service. The notion of a civil servant has a broad interpretation in the case law (see HR 30 January 1914, W 9149; HR 1 December, *NJ* 1993, 354; HR 30 May 1995, *NJ* 1995, 620) and according to the law (Article 84 Penal Code in which it is explained that members of parliament and members of city Councils are also civil servants in this context). In the law, special attention has been given to situations before and the situation after the fulfilling of the function of the civil servant. The third element of corruption is that there is a third party who will profit from the (non-)action of the civil servant and the civil servant will receive something in return for this (non-)action. This party will be mostly somebody outside the public organization. The fourth aspect is that we can speak

[65] Amsterdam Report 2005, 4. [66] Ibid, 5.

about corruption in situations where there is not only a situation of receiving gifts, but also the prospect of receiving such gifts.

The definition provided here is more or less in line with the Dutch Penal Code, especially Articles 362 and 363. To explain this definition we have to study, first, these articles concerning gifts, promises, or services and also the articles on bribery (Articles 177 and 177a). Then we have to highlight the difference between corruption and fraud and what the limitations of these factual illegal activities are exactly. We will see that not only the negative qualifications (corruption and fraud) are relevant, but that for an administrative (preventive and repressive) approach we have to look at the standards which are relevant for the administration. These standards are especially integrity and the principles of good governance and these norms complete the national and international legal framework. But in administrative law we have a more narrow definition of a civil servant and, as a consequence, also a more restrictive content of corruption in which there is only discussion about civil servants, politicians thereby being excluded.

(h) Violations of integrity

Often, in a report, a difference has been made between corruption and fraud; however, the two terms are related because both terms concern personal favours or promises. With regard to fraud, there are two parties involved: the fraudster and the harmed person or institution. Corruption takes place between three parties: the civil servant who profits, the public organization, and the person who induces the civil servant to benefit from his (non-)actions.[67] This difference can also be found in the administrative case law[68] and administrative policy[69] of the Netherlands.[70]

There is in general an important difference in the Netherlands between the Penal Code and Administrative Legislation. In the Administrative Legislation a distinction is made between a legal fact, a legal norm, a legal consequence, and a legal act. In the Penal Code attention is given to the punishable act and the punishment. From our point of view a fundamental point is lacking in the Amsterdam report: specifying the norm. We found only general reflections concerning integrity. In another report good governance principles were mentioned, but there was also no specification in relation to corruption.[71] There is a need for a positive administrative law norm which can be found in the principles of good governance.

There is a second much broader approach of integrity violations which have been developed by van den Heuvel and Huberts[72] and which have also been used by other authors. The following types are distinguished:

- *Corruption*, including bribing, 'kickbacks', nepotism, cronyism, and patronage (with gain for oneself, family, friends, or party).

[67] Ibid, 5 and para. 1.2.1.

[68] Corruption: Central Appeals Tribunal 7 November 2002, 00/5791 AW, LJN AF3553; Fraud: Central Appeals Tribunal 1 November 2003, 02/1004 AW, 03/1535, LJN AN8809.

[69] See about fraud policy: *Kamerstukken (Parliamentary documents) II* 2004/05, 17 050-29 810, nr. 295.

[70] Addink and Ten Berge 2006.

[71] Huberts 2001, 4.

[72] Huberts' classification has subsequently been used in research into the occurrence of integrity breaches in local government (J.H.J. van den Heuvel, L.W.J.C. Huberts, and S. Verberk, *Het morele gezicht van de Overheid: Waarden, normen en beleid, Utrecht* 2002) and into the implementation of integrity policies in local government (J.H.J. van den Heuvel and L.W.J.C. Huberts, *Integriteitsbeleid van gemeenten*, Lemma 2003); L.W.J.C. Huberts What can be done against public corruption and fraud. Expert views on strategies to protect public integrity *Law and Social Change* 29: 209–24, 1998.

- *Fraud and theft* of resources, including manipulation of information to cover up fraud.
- *Questionable promises, gifts, or discounts.*
- *Conflict of interest* through jobs and activities, outside the organization (eg 'moonlighting').
- *Improper use of violence* towards citizens, suspects.
- *Other improper (investigative) methods of policing* (including improper means for achieving noble causes).
- *Abuse and manipulation of information* (unauthorized and improper use of police files; leaking confidential information).
- *Discrimination and (sexual) harassment*; indecent treatment of colleagues/citizens.
- *The waste and abuse of organizational resources*, including time.
- *Misconduct at leisure* (domestic violence, drunken driving, use of drugs etc).

This list of violations of integrity norms has been linked to some principles of good governance by Dadan Anwar (2015). The following principles of good governance are relevant in this context: properness, human rights, transparency, and accountability (see Figure 4.2).

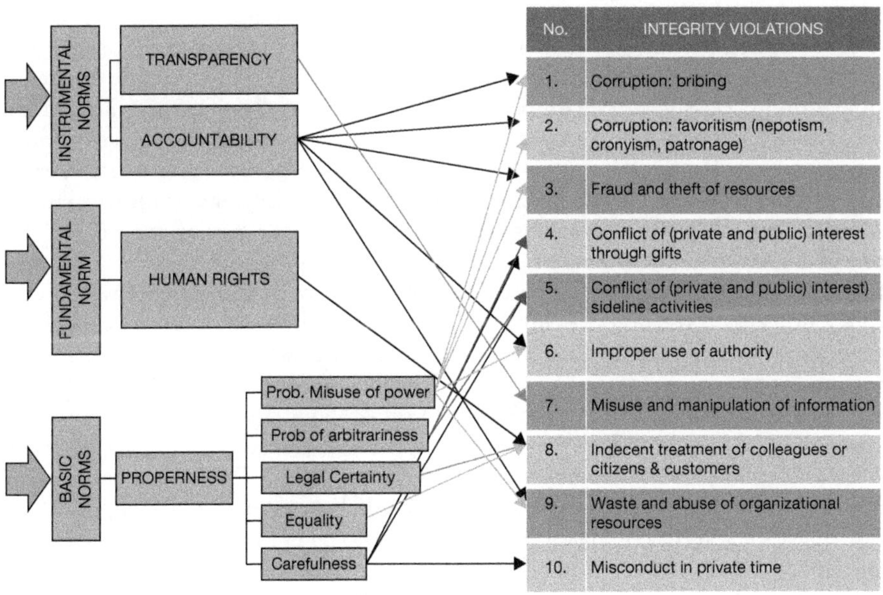

Figure 4.2 The applicability of good governance norms in situation of integrity violations (Dadan Anwar 2015)

6. Concepts of Values

Principles and values are connected to each other, especially when it comes to a balance of competing principles and values. Values are often regarded as the ground for principles. In both situations gradation is possible. There are three different concepts: axiological, deontological, and anthropological concepts of values.[73]

The axiological concept refers to the adhered framework of values. It resembles what is regarded as the ultimate good. Axiological concepts are used whenever something is described as beautiful, effective, reliable, valuable, democratic, socially just, liberal, or consistent with the rule of law. The deontological concept relates to the axiological concept as norms relate to values. It concerns the framework of obligations or duties. The anthropological concept, by contrast, refers to the concept of will, interest, need, decision, and action. One could say that these groups of concepts cover the whole range of basic disputes both in practical philosophy and in jurisprudence.

Taking this threefold division into account, the significant difference between principles and values is easy to see. Principles are requirements of a particular nature. They resemble values, but more importantly, they are requirements. By contrast, values are located on the axiological plane. However, this does little more than crudely identify the nature of values. In order to identify their relation to principles more precisely, a deeper analysis is necessary.

The idea of values is used in many different ways in ordinary speech, as well as in philosophy and in the jargon of various disciplines. The comparison of values with principles can be based on a few general and basic structural characteristics of values. These become apparent in a basic distinction in frequent usage: the difference between the idea that something *has* value and that something *is* a value.

If someone says that something *has* value, that person is engaging in evaluation. Value judgements, along with the concepts of value they include, can be divided in three groups: classificatory, comparative, and metric. A classificatory value judgement is made when, for example, someone identifies a particular constitution as 'good' or not. The function is to divide things with a positive and negative value and, if permitted, a neutral value. Comparative value judgements allow someone to make differentiated evaluations. This is used when one says of two objects that one is better than the other, or that they are perhaps of equal value. The most precise form of evaluation is offered by the metric value judgements which allocate a number to the object being evaluated as an indication of its value. A classic example of metric evaluation is the evaluation of a piece of property in terms of a sum of money.

When something *is* value then we have to think about criteria of evaluation. These criteria can be diverse and they can also compete with each other and have an overall evaluation. 'Good' is the expression of an overall evaluation. The application of evaluative criteria which have to be balanced to each other corresponds to the application of principles. Only those criteria for evaluations which can be balanced against each other will be termed evaluative criteria. Their counterparts are criteria which, like rules, are applicable without balancing. These are called evaluative rules.[74]

All sorts of things can be the object of evaluation: natural objects, artefacts, ideas, experiences, actions, and states of affairs. The criteria of evaluation can also be highly diverse. A car can be evaluated according to various qualities, like its speed, safety, comfort, price, economy, and beauty. Furthermore, criteria of evaluation may compete with each other.

[73] Alexy 2002, 87. [74] Ibid, 89.

(a) Principles and values

The difference between principles and values is reduced here to just one point. Norms are distinguished in axiological norms and deontological norms. The first refers to an evaluative criterion or value. The second concerns the existence of a rule or principle. What, under a system of values, is *prima facie* the best, is under a system of principles what *prima facie* ought to be; and what under a system of values is definitively the best, is under a system of principles what definitively ought to be. Principles and values are distinguished by their respective deontological and axiological characteristics only.[75]

(b) Position of law

Law is concerned with what ought to be. This counts in favour of the model of principles. On the other hand, it is not difficult to move from the idea that a certain solution is constitutionally speaking the best in terms of positive law, to the idea that certain principles stem from the constitution. The moment one accepts such transitions as possible, they are entirely acceptable for legal reasoning to proceed from a model of values instead of a model of principles. However, the model principles have the advantage that they express the obligatory nature of law quite clearly. In addition, the concept of a principle gives rise to fewer misconceptions. Both of these points are important enough for us to prefer the model of principles.

7. Conclusions

From the interpretative approach of Dworkin there is more room for the development of new good governance principles. Also, Hart would accept such principles, as long as they are laid down in positive law. There are different conceptions around a common fundamental value. These different conceptions are, to a large extent, expressed in the principles connected with the interpretive legal concept. But we also have to see that it is important for legal certainty and equality that these principles have to be codified as much as possible in the positive law. Having the principles of good governance as solely unwritten principles is not enough.

These concepts of the importance of the principles and the codification of the principles in positive law can be developed on national, regional, and international levels. There is a continuous line from one level to another in which these concepts become increasingly developed. Good governance is related to positive law and to its underlying principles. These principles are linked to the underlying values.

From a legal perspective, the discussion between principles and rights in the context of good governance is also relevant. We see a difference in the more or less abstract character of the legal norm. The principle can be seen as an abstract legal norm and the right is a concrete legal norm. Alexy and Dworkin both have an open eye for the principles and the rules, but on the topic of principles they do not have exactly the same opinion. Alexy gives legal weight to principles whereas Dworkin seems to be of the opinion that the legal effect will be realized by the rules in which the principle has been codified.

The theory of principles and the principle of proportionality are related to each other and the principle of proportionality has been specified. It is interesting to see

[75] Ibid, 92.

that in relation to fundamental rights Alexy works with the concept of optimization requirements in relation to these rights. This is also a norm which presents the principles of good governance in context.[76]

Furthermore, principles are differently 'valued', so their role in particular cases may differ depending on how much weight they bear in that particular case. Values are often regarded as the ground for principles. Different concepts have been developed in relation to this relationship. Most importantly, the principles are requirements of a particular nature, while values are seen as what is ultimately good. A distinction also can be made with the comparison between the notion that something has value and something is a value.

We conclude by looking at good governance as a principle and good governance as a value. The difference between principles and values is reduced to just one point. Norms are distinguished in axiological norms and deontological norms. The first refers to an evaluative criterion or value. The second concerns the existence of a rule or principle. What, under a system of values, is *prima facie* the best, is under a system of principles what *prima facie* ought to be; and what under a system of values is definitively the best, is under a system of principles what definitively ought to be. That is relevant in the context of principles of good governance.

[76] Boustra 2010.

5

The Rule of Law and Good Governance

Good governance is a meta-concept and as such it is easily linked to other meta-concepts such as the rule of law and democracy. Together, they form the cornerstones of the modern state. This chapter and the next deal with such relationships. This chapter focuses on the rule of law and good governance, and the next is concerned with democracy and good governance.

The structure of this chapter is as follows: first, the rule of law in the classical liberal tradition is outlined, the different powers in the state and the relations between these powers is also discussed; second, the historical roots and the traditional perspectives on the rule of law are explored, with specific attention paid to some differences between the narrow concept of the common law tradition and the broader concept of civil law tradition; third, some difficulties and the developments in relation to the traditional approach of the rule of law are addressed; finally, the relationship between good governance and the rule of law is elaborated upon. The conclusion is that the modern approach of the rule of law needs the concept of good governance.

As addressed briefly in Chapter 1, good governance is the third cornerstone of the modern state. Although good governance is rooted in both the rule of law and democracy, it has developed into a full-fledged cornerstone which has its own core dimension. This means that aspects of good governance are still recognizable in the rule of law and democracy, but that good governance also has new elements which cannot be found there, such as the principles of effectiveness and accountability. The processes of development of all three cornerstones are strongly intertwined.

It is important to recognize that these meta-concepts could be interpreted differently. These concepts are models which are to be implemented in the modern state. Each state has to take into account its own features, its own traditions and its own cultural and economic factors.

The rule of law itself is used differently in Western European countries. The scope of the rule of law has different particularities in the common law tradition and in the German *rechtsstaat*, the French *l'État de dro*it, and the Italian *Stato di diritto*. Although all adhere to the idea that the government's exercise of power should always be conditioned by law,[1] the precise convictions concerning the law vary. Roughly speaking, the differences between the thick and the thin concepts of the rule of law correspond with the rough division of the common law and the civil law traditions.[2]

1. Rule of Law in the Classical Liberal Tradition

(a) Elements instead of a definition

It has been disputed whether a definition of the rule of law could be stated. It would result in either a fragmentary, vague description or to an unintended expansion of the

[1] O'Donnell 2004, 33. [2] Urbina 2002, ch 4, 225–43.

concept.[3] One should be careful whether such a definition refers to the scope and interpretation of the rule of law as such or to some of its elements.

In the introduction it is explained that the rule of law is a meta-concept and as such it needs interpretation and adoption to fit in with the national legal system. In practice, this has been done for several countries and although this interpretation differs, the core elements turn out to be the same. One could say that a formal rule of law is shared, though the material rule of law may differ. This is often explained by the historical backgrounds of the rule of law. For example, the rule of law in Britain emerged in the seventeenth century in a situation where the political and the civil society worked together, while the German *rechtsstaat* emerged in the nineteenth century, when the political and the civil society were vigorous opponents.[4]

The concept of the *rechtsstaat* first appeared in a German book[5] and was placed in contrast to the aristocratic police state. German writers usually place Kant's theories at the beginning of their accounts of the movement towards the *rechtsstaat*.[6] The German rule of law, the *rechtsstaat*, consists of the following principles:[7] (1) the separation and differentiation of state power; (2) the principle of legality; (3) the principle of legal certainty; (4) the principle of trust; (5) independent judicial control; and (6) the principle of proportionality.

The Anglo-American rule of law is connected with the work of Dicey. He has articulated some characteristics as to the situation in Britain, which are contained in the following elements:[8] (1) constitutionalism; (2) rule-based decision-making; and (3) a commitment to neutral principles, such as federalism, separation of powers, and textualism. This rule of law is to be defended by an independent judiciary.[9]

(b) A shared basis

When these two archetypes are brought together, four elements appear to correspond. The first one is the principle of legality, which requires a legal basis and legal implementation preceding state actions. The second element is the division and balance of powers. More specifically, this concerns legislative, executive, and judicial actions. The third element is independent judicial control. The judiciary applies written and unwritten legal principles. The fourth and final element concerns the protection of fundamental rights which flow from various legal sources, for example international treaties, case law, a human rights bill, or a constitution. These four elements are elaborated upon below.

(c) The principle of legality

The principle of legality is a fairly strong requirement which must be adhered to. This principle demands that representatives of the people should have adopted the legislation; that statutes find general application; and that the legislator is himself bound by such legislation. An important safeguard flowing from the rule of law is entrenched by a constitution: the democratically elected legislator alone can authorize any limitations

[3] Ibid.

[4] Walker 1971, Pt III. German home towns have had quite a strong identity. The liberal bureaucracy has been their firm opponent. Home towns reacted to the developing liberal bureaucracy with the Biedermeier culture.

[5] Von Mohl 1866. [6] Hayek 1960. [7] Blaau 1990, 81–2.

[8] Zywicki 2003, 2–3. [9] O'Donnell 2004, 32.

of fundamental rights. This is relevant since the legislator has received the power to determine the concrete scope and the content of such a right.[10] In the meantime, the principle of legality limits the exercise of governmental power. In the written constitutions, this principle of legality is often explicitly expressed. The German Constitution, for instance, states in article 20 that 'the Executive and the Judiciary are bound by the law'. The United Kingdom does not have such a written constitution. Its constitution is composed of the set of laws and principles under which the United Kingdom is governed: court judgments, treaties, and unwritten sources, such as parliamentary constitutional conventions and royal prerogatives.[11] In its constitution, the principle of legality operates as an important constraint ensuring that officials act in accordance with the law.[12]

(d) Separation and balancing of powers

The separation and balancing of powers protect against coagulation of power. This is a compelling requirement. As said by Lord Acton: 'power tends to corrupt and absolute power corrupts absolutely'.[13] Originally, the separation of powers meant that the three traditional branches of state authority—the legislator, the executive, and the judiciary—are to be kept distinct and that none of them should have excessive power, which is of the utmost interest to the democratic liberal state.

Separation of powers is a political doctrine and, like the rule of law, a key element of constitutionalism. Most countries employ a balance of powers rather than a strict separation of powers. In those terms, the balance of power translates to a certain separation of state activities rather than a separation of the institution involved. For instance, Australia is a constitutional parliamentary democracy that does not adhere to the strict separation. On the contrary, to separate the executive branch from the legislature would entail significant constitutional implications. In that case, another balance of powers must be sought. The fourth power institutions might prove to be helpful in this process. They could serve as a check on the traditional institutions, regardless of their position in their respective constitutional systems.

The doctrine of separation of powers can be traced back to ancient Greece, particularly to Aristotle. He identified three elements of a constitution: the deliberative body which discusses community affairs, the magistracies formed by the officials, and the judiciary. If these three elements are well arranged, the constitution is bound to be well arranged, and the differences enshrined in the constitution are bound to correspond to the differences between each of these elements.

In the developments of the different countries, there has been a move towards a more separated approach to these main functions in most situations. The views of Locke, Montesquieu, and Bolingbroke became very influential in the seventeenth and eighteenth century (Locke's *Second Treatise of Civil Government* 1689 and Bolingbroke's *Remarks on the History of England* in 1748). However, the writings of Montesquieu[14] are credited with the modern expression of 'separation of powers'. In book XI, chapter 6 of his book *The Spirit of Laws*, he has given an account of the English Constitution, outlining the doctrine of separation of powers. There are three elements contained within Montesquieu's theory on separation of powers. First, he recognized that government has three main functions 'that of making laws, that of executing public affairs, and that of adjudicating on crimes or individual cases'. Second, he stipulates that there

[10] Giussani 2008, 63. [11] Ibid, 5. [12] *Entick v Carrington* (1765) 19 St Tr 1029.
[13] Lord Acton, 3 April 1887. [14] Montesquieu 1748.

should be three corresponding organs of the government: the legislator, the executive, and the judiciary. Finally, he states that these three functions should be held by three separate branches in order to uphold and protect liberty.

In the literature, there are two stances towards Montesquieu's opinion. The first adheres to a complete or strict separation of powers.[15] The second is that there is some overlap and interaction possible between the powers. Again, it is not clear whether the separation refers to the institutional functions or activities. On one point, Montesquieu was outspoken; the independence of the judiciary must not be compromised in any way.

It is generally accepted that a strict separation of powers is impossible both in theory and practice and therefore many have advocated for a system of checks and balances. This is certainly a justifiable position, considering that the doctrine's desired end, the avoidance of tyranny, could be compromised by a strict interpretation. The avoidance of tyranny, or any hindrance of the state, may be better achieved through efficient checks and balances and could represent the doctrine in its highest form.[16] Nowadays, and in the context of this book, we not only have three powers but also a fourth power[17] and the good governance concept can bring a better equilibrium to the separation and the balance of the four powers in the state.

(e) Judicial control

There are several aspects to judicial control. First, the judiciary must be independent. Second, the legislation and administration must be subject to control by an independent judiciary. Finally, there must be judicial control over the fundamental principles of law. These fundamental principles stem from three elements: the legal certainty principle, the principle of trust, and the principle of proportionality.

The principle of legal certainty is very important. It means that legal measures and legal rules must be clear and consistently applied and that state action must be sufficiently defined in order to remain predictable. According to the principle of trust, legitimate expectations are protected. If the state has created a specific situation and a person has acted on the reasonable assumption that this situation will remain unchanged, then he or she can rely on that assumption.

The principle of proportionality is also an important aspect of the *rechtsstaat* concept. Proportionality is a method for determining whether the reasons advanced by the state for limiting a specific fundamental freedom outweigh the values which underlie the constitutional commitment to the protection of that freedom. It is clear that the state's actions could come into conflict with the scope of protection offered by the citizens' right, and thus the principle constitutes the very last stage in an enquiry into the constitutionality of a particular infringement on fundamental freedoms. The principle entails that laws, actions, and measures of state organs should not exceed those strict limits within which a specific legal purpose is pursued. Proportionality is usually tested as to the objective suitability of the law, action, or measure, the question of its necessity, and the question of its reasonableness or its 'proportionality' in the narrow sense. By applying the proportionality principle at the point where the justifiability of a specific restriction has to be determined, the Court endeavours to come to an optimal decision based on the hypothetical relationship between an intended infringement and the intended goals to be attained by it.

[15] Munro 2001, 301. [16] Giussani 2008, 28. [17] Addink 2005b, 269–302.

(f) Human rights protection

In relation to human rights, a state's respect for the individual's fundamental rights and freedoms is relevant to any power emerging from collective authority. Such authority is vested in the legislature and the executive, and the systematic protection of these rights and freedoms by the judiciary.[18]

In the Magna Carta, we find guarantees against arbitrary power of the nobility and their liege (lord) to land owners' rights. The guarantee meant to curtail the possible misuse of royal power. But for centuries it was considered as a self-evident truth that any ruler would take care of his subjects in the most appropriate fashion. In Europe, all the kings and other princes understood themselves as committed to the values of the Christian faith. Thus, they perceived no need to take action with a view to protecting the rights of people in another state. It was the general understanding that the king will always do the best for the well-being of his subjects. In France, Jean Bodin (1530–95)[19] sought to confirm the royal authority; the king enjoyed the right of sovereignty which no one was entitled to call into question. The relevant issue was the independence of the king of France versus any other outside powers. At the same time, the English writer Thomas Hobbes[20] stressed the rights of the sovereign power of the state over all the members of the common polity.

A more modern development in human rights can be found in the publication of John Locke's *Two Treaties of Government* from 1690, in which (diametrically opposed to the recipes advocated by Thomas Hobbes) a systematic theory of the state was worked out and human rights were attached to individual persons. Locke writes: 'nobody can transfer to another more power that he has in himself, and nobody has an absolute arbitrary power over himself, or over any other, to destroy his own life, or take away the life or property of another. A man […] cannot subject himself to the arbitrary power of another.' In this sense, a societal treaty has the function to protect life, freedom, and ownership of all the citizens. Here human rights already have a pre-constitutional character.

Then we have the phase of the first constitutions and human rights. The American Declaration of Independence from 1776 says: 'We hold these truths to be self-evident, that all men are created equal, that they are endowed by their Creator with certain unalienable Rights that among these are Life, Liberty and the pursuit of Happiness. That to secure these rights, Governments are instituted among Men, deriving their just powers from the consent of the governed.' As a result, some fundamental rights and freedoms were worked out in the American Constitution, ratified by sufficient states in 1788 and came into force in 1789.

In 1789, the French *Déclaration des droits de l'homme et du citoyen* was proclaimed in the Netherlands, and the rights were introduced for the first time in the 1798 *Bataafse Regeling*. During these times, fundamental rights were codified on a national level in many European countries. Rights relating to freedoms were more often codified in the beginning, but later (especially after the Second World War) more social rights were codified. In the codification process, rights were further developed on both a national level and international level.

In the nineteenth century, there were some early developments in humanitarian law but, unfortunately, there were no general guarantees of human rights internationally. Between the two world wars of the twentieth century, some first steps were taken on

[18] Tomuschat 2003; Burkens and others 2006, 119 ff.
[19] Bodin 1576.
[20] Hobbes 1642.

the international level, such as the mandate system of the League of Nations, the international protection of minorities, and the development of the International Labour Organization. However, the greatest steps were taken after the Second World War.

Three generations of human rights jurisprudence can be distinguished. Human rights of the first generation are 'negative' human rights, or civil liberties, which enjoin states to abstain from interfering with personal freedom. Human rights of the second generation are 'positive' rights; these concern economic or social rights, such as the right to work or the right to social security, which entitle individuals or collectives to the provision of certain goods or social services. Human rights of the third generation are highly complex composited rights, like the right to development, the right to peace, and the right to a clean environment. Several of these rights, especially the first and second generation, were originally codified on a national level and, eventually, there was a development on the current system of international protection of human rights. Rights and obligations are explicitly regulated under the human rights treaties.

The developments of human rights have also depended upon the basic principles which make up the bedrock of our legal system. The conduct of governmental institutions is a decisive factor in bringing the prevailing societal climate in a given state up to the level of the expectations raised by those soft principles. In that context, the concept of good governance plays a crucial role.

In Chapter 12 of this book, the actual situation on human rights and its relation to the principles of good governance is discussed.

2. Different Historical Roots and Traditional Perspectives

The rule of law—in both the broad and narrow senses—has to do with the different historical roots of the common law and the continental legal systems. The historical roots of the two legal systems have critically influenced the major differences, as described below.

(a) Common law and continental law tradition

The common law tradition sees law only as an instrument to limit the powers of the state, whereas in the continental tradition, law is used not just to limit but also to empower the government. If the constitution is seen as an instrument that not only limits state power but also empowers state agencies to change the society, it may have a more direct effect upon the development and peace processes.

As we saw before, it is crucial to know what the substance behind the label 'rule of law' is in a legal system. It may have two totally different meanings according to the country's tradition. It can mean obedience to the existing positive law (as in the continental law system), or it may signify (according to the common law tradition) that inalienable rights are to be respected even by the sovereign.

Depending on the legal system of the country, one has to carefully investigate the remedies available to the citizens, the procedure and fact finding, the status of the administration (including the police), the jurisdiction and the power of the court, and in particular the independence of the courts. In civil law countries, decentralization needs to be implemented by the local authorities legislating on several specific areas. In common law countries, one has to examine the possibilities for local authorities to issue bylaws and to find out the extent of the parliament's competence.

(b) Rule of law and *rechtsstaat* distinguished

In the literature, some authors have shown that the concept of *rechtsstaat* is in fact incorporated in the principle of the constitutional state, and that it must be distinguished from the concept of the rule of law. The rule of law originated in England as a symbol of resistance against attempts by the Stuart kings to institutionalize an absolutist regime at the cost of sovereignty of Parliament, which was regarded as the representative of the people.

By contrast, the notion of a constitutional state—evolving from the principle of *rechtsstaat*, which in turn originated in Germany as a solution to unchecked power—denotes a rigid, written constitution (as opposed to parliamentary sovereignty) as the highest directing normative principle.[21] In relation to the unchecked power in the literature,[22] it was shown that the *rechtsstaat* was developed as a counterpoint against the police state (ie in the sense of the welfare state), as well as against a system of despotic rule and absolutism. The meaning of *rechtsstaat* has changed drastically over the last two centuries. In the nineteenth century, it originated from Kant's concept of the state (that freedom had to be governed by law), and thus denoted the importance of legality in a legal system. After the Second World War, the principle symbolized the state's commitment to the realization of justice. In Germany, this is sometimes described as the progression from the 'formal' *rechtsstaat* to the 'material' *rechtsstaat*.[23]

Despite the different developments of the concepts, it must be said that in modern versions there is some overlap between rule of law and *rechtsstaat*. This overlap can be found on topics where there is a need for realization of the ideals of equality before the law, substantive liberties and rights, and the notion of law as a general principle.

3. Rule of Law and Rechtsstaat: Specification of Differences

(a) Different concepts of the state

In relation to the concept of the state, we can distinguish between two approaches. First, the Lockean concept of the state which has limited sovereignty, where government is perceived only as a moderator of individuals and social groups to the extent minimally needed to protect individual liberty and men. The second approach is the Leviathan (Hobbesian) concept of the state where authority or sovereignty is the true and only source of law and justice; the main *holder* of sovereignty is the legislature as the only law-maker and where the 'pouvoir constituant' instituting the state can be seen as the 'big bang' out of which the universe of justice, law, and legitimate state authority (including the rule of law and human rights) evolves. This universe is defined by the territory of the state and its authority. The state is conceived as a collective unit containing all elements of justice and law and is established by the social contract.

(b) Mixed legal systems

From the perspective of a mixed legal system, we have to conclude that both approaches are complementary to each other. In a modern state there are tasks for the government to do as well as restrictions on the government so as to preserve the liberty of individual

[21] Sobota 1997, 27 ff, 39 ff. [22] Mohnhaupt 1993. [23] De Waal 1995.

persons. However, both the task of the government and liberty are not absolute, since there is always a balance between them. To make the task possible, the government will need authority and sovereignty in which the rule of law and human rights play an important role. This line can be seen as a detailing of the first line.

(c) Constitution from both approaches

The concept of a constitution can be approached from different perspectives.

According to Locke's natural law, the American Declaration of Independence is based on the concept of natural law: the right of resistance and the right of self-determination. This can be seen in the following examples:

1. In the American Declaration of independence, it is written that 'We hold these Truths to be self-evident, that all Men are created equal, that they are endowed, by their Creator, with certain unalienable Rights, that among these are Life, Liberty and the Pursuit of Happiness.'
2. In 1787, the American Constitution constituted not only a new government but, much more, it constituted a new state composed of several already-existing sovereign states and members of the Confederation.

The American Declaration of independence itself has six basic pre-conditions: (1) it had to be based on the universal principle that people have been given inalienable rights by the Creator; (2) it had to prove that the English Colonial Government violated inalienable rights; (3) it had to give evidence that people have as inalienable the right of resistance against a state power which is violating those rights; (4) it had to demonstrate that the power to govern people comes from the people, but that this power is limited to the inalienable rights; (5) it had to determine that people have the power to set up a new government; (6) it had to give evidence that the new government will be a government of consent and will thus apply and fully respect the inalienable rights of the governed people.

The second perspective is Rousseau's *volonté générale*. The French Revolution established the parliament as the sovereign power which enacts statutes, and the statutes implement the *volonté générale*. Some examples are the following: (1) Article 6 of the Déclaration des Droits de l'Homme 1789 mentioned: '*La loi est l'expression de la government*' and not the state; (2) constitutions are not only conceived as instruments to limit governmental power, but they are also seen as the tools to set up, organize, and empower the governmental branches in order to establish the liberal state and the social welfare state.

But a general will of the majority can lead to the oppression of minority factions and the stability of such a society is not immune to the manipulations of a single individual. Good governance can play an important role from that perspective.

The constitution, especially a written constitution, is very important because the fundamental governmental responsibilities in the area of human rights protection are guaranteed according to a special constitutional procedure. It is logical that the Parliament, as part of the legislature, plays a significant role.

(d) Human rights from both perspectives

The concept of human rights can first be looked at from the common law perspective: (1) human rights are taken to be pre-constitutional rights limiting the entire state authority; (2) the individual's pursuit of happiness is on the same level as individual liberty; and (3) welfare is not a responsibility of the state or the political community.

From the continental law perspective, different concepts are embraced: (1) human rights are created by the constitution (often in the context of international treaties); (2) rights are given by the state or the political authority; and (3) the pursuit of happiness depends on the common welfare and, thus, depends on the policy of the state.

The concept of human rights has two sides. The first is the expectation that the government will fulfil its task by providing social, economic, and cultural rights, and second is the expectation that the government will protect the citizen's civil rights.

4. Rule of Law and Rechtsstaat: Formal and Substantial Perspectives

(a) Formal elements of the concept of the rule of law

One can imagine—depending on which elements are in the description—that there are different concepts of the rule of law, from very strict to rather broad. A more formal approach consists of the following elements. First, in all the legal systems there is the idea that one of the cornerstones of the rule of law is the legality principle—legal basis and legal implementation. By law, the parliament is involved in the process of legislation and the court can, by way of judicial review and ultra vires, check if the legality principle has been followed. Second, there are some more significant elements, such as the powers of the state, the division of those powers, and by whom these powers will be applied. This should be a division of powers and also the balance of powers. More specifically, there should be a balance between the legislative, the executive, and the judicial powers; we will add the role of the fourth power in this context. The third element is the independent position of the judiciary, which not only applies the law, but also the non-written legal principles in addition to the written legal principles. These legal principles are not only the principles of proper administration but also the principles of good administration, which not only restrict the government but can also be focused on broadening the task of the government from a legal perspective. Finally, all the powers, including the fourth power, have to follow the fundamental rights as they are laid down in international treaties and the case law based on these treaties. The developments of these four elements of the rule of law are elaborated in this chapter.

(b) A more continental law perspective of rechtsstaat

Rechtsstaat is a concept of the continental European legal thinking originally borrowed from German jurisprudence. It can be translated as 'state of law', 'state of justice', or 'state of rights'. It is a constitutional state in which the exercise of governmental power is constrained by the law[24] and it is often, as we saw before, tied to the Anglo-American concept of the rule of law. The power of the state is limited in order to protect citizens from the arbitrary exercise of authority. In *rechtsstaat*, the citizens share legally based civil liberties and can also use the courts.

The concept of the *rechtsstaat* first appeared in a German book[25] and was contrasted with the aristocratic police state. German writers usually place Kant's theories at the beginning of their accounts of the movement toward the *rechtsstaat*.[26]

[24] Schmitt 1996. [25] Von Mohl 1866. [26] Hayek 1960.

The most important principles of the *rechtsstaat* are as follows.[27] First, the state has monopoly over power, meaning the state alone exercises coercion and guarantees the safety of its citizens. There is also separation of powers, with the executive, legislative, and judicative branches of government limiting each other's power and providing a system of checks and balances. Then, the judiciary and the executive are themselves bound by law, and the legislature is bound by constitutional principles.

Both the legislature and democracy itself are bound by elementary constitutional rights and principles. Transparency of the state's actions and the requirement of providing justification for all those actions are relevant conditions. There should be a possibility for reviewing against the state's decisions and acts by independent organs, which will also include an appeal process. In addition, a clear hierarchy of law and the requirement of clarity about the definitiveness of public acts are conditions which have to be fulfilled. The other conditions are the reliability of state actions, the protection of past dispositions made in good faith against later state actions, and the prohibition on retroactive punishment. Finally, there should also be a principle of proportionality regarding state action.

(c) A common law perspective on the rule of law

The rule of law is a concept that is notoriously difficult to define. In essence, it means that government must act under the law, and its rationale is to control the exercise of public power and ensure that it is exercised according to the law and within legal limits. In this sense, the rule of law is part of the principle of constitutionalism.[28]

There are two main interpretations of the rule of law: the procedural or formal conception and the substantive conception.

(d) Procedural or formal conceptions of rule of law

In procedural or formal conceptions, this principle is seen as a procedural mechanism which emphasizes the need for rules and procedures to control and limit power. Formal conceptions of the rule of law do not say anything about the content of laws but are merely concerned with passing legislation in the correct manner.

A suitable example would be the UK case of *Malone v Met Police Commission*.[29] Here, the use of tapped telephone conversation as evidence in criminal proceedings was contested, but because no statute or case law expressly forbade telephone tapping or required a warrant, the conduct was held not to be trespass. However, when the same facts were presented to the European Court of Human Rights (ECtHR), which concerned itself with substantive rule of law, it was held to be a violation of Article 8 (respect of the private life and correspondence). This shows us that when a purely formal rule of law is applied, fundamental rights may be at risk unless they have been protected by legality.

Joseph Raz[30] believes that the rule of law is a political ideal which theorizes that individuals should be ruled by the law and the law must be able to guide individuals so that they can plan their life accordingly. His theory contains eight principles: (1) the law should be general, prospective, open, and clear; (2) the law should be relatively stable and not subject to frequent and unnecessary alterations; (3) open, stable, clear,

[27] Venice Commission, *Report on the rule of law*, March 2011, CDL-AD (2011).
[28] Giussani, 2008, 60. [29] [1979] Ch 344 (Sir Robert Megarry V-C).
[30] Raz 1977, 195.

and general rules should govern the executive's law-making, meaning that delegated legislation should be enacted in the context of more detailed ground rules laid down in general laws; (4) the independence of the judiciary must be guaranteed; (5) the application of law should accord with the rules of natural justice, which includes the right to a fair hearing and the right to have a decision made free from bias;[31] (6) courts should have power of review over law-making and administrative action to ensure compliance; (7) courts should be easily accessible;[32] and (8) the discretion of the police, prosecuting authorities, and courts should not be allowed to pervert the law.[33]

The principles exposed by Raz are also key principles of the ECHR which, by virtue of the Human Rights Act 1998, is now applicable domestically in the United Kingdom. For any interference to be legitimate under the ECHR, it must be 'in accordance with (or prescribed) by a law'. In *Sunday Times v UK*,[34] the ECtHR gave consideration to the meaning of the phrase and found that it must meet the following requirements:

1. There must be a legal basis for the restriction, ie there must be a law. This can be either statute or common law (this is the principle of legality).
2. The law must be adequately accessible. This means that an individual must be able to have an indication of the legal rules applicable in any given case. This must be what is adequate in the circumstances.
3. The law must be formulated with sufficient precision to enable citizens to regulate their conduct. This means an individual must be able to foresee, to a degree that is reasonable in the circumstances, the legal consequences of this action. This does not equate to absolute certainty; as excessive rigidity should be avoided. Laws are often couched in vague terms requiring judicial interpretation.

One key point is that the rule as articulated by Raz is concerned with whether or not a system is a legal system, not whether we approve the outcomes it produces. The rule of law is not concerned with the content of the law. This of course means that a government could pass laws that are open, clear, and prospective but morally wrong or that interfere with individual rights.[35]

While adherence to the conceptual rule of law provides no guarantees as to the outcomes a legal system may produce, it works to ensure internal consistency. If the above premises are observed, an individual will be guided by the law and his/her position within society in given circumstances will be guaranteed. This is the value of Raz's analysis.

(e) Substantive conceptions of the rule of law

In other conceptions, one sees the rule of law as having a substantive element to it. In essence, laws passed should conform to the procedural requirements and encapsulate certain fundamental values, such as human rights.

Dworkin incorporates this conception in his concept of human rights. He sees the rule of law as requiring substantive justice stating that 'it requires, as part of the ideal of law, that the rules in the book capture and enforce moral rights'.[36] Also, other authors

[31] Dowell 2011.

[32] This principle is also enshrined within Art 6 of the ECHR which guarantees the right to a fair trial and access to the Courts.

[33] *Philips v Eye* (1870) LR 6 QB1.

[34] Case: 1979–80, 2 EHRR 245, 26 April 1979.

[35] *Inland Revenue Commissioners v Rossminster Ltd* [1980] AC 952.

[36] Dworkin 1985, 11–12.

choose a similar line. Those include Sir John Laws,[37] Trevor Allan,[38] and Lon Fuller. Fuller's focus was on the morality of law. He believed that for a system to be a legal system, it must have an 'inner morality'. A government must seek to provide the environment in which each citizen can reach maximum potential in a society that must be free and directed to the good of each of its members. Failure to achieve this would mean that the system has failed to meet the standards of a legal system.[39] Jeffrey Jowell also believes the rule of law must have a substantive element. In his opinion, the rule of law is a principle of institutional morality which, he argues, is manifested in the courts' willingness to strike down executive action if the action is unreasonable, arbitrary, or capricious.[40]

(f) Summary of formal and substantial conceptions of the rule of law

Paul Craig[41] summarizes these two conceptions by saying: 'Formal concepts of the rule of law address the manner in which the law was promulgated, the clarity of the ensuing norm and the temporal dimension of the enacted norm.' Formal conceptions of the rule of law do not, however, seek to pass judgement upon the actual content of the law itself. This formal conception is concerned with whether the law was a good or bad law, which looks like a contradiction with the previous statement but brings the two lines closer. Those who espouse substantive conceptions accept that the rule of law has the abovementioned formal attributes. However, these people wish to take the doctrine further. Certain substantive rights are said to be based on or derived from the rule of law.

The rule of law is often used in an international context and, as we have seen, it finds expression in the ECHR. The European Union is based on the rule of law. This means that every action taken by the EU is founded on treaties that have been approved voluntarily and democratically by all EU member countries. The Preamble to the Universal Declaration of Human Rights (1948), adopted by the General Assembly of the United Nations, also confirms respect for human rights and the rule of law by saying:

> Whereas it is essential, if man is not to be compelled to have recourse, as a last resort, to rebellion against tyranny and oppression, that human rights should be protected by the rule of law.

The link between human rights and the rule of law is clear here, which gives the interpretation of the principle a substantive element. One can also see this in the Declaration of Delhi issued by the International Commission of Jurists in 1959, which was criticized by Raz.

The rule of law in the United Kingdom has been closely associated with the work of Dicey[42] but in the Anglo-American literature it goes beyond Dicey. Here Dicey's work is referred to. There, we find three meanings of the rule of law: (1) an individual would only be punished for a distinct breach of the law and there is a predominance of regular law by arbitrary power; (2) equality before the law; (3) the principles of the constitution are the result of the ordinary law decided by the courts, especially concerning the area of national security and discretionary power. Historically, in such cases, the courts

[37] Laws 1995 and 1996. [38] Allan 2003. [39] Fuller 1964.

[40] Jowell 2007, 5; Cases: *R v Secretary of State for Home Department* (2004) UKHL 56 and (2005) UKHL 71.

[41] Craig 1997. [42] Dicey 1959.

have been very deferential to the actions of the executive. In doing so, they allow discretionary power to be potentially abused by not providing an effective check on its use. By not checking the executive, they are compromising the rule of law. This compromise may be accepted if there is an emerging threat to the life of the nation or the power is strictly required by the exigencies of the situation (proportionality).

David Herling and Ann Lyon[43] present a list of key elements of the rule of law, according to the practices used in the United Kingdom. These are: (1) government according to the law; (2) the courts are independent of the executive in the administration of justice; (3) the powers of the executive do not exceed those known to the courts; (4) the rule of law imposes duties upon the law-makers; (5) retroactivity and the common law; (6) the necessity for the publication of laws; (7) the principle that laws should be stable; (8) judicial creativity and the stability of laws; (9) equality before the law; (10) the law's application to the executive; (11) rights are declared by the common law; (12) the principle is in the keeping of the courts.[44]

5. Difficulties and Developments of the Traditional Rule of Law

The narrow and broad concepts of the rule of law have gradually come closer. This means that there is (or should be) a legal basis for the activities of the government and the government should act according to the law. Also, in the narrow view of the rule of law there is a need for control by the independent judicial court.

But what do we see in the law? There are more and more powers given to the administration and these powers include broad discretionary space. In the law, we also find several open norms which have to be filled in by the administration.

The administration is developing more policy rules, and in those rules we find the norms according to which the administration is acting. It is impossible for parliament to control all these regulations and, in practice, parliament never discusses individual cases. When there are conflicts between the administration and the citizens, it is often too difficult for individual citizens to start a legal procedure.

These developments are not only in one or two fields but almost in all the policy fields of the government, perhaps more than twenty broad policy fields in all. There is a direct link between the general and specific aspects of administrative law. The consequence is that the traditional concept of rule of law no longer works due to the very loose legislation, the strong development of policy rules, and the difficulties for parliamentary and judiciary control. The need for general and substantial norms for the government is clear, and these should be norms which have to be followed by each branch of the government.

The meaning of the rule of law has gone through a process of change which runs roughly parallel with the view on the role and objectives of a national government. As that view has evolved, so too has the concept of the rule of law. This is a dynamic concept and does not stand for an abstract, unchanging set of unambiguous rules, but rather for a range of principles which have to be filled in on a case-by-case basis. The rule of law should be seen as a series of legal standards which bind governments and subjects. The exact content of these standards is determined by several factors,

[43] Herling and Lyon 2004.

[44] This principle is also enshrined within Art 6 of the ECHR which guarantees the right to a fair trial and access to the Courts.

including public opinion, political consciousness, and the prevailing sense of justice.[45] The rule of law is constantly changing but the basic principles remain. Society is also constantly changing, and now there are difficulties in society's relationship with the traditional rule of law.

(a) Two levels of development

The rules of law and administrative law have a long common development in history, so that the rule of law seemed to be a well-ordered administrative law.[46] Nevertheless there are two levels of developments in the present idea of rule of law.[47] The first is the objective legal structuring by law and the second is a series of subjective individual legal positions. Both can be explained as followed.

In the first level, the relationship is based on a model in which law is a way of structuring and restricting the power of the state. This idea has a strong dualistic concept about the relation between state and society, and the task of the state is to do only specific intervention which adheres closely to this legal concept. Here we have to be careful not to colour the contrasts between the older liberalism and the younger concept of the social rule of law. A convergence between the social model and *rechtsstaat* understanding can be seen. According to the *rechtsstaat*, a legal and legally controlled executive must exist. The goal is the 'most practicable formal justice of the administration' and the legal steering function is based upon a degree of rationality behind the law. This again relies on the separability of causes, the reliability of effects, and a division of legislation and law application, following the prerequisite norms and schemes.

The second level is more subjective and has important individual legal positions. The concept of *rechtsstaat* has developed further according to this level. In the newer view, all national powers are bound decisively by basic rights. The basic rights permeate the entire administrative legal system. They are in the single fields of special administrative law as well as generally omnipresent. This is a mark of the *rechtsstaat* development under the constitution. This includes: the constitutional rights and norms of proportionality; equality and legal certainty; and the concept of the *rechtsstaat* based on the elementary human needs for rationality, attention, and orientation. Administrative action was, according to the *rechtsstaat*, an objective-legal principle in the beginning. In the current development, the individual as a subject is the centre of the administrative legal scope.

(b) Three points of attention related to these developments

From this perspective on administrative law, let us focus on the following points. On one side, all the administrative law components have a strong individual aspect. An emphasis on effects, proportionality, reasonableness, and fairness has become drastically more important in administrations' legal systems. Now one may see a clear subjective euphemism of administrative law as a second mark. The subjective right is no longer attached to a specific award but has become the protection standard everywhere where there are standards of objective interests. The law has not only its general regulation function, but it also wants to bring this function in balance with individual rights.

[45] Van Banning and Van Genugten 1993, 42.
[46] Schmidt-Assmann 2006.
[47] Schmidt-Assmann 2003, § 26.

The context of the effects of specifying control methods and private interest positions are examined after determining their intensities from different dimensions. The dimensions' effects are related to the appropriateness of its constitutional securities. The effect of these basic rights has been proven to be a motor for the development of new administrative law questions. The meaning of procedural law for the protection of material legal positions is an example of this legal sensitization.

6. The Role of Good Governance Related to these Developments

Objective suitability means that the restriction tested against the constitutional provisions should be appropriate or suitable to achieve the objective intended. The intended aim of the legislation in question must be measured against the possible means to achieve it in order to determine whether a rational relationship exists between them.[48]

This means a cost-benefit analysis is necessary. The measure taken must not, in other words, be harsher than is necessary to achieve the specific goal.[49] Reasonableness is proportionality in the narrow sense. In relationship to the importance and meaning of the fundamental right, no lesser restriction of the right could be able to achieve the same result.

This element is also sometimes referred to as proportionality in the narrow sense.[50] The proportional evening out of the interests of the involved parties (ie proportionality in the wider sense) should not be confused with the classical investigation into the proportionality in the narrow sense (a specific infringement with a concrete purpose).

(a) Basic presumption of the rule of law: need to broaden concepts

Of course, this expansion leads to doctrinal difficulties. An important premise of the rule of law remains the individualization of interest and the possibility to make a normative allocative decision on the general and abstract level of the law. Where these prerequisites are missing because of diffuse interest positions, the clear rule of law instruments related to protection will lose focus. This forces not an abdication of constitutional requirements, but must rather be an impetus for thinking about new, functionally equivalent rule of law protection. It turns out that the rule of law, although a shaping principle, is not limited to a strict formalization—it is not set in stone. Even in the older rule of law practice, its formal clarity is not in the sense of a mathematical model. Nor is the rule of law legal concept exhausted in the regulatory/steering aspect of law, it rather exists more to create advanced concepts of law. The legal order of complex interests, finding the right method for them and patterns of organization are a basic concern of the modern rule of law. Here, the view of the administrative law is especially focused on the 'medium level', not fixed by a definitive, binding administrative decision. Above, we already pointed out the importance of the administrative rule-making. In particular, regulations, concepts, plans, and programmes have their function. In this respect, one can speak of a return to the objective legal side of the rule of law. It is generally a question of law to be understood as encompassing recovering public rationality.

[48] Degenhart 1998, 278. [49] Ibid, 279. [50] Ibid, 281.

7. Conclusions

The rule of law is one of the cornerstones of a modern state, but we find in the literature several variations on the converging theme that is the rule of law. In the narrow approach, only principles of procedural fairness are accepted. In the broader approach, there is a more substantive specification of the elements of the *rechtsstaat.* These elements are legality, division of powers, independent judicial control, and protection of human rights. Three generations of human rights have been developed: civil rights, social and economic rights, and finally complex composited rights like the right to development and the right to a clean environment. There are important differences between the common law and the continental law tradition. In the common law tradition, the focus of the law is to limit the power of the government. In the continental tradition, the law also gives the basis for empowerment of the government.

The basis of the different approaches of the rule of law and the *rechtsstaat* is the differing concept of the state. Originally, we had the two different legal systems, but more and more countries have a mixed legal system. In such a mixed legal system the rule of law and the *rechtsstaat* concepts are getting closer to each other. It becomes increasingly important to distinguish the formal and the substantial aspects of these concepts.

There are some difficulties in the traditional concept of the rule of law, but there are important developments of the rule of law on two levels. The first level is the objective legal structuring of the state by law, and the second is the subjective individual legal positions.

Finally, we see that the developments on these two levels make clear that there is a need for a further development of the concept of the rule of law. In this process of broadening the scope of good governance, a new dimension can be added. The good governance concept specifies the two aforementioned levels of the rule of law, and this combination gives more adequate answers to the normative side of the functioning of the public sector nowadays.

6

Democracy and Good Governance

Democracy is about government and governance by the people in a direct or indirect way. Sovereignty of the people, however, is not the same as democracy. The position of minorities in relation to majorities, in a democracy, is not always easy to regulate. This situation has made clear that democracy also has its qualitative contents and it is even clearer when we speak about democracy in the sense of a liberal democracy or of a social democracy. Two key elements in and topics related to democracy are the participation of the people and the elections by the people and the transparency of the government. There are some restrictions in a representative democracy and, for that reason, participation will be necessary to maintain the connection between the government and the people. But in order to have an adequate functioning of this participation and also of the elections, transparency on behalf of the government is a necessary condition for a democracy.

1. Democracy: Different Forms of Government

Democracy is a political form of government in a state carried out either directly by the people (direct democracy) or indirectly by means of elected representatives of the people (representative democracy). The term comes from the Greek and means 'rule by the people'. Democracy is also linked to the broader concept of the rule of law.[1]

There are several varieties of democracy; some of them provide better representation and more freedoms and rights for their citizens than others. However, if a democracy is not carefully legislated—for example, through the use of balances or separations of powers in order to avoid an uneven distribution of political power—then a part or a branch of the government could accumulate power and become harmful to the democracy itself. Even then, there can be a discussion about some aspects of a democracy. The majority rule is often described as a characteristic feature of democracy, but without responsible government or constitutional protections of individual liberties from democratic power, it is possible for dissenting individuals to be oppressed by the 'tyranny of the majority', as phrased by the philosopher John Stuart Mill. The people may decide to oppress a part of their number and precautions are as much needed against this as against any other abuses of power.[2] James Madison, Founding Father, fourth US President and 'Father of the US Constitution', also claimed that human nature is such that one cannot simply trust that majority will necessary work for the common good, and advocated the adoption of safeguards in the constitutional model to be created by the Americans after their independence.[3]

An essential process in representative democracies is the organization of competitive elections that are both fair substantively and procedurally. Furthermore, freedom of political expression, freedom of speech, and freedom of the press are essential for

[1] Burkens and others 2001, pp. 21 and 193; Sepúlveda and others 2004. [2] Mill 1859.
[3] Madison 1787.

citizens to enable them to be informed and to be able to vote in accordance with their personal interests.

Popular sovereignty is a common but not universal motivating subject for establishing a democracy. In some countries, democracy is based on the philosophical principle of equal rights. Many people use the term 'democracy' as shorthand for liberal democracy, which may include additional elements such as political pluralism, equality before the law, the right to petition elected officials for redress of grievances, due process, civil liberties, human rights, and elements of civil society outside the government.

In the United States, separation of powers is often cited as a supporting attribute, but in other countries, such as the United Kingdom, the dominant philosophy is parliamentary sovereignty—even if in practice judicial independence is generally maintained. In other cases, 'democracy' means direct democracy. Although the term 'democracy' is typically used in the context of a political state, the principles are also applicable to private organizations and other groups.[4]

For common law countries like the United Kingdom in which there is a dominant position of the parliament, Young[5] recently provides a normative account of democratic dialogue across a range of constitutional systems and examines the emerging dialogue between domestic and regional courts like the European Court of Justice and European Court of Human Rights. Constitutions divide into those that provide for a constitutionally protected set of rights, where courts can strike down legislation, and those where rights are protected predominantly by parliament, where courts can interpret legislation to protect rights, but cannot strike down legislation. Democratic dialogue is an inter-institutional interaction between the parliament and the judiciary related to human rights but also between national and international courts. Both forms of democratic dialogue are especially needed in common law countries in which a more horizontal concept on human rights is created and which brings more balance between the different powers in the state. In this situation, there is no longer a dominance of the political, parliamentarian power or the legal, judicial power.

Democracy has its origins in Ancient Greece. However, other cultures, such as Ancient Rome, Europe, and North and South America, have also significantly contributed to the evolution of democracy. The concept of representative democracy arose largely from ideas and institutions that developed during the European Middle Ages, the Age of Enlightenment, and also in the American and French Revolutions. The right to vote has been expanded in many jurisdictions over time from relatively narrow groups, such as wealthy men of a particular ethnic group, with New Zealand being the first nation to grant universal suffrage for all its citizens in 1893.[6]

In the concept of democracy, the people are the most important element. The people can govern themselves in a direct way or can elect representatives in a parliament to represent them in discussing legislation and controlling the administration. We must distinguish between direct democracy and representative democracy. However, sometimes semi-direct democracy is promoted, especially in situations where citizens can develop initiatives. One form of semi-direct democracy is deliberative democracy, a form of democracy in which deliberation is central to decision-making. It adopts elements of both consensus decision-making and majority rule.[7] It differs from traditional democratic theory in that authentic deliberation, not mere voting, is the primary

[4] Craig 1990. [5] Young 2017.

[6] See for the universal suffrage: the Electoral Act, signed by Lord Glasgow. See: http://www.nzhistory.net.nz/Gallery/suffragists (accessed 4 October 2011).

[7] Bessette 1980.

source of legitimacy for the law-making processes. Deliberative democracy combines elements of both representative democracy and direct democracy, which relies upon the deliberation of the citizenry to reach a sound policy.

2. Democracy: Direct and Representative

Direct democracy, classically termed 'pure democracy', is any form of government based on a theory of civics in which all citizens can directly participate in the decision-making process, rather than relying on intermediaries or representatives. Some adherents want legislative, judicial, and executive powers to be handled by the people, but most extant systems only allow legislative decisions. These acts are often specified, for example certain regulations or contractual activities of the administration. However, even on the decisions concerning factual activities there can be a direct participation. Two elements are often seen in modern democracies: citizen's initiatives and referenda. If there is a large number of citizens in a state, it places greater difficulties on the implementation of a direct democracy since all citizens must be actively involved in all issues all of the time. So, the need for representative democracy increases as the number of citizens grows. There are concerns about how such systems would scale to larger populations. With the advent of the internet, there have been suggestions for 'e-democracy' in which the internet plays an important role comprising various mechanisms for implementing direct democracy concepts.

Representative democracy involves the selection of government officials by the people and by those represented. If the head of state is also democratically elected, then the state is called a democratic republic. The most common mechanisms involve election of the candidate with a majority or a plurality of the votes. Representatives may be elected as ones of a particular district or a constituency, or represent the entire electorate proportionally. Some countries use a combination of both. Some representative democracies also incorporate elements of direct democracy, such as referenda. A characteristic of representative democracy is that while the representatives are elected by the people to act in their interest, they retain the freedom to exercise their own judgement as how best to do so.

Parliamentary democracy is a representative democracy where government is appointed by parliamentary representatives as opposed to a 'presidential rule' where the president is both head of state and the head of government and is elected by the voters. Under a parliamentary democracy, the country's government is exercised by delegation to an executive ministry, subject to ongoing review, checks, and balances by the legislative parliament elected by the people.

A liberal democracy is a representative democracy in which the ability of the elected representatives to exercise decision-making power is subject to the rule of law. It is usually moderated by a constitution that emphasizes the protection of the rights and freedoms of individuals and which places constraints on the leaders and on the extent to which the will of the majority can be exercised against the rights of minorities. Liberal democracy—bourgeois or constitutional democracy—is a common form of representative democracy. According to the principles of liberal democracy, elections should be free and fair, and the political process should be competitive. Political pluralism is usually defined as the presence of multiple and distinct political parties. A liberal democracy may take various constitutional forms. It may be a federal republic, such as the United States, India, or Germany, or a constitutional monarchy, such as the United Kingdom, Japan, or Spain. It may have a presidential system (United States), a parliamentary system (the United Kingdom and the Commonwealth countries), or a hybrid, semi-presidential system (France).

Even in a representative democracy with a parliament we find different opinions for the role of the parliament. The traditional view is the unitary, self-correcting democracy, in which there is sovereignty in the sense of omnipotence and legislative monopoly of the parliament. Later, more modern types of pluralist democracy were developed. This pluralist approach to democracy is more focused on rights and certain standards of legality and is designed to prevent misuse of power by public bodies, but also by other quasi-public or private bodies which possess a certain degree of power. The controlling bodies, including the judiciary, do not just apply the legislative will but articulate principles which should guide the exercise of administrative action and interpret legislation in the light of these principles. Different forms of pluralism have been developed: traditional pluralism, market-oriented pluralism, and another forms of pluralism which are often called the third way. Pluralism has different forms, but, in all of them, principles and especially the principles of good governance play an important role. The good governance concept will influence the concept of democracy, for instance on the issue of a good balance between the majority and the minority in a democracy.

Transparency and participation are two key words in the different types of well-functioning democracy, be it direct or representative. Both ideas are directly linked to the citizens and the opportunities they should have for being well-informed and for influencing the activities of the government.

3. Democracy and Transparency

The term 'transparency' has different meanings. Often, a general distinction between a broad and a narrow notion is made. In the broad notion, transparency implies openness, communication, and accountability. Of course, there is a link between transparency and accountability and one can say that this is a means of holding public officials accountable and of fighting corruption. The transparency principle has to be distinguished from the accountability principle.

The narrow notion of transparency is more closely related to the essential meaning in the context of a 'transparent' object, which is one that can be seen through. It means openness in relation to the work of the government. In that context, transparency includes open meetings, financial disclosure statements, freedom of information legislation, budgetary review, audits, and the like. This openness is necessary in the two forms of democracy discussed above.

In general, we can distinguish three types of transparency: transparency of meetings, transparency of the administrative actions, and transparency of access to public information. When government meetings are open to the press and the public, when budgets and financial statements may be reviewed by anyone, when laws, rules, and decisions are open to discussion, they are seen as transparent and there is less opportunity for the authorities to abuse the system in their own interest.

In government, politics, ethics, business, management, law, economics, sociology, transparency is posed as the opposite of privacy. An activity is transparent if all information about it is open and freely available. Thus, when courts of law admit the public, when fluctuating prices in financial markets are published in newspapers, those processes are transparent. When military authorities classify their plans as secret, transparency is absent. This can be seen as positive or negative: positive, because it can increase national security, and negative, because it can lead to secrecy, corruption, and even a military dictatorship.

While a liberal democracy can be a plutocracy, where decisions are taken behind closed doors and the people have almost no opportunity to influence the politics between elections, a participative democracy is more closely connected to the will of the people. Participative democracy, built on transparency and everyday participation, has been practised officially in Northern Europe for decades. For example, Sweden allowed public access to governmental documents from 1766, when Sweden passed its Freedom of the Press Act.[8] It has been adopted as an ideal to strive for by the other European Union states. Many countries in the world still have older forms of democracy, or other forms of government.

4. Democracy and Participation

Participation refers to different mechanisms for the public to express opinions—and ideally exert influence—regarding different types of governmental activities. Participatory decision-making can take place along any realm of human social activity like participative democracy. There is also a strong development in deliberative democracy which is directly related to participation.[9] For well-informed participation to occur, it is argued that some version of transparency is necessary, but not sufficient. It has also been argued that those most affected by a decision should have the greatest say, while those least affected would have the least say.

Participation has different objectives. Participatory activities may stem from an administrative area or a citizen's perspective. From the administrative viewpoint, participation can build public support for activities. It can educate the public about an agency's activities. It can also facilitate useful information exchange regarding local conditions. Furthermore, participation is often legally mandated. From the citizen's viewpoint, participation enables individuals and groups to influence agency decisions in a representational manner.

Participation can be classified in different ways. Sherry Arnstein discusses various types of participation.[10] These are broadly categorized as non-participation, tokenism, and citizen power. She defines citizen participation as the redistribution of power that enables the have-not citizens, presently excluded from the political and economic processes, to be deliberately included in the future. Archon Fung presents another classification of participation based on three key questions: Who is allowed to participate, and are they representative of the population? What is the method of communication or decision-making? And how much influence or authority is granted to the participation? Other 'ladders' of participation have been presented by Connor,[11] Wiedemann and Femers,[12] and Rocha.[13]

Participation can refer to participation as part of decision-making, a notion in legal theory. But participation can also mean ownership and, in that case, it means having something in common with others. Participation in the context of finance means getting some benefit from the performance of a certain underlying asset. Finally, we see more and more e-participation and that refers to participation in e-government, and is related to the involvement of the citizen in the democratic process.

[8] Banisar 2004. [9] Akerboom 2018. [10] Arnstein 1969. [11] Connor 1988.
[12] Wiedemann and Femers 1993. [13] Rocha 1997.

5. Conclusions

Democracy is a political form of government which can be worked out in different ways. For that reason, we speak about different forms of government. In this chapter, we discussed some aspects suggesting that they are strongly related to democracy. These aspects are representation after the elections, the relevance of the majority rule, the relation between direct and representative democracy, and the topics of transparency and participation. We saw the importance of representative democracy but also the tyranny of the majority. Care for minorities in a democracy is crucial. It is also interesting to consider the different ways of thinking about popular sovereignty and how it is related to the idea of separation of powers.

We noted the difference between direct and representative democracy. The questions we need to ask are: What should be the link between the powers of the state and the citizens? Which type of direct democracy is possible and how is it linked with representative democracy?

There are different types of direct democracy, because in a representative democracy not all the matters in a state can be carried out by the representatives. There are different opinions about the role of the parliament in a representative democracy.

On the issue of transparency, we distinguished between the narrow and the broad notions, which can be summarized as a more or less open functioning of the institutions of the state. This topic of transparency is often related to the following activities of the government: meetings, access to information, and government action. The existing restrictions become significant when dealing with issues of privacy.

Direct democracy can be realized—in addition to representative democracy—in different ways. Often it depends on the topic, but citizens' initiatives and referenda are examples. The objectives of participation can be different: it can be from the perspective of the citizen, but it can also be done for management reasons. For the legitimizing aims of the government, different forms of participation can be very relevant.

PART II

GOOD GOVERNANCE: SPECIFICATION BY PRINCIPLES

7

The Principle of Properness

In general, the principle of properness and its sub-principles, including the 'principles of properness', have (in most countries) the longest history of all principles of good governance. The principles of properness were developed because the traditional formal approaches to legality were too narrow for adequate control of the government. These principles were often developed by the judiciary as unwritten principles, as well as by the ombudsman or as policy principles in policy papers. Several of these unwritten and policy principles have been codified in the laws of different countries.[1]

It is important to note that these properness principles do not have the same content and qualifications in all countries. In many countries, the process of codification of unwritten norms is at a different stage. The foundations of the principles are often comparable. The judiciary started to develop these principles as they found a pure legality review too narrow, especially in situations in which the legislator did not specify the norms to be fulfilled by the administration. Different courts developed a more sophisticated way of protecting the rights of individuals: sometimes by developing unwritten principles or by having a more extensive interpretation of the law.

The lines of development of the principles of properness were illegality, irrationality, and then impropriety. This means that in the beginning, the focus was on the aim of the regulation or power, which was sometimes a written but often an unwritten legal norm. A more general perspective was the rationality and irrationality of actions. The third step in this development was the specification of other principles, such as equality, legal certainty, carefulness, and motivation. Each of these categories was specified by means of a principles-based approach and a rights-based review. This development sometimes went faster under the influence of international human rights treaties. However, the innovation of judicial review went through. In Belgium, a distinction between the formal and material principles was made initially. Examples of the formal principles are: the duty to hear the addressee of a decision, rights of due process of law, impartiality, and independence. Most of these principles are forced on the judicial procedure. The material principles, however present, determine the substance of the acts of the administration.[2]

In the principles of properness, we distinguish the following elements:[3] formal carefulness (hearing as part of natural justice), abuse of power (abuse of discretion), rationality (substantial carefulness), proportionality, legal certainty, legitimate expectations, and equality and reasoning.[4]

1. Development of the Principle of Properness

The first question is, 'why have the principles of proper administration been developed?' By describing the developments of the role of the Dutch judiciary, the *Benthem*

[1] Addink 1999. [2] Lust 2007, 28–9. [3] Seerden (ed) 2012; Seerden (ed) 2018.
[4] Craig 2008; Harlow and Rawlings 2009.

case deserves some attention. This case before the ECtHR led to an important and impressive reform in the Dutch administrative courts, including the strong development of a general high administrative court in combination with already existing specific high administrative courts. These specific courts were the Central Appeals Tribunal on legal areas pertaining to social security and the civil service (based in Utrecht) and the Trade and Industry Appeals Tribunal in the area of socio-economic administrative law, based in The Hague. The high general administrative court is the Administrative Jurisdiction Division of the Council of State. The introduction of the Administrative Jurisdiction Division of the Council of State as a general higher administrative court in particular has prompted the strong development of the principles of properness.[5]

There are several reasons for this, depending on the function of the institutions involved. The main reason is that there was, for a time, a too restrictive interpretation of formal legality and, therefore, there was a need for unwritten principles. There was also a need for a broader judicial control, more than a simple legality check. In a situation where the controlling mechanisms of parliament are more focused on general aspects, there is a need for more intensive control by the judiciary for individual cases. At the same time, there are restrictions on the court because of its constitutional role. We also see that national administrations increasingly developed policy rules where principles of good governance are stipulated. But most of the unwritten principles of good governance have been codified in a general administrative law act or in a specific act which deals with specific points.

2. The Concept of Properness

General administrative law is often about decision-making and about legal certainty for citizens and organizations. Decision-making by the administration implies the application of general rules to specific cases. When regulations are unclear because of vague language of structural matters, the administration increasingly gains discretionary power. Choices with regard to discretionary power in specific cases are made by the application of relevant regulations and by identifying and balancing the interests concerned. In many cases, the administration acts as an intermediary between the conflicting interests of different parties. If an administrative order is correctly made, at least procedurally, the parties involved often accept the outcome of the case more easily. The administration has to act in accordance with the law. A party who disapproves of a ruling, however, may appeal to a court. If the court is competent in the reported matter, it can by exception consider the (legal) act at hand.

As the law is unclear in many cases, it is often almost unpredictable whether or not a ruling is lawful. This unpredictability of the law is reinforced by conferring and delegating discretionary powers to lower administrative bodies and agencies. Furthermore, many kinds of regulations change rapidly. From the point of view of the classic continental version of rule of law, legal certainty is sometimes undermined by interwoven and somewhat unpredictable societal, political, and judicial processes.

In the administrative law of many countries, the general principles of proper administration were developed as tools to cope with these unavoidable legal uncertainties. These principles contributed to the development of procedural legal certainty, which replaced the unreachable ideal of substantive legal certainty, the continental version

[5] Addink 1999, ch 1.

of the rule of law. Thus, the principles of proper administration are generally about decision-making, administrative discretionary powers, and judicial control. That includes the relationship between the courts and the administration. In this and some of the following chapters, the situation in the Netherlands is taken as an illustration. The General Administrative Law Act (GALA) is in fact an elaboration of the general principles of proper administration. It is, however, more than a codification only, it is also an instrumental statute that regulates the relations between administrative authorities and citizens. On the other hand, it does not codify all the principles of proper administration and therefore there are written and unwritten principles of properness.

The written and unwritten principles of proper administration can be divided into two groups: the formal and the substantial (or material). This distinction partly clarifies the differences between the several principles of proper administration. The substantial principles are: legal certainty, equality, and proportionality. The formal ones are carefulness and motivation. Two remarks have to be made in relation to this distinction. First, some principles have both formal and substantial aspects. That is actually the case with legal certainty, carefulness, and motivation. Second, the annulment by the judge based on a formal or a substantial principle is relevant. After an annulment based on a formal principle, substantially speaking, the same decision can be reached once again by the administration. Annulment based on a substantial principle means that a completely new decision must be reached by the administration.

When we look at the functions of the principles of proper administration, we can distinguish two different functions in the course of public decision-making and in judicial review.

First, there are rules of conduct for administrative bodies and other legal entities. Because most principles are linked to a certain stage in the decision-making process, it is quite possible to apply them from the start. Of course, the same principles are to be applied in the objection procedure. Many of these principles have been codified in GALA. Its chapters and paragraphs concern dealings between individuals and administrative authorities, general provisions on orders, and the application and publication and communication. For instance, articles 4:7 and 4:8 indicate that before a burdensome order can be enacted, the applicant and the aggrieved must be invited to give their views on the matter; this is directly related to the principle of carefulness.

Second, the principles of proper administration are tools for judicial review. There are principles relating more to the procedure of decision-making and principles relating more to the content of the administrative order. For instance, the principle of justification and the principle of prohibition of arbitrariness; judges can often choose between different kinds of principles.

3. Specification of the Concept

The following eight sub-principles of properness have been distinguished: (1) the prohibition on misuse of power; (2) the prohibition on arbitrariness; (3) legal certainty; (4) legitimate expectation; (5) equality; (6) proportionality; (7) carefulness; and (8) reasoning. These sub-principles are explained in turn.

(a) The prohibition on misuse of power

This is also called '*la défense de détournement de pouvoir*'. This principle has been codified in the Netherlands GALA. We read in article 3:3 that 'An administrative authority shall not use the power to take a decision for a purpose other than that for which it was conferred'.

The prohibition on misuse of power means that an administrative authority may not use its power for other purposes than it was intended to be used for by the legislator. We find this principle in France in the context of alleged illegality in the purpose of the decision.[6]

Instead of an abuse of power, the literature sometimes refers to abuse of discretion. But in essence, this is a different situation. The first situation resembles a situation in which power has been used for an illegal purpose. The second refers to a case which the court finds the decision to be unreasonable, irrational, or disproportionate. So, it is about the difference between illegality and irrationality. Nevertheless, the second may become relevant as well, although the court can choose to make use of more specified principles of fair administration. The illegality line in the UK case law is formulated according to the lines of improper purposes, but less with reference to the line of relevance, and only incidentally according to the concept of bad faith.[7] Peculiar situations occur when there is a duality of purpose or overlapping motives.[8] In both situations, the court refers to the dominant purpose.

As an illustration, after the liberation of the Netherlands in 1945 from German occupation, there was an enormous shortage of housing. The Dutch government weighed in on the distribution of living accommodation. The Act on Living Accommodation 1947 was enacted. The purpose of this Act was to enhance the correct distribution of living accommodation. To pursue the Act's aim, a mayor of a municipality, appointed by the Crown, could requisition accommodation from homeowners and rental owners. In 1947, the mayor of Zandvoort, a seaside resort, requisitioned a house and summer cottage, claiming that the rent for them was too high. The mayor intended to give the house in use to a police officer, Mr Douma, who was newly employed by the municipality of Zandvoort. As a consequence, the owner, Mr Van Spingelen, could not earn his higher market price. The owner appealed to the civil court. The case ended when the Supreme Court held that the conflict in hand was about the question whether claiming the house and the summer cottage enhanced the just distribution of living accommodation or if the claim was for another purpose. According to the Supreme Court it was clear that the mayor of Zandvoort, in claiming the summer cottage, primarily aimed at housing a municipal civil servant and at levelling rental prices, and not at achieving a just distribution of living accommodation.[9] This was contrary to the general principle of '*défense de détournement de pouvoir*'. Of course, this principle is derived from the principle of legality. So, in cases where the prohibition of misuse of power applies, the enacting administrative authority is not competent to use its power for the aim it tries to achieve.

Generally, in the case law of the Netherlands, four aspects of this principle have been developed. We find a specification of the aim for which the power has been attributed. The first aspect is the administrative authority which uses the power *against* the aim of the power, for instance if an environmental licence has been granted only based on economic and not environmental argumentation. The second aspect is the use of the power for an *incorrect* aim, like granting a licence for money laundering.[10] The third

[6] Auby and Cluzel-Metayer 2007, 87.
[7] Craig 2008, 531–44.
[8] Wade and Forsyth 2009, 349–52.
[9] Dutch Supreme Court, 14 January 1949, NJ 1949 nr 557 (*Zandvoort's legal claim of a living accommodation*).
[10] Stouten 2012.

aspect is the situation where an environmental licence has been granted by using the power in an *appropriate* way, like conditions to prevent dumping waste. The fourth aspect is using the power *consistently* with the aim of the power like environmental conditions in combination with an environmental licence.[11]

(b) The prohibition on arbitrariness

The prohibition on arbitrariness is sometimes called the principle of reasonableness. This principle has been codified in GALA in two ways, first, in general and then in the context of the enforcement of administrative law. The first codification can be found in article 3:4 where we read:

> An administrative authority shall consider the interests directly affected by a decision, subject to any limitations following from a provision of law or the nature of the power to be exercised ... The adverse consequences of a decision for one or more interested parties may not be disproportionate to the objects to be served by the decision.

The second codification is in article 5:13 where we read that 'An inspector may only exercise his powers to the extent that this is reasonably necessary for the performance of his duties'.

The prohibition on arbitrariness means that administrative orders should result from a balance of interests which is obviously not unreasonable. This principle is one of the first principles of proper administration. The use of this principle by a court implies a limited review of the administrative order or other legal act in hand. As a consequence, only severe mistakes by administrative bodies or other legal entities compel a court to nullify the legal act subjected to review. However, in daily court practice, the mere suspicion that a decision may be regarded as unreasonable often leads to a quite comprehensive review of that decision.[12]

This principle can be found in most European countries, like the United Kingdom, France, and Germany. In the United Kingdom, the deciding authority has genuine full discretion within the bounds of legal reasonableness. But the decision is unlawful if it is one to which no reasonable authority could have come to (this is called '*Wednesbury unreasonableness*').[13] It is described as a situation 'so irrational that *no* properly directed authority could ever have come to this conclusion'. There is a direct line with what was earlier called rationality. Wednesbury unreasonableness is an exception to judicial review in common law systems because it looks at the substantive merits of the decision. Since the judges do not make a new decision, it is not considered a breach of the separation of powers. In France, the norm is the manifest error of appreciation.[14] In Germany, it is crucial if all the circumstances are relevant. If these do not belong to the case, there is misuse of power and the court also reviews by using indefinite legal terms for the interpretation.[15]

Generally, we find the following manifestations of this principle: arbitrariness in the context of evidently unreasonable actions by the administration, visible unreasonableness (which means that a balance of interests was made by the administration, but this was not acceptable); 'in reasonableness it cannot be done' is the formulation used when there is a situation of marginal judicial review, and 'in fairness' which is a more substantial interpretation: that it was not only reasonable in the strict sense, it was also fair.

[11] Addink 1999, ch 7. [12] Stroink 1995, 83, note 5.
[13] Wade and Forsyth 2009, 302–5. [14] Auby and Cluzel-Metayer 2007, 78.
[15] Schröder 2007, 130.

(c) The principle of legal certainty

The principle of legal certainty has two dimensions, a formal and a substantive dimension. The formal dimension means that all rights and the duties are formulated carefully so that they are recognizable and foreseeable to the addressees. At least they must know which conditions have to be fulfilled. The substantive dimension means that there is a durability of rules. It also means that there should be no infringement of rights without any legal basis and, in general, there is a prohibition on retroactive effect for restrictive rules.

We find a codification of this norm in two different chapters of GALA, one in the chapter on subsidies and one in the chapter on enforcement of administrative norms. Article 4:23 reads as follows:

1. An administrative authority may only provide a subsidy pursuant to a provision of law that specifies the activities for which subsidies may be provided.
2. If such a provision of law is part of a general administrative measure not based on a statute, the provision shall cease to have effect four years after it enters into force, unless a bill regulating the subsidy has been presented to the States General before this date.
3. Paragraph 1 does not apply:
   a. for a period of one year at most pending the adoption of a provision of law or until a bill presented to the States General within that year has been defeated or has been passed and entered into force;
   b. if the subsidy grant is based directly on a programme adopted by the Council of the European Union, or the European Parliament and the Council jointly, or the Commission of the European Communities;
   c. if the budget specifies the subsidy recipient and the maximum amount at which the subsidy may be determined, or
   d. in isolated cases, provided the subsidy is given for a maximum of four years.
4. Each year the administrative authority shall publish a report of the subsidies provided in accordance with subparagraphs 3.a and 3.d.

We read in article 5:22: 'The power to take enforcement action exists only if it has been granted by or pursuant to act of Parliament.'

(d) The principle of legitimate expectation

This is also called the principle of confidence. In general, one can say that by enacting policy rules, directives, or circulars, expectations have been created and they have to be followed. In a concrete situation, when an expectation has been created by an administrative authority, this has to be followed, under certain conditions. In the literature, connected to this principle is the principle of consistency. Consistency plays a big part in the principles of proper administration. It is also strongly connected to the principles of equality and legal certainty.

This principle of legitimate expectation is only partly codified in GALA. It can further be discovered in the regulations concerning the withdrawal of subsidies. These are articulated in paragraph 4.2.6 of GALA. From that paragraph we only read article 4:48:

1. Until the definitive amount of the subsidy has been determined, the administrative authority may withdraw the decision granting the subsidy or amend it to the detriment of the subsidy recipient if:
   a. the activities or part of the activities for which subsidy has been granted have not taken place or will not take place;

b. the subsidy recipient has failed to comply with the requirements attached to the subsidy;
c. the subsidy recipient has provided incorrect or incomplete information and the provision of correct or complete information would have resulted in a different decision on the application for a subsidy grant,
d. the subsidy grant was otherwise incorrect and the subsidy recipient knew this or should have known this, or
e. the administrative authority, applying article 4:34.5, invokes the condition that sufficient funds be allocated.

2. Withdrawal or amendment has retroactive effect to the date when the subsidy was granted, unless otherwise provided in the decision to withdraw or amend the subsidy.

A legal entity enjoying the public power to decide should live up to the legitimate expectations it has created. The meaning of this principle is strongly related to the ways in which legitimate expectations can be raised. This has to do with the information given to subjects of law (with decisions taken in comparable matters) and with publicly announcing policies, possibly by stating policy rules. As a matter of course, this principle is derived from the general standard of legal certainty. This does not mean, however, that administrative policies concerning the implementation of unclear or vague regulations are to remain unchanged.

As an example, the Ministry of Development Cooperation sends a letter to Parliament, stating that Surinamese students may apply for a student's grant because the Surinamese government had problems with foreign currencies. A Surinamese student applied for such a grant, but the Ministry of Education refused the allowance because the student had changed the subject of her study. The administrative court ruled that the condition that applicants should not change their study was mentioned in the administrative order for the first time. This condition was neither published in any printed matter of the Ministry of Education, nor in the Student Finance Act. Since the student was not informed in any other way, the Judicial Section judged that the principle of legitimate expectations was violated. Therefore, the subsidy should be granted.[16]

According to the case law, the judge must discover the following elements. The first aspect is *who* created the confidence. Relevant is, for instance, the question: has this person the power to create such confidence? The following aspect is *in what way* has the confidence been created: was it orally or was it created by a letter? Another aspect is *by which act* was the confidence created: was it in an informal setting or was it part of a public decision of the administrative authority? Finally, has the person made some decisions or conducted some activities based on this confidence ('*disposed of*'), so as to create legal consequences?[17]

(e) The principle of equality

The principle of equality has been codified in Article 1 of the Dutch Constitution and for that reason there was no codification of this principle required. Other countries have these provisions as well, including Germany, South Africa, and Latvia:[18]

[16] ARRS, 5 January 1989, tB/S 1989 nr. 2. [17] Addink 1999, ch 10.
[18] The provisions are translation of original texts in Dutch, German, English, and Latvian.

Article 1 Dutch Constitution

All persons in the Netherlands shall be treated equally in equal circumstances. Discrimination on the grounds of religion, belief, political opinion, race or sex or on any other grounds whatsoever shall not be permitted.

Article 3 Grundgesetz

(1) All persons shall be equal before the law.
(2) Men and women shall have equal rights. The state shall promote the actual implementation of equal rights for women and men and take steps to eliminate disadvantages that now exist.
(3) No person shall be favoured or disfavoured because of sex, parentage, race, language, homeland and origin, faith, or religious or political opinions. No person shall be disfavoured because of disability.

Article 9 South African Constitution

1. Everyone is equal before the law and has the right to equal protection and benefit of the law.
2. Equality includes the full and equal enjoyment of all rights and freedoms. To promote the achievement of equality, legislative and other measures designed to protect or advance persons, or categories of persons, disadvantaged by unfair discrimination may be taken.
3. The state may not unfairly discriminate directly or indirectly against anyone on one or more grounds, including race, gender, sex, pregnancy, marital status, ethnic or social origin, colour, sexual orientation, age, disability, religion, conscience, belief, culture, language and birth.
4. No person may unfairly discriminate directly or indirectly against anyone on one or more grounds in terms of subsection (3). National legislation must be enacted to prevent or prohibit unfair discrimination.
5. Discrimination on one or more of the grounds listed in subsection (3) is unfair unless it is established that the discrimination is fair.

Article 91 Latvian Constitution

All human beings in Latvia shall be equal before the law and the courts. Human rights shall be realized without discrimination of any kind. International and European documents state the right to equal treatment as well, such as Art. 26 of the International Covenant on Civil and Political Rights, and Art. 14 of the European Convention on Human Rights.

The literature distinguishes the following three aspects of the principle of equality. First, the equality of law, which means that law is applied for all. Second, the equal treatment of individuals, as individuals, by the administration. This second aspect has these elements: no predisposition, no negative discrimination, and no positive discrimination. Third, the equal spread of costs which have been made in the general interest.

The principle of equality seems to be convenient: equal cases should be treated equally. The difficulty is, of course, which cases are equal and in what relevant aspects are similar cases different? The function of this principle is to prevent arbitrary distinctions being made, and to avoid differences in treatment without reasonable grounds. For an applicant in an administrative procedure, it is difficult to prove that there is a violation of the principle of equality. Appeals based on the principle of equality in administrative procedures only seldom succeed and usually one has to prove deemed discrimination.

(f) The principle of proportionality

In the Netherlands, this has been developed especially in the context of administrative sanctions. But in other contexts, for example in Germany and at the European level, one finds a broader application of this principle. In this broader application, a right balance between the means and aims should exist. This principle is codified in article 3:4, under 2, of GALA, as follows:

1. An administrative authority shall consider the interests directly affected by a decision, subject to any limitations following from a provision of law or the nature of the power to be exercised.
2. The adverse consequences of a decision for one or more interested parties may not be disproportionate to the objects to be served by the decision.

Once enquiries are made and the interests identified, an administrative authority weighs these interests against the others, and constructs the contents of the administrative order. The principle of proportionality requires that the content of an administrative order is proportionate to its aim. For example, let's say a shed was built illegally; it is not always proportionate to bulldoze it away, despite its illegality. If the administration should inform the owner about the situation and notify him that the shed should be torn down and the shed remains, the administration may impose a penalty, whether timely or occasionally.

In the Netherlands, the following aspects of the principle of proportionality in relation to the decisions of administrative authorities are examined. First, the authorities have the obligation to balance interests. The second element is the prohibition on reaching a manifestly unreasonable result as an outcome of balancing the different interests. The third element is the choice of the least painful burden for the citizen. And finally, administrative sanctions have to be proportional to the offence.[19] In other countries, like Germany, proportionality is based upon sustainability, necessity, and proportionality in a strict sense.[20] In the case of the ECJ, the intensity of the review plays an important role because the principle of proportionality is often mentioned and applied in EU law.

Gerards mentioned that the ECJ does not systematically and consistently apply the three main elements of proportionality review and instead uses wide variations. She concludes that most of these variations can be explained by the variation in the intensity of its proportionality review and by the highly different contexts in which the principle may be applied. The intensity of the Court's proportionality review itself appears to depend on a number of factors, of which the nature and specificity of the discretionary powers and the nature of the affected interests seem to be the most important.[21]

(g) The principle of carefulness

This is one of the most often used principles of proper administration. This principle is developed not only by the judiciary, but by the ombudsman as well. The meaning of the principle of carefulness has not been defined exhaustively yet. Nevertheless, it is one of the most prominent administrative principles. The principle of administrative carefulness is sometimes defined as 'the careful preparation of an administrative order'. The notion 'careful' is used in the name of the principle as well as in its definition. 'Careful preparation' has different meanings. It concerns the obligation of any legal entity as a part of the state to gather information concerning the matter to be decided. This implies the obligation of administrative bodies to:

- do research in order to find the information which must be taken into account in a decision;

[19] Fennel 2004, 14. [20] Gerards 2010. [21] Gerards 2009.

- give interested parties procedural opportunities to give the deciding administrative authority additional information on their concerns and their interests before a decision is taken;
- identify adequately the relevant facts and interests concerning a decision.

This principle is explained in its substantive and formal aspects. The substantive part of the principle means that there should be a careful balance of interest. The formal side of the principle of carefulness can be described by the four phases: (a) treatment; (b) research; (c) consultation; and (d) publication.

This interesting article concerning carefulness is stated in article 2:3 of GALA:

1. An administrative authority shall forward documents which manifestly come within the competence of another administrative authority to the latter authority without delay, while at the same time informing the sender.
2. An administrative authority shall as soon as possible return to the sender any documents which are not intended for it and which are not passed on to another administrative authority.

Another, even more important illustration on the preparation of a decision is stated in article 3:2 of GALA:

When preparing a decision an administrative authority shall collect the necessary information concerning the relevant facts and the interests to be considered.

(h) The principle of reasoning

Often, we see in the non-legal literature a qualification of reason: adequate, sufficient, or valid reason. A valid reason can mean a well-founded reason or a reason which produces the desired result or a reason which has force. The principle of sufficient reason is a powerful and controversial philosophical principle stipulating that everything must have a reason or cause. There is a long philosophical debate about it and it has links with the history of metaphysics.

The principle of reasoning in the legal context has two dimensions, like many other principles. The substantive dimension means that the decision of the administrative authority should include reasons in relation to the relevant facts, the interests involved, and the rules applicable. The formal dimension means that there must be recognizable reasons or motives given by the administration. Both dimensions have been codified in GALA, in a special paragraph for reasoning.

Article 3:46

An order shall be based on proper reasons.

Article 3:47

1. The reasons shall be stated when the order is notified.
2. If possible, the statutory regulation on which the order is based shall be stated at that same time.
3. If, in the interests of speed, the reasons cannot be stated immediately when the order is published, the administrative authority shall give communication of them as soon as possible thereafter.
4. In such a case, articles 3:41 to 3:43 inclusive shall apply mutatis mutandis.

Article 3:48

1. The reasons need not be stated if it can reasonably be assumed that there is no need for this.
2. If, however, an interested party asks within a reasonable period to be informed of the reasons, they shall be communicated to him as quickly as possible.

Article 3:49

To state the reasons of an order or part of an order, it is sufficient to refer to an opinion drawn up in this connection if the opinion itself contains the reasons and communication of the opinion has been or is given.

Article 3:50

If the administrative authority makes an order which derogates from an opinion drawn up for this purpose pursuant to a statutory regulation, this fact and the reasons for it shall be stated in the reasons of the order.

These illustrations show how important it is to state reasons. It has to do with procedural justice and with the openness of the administration. The obligation to state reasons may prevent arbitrariness. It has a 'reason' and the obligation to give that reason was found so important that this was included extensively in GALA

4. Institutions Involved

In general, all government institutions are involved in the development of the principles of properness. The legislator is involved because of the codification of the different principles of properness in GALA. This codification is related to the execution and its standardization. Other parts of the codification relate to the controlling standards to be applied by the judiciary. The consequence of these two types of codification is that the administration is bound by these norms. Thus, the parties could probably rely on these norms as standards of judicial control. Other controlling institutions, like the Ombudsman and the Court of Audit, use one or more of these principles of properness in their overall control. Finally, citizens can rely upon these norms. They expect that these norms will be applied by the administration and that the application of the norms will be controlled by the controlling institutions.

5. Conclusions

The principles of proper administration can be found in legislation, case law, policy rules, and in ombudsman reports. Eight sub-principles of proper administration are distinguished below.

1. The prohibition on misuse of power, with its four aspects: against the purpose of power, striving for an incorrect goal, inappropriate use, and inconsistent use.
2. The prohibition on arbitrariness, with its three earlier explained aspects: arbitrariness grasped as evident unreasonableness or visible unreasonableness that cannot be done reasonably and is not unfair.
3. The principle of legal certainty with its two aspects: formal legal certainty in the sense of recognizable rights and duties, and substantive legal certainty in the

sense of durability of rules, orders that have to be complied with, protection of rights, and the prohibition of retroactive effect.

4. The principle of confidence as worked out in general by policy rules, directives, or circulars. In concrete cases, the following specification criteria have been developed: by whom, in what way, by which act confidence has been created, and which aspects of disposition are important.
5. The principle of equality which is split into equality for the law and equality of administration: no predisposition, no negative discrimination, no positive discrimination, and equal spread of costs made in the general interest.
6. The principle of proportionality is used in the context of administrative sanctions (individual and general), and more broadly in the sense of a right balance between means and aims.
7. We distinguish in the principle of carefulness the substantive and the formal parts. Substantive carefulness means a careful balance of interest. In formal carefulness steps in procedure of ordering are distinguished as follows: (a) treatment; (b) research; (c) consultation; and (d) publication.
8. Finally, within the principle of reasoning, there is also a distinction between substantive reasoning (bearing reason in relation to facts, interest, and rules) and formal reasoning (recognizable reason by giving/publication of administrative motives).

Furthermore, understanding administrative law is easier if we know the history of administrative judicial review. The history of administrative judicial review is mainly linked to growing competences at the cost of review powers of higher administrative bodies. Many principles of proper administration were developed mainly by the courts. The judiciary did so in order to counterweigh the increase of discretionary powers of the administration. For this purpose, the courts generated discretionary powers for themselves, in creating and applying the different general principles of proper administration. In many cases they could choose between a restricted and a comprehensive review of an administrative order. At the moment, the courts do not always extensively justify this choice. Contradictorily, this sometimes leads to legal uncertainty as to judicial review.

In the Netherlands, the introduction of GALA has two faces. It is a codification of a hundred years of judicial review on administrative decisions. It is also a modification of the status quo reached in 1994. This modification implies a severe formalization of judicial review in Dutch administrative law, especially when courts refer to their competences as restricted to subjective law enforcement. This may be perfectly suited to citizens and organizations that are used to taking care of themselves in judicial matters. For people who are not used to that, the system has become harder and less predictable. Today, it is hard to say in which way judicial review will develop in the future. The Council of State has been gravely attacked by some academic lawyers, in such a manner that the Council of State has sought publicity to defend itself for the first time in its existence. Nevertheless, we must not close our eyes to the fact that GALA brought unity to a situation where almost each governmental field had its own administrative court with its own rules of procedure. Given that unity, differences that could not be seen before have become visible based on the codification in the GALA. Most important is that this effort to create unity and coherence has provided for much more legal certainty and standardization in administrative law.

8

The Principle of Transparency

The most fundamental reason to have a principle of transparency is the need for legitimacy of the government. But transparency also assists internal accountability and enhances the opportunity for outside comment. Several developments have caused the increasing need for transparency.

First, rules have become more technical and the bureaucracy has expanded. Thus, the idea that transparency and accountability flourish when the administration is more rule-bound is not necessarily true. As rules have become more intricate, the public at large often finds itself defeated by this technical language.[1] The enlarged bureaucracy created an enormous number of rules, which is out of the scope of the Parliament. This form of 'new despotism' should be diminished by means of transparency.[2] Further, as a consequence of developing science and technology, more and more experts are hired. But experts cannot be relied upon in order to know what is good for us. Here, protection by means of the principle of transparency is needed.

Second, national law in general and administrative law in particular are increasingly influenced by international and regional legal institutions.[3] At the same time, we see that transparency has declined as a result of the opacity of international law-making and policymaking processes. Apart from this kind of internationalization, states increasingly cooperate by means of ad hoc agreements as to certain activities. The legitimacy question then requires further-reaching transparency, as these activities are undertaken at a distance from the individual citizen. Third, competences are more frequently transferred to regulatory agencies that hold a considerable degree of discretion. These institutions should inform the public about their regulations and policies under the principle of transparency. Finally, the increasing number of private finance initiatives and public-private partnerships make it necessary to think about the actual transparency of these activities.

1. The Development of the Principle of Transparency

In the context of governmental transparency, different terms—information, transparency, and openness—are used. Therefore, it is useful to explain these terms.[4]

First, the term 'information' often refers to access by individuals as a presumptive right to information. Reasonable and clearly defined time limits for the right must be in operation. In some regimes, access to information can be restricted to citizens or permanent residents only, but it may be extended. Over fifty countries possess access to information bylaws. Second, access to information is only one component of transparency. The term transparency has a much broader scope and also entails the conducting of affairs in all candour so these affairs can be subject to public scrutiny. It refers to records of official decisions and activities. Transparency includes the provision

[1] Harlow and Rawlings 2009, 75. [2] Roberts 2006. [3] Buijze 2013.
[4] Birkinshaw 2006.

Good Governance: Concept and Context. Henk Addink. © Henk Addink 2019. Published 2019 by Oxford University Press.

of reasoned explanations for decisions. It also refers to policymaking and law drafts which should be as accessible and as comprehensible as possible, simplifying them so that they are more easily understood by the public. Complexity, disorder, and secrecy are features that transparency seeks to combat. The term 'openness' is quite similar to transparency. Openness goes beyond access to documents to cover such items as opening up the processes and meetings of public bodies. Openness means concentrating on processes that reveal the operations and activities of government. Often the term is used in combination with open government, which means actively providing access to information. But how should that be interpreted? When there is only a non-legally binding code, then no rights are created. Here, openness and transparency are seen as equal terms but we prefer the term transparency because it entails the most protection. Openness alone is not the same as protection.

2. The Concept of Transparency

The concept of transparency is regarded as a central notion of modern democracy.[5] Important elements of legal transparency include clarity of procedures, clear drafting, the publication and notification of legislation and decisions, and the duty to give reasons[6] as well as 'clear language, the predictability of public authorities" actions or behaviours, and consistency in the interpretation and application of the law. Secrecy is a cloak for arbitrariness, inefficiency, and corruption. Access to the relevant documentation is crucial for understanding the reasons behind governmental actions. Transparent information creates the trust that the people place in the government. It facilitates the construction of a reasoned argument by those opposed to a measure. Government should be accountable for its actions and this is difficult if it has a monopoly over the available information. Accountability is based upon reliable information, which is a prerequisite to establish effectiveness and efficiency of government. Some authors argue that having accountability through transparency can, in a very practical way, hinder the effectiveness of decision-making. For example, transparency may lead to defensive thinking and excessive caution, a return to the 'avoid personal risks at all costs' culture that new public management sought to eliminate.[7] Individual citizens should know about the information held about them in order to check its correctness and the use to which it is put. So, it is necessary for the idea of citizenship. Furthermore, it is hoped that public disclosure of information will actually improve decision-making and its processes. Then, it strengthens the reliability of government decisions and aides those in government to identify the public interest.[8]

But what are the arguments against the concept of transparency?[9] Some authors are of the opinion that we are not thinking critically enough about where and when transparency works, where and when it may lead to confusion, or worse. Lessig gives many reasons in favour of limited administrative transparency. He says: 'understanding how and why some stories will be understood, or not understood, provides the key to grasping what is'.[10] This is clarified as follows. The first argument, which is addressed in the literature, is that of representative democracy. Citizens are represented by government and parliament, who have to solve problems. Disagreement within the government should not be revealed. Because of the need for an efficient and strong

[5] Birkinshaw 2005. [6] Prechal and De Leeuw 2007, 51.
[7] Bannister and Connolly 2011. [8] Craig 2006, 350. [9] Birkinshaw 2006.
[10] Lessig 2009.

government, too much information will deflect resources away from the provision of essential public services. Allowing public access to the government's information would undermine ministerial responsibility. But how is this argument related to the argument that, by transparency, citizens' trust in the government is promoted? One can never be sure that sensitive or controversial information is used appropriately. Seemingly innocuous information may be lethal in the hands of terrorists or psychopaths. What about unjustified invasion of personal privacy or commercial confidentiality? In the end, it might undermine the trust that must exist between those in government and the governed. But some will say: is it not the task of the representatives to ensure that the government functions correctly? They do need information, and because the people elect the representatives, we also need the information to make a good choice during the elections.

Nevertheless, we should not exaggerate the transforming effect of these developments. Openness in government is not altogether new, and it is not guaranteed. We should keep in mind that the government has had to live with forms of openness for centuries. The questions in parliament from the parliamentarians and the openness of the courts already existed for a long time. Various forms of public inquiry are part of a longstanding tradition in many countries, whereby public inquiry commissions of the parliament or the government were formed. Open government really is partly new and cannot be taken for granted. The principle that administrative information in general is to be open is a new principle, which has been developed since the 1990s. It is of constitutional importance because of its contribution to political control of government. But it has a more basic importance, because it makes the government face up to people: it is in itself an accountability technique.[11]

The description of transparency has two sides: the active and the passive one. The active side means that the government has to inform the public by itself and on its own initiative. The passive side means that anyone can request specific information. This access to information is one of the most important elements of the concept of transparency, but there are more. The active side is related to the openness of the government. It means that the government is open in their activities related to public interests. This obligation does not mean that every single meeting is announced, but in principle, citizens should be able at least to attend meetings that are of any importance to them. The same applies for decisions taken by the government, and the final decisions which could have consequences for third parties should be published. The second is about inquiries done by specific committees. Often these committees are chaired by an independent person and can have different functions. A few possible functions are: to establish the facts; to learn from events; to provide trust for 'stakeholders'; to reassure the public; to make people and organizations accountable; and to serve the political interests of government.[12]

Until now, the focus was on the transparency of the government, and especially on the administration. But because we speak here about transparency as a principle of good governance, this principle is applied in the context of the legislative power and the judicial power too. Traditionally, legislators mostly act transparently, so the principle is well recognized here. But also, in the judiciary, there is a tendency to be more transparent in the trial as well as in the publication of the final judicial decision. The transparency of information in the framework of (quasi-)judicial procedures is also relevant. Some examples for the Netherlands are article 121 of the Dutch Constitution

[11] Endicott 2009, 31; Endicott 2015.

[12] Howe 1999.

and article 8:79 of GALA. Article 121 of the Constitution, in short, is about the obligation that judgments shall be held in public and specify the grounds on which they are based. Article 8:79 of GALA is about the obligation to send judgments to the parties and the possibilities for others to ask for judgments. It is about the question of whether one party can get information from the other party in the trial in which the first party wants to build up its argumentation. Mostly, there are specific regulations about transparency on this type of information.

Finally, there is a topic where the principle of transparency has already functioned for a long time and in a rather different way. Sometimes the government uses market competition to get a contract with the lowest price, or at least with the best price-quality ratio. There are different examples in the field of economic law but we find it also in the field of public procurement law.[13]

3. Specification of the Concept

Transparency and transparent governance are—as we saw earlier—related to democracy. In essence, three sub-principles are distinguished here: transparent meetings of the government; transparency of governmental acts; and transparency of governmental information.

(a) Transparent meetings of the government

This paragraph will show how these three sub-principles have been specified in the Dutch legislation as a case study. Meanwhile, we have to make it clear that these three sub-principles are relevant for all the four powers in the state. First, the principle of transparency of meetings of the administration can be explained by an example of a regulation about the meetings in the Parliament of the Netherlands. In the Rules of the House of Parliament we read:

Article 38. Breach of confidentiality

1. Secrecy shall be observed with regard to the content of confidential documents and the exchange of views in a private Committee meeting, with the exception of what the Committee states in its report.
2. The Committee may permit the members and the Ministers to disclose what they themselves have said in a private meeting, provided that the confidentiality of statements made by other persons is not thereby breached.
3. The Presidium may propose to the House that a member who has breached the confidentiality of a Committee meeting or of a document be excluded from all meetings of one or more Committees and/or be barred from receiving confidential documents for a maximum of one month.
4. The proposal may not be made until after the member to be excluded and the chairman of the Committee meeting whose confidentiality has been breached have been heard or in any event properly summoned to attend.
5. The proposal shall be put to the vote at the start of the first meeting after the day on which the Presidium decides to make the proposal. No debate shall be held on this proposal.
6. A decision to exclude a member shall be immediately communicated in writing by the President to the members of the House.

[13] Wibowo 2017, 21.

This type of regulation on transparency in relation to the parliament can be found in almost every country. Similar regulations have often been developed for the meetings of the council of ministers and other institutions. These regulations can be found not only at the central level but on the level of the decentralized government as well.

(b) Transparency of governmental acts

The second sub-principle of transparency is related to the transparency of other types of acts of the administration. For public acts, the most common are orders, regulations, decisions, policy rules, and plans, but sometimes public contracts and factual acts are also seen as examples of public acts.[14] As an example, we will take the transparency regulation on 'orders' in the Dutch GALA. In this Act, a special paragraph is dedicated to 'Notification and communication'. The content of some of the articles in this paragraph is as follows:

Division 3.6 Notification and communication

Article 3:40

An order shall not take effect until it has been notified.

Article 3:41

1. Orders which are addressed to one or more interested parties shall be notified by being sent or issued to these, including the applicant.
2. If an order cannot be notified in the manner provided in subsection 1, it shall be notified in any other suitable way.

Article 3:42

1. Orders which are not addressed to one or more interested parties shall be notified by means of a notice of the order, or the substance thereof, placed in an official government publication, newspaper or free local paper, or in any other suitable way.
2. If notice is given only of the substance, the order shall at the same time be deposited for inspection. The notice shall state where and when the order will be deposited for inspection.

(c) Transparency of governmental information

Finally, some examples of Dutch regulations in the context of the principle of transparent governmental information are provided. The transparency of governmental information has been developed in the Dutch Information Act. Since the Information Act contains obligations addressed to all the government institutions, including those operating on the regional and international level, it is interesting to mention the European side of the grounds for refusal of information. It is interesting to see that in EC Regulation 1049/2011, another system of grounds for refusal is used (eg article 4), which could lead to different outcomes. So, a European institution is involved in a (European) citizen's case. Instead of a Dutch institution, legal consequences may differ.

In the context of an information act, it is important to ask: what rights do people have to get information from state authorities? In this context, it is relevant to have the right to access your own personal file, 'which may be considered as an individual

[14] Zigirinshuti 2013, 37.

manifestation of access to documents and is explicitly recognized in Article 41(2) of the Charter of Fundamental Rights as part of the right to good administration'.[15] Is there any absolute obligation for government authorities to provide this information? The questions in relation to public information are: to whom, about what, which rights, and when?

We first illustrate the passive obligation to inform and then the active obligation of the administration. We read in section 3 of the Netherlands Information Act:

1. Anyone may apply to an administrative authority or to an agency, service or company carrying out work for which it is accountable to an administrative authority for information contained in documents concerning an administrative matter.
2. The applicant shall specify the administrative matter or the document relevant to it about which he wishes information.
3. An application for information shall be granted with due regard for the provisions of sections 10 and 11.

Thus, anyone can ask for information from an administrative authority and has to specify his request. This request should usually be granted, unless one of the provisions of sections 10 and 11 has to be followed. The active obligation or duty of the administration is formulated as follows:

Section 8

1. The administrative authority directly concerned shall provide, of its own accord, information on its policy and the preparation and implementation thereof, whenever the provision of such information is in the interests of effective, democratic governance.
2. The administrative authority shall ensure that the information is supplied in a comprehensible form and in such a way as to reach the interested party and as many interested members of the public as possible at a time which will allow them to make their views known to the administrative authority in good time.

Section 9

1. The administrative authority directly concerned shall ensure that the policy recommendations which the authority receives from independent advisory committees, together with the requests for advice and proposals made to the advisory committees by the authority shall be made public where necessary, possibly with explanatory notes.
2. The recommendations shall be made public no more than four weeks after they have been received by the administrative authority. Their publication shall be announced in the Netherlands Government Gazette or in some other periodical made generally available by the government. Notification shall be made in a similar manner of non-publication, either total or partial.

This means that the administrative authority is obliged to provide information about its policy of its own record in an adequate way when the information comes from an advisory institution. In the following articles one may find examples of exceptions and restrictions:

Chapter V. Exceptions and restrictions

Section 10

1. Disclosure of information pursuant to this Act shall not take place insofar as:
   a. this might endanger the unity of the Crown;
   b. this might damage the security of the State;

[15] Prechal and De Leeuw 2007, 52.

c. the data concerned relate to companies and manufacturing processes and were furnished to the government in confidence by natural or legal persons.

2. Nor shall disclosure of information take place insofar as its importance does not outweigh one of the following:
   a. relations between the Netherlands and other states or international organizations;
   b. the economic and financial interests of the State, other bodies constituted under public law or the administrative authorities referred to in section 1a, subsection 1 (c and d) and subsection 2;
   c. the investigation of criminal offences and the prosecution of offenders;
   d. inspection, control and oversight by administrative authorities;
   e. respect for personal privacy;
   f. the importance to the addressee of being the first to note the information;
   g. the prevention of disproportionate advantage or disadvantage to the natural or legal persons concerned or to third parties.
3. Subsection 2, chapeau and at b, shall apply to the disclosure of environmental information concerning confidential procedures.
4. Subsection 2, chapeau and at g, shall not apply to the disclosure of environmental information. It is possible to refrain from disclosing such information pursuant to this Act if its publication would make damage to the environment more likely.

Section 11

1. Where an application concerns information contained in documents drawn up for the purpose of internal consultation, no information shall be disclosed concerning personal opinions on policy contained therein.
2. Information on personal opinions on policy may be disclosed, in the interests of effective, democratic governance, in a form which cannot be traced back to any individual. If those who expressed the opinions in question or who supported them agree, information may be disclosed in a form which may be traced back to individuals.
3. Information concerning the personal opinions on policy contained in the recommendations of a civil service or mixed advisory committee may be disclosed if the administrative authority directly concerned informed the committee members of its intention to do so before they commenced their activities.

Articles 10 and 11 of the Act contain the grounds for refusal of information:

- Article 10 Subsection 1: absolute grounds of refusal of information; if this ground applies, information must remain secret;
- Article 10 Subsection 2: relative grounds of refusal of information = whether or not the information needs to be given, depends on a balancing of interests between the interests of making the information public (the interest of the person who requests the information) and those of keeping the information secret (the general interest of society and/or the interest of the person about whom the information is requested);
- Article 11: keeping secret information on internal debates; this is to protect personal opinions of civil servants, because they need to express their opinions freely without these being made public (it is essential in a parliamentary democracy).

If the information requested is refused, a person can go to an administrative court to challenge the decision.

4. Institutions Involved

All the government institutions on the national level, in the broader sense, have regulations regarding the transparency aspects of their behaviour. This means that not only the three traditional powers have to deal with it, but also the fourth power institutions. The relevance of this principle is multilevel. Transparency has been developed in different countries through civilians rebelling against official secrecy by utilizing the access to information laws with a 'right to information approach'.

The first steps to transparency in relation to access to information in the EU faltered and were attacked for failing to appreciate the fundamental nature of the right in question.[16] For example, many criticized the Council of Ministers because it merely adjusted its internal rules of procedure to allow public access to documents. In *Netherlands v Council of the European Union*, the Advocate General noted in his opinion for the ECJ that:

> The basis for such a right should be sought in the democratic principle, which constitutes one of the cornerstones of the Community edifice . . . in the Preamble to the Maastricht Treaty and Article F of the Common Provisions of the Treaty . . . The right of access to official documents is now . . . part of that democratic principle.

Thus, the Advocate General referred more broadly to a right of access to documents as a constitutional or legislative principle enshrined in the legislation of most Member States. The European Parliament, in its intervention before the ECJ, 'rightly stress[ed]' the democratic nature of the Community legal order. '[O]penness is a fundamental characteristic of a democratic system', the European Parliament claimed. The Dutch government argued that the categorization of access as an internal bureaucratic matter—that is, a 'right' governed by internal rules of procedure—by the Council was misconceived. The reason was that procedure was a 'fundamental right', especially the public's right of access to information, the rules governing which must be accompanied by the necessary safeguards. The right was an 'innate feature' of any democratic system. The ECJ declined to accept that it was such a fundamental right, although it acknowledged that the right of access has been reaffirmed by the Community 'on various occasions'. To amend the rules governing its internal administration, which were based on confidentiality in order to allow access by the public to its documents, the Council confirmed this trend of openness that 'discloses a progressive affirmation of individuals' right of access to documents held by public authorities'.

The ECJ held that the Council was empowered to amend its internal organization in this manner, by an administrative code which is backed up by formal legal decisions. The ECJ and Court of First Instance (CFI)—the latter deals with most of the cases on access to information at first instance and from which there is an appeal to the ECJ—have subsequently avoided any ruling on the general principles of openness and access, finding technical or reviewable faults when the Council and Commission have denied access under the 1993 code and decisions. In *Hautala v Council*, both the CFI and the ECJ on appeal found for Ms Hautala, a Member of the European Parliament, in her claim for access to documents relating to Title V information, the common foreign and security policy, which the Council had wrongly refused to disclose in redacted form. In other words, the Council refused to fillet out information that was not covered by an exemption and claimed that the exemption covered every item of information in the documents. A failure to consider redaction rendered the decision null. Both courts found it unnecessary to rule on Hautala's third claim that denial constituted a 'breach of the fundamental principle' of Community law that citizens of the EU must be given the widest and fullest possible access to documents of the Community institutions. That refusal amounted to a denial of Ms Hautala's legitimate expectations. The ECJ did

[16] Birkinshaw 2006.

not find it necessary to rule on the Council's ground of appeal that the CFI wrongly based its decision on a 'right to information', finding that the refusal to consider disclosing redacted documents was illegal and disproportionate. General principles of law, such as proportionality, help to interpret the right to access, but according to the ECJ, access is not yet a general principle itself. It should be emphasized that the general principles of law include fundamental rights taken from national constitutional systems, international treaties, and legal traditions, as well as principles of judicial review within the member states.

A lot has happened since *Hautala v Council*. In 2001, the ECJ had not yet found the right of access to information a 'principle', but in the case *Sison v Council*, the ECJ did precisely that in paragraph 63.

> As they [exceptions as found in Article 4 of Regulation 1049/2011] derogate from the principle of the widest possible public access to documents, such exceptions must, as the appellant has correctly observed, be interpreted and applied strictly.

Other cases related to the development of the right of access to information are *Kuijer v Council*[17] and *Turco v Sweden*.[18]

The Amsterdam Treaty on the European Union declares in article 1(2) that the EU should operate as 'openly and as closely as possible to its citizens'. Specifically, article 255(1) provides for a right of access to documents of the European Parliament, Council, and Commission. The general principles and their limits are set out in Regulation 1049/2001. Recital 2 of Regulation 1049 notes that openness contributes toward strengthening democracy and the protection of human rights within article 6 EU and the Charter of Fundamental Rights. The purpose of Regulation 1049 is, among other things, 'to give the fullest possible effect to the right of public access to [EU] documents' that establish general principles and limitations (Recital 4). Subsequently, a Directive of the European Parliament and Council of Ministers has set out provisions that seek to facilitate the reuse of public sector information by private sector bodies.

The draft EU-Constitution (EUC) extended the right of access to cover all institutions, bodies, offices, and agencies of the EU, including the European Council, which has to conduct its work 'as openly as possible' in accordance with the draft-EUC article 1-50.[19] The European Council of the EU is a meeting of the heads of state or government. It has no formal legal status within the EU Treaty, remarkably similar to the UK Cabinet within the British legal system. The European Council is the body that sets out the most important agendas for future development of the EU. The draft-EUC gave legal status to this body for the first time in article 1-19(1). No working group in the Convention on the Constitution, which drafted the Constitution, dealt with access

[17] ECJ 7 February 2002, T-211/00, *Aldo Kuijer v Council of the European Union*, ECR II-488.

[18] ECJ 1 July 2008, Joined cases C-39/05 P and C-52/05 P, *Sweden and Turco v Council*, ECR, 2008 I-04723.

[19] The draft-EUC does this in a number of ways, which include simplifying the EU Annex. For 2004, see COM (2005) 348 final and Annex; for the general report on implementation of Regulation 1049/2001, see COM (2004) 45 final. See, eg, ECJ 17 September 2003, T-76/02, *Messina v Commission*, ECR II-03203 (finding the documents to be an exception to disclosure under art 4(5) of Regulation 1049); ECJ 23 November 2004, T-84/03, *Turco v Council*, ECR II-04061 (dismissing the request for access to documents under the art 4 exception); ECJ 30 November 2004, T-168/02, *Internationaler Tiershutz-Fonds (IFAW) GmbH v Commission*, ECR II-04135 (dismissing the request for access to documents under art 4(5)); ECJ 13 April 2005, T-2/03, *Verein für Konsumenteninformation v Commission*, ECR II-01121 (annulling the Commission's decision to withhold access for lack of concrete examination, and setting a demanding test for examination of large files of documents by the Commission); ECJ 26 April 2005, Joined cases T-110/03, T-150/03,

as a distinct topic, because the Convention believed that what was required was more transparency and simplification of structure in the EU.

The EU (2004) draft constitution placed access to documents in article 1-50 within Part I of the draft-Treaty and places the basic constitutional measures under the title (nr. VI) on 'Democratic Life' within the EU.[20] The right covers access to documents in the possession of the institutions, including the European Council, the agencies, offices, and bodies of the EU. Its scope was far wider than the at that moment present Regulation since it covered agencies and committees of the Council and Commission. The right of access was accompanied by the principles of democratic equality (article 1-45), representative democracy (article 1-46), participatory democracy (article 1-47), and, among other things, data protection (article 1-51).

Access founded also its way into the Charter of Fundamental Rights in Part II (at that moment as a part of the draft constitution) as article 11-102 (article 42 final version of the Charter), together with a right to good administration (article II-101; article 41 final version of the Charter) and in Part III, article 111-398 makes provision for an 'open, efficient and independent European administration'. Article 111-399 conferred a right of access to documents held by the bodies covered in article 1-50. In addition, the ECJ and European Central Bank were for instance covered when exercising 'administrative functions'. Some of the norms in the draft-constitution, like the norm for an 'open, independent and efficient European administration', are still under discussion as we can see from the European Parliament study of July 2018 and can be found in the frame of the different principles of good governance as explained here.

The Convention on Fundamental rights was proclaimed on 7 December 2000. A modified Charter formed part of the defunct European Constitution of 2004. In 2007, the Lisbon Treaty gave force to the Charter by referencing it as an independent document rather than by incorporating it into the treaty itself. But, following the entry into force of the Lisbon Treaty in 2009, the fundamental rights treaty became of the same legal value as the European Union treaties.

Despite some possible criticisms about the process, these are crucial developments in the EU, and there is no doubt that the freedom of information is treated as a constitutional and fundamental human right. In a 2005 European Data Protection Supervisor publication, public access to information is described as a fundamental right along with privacy, data protection, and integrity of the individual established under the EC Data Protection Directive.

5. Sources of the Principle of Transparency

Most of the norms pertaining to the principle of transparency have been worked out in the regulations and, therefore, the sources are these regulations on transparency and the three sub-principles as explained before.

On the European level three sources are elaborated upon: the Directive on Data Protection; the Directive on Environmental Protection; and the European Convention on Human Rights. The international level is covered by transparency on the WTO level.

and T-405/03, *Sison v Council*, ECR II-01429 (rejecting the plea for access to documents as unfounded and refusing the access); see also Stolk and others 2005, *Transparency in Europe 11*: public access to documents in the EU and its member states.

[20] Birkinshaw 2006.

(a) Transparency, access to information, and data protection

In the public eye, data protection laws are the most vivid example of access to information laws including access to information or data about oneself.[21] There is an EC Directive (95/46) on Data Protection. Data protection laws are also derived from article 8 ECHR which concerns the protection of privacy. Some see it as incongruous that the Directive also seeks to facilitate cross-border flows of personal information for purposes of the single EC market. While the thrust of this chapter has been an argument in favour of freedom of information as a human right, we have no doubt of the essential importance of privacy protection. Data protection is not a complete privacy law, but it has a vital role to play in securing the integrity of individuals. It has been noted, however, that it can be abused by national governments, the Commission, and individuals. This particular subject emphasizes the importance of right to transparency, not only as a right to invoke in special situations but also as a right that is of continuing weight, especially in the digitalized 'environment'.

The Directive and national laws implementing transparency have been invoked in order to deny access to information about the identity of individual officials or persons with whom citizens had met when there were no security or safety reasons not to allow disclosure of identity. These laws have also been used to prevent individuals from obtaining access to information because it contained personal data that was irrelevant to the request and in every other respect completely marginal to it. Data protection was sometimes simply a convenient excuse not to disclose. This begs a series of questions about the proper scope of privacy and the extent to which officials are themselves protected by privacy when performing public business. I have no doubt there is a serious issue in this wider question when personal safety is, or may be, in question. Too often, however, governments resort to overreach and don't choose the genuine protection of personal privacy that is necessary and desirable.

(b) Transparency and access to environmental information

Reference should be made to Directive 2003/4/EC of the European Parliament and of the Council of 28 January 2003 on public access to environmental information.[22] The Directive followed the Aarhus Convention on Access to Information, Public Participation in Decision-Making, and Access to Justice in Environmental Matters. This measure had to be implemented into the Member States' law and it allows individual rights of access to environmental information, which is very broadly defined. Its scope is truly enormous; it also covers the security and intelligence services in the member states, although a national security exemption will apply to much of the work of these bodies. There is no doubt that access to environmental information will have significant human rights implications, a factor included in the decisions of the European Court of Human Rights (ECtHR) outlined in the following part. Environmental rights are referred to as one of the 'third generation of human rights', which will be detailed in Chapter 12. It seems appropriate to place access to information rights generally within this category of third generation rights.

[21] Ibid. [22] Ibid.

(c) Transparency and the European Convention on Human Rights

Reference has been made to the articles of the ECHR and various recommendations of the Committee of Ministers above on access to information.[23] Article 10 is not a provision concerning access to information. Instead, it is one on free speech and freedom to pass on information. However, in *Gaskin v United Kingdom*,[24] the ECtHR ruled that article 8 (which guarantees a right to family life and privacy) may provide a right to independent arbitration of a contested claim to records held about an individual by a public authority. Access had been refused by the authority when the applicant, who had been brought up in the statutory care of the local authority, claimed that he had suffered damage as a consequence of the authority's negligence. The refusal to give access was not subject to any independent system of arbitration to determine whether grounds for withholding personal information under article 8(2) were justified. *Sdruženi Jihočeské Matky v Czech Republic*[25] must be mentioned here because this case was the first time the ECtHR actually applied article 10 ECHR in an access of information case. There has been a reluctance to recognize a positive obligation to supply relevant information regarding matters of public interest, but this case held that 'there are indications that the Court's position is changing'.[26]

In *Guerra v Italy*,[27] the former European Commission on Human Rights (CHR) believed that local residents had an entitlement under article 10 to access environmental information about a chemical works programme that was causing pollution. The CHR disagreed with this finding on article 10 but did find a breach of duty by the state under article 8, insofar as there was an interference with family and private life by not ensuring disclosure of information about harmful substances. In *McGinley and Egan v United Kingdom*,[28] the ECtHR determined that members of the British armed forces would have a right under article 8 to access documentation on the effects of experimental atomic explosions on those members of the armed forces who had witnessed them. However, since they had not yet exhausted all domestic provisions, their rights had not been breached in the case. The following excerpt from the judgment is full of potential:

> When a government engages in hazardous activities, such as those in issue in the present case, which might have hidden adverse consequences on the health of those involved in such activities. Article 8 requires that an effective and accessible procedure be established which enables S165 such persons to seek all relevant and appropriate information.

One only needs to refer to *Fressoz v France*[29] to demonstrate the close relation between the right to free speech under article 10 and the right of access to information. On many occasions, courts have determined that a criminal defendant's right of access to information held by the prosecutors is a requirement to guarantee a fair trial under article 6. It has also illustrated a very difficult dilemma of ensuring a fair criminal trial in circumstances in which state security or informers' identities may allegedly be compromised.

[23] Ibid. [24] ECtHR 7 July 1989, 10454/83 (*Gaskin v The United Kingdom*).

[25] ECtHR 10 July 2006, 19101/03 (*Sdruženi Jihočeské Matky v Czech Republic*).

[26] Hins and Voorhoof 2007, 114.

[27] ECtHR 19 February 1998, 14967/89 (*Guerra and others v Italy*).

[28] ECtHR 9 June 1998, 10/1997/794/995-996 (*McGinley and Egan v United Kingdom*).

[29] ECtHR 21 January 1999, 29183/95 (*Fressoz v France*).

These are European cases, but one should not ignore developments from the American continent. The meaning of freedom of expression has been tested in the Inter American Court on Human Rights (IACHR) in relation to access to information. Article 13 IACHR (a free speech provision) has been invoked to provide an access right to state-held information. The litigation concerns a refusal by Chile to provide information about inward investment and its environmental impact. The dependence of freedom of speech upon freedom of information is raised once again in these proceedings.

The transparency principle has now also made its entry on the European stage. Here, it is also about increased publicity of the work of European institutions like the Council of Ministers and the European Commission as well as increased access to EU documents.[30] The EU Publicity Regulations, effective since 1 December 2001, are very important in this respect. These Regulations primarily regulate access to documents in the hands of European institutions as well as contain restrictions. However, because there is an intensive exchange of documents among the EU and member states, many European documents are in the hands of member state governments. For this reason, the European Publicity Act also applies to European documents that are kept by the Dutch government, ministries, and other public bodies among others. On 18 April 2007, the European Commission presented a green paper[31] about the effects of Regulation 1049/2001 on public access to documents from the European Parliament, the Council, and the Commission. This can be seen as an assessment of the impact of the law on the accessibility of documents. Meanwhile, judicial experience has been gained with regards to the Regulation and judicial decisions have been reached explaining the Regulation. The European Ombudsman has also published advice on this matter. In addition, in 2005, the Commission initiated the European transparency initiative which calls for the revision of the Regulation to facilitate increased publicity. The European Parliament has since called on the Commission for proposals regarding the Regulation's revision.[32] The transparency principle has further entered into specific areas of European administrative law, for instance, competition[33] and environmental law[34] and, it is also included in two European tender regulations.[35]

Besides legislation, the Court's jurisdiction also pays attention to the transparency principle.[36] In some cases the transparency principle is connected to, or is part of, the principle of equality.[37] In other cases it is applied without violating the equality principle. It goes without saying that the transparency principle often precedes the principle of equality. The transparency principle can sometimes also be connected with the

[30] Widdershoven and others 2007, 85ff; in addition, see Prechal and De Leeuw 2007, 51–61.

[31] European Commission, *Green Paper on Public Access to Documents held by institutions of the European Community*, 18 April 2004, COM(2007)185.

[32] The consultation round on this Green Paper runs up to mid-July 2007. According to the Commission's schedule it will respond to the consultation in September and make propositions for any adjustments of the regulation as soon as October 2007.

[33] Articles 5 and 6 of Directive 2002/21/EC for market supervisors.

[34] A separate regulation has since been effected concerning access to environmental information, see Regulation (EC) 1367/2006 of the European Parliament and the Council, 6 September 2006. It is based on the implementation of the Aarhus Convention.

[35] Article 2 of Directive 2004/18/EC, coordination of the procedures for placing government commissions for works, provisions and services; art 10 of Directive 2004/17/EC, coordination of the procedures for placing commissions in the departments of water and energy supply, traffic and postal services.

[36] For the first time, ECJ 25 April 1996, C-87/94, *Commission v Belgium*, ECR I-2043.

[37] ECJ 18 November 1999, C-275/98, *Unitron*, ECR I-8291; ECJ 12 December 2002, C-470/99, *Universale-Bau*, ECR I-11617; and ECJ 4 December 2003, C-448/01, *Wienstrom*, ECR I-14527.

principle of legal certainty, although they do not completely overlap. A natural conclusion is that the transparency principle at the European level has grown from a principle of contract law into a general legal principle especially in the administration of justice. However, it still depends on, and is discussed in connection with, other legal principles like the principles of equality and legal certainty.

(d) Transparency on the WTO level

For a long time, there has been talk with respect to the WTO and the desirability of giving further meaning to the transparency principle.[38] This talk has not only come from within the WTO but also from many governments,[39] NGOs,[40] individuals, and (European) institutions[41] insisting on more transparency in the administration of the WTO as well as the processes that take place. In Cancun, 2003, it was ascertained that there is a great need for more democracy and transparency in WTO processes and procedures. An end must be brought to the confusion among the legislative, executive, and judicial powers of the WTO; to the secrecy surrounding the functioning of most WTO organs; to the 'Green Room' and 'Mini-Ministerial Conferences'; and to the sham democracy that is based on the method of implicit consensus. The critique on the lack of transparency at the WTO has become fiercer and, at the preparations for the meeting in Hong Kong in June 2005, there were further pleas made for revision of the conciliation mechanism[42] to make it more transparent and accessible to the member states, thereby enhancing legal security through publicity and independence. The European Parliament has also insisted on the reform of the WTO, not only in terms of more internal transparency, but also more external transparency in cooperating with other international organizations and developing countries.[43]

Despite the internal and external unrest and the associated political pressure, attempts at implementing the transparency principle with respect to the internal and external functioning of the WTO regulations have so far been unsuccessful.[44] The usual explanation for this is that the transparency principle is a typically western product and that it is only beneficial to western countries, not to the other countries in the world. This argument then invariably leads to stagnation in the substantive exchange of thoughts on, arguments for, and the further development of, the

[38] Among others: Wolfe 2003 and Mori 2007.

[39] In a response to the Seattle meeting, the Dutch government advocated more external transparency.

[40] At the time of the WTO meeting in Seattle in December 1999, there was an appeal for more transparency in the WTO; in June 2005, a similar appeal was made from Belgian NGOs at the preparation of the WTO meeting in Hong Kong.

[41] In 1994, the European Parliament, in a motion, demanded maximum transparency of WTO activity; in 1997, a motion was accepted for an annual report to be handed to the parliament by the Commission regarding its WTO activity.

[42] One task of the WTO is to mediate business disputes between members. The existing GATT procedures for conciliation are, compared to the WTO, easier to execute and more efficient. Individual WTO members cannot stop a decision made by the organ responsible for conciliation. Besides a direct appeal to the WTO to act as referee, a member state is also able to appeal to two specific regulations.

[43] See the defence of member of the European Parliament, Van Hecke, on 5 March 2008.

[44] The WTO regulations are concerned with the stipulations of the GATT and agreements that were made during several GATT rounds. This means that countries that want to become members of the WTO have to abide by all these GATT stipulations. In addition to the GATT agreements, the WTO covers a large set of further rules on trade in goods, agreements on disruptions in agricultural trade, among which are disciplines for market access and agricultural grants, as well as rules for trade in services and protection of so-called 'intellectual property'.

transparency principle as it relates to the WTO.[45] Whilst 1 January 2008 marked the multilateral trade system's sixtieth year of existence, a milestone in the history of GATT and its successor WTO, the transparency principle as it relates to the WTO finds itself at an impasse.

Complaints about the lack of democracy at the WTO, such as the lack of transparency in decision-making processes and other procedures of the organization, were earlier discussed. In *The Glass Case*, Roberts[46] points out that there is 'a host of disclosure requirements now imposed on countries through WTO agreements'. If the WTO requires its members to participate in its disclosure requirements without being transparent itself, how would it expect WTO members to fully embrace the legitimacy of its decisions? I think that this point should be discussed in the book to assist it in enabling the expectation of transparency on the part of the WTO as much as it does from its WTO members The WTO will have to further engage in discussions with social organizations without losing its character as an intergovernmental organization. Moreover, it will have to pay significant attention to existing issues regarding the environment, health, and fundamental work standards connected to international trade. The WTO has created a conciliation mechanism and, thanks to this mechanism, the law of the jungle does not apply. However, the capacity and quality of conciliation needs to be investigated, especially the real-life effectiveness of this mechanism in developing countries. The problem is how compliance with panel jurisdiction can be ensured. Revision of the conciliation process within the WTO is currently needed especially in terms of which conciliation panels and hearings of the board of appeal should be opened to the public. UN agencies should play a role in these panels. In short, a revision of the conciliation mechanism so that it becomes more translucent and accessible to all member states would increase legal security in the area of publicity and independence.

These seemingly secondary aspects keep the WTO from doing its actual job, which is obviously to stimulate trade. This is achieved by encouraging countries to negotiate the lowering of import duties, the abolition of rules that restrict trade, and by applying the same rules for all countries. The WTO cannot make rules itself; decisions can only be made if all countries are in agreement. The foregoing makes it appear as if the WTO pays little attention to the transparency principle, however, this is not the case. For this reason, the current elements of the transparency principle at the WTO will be discussed in order to determine which additions and adjustments are possible and desirable.

In the original GATT there were a number of articles that implied a requirement of transparency.[47] First, article X stipulated that certain regulations and judicial decisions were to be published quickly and in such a way that the governments and trade organizations could become acquainted with them. The second clause stated the same regarding measures that could influence international trade and agreements. The third clause stipulated that measures were to be applied in a uniform, impartial, and reasonable way.

Besides these (mainly procedural) requirements for publicity in article X, there were also some more substantive references to the transparency principle. Article XI:1

[45] The WTO is based on several principles, the most important of which are: the 'Most Favoured Nation' principle, the 'National Treatment' principle, the principle of preferred rates, and the principle of conciliation.

[46] Roberts 2006. [47] Zoellner 2006.

stated that all duty-free borders should be removed. This was also stipulated in article VIII:1b and 1c, which stated that parties should recognize the need to limit the number and diversity of duties and taxes. This was also concerned with lifting duty-free borders.

Third, the more recent WTO agreements contain obligations for publishing that go further than those contained in GATT. These requirements are not only to publish standards that are agreed upon, but also to supply them together with reasonable explanations and to provide ample opportunity for foreign governments to comment, in advance, on proposed standards.

Fourth, the deals that were made during the Uruguay round of negotiations elaborate further on the content of the transparency principle. According to these deals, standards should be based on achievements of products and on scientifically accepted assumptions.

The foregoing does not alter the fact that the transparency principle has been a controversial subject on the WTO agenda since 1996. That year, the controversy led to the establishment of the 'Working Group on transparency in Government Procurement', which had the task of conducting a study on the meaning of the transparency principle in public contract practice. Within the WTO, it is clear that whilst some countries are very sceptical and only class a limited number of cases under it, for example India, Pakistan, Malaysia, and Egypt; other countries that already have much further advanced systems want to class more cases under the regulations, such as EU countries and the United States. It appears that the second group ultimately gained the upper hand.

(e) Improving the transparency principle at the WTO level

The transparency principle, with respect to the WTO, could be specified through several paths. Articles X and XI oblige publication in more recent WTO agreements, and concrete suggestions fit within the WTO developments could be made from the experience of the European and Dutch development of the transparency principle.

First, there is the need to specify the possibilities for more internal transparency. This involves making the internal organizational structure less opaque, especially the publicity of the processes taking place and the procedures followed. There are a number of bodies involved in the execution of agreements between member states of the WTO including the Ministerial Conference (MC), the General Council (GC), and the Secretariat. There should be regulations on the announcements of MC and GC meetings and the preparations for them as well as post-hoc reports. The same is true for national parliaments. This type of publicity would enable citizens, companies, and NGOs to discern which aspects are under discussion. After the purportedly positive experience with the EU Publicity Regulations, the Netherlands should—as was concluded in June 2006 regarding increased publicity of Council meetings—take the initiative to apply the same publicity regulations to the MC and GC. The MC and GC's Code of Order would need to be adjusted to such an extent that all MC and GC meetings with a public interest would be made public. The Netherlands would have to closely follow this process and actively contribute to it. Such government regulations for MC and GC meetings would then have a positive effect on the democratic legitimacy of the WTO.

Second, the publicity of WTO documents should be regulated in a more precise way. The current regulations contained in articles X:1, X:2 and X:3a are imprecisely formulated, as they should also focus on external transparency in the narrow sense. The EU Publicity Regulations and the experience gained from them can be taken as an example. Several national governments consider it highly important to increase the transparency of the government further. This is not only in the interest of democratic legitimacy, but it would also increase the people's confidence in the WTO.

Third, some specific regulations regarding the transparency principle within the sphere of the WTO should be developed. The following subjects should be taken into account in any case:

a. The transparency principle as part of the WTO conciliation process

Revision of the conciliation process within the WTO so that conciliation panels and hearings of the board of appeal are opened to the public is desirable. UN agencies should also play a role in the panels. Revision of the conciliation mechanism to make it more translucent and accessible to all Member States will result in more legal certainty in the area of publicity and independence.

b. The transparency principle in regional trade agreements

Within the scope of the Doha development agenda (DDA), negotiations are held to clarify and improve existing WTO regulations for regional trade agreements (RTAs) which concern transparency procedures. On 26 June 2006, the negotiators reached agreement on a draft text for an RTA transparency mechanism. The RTA transparency mechanism implies the establishment of a uniform procedure for notification and research, based on factual reports from the WTO Secretariat, for all RTAs. This strengthens the capacity and role of the WTO as supervisor of developments in the area of RTAs throughout the world. The General Council of the WTO formally approved the transparency mechanism on 10 October 2006. Progress has been made in 2011 in relation to TRIPS (intellectual property rights).

c. The transparency principle with respect to public contracts

In the past, Sue Arrowsmith[48] has made propositions concerning the effect of WTO agreements on public contracts. The following proposals for such agreements are based on her article. Such agreements should have a broader content than the Government Procurement Agreement (GPA). Rules governing contractual procedures should be published. Publicity should be given to contractual opportunities. Rules should be established to restrict the discretionary power of contract services. These rules must be controlled and maintained.

6. Conclusions

The traditional relevance of the principles of transparency, such as access to information, has been developed into many regulations. That is also the situation with the

[48] Arrowsmith 1998; Arrowsmith 2003.

other two sub-principles related to the transparency of meetings and the transparency of administrative acts. But less known is the information developed and published in the framework of public inquiries by specific committees, or the effects this information could have for those who have been investigated. Often, this can include the possible criminal effect of publications and the violation of fundamental rights by these publications. Therefore, these interests ought to be balanced in order to constitute constructive legislation. This legislation should at least try to expel the dangers inherent to transparency, and in the meantime strengthen public participation.

9

The Principle of Participation

Participation is defined as the active involvement of a group of individuals in a collective process. Within the context of public administration, participation refers to the involvement of citizens in actual or intended actions of administrative authorities. It has strong links with democracy and the theory on deliberative democracy.[1] Involvement can have different outlooks depending on the context in which it occurs. Participation can refer to taking part in preliminary arrangements, influencing decision-makers, or taking part in actual decision-making processes.[2] But participation can also be justified from the point of view of a sensible government discovering potential flaws and realizing ownership.

Is there any obligation of the administration to pay deference to the views of the citizens? It should be noted that although the term 'public participation' presumes that the initiative and procedures are in the hands of citizens, the participation process is generally managed by public entities. A definition formulated by the African Development Foundation seems to be both clear and concise:

> Participation is a process through which all members of a community or organization are involved in and have influence on decisions related to development activities that will affect them. That implies that development projects will address those community or group needs on which members have chosen to focus, and that all phases of the development process will be characterized by active involvement of community or organization members.[3]

An interesting aspect is the development of the participation principle with regard to participation as a right, and the question of what consequences there are for the direct and guiding function of the administration.[4] The significance of participation is an important part of the development of the principles of good governance under the democratic rule of law as well.

Public participation can be motivated by various reasons aside from genuine motives of public participation. The literature[5] distinguishes between democratic, constitutional, corporatist, and administrative motives. Democratic motives are opportunities for citizens and groups of citizens to influence and regulate policy. An aim of the constitutional motive for participation is participation as means of protecting individual interests in the context of the balance of powers in the state. The corporatist motive is described as a means for social organizations to achieve their own responsibility. The administrative motive is to have participation serve the interests of the public body. While the distinction between these motives for participation is not always unequivocal, these do offer an indication of the various perspectives—and consequently motives—of the parties involved in public participation.

With regards to participation, a distinction can also be made between which type of participation is pursued and the levels of which type of actual participation are achieved, that is, form and degree of participation. A distinction between the various

[1] Akerboom 2018. [2] Vucsán 1995. [3] ADF 2014. [4] Addink 2008.
[5] Vucsán 1995.

forms of participation is made below. In this book, we consider popular initiative, the citizen's panel, the referendum, and the community-level forms of participation.

The degree of participation is quantified using certain indicators, including the number of individuals, the time invested in and the frequency of participation, the involvement of individuals, the extent of influence on the process with respect to the issues addressed by the public authority, and the level of participation that citizens are entitled to. For instance, should citizens' views be taken into account in their decision-making, or is it just an opportunity to voice an opinion? In community-level participation, it is uncertain as to whether the opinions expressed will actually result in action, and in popular initiatives there is limited influence once the initiative has been completed.

Further distinctions can be made among those who are given the opportunity to participate, including individuals acting independently, individuals who form groups to promote collective interests, and organizations established to promote all or specific elements of a common interest. Certain target groups or stakeholders may also be explicitly given the opportunity to participate.[6] It is clear that these cases involve different interests and motives that form the basis for participation.

For participation on local level, a significant consideration for the Dutch situation is that since the implementation of the separation of powers at local level in 2002, the mayor and the Queen's Commissioner must both publish an annual report on public services provided to residents (*burgerjaarverslag*), including an indication of the quality of procedures governing public participation.[7] In addition, the report addresses the quality of procedures for community-level participation and the application, if any, of non-binding referenda or a popular initiative. This annual reporting duty should ensure periodic consultation with public representatives on any shortcomings of procedures for public participation. These reports are usually published online. However, it is unclear how the intended consultation should be put into practice.[8] The Dutch Ombudsman has recently published a study 'Strengthening citizen's participation' in which he has developed ten recommendations for good local citizens' participation.[9] These recommendations include how the municipality should explain and motivate if and how citizens are involved, that they make municipality participation an integral part of the political and administrative decision-making process, and determine the participation pathway before it begins. Citizens could play different roles, for example one of co-decision-making, co-producing, counselling, consultation, or of distributing information.

1. The Development of the Principle of Participation

Democratic systems are in principle open to criticism and adjustment. For instance, this criticism can address strong party discipline in parliament, the intense monistic relationship between government and parliamentary majority, the exercise of ministerial responsibility, or the legitimacy of decisions and the decision-making process. There is also a direct link with the transparency principle. Sometimes, transparency is

[6] De Graaf 2007.

[7] Section 170 of the Dutch Municipalities Act and s 175 of the Dutch Provinces Act.

[8] Press releases have been issued stating that the Minister of the Interior wants to delete this stipulation.

[9] Brenninkmeijer 2009.

even a *condition sine qua non* with regard to participation.[10] While these issues are also relevant to local authorities, at the local level matters are sometimes different due to the close proximity to citizens.

The accuracy of the classical concept of the rule of law, in which legislation and regulations define the exercise of government power, has diminished. Nowadays, the growing body of discretionary powers wielded by public entities and the countless vaguely defined terms and standards in legislation continue to distract attention from the normative character of the law. In the literature,[11] the claim is made that—with respect to the acceptance of government decisions—it is no longer enough that policies and legislation arise as part of a procedure in accordance with constitutional requirements and the principles of a representative democracy. In addition to a reduction of regulations and a striving for private self-regulation, the solution now requires the involvement of citizens in the decision-making process more than ever. The government's desire does not only cause this to increase the legitimacy of decisions taken, but also by initiatives undertaken by citizens. The discussion is not limited to decisions, but also covers all of the practices of public entities. Of course, the involvement of citizens will also lead to a defence of the norm by the administration.[12] See the problems related to public participation and energy transition in the context of windfarms.[13]

With this in mind, forms of participation can be distinguished according to the practices of public authorities—decisions, contracts, and specific activities—as well as the phase in which these practices occur during the policymaking process. The number of citizens affected by the particular practices of a public authority is also important. As the scope or impact of such practices increases, a larger number of people should be given the opportunity to participate. In addition, the more far-reaching the practice of the authorities, the earlier the citizens affected by such practice will have to be involved.[14]

2. The Concept of Participation

How should the forms of participation be valued or what is, in essence, the concept of participation? Three key reference points include the necessity of participation to supplement representative democracy, the consequences for the government's legitimacy, and the special situation for participation options at the local and regional levels. The importance of legitimacy as part of the traditional rule of law, as well as the content of legitimacy in terms of notions, are similar to ideas of the principles of good governance.[15] In the literature, it is also explained that the notion of the rule of law is based on 'a state-consideration of self-conscious people … and who want to be involved when major decisions are made'.

Participation is a necessary addition to representative democracy. In a representative democracy, the citizens either directly or indirectly elect their representatives. These representatives then make up the legislative authority, whose task it is to monitor the administration. Why then speak of a necessary addition to representative democracy? There are several reasons for this. First, it appears that public representatives limit themselves in their monitoring task to the main points of the policy being implemented by the administration. Second, party discipline has resulted in public representatives

[10] Curtin and Dekker 2005. [11] Burkens and others 2006, 255.
[12] Vucsán 1995. [13] Akerboom 2018. [14] Damen 2009.
[15] Burkens and others 2006, 17, 41–7, 87–8, 94–100.

increasingly expressing the party's standpoint rather than their own. Third, a minority does not always get what it deserves due to dominant majorities.

People sometimes speak of 'legitimacy erosion', which is explained as a gradual, but fundamental deterioration of the legitimacy of the performance of public administration. Legitimacy refers to the competence of the public administration or representatives to govern.[16] Recent research has been conducted to map out the perceived legitimacy of acts associated with the Dutch Ministry of Justice.[17] In studying these, the researchers considered it important to first assess issues related to the perceived legitimacy of formal institutions, legal officials, and rules and regulations. In addition, three dimensions of legitimacy were established, which subsequently define legitimacy as: (1) trust; (2) satisfaction; and (3) acceptance.[18] According to the study, empirical data does not suggest large-scale erosion but legitimacy is practically affected. Legitimacy of performance is not self-evident, but more often disputed. It should be noted, however, that a relatively small amount of empirical data is available, especially in the social science literature. Finally, the research showed that familiarity among the citizens with certain parts of the judicial authorities is relatively high, while familiarity with other parts is particularly low.

It can be expected that participation leads to more trust, more satisfaction, and more acceptance on the part of the citizens. As a result, the legitimacy of the public administration performance increases. People generally agree that it is sensible to bring the exercise of power as close as possible to the citizens. One way of achieving this involves decentralization in either functional or territorial terms. Territorially decentralized authorities are municipalities and provinces, whilst the functionally decentralized authorities are the public bodies for employment and business. We also see that governing committees have been established within municipalities and provinces with a specific task. Advantages of functional decentralization include the significant influence of stakeholders, increased expertise, and increased participation. However, territorial decentralization also offers substantial advantages as the distance between government and citizens is significantly smaller. Furthermore, public representatives can also be called to account relatively easily and in a direct manner. In short, participation—particularly at local and regional level[19]—enables a greater influence for citizens and increases the willingness to cooperate.

3. Specification of the Concept

The focus here is on four forms of participation: (1) popular initiative; (2) citizens' panel; (3) referendum; and (4) community-level participation. It is essential to clearly describe these four forms and the three policymaking phases: (1) the policy agenda development phase; (2) the policy development phase: and (3) the decision-making phase.

(a) Participation: term, motives, distinctions, and forms

Participation has already been defined as active involvement of a group of individuals in a collective process. Within the context of public administration, it refers to the involvement of citizens in the actual or intended actions of administrative authorities

[16] Addink and others 2000, 87–8. [17] Weyers and Hertogh 2007.
[18] Tyler and Huo 2002. [19] Addink 2009.

and public entities. We have seen that public participation can be motivated by various participation motives.

There have been many successful examples of direct democracy. In villages with less than 200 inhabitants in Spain, there is a community-level participation system called '*Concejo Abierto*'. In this system, the outcomes are indeed binding on the public authorities, because this system is itself the town hall: an assembly where all neighbours speak and decide in a construct with different decision-making mechanisms and required majorities. This system, which also rules in villages with more than 200 inhabitants (if they decide to), is old and traditional in some regions. It is nowadays regulated by Spanish national law[20] and even officially recognized in article 140 of the Spanish Constitution.

With regards to participation, another distinction is made between the forms and degrees of participation. Among the four forms of participation considered here, some authors deem community-level participation as the main form of participation. Other forms of participation are also identified here, in addition to or instead of those already mentioned, namely citizens' panels and public consultation. For the various forms of public participation, there is a sliding scale that reflects the potential degree of participation, divided into informing, consulting, and co-deciding activities. The degree of participation is quantified using certain indicators, including the number of individuals, the duration, the frequency of participation, the level of involvement of individuals, and the extent to which participation influences the process with respect to the issues addressed by the public authority.

(b) A popular initiative

A popular initiative involves a citizen entitled to vote taking the lead to make sure that a certain issue is placed on the agenda of a public entity. The initiator must often meet certain conditions for the initiative to be binding and placed on the agenda, such as place of residence and age. In some cases, support from a minimum number of citizens who are entitled to vote is required, or these citizens should have a direct and personal interest. Furthermore, it is sometimes stipulated that popular initiatives are only possible with regard to a kind of predetermined policy area.

Moreover, the proposal must often satisfy additional requirements, including that it must be a clear and written proposal and that it must go through a predetermined procedure. The standard decision-making protocol is followed once the initiative is placed on the agenda of the public entity. Popular initiatives differ from the classic forms of popular referenda in which citizens are asked to approve or reject a particular proposal. In some countries, popular initiative is also implemented at the local level, and some municipal authorities have rules for having popular initiatives in place.

The development of ideas by citizens and renewing policy from outside the administration can provide useful insights to a public institution. The disadvantages include a certain kind of uncertainty as to whether the initiative is actually placed on the administrative agenda and the limited influence of citizens once the initiative has been completed.

[20] Law 7/1985, of 2 April 1985, Reguladora de las Bases de Régimen Local and Reglamento de Organización, funcionamiento y regimen Jurídico de la Entidades Locales, aprobado por Real Decreto 2568/1986, of 28 November 1986.

(c) A citizens' panel

Citizens' panels are usually established by and make recommendations to the public entity responsible for the issue at hand. However, they operate independently of the public entity in question. The panel, whose membership is permanent and often involves a fairly large number of citizens, can be asked for recommendations during various phases in the policymaking process and can make recommendations of its own accord.

Even though the practical implementation differs, we currently see that in certain countries the panel members must answer a questionnaire of at least ten questions per subject. The members are, however, not obliged to complete the questionnaire. As the process is often conducted electronically, only those who have access to a computer can serve as citizens' panel members. Members usually have a week to complete the questionnaires. As the information processing is fully automated, the outcome is known almost immediately afterwards.

There are several conditions for serving on local level citizens' panels, including that the prospective member must be a resident of the municipality in question, must be eighteen or over another minimum age required, must be able to go online, and must have a personal email address.

The advantages of citizens' panels are the availability of a permanent group for recommendations and that, due to their professional guidance, these panels are better at fulfilling the role of a consultant than the traditional advisory bodies. Disadvantages include the permanent character that might cause higher costs and that the development of citizen expertise gives them and the council members a certain status which consequently leads to a certain position of power. The cost of decision-making is usually only a fraction of the cost to society of implementing the regulation.[21] If the panel is better at fulfilling the role of a consultant, the absolute cost of the decision is generally less to society. The real problem with council members acquiring a 'certain status' is that the panel becomes a skewed representation of society.

(d) Referenda as forms of participation

In a referendum, the electorate is asked to vote on a proposed decision of a public entity. A popular referendum originally involved a vote called by the electorate, whereby representative entities were compelled to raise the status of a broadly supported measure to law. This version of the referendum is still applied in Switzerland, where the electorate is asked to approve or reject a legislative proposal made by public representatives. More restricted forms of referenda can be found in several other countries. A popular referendum is currently defined as the right of a minimum number of citizens to take the initiative to propose legislation or make other proposals. Although there are different variations of this form of participation, the proposal is usually put to popular vote in the end.

The referendum has a long tradition in many countries and has therefore reached a more advanced stage of development than most other forms of participation. This is demonstrated by the fact that various forms of referenda can be distinguished. Referenda can be either non-binding or binding in terms of their legal implications. While the vote is decisive in the latter case, the public entity is not bound by the outcome in the former. A distinction can also be made according to legal basis. While a

[21] Vucsán 1995, 372.

mandatory referendum is prescribed by procedure, a facultative referendum is initiated at the request of the authorized authorities.

Australia is one example. In Australia, referenda are used to propose parliamentary-approved changes to the Australian Constitution. For instance, the infamous 1967 referendum transferred legislative powers in respect to indigenous Australians from the states to the Commonwealth government. As such, a positive outcome in a referendum results in a binding obligation on parliament. In that sense, a referendum is an indirect mechanism of compelling the public to participate in a legislative process that could have administrative implications in society. Therefore, it is almost impossible to have a non-binding referendum in Australia.

Furthermore, a distinction can be made according to how the matter is put to a referendum. There are both multiple-choice and single-choice referenda. Multiple-choice referenda do not involve the approval or rejection of a particular proposal like single-choice referenda do, but rather the selection of one of several alternatives. As identified in the literature, the advantages of the referendum include the expansion of political monitoring and the ability of citizens to have a say in decision-making, as a result of which they become more involved. This has the effect of legitimizing the performance of the public administration. Disadvantages of the referendum include possible abuse by public representatives, the fact that it is not a neutral instrument, and also that the effect often depends on the expertise of the voter. It must be added that is also relevant in the context of other forms of participation and, in a more general way for the concept of democracy.

In the United Kingdom, eleven referendums have been held since 1973. At the time of writing, their present government is currently promising that referendums will be held on any EU treaties transferring sovereignty from the UK government to the EU. However, despite this apparent display of participation, referenda in the United Kingdom are not constitutionally binding due to parliamentary sovereignty. This means that, although an act of parliament may give effect to the result of a referendum, this can be retracted. However, political speaking, to retract an act of parliament is not so easy. Some may argue that referenda could serve as merely an opinion poll rather than a means for active participation for the public. We see the relevance of the participation principle in relation to referenda on BREXIT and the roles of the government and the Parliament in the United Kingdom.

(e) Community-level participation as form of participation

Community-level participation can be described as an informal or structured opportunity for individuals and organizations who are not affiliated with public authorities to express their views and thoughts regarding policy principles and policy proposals as well as to engage in debate about these matters with public representatives. This type of participation can take a variety of forms, involving such elements as public hearings, the right to speak during meetings, surveys, and other opportunities to respond to the draft proposal made by the public entity to undertake a certain activity.

A characteristic of community-level participation is that the outcomes are not binding on public authorities. The outcomes of consultation procedures are at times far from encouraging. However, public input is at least theoretically considered beneficial, particularly with a view to exercising due care in the decision-making process. In the Netherlands, the optional uniform public preparation procedure has been incorporated into GALA. In addition, general regulations for community-level participation at the local and regional levels are contained in the Municipalities Act and the Provinces Act.

The advantages of this form of participation are that citizens can influence the policymaking process and, as a result, the administration starts paying more attention to the various social interests involved in the proposal. This means that, in theory, the quality of administrative practices improves. Disadvantages include uncertainty as to whether the views and opinions expressed will actually be translated into action by the public administration. Furthermore, there is only a limited chance that the intended administrative practice will be affected if there are opposing opinions and interests on the citizens' side.

4. Institutions Involved

All the government institutions, in the broad sense, have regulations about the participation aspects of their behaviour. This means that not only the three traditional powers should adhere to these norms, but the fourth power should as well. These institutions encourage public participation. In fact, the type of participation in administrative departments varies depending on their individual characteristics. The situation in the Netherlands is similar to one in Australia, where legislators are the main codifiers of effectiveness in public authorities and controlling institutions. For instance, the Commonwealth Ombudsman Act empowers the Commonwealth Ombudsman to investigate any unreasonable delays in the exercise of power (section 10). The need for administrative agencies to not be unreasonable in exercising their competences underlies these systems.

The actual effectiveness of participation is relevant as well. Various analyses of local-level public participation have been developed in the literature[22] of why or how citizens are motivated to participate. Three models have been developed: (1) the civic voluntarism model in which citizens are prepared to participate if given sufficient opportunity, are politically active, and are encouraged to do so; (2) the rational choice model in which citizens are prepared to participate if the advantages outweigh the disadvantages; and (3) the social capital model in which citizens are prepared to participate when there is mutual trust between the citizen and the institution involved. One of the more recent models, the CLEAR model,[23] is intriguing as it links the three models mentioned above:

CLEAR stands for:
C = **C**an citizens participate? — Suitable (skills)
L = Do they **L**ike to participate? — Involved (commitment)
E = Are they **E**nabled to participate? — Organized (collaboration)
A = Are they **A**sked to participate? — Asked (by public authorities)
R = Are they **R**esponded to if they do participate? — Appreciated (by public authorities)

The five relevant factors to be studied are: (1) suitability; (2) sense of involvement; (3) degree of organization; (4) whether the citizens have been asked to participate; and (5) whether the citizens' participation is appreciated. For each factor, there are several variables. Suitability depends on the level of education, profession, age and social

[22] Steur and Van der Groot 2006.

[23] Lowndes and others 2001.

group, sources, skills, and knowledge. The sense of involvement depends on identity, homogeneity, trust, and citizenship. The degree of organization is based on the type of organization, its activities, and its organizational structure. Whether the citizens have been asked to participate varies depending on the forms of participation, strategy, and diversity. Whether the citizens' participation is appreciated is monitored by the extent to which the authority actually listened to the citizen's advice, the prioritization of public opinion, the feedback and training that participants receive. These variables are in turn associated with a range of facets, which partly served as the basis for the standard questionnaire which is used.

5. Sources of the Principle of Participation

The principle of public participation has been developed in different ways and the most important ones are the development by legislation and the development by policy. I mention here, as some examples, the Charter on Local Government and the Aarhus Convention. The last one has had an enormous impact on Dutch procedures in environmental law. The relevant act is EC Regulation 1367/2006 on the application of the Aarhus Convention on Access to Information, Public Participation in Decision-making and Access to Justice in Environmental Matters to EC institutions and bodies. It enforces the position of NGOs in their possibilities to request an internal review of 'an administrative act under environmental law'. In addition to this EC Regulation, it might also be interesting to refer to the EC White Paper on European Governance. Curtin and Dekker are very critical of it, especially on the position of NGOs.[24] The value of mentioning these laws and policy papers shows how dynamic this principle still is.

(a) Features of the principle of participation

General elections can be seen as an aspect of the principle of public participation, but more in the constitutional law context reflecting indirect democracy. But in the administrative law context we also find elements of more direct democracy in which the following three aspects are relevant: who can participate, about what, and at what moment?

The principle of public participation in the administration is allocated according to two features: the people involved in the competence or act concerned, and the stage of the decision-making process. This is illustrated with some articles of GALA:

Article 3:10

1. The procedure for the preparation of orders provided in this division shall be followed if this is required by statutory regulation or by order of the administrative authority.

Article 3:13

1. Interested parties may state their views on the application or the draft either orally or in writing, at their discretion.
   (Article 1:2: 1. 'Interested party' means a person whose interest is directly affected by an order.)

[24] Curtin and Dekker 2002.

Article 3:24

1. Anyone may submit written reservations to the administrative authority within four weeks of the date on which the draft is deposited for inspection.

The following phases in the policymaking process can be distinguished: policy agenda development; policy development; policy determination; policy implementation; policy compliance; policy enforcement; and policy evaluation. While the steps in the policymaking process can be gleaned from this phase structure, there is a certain degree of overlap between the phases identified. In other words, the distinctions carry no legal significance and are no more than an indication of focus on the activities undertaken by public entities. This does not preclude the possibility that some of the phases will be skipped, whether entirely or in part, when addressing certain policy issues. In short, the distinction is more practical in nature than a legal standard.

(b) Participation models

When ordering the various forms of participation, it is not only important to clarify which forms can be distinguished; it is also interesting to know which combinations of these forms appear in the various countries at local and regional levels. It should be determined whether certain forms, or combinations of forms, only occur in combination with certain phases in the policymaking process or whether these forms, whether alone or in combination, occur independently of phases in the policymaking process.

What kind of participation models in terms of the degree of participation can be distinguished, and are these varying degrees of participation related to a specific phase in the policymaking process? The preceding section simplifies the selection of substantively defined forms of participation. As the various forms of participation can have legally significant implications, they are used as the basis for distinguishing between the models.

In the case of the popular initiative, any citizen can take the lead to raise an issue for consideration, but the matter will be handled in accordance with established protocols and procedures, and the government must first explain what their activity entails and what the approach is. This can be qualified as a 'minimum' participation model.

In the case of the citizens' panel, a group of citizens can issue recommendations on a matter submitted to them by the public entity or by someone from among its own ranks. This is a more involved form of participation, as the citizens' panel issues a recommendation on the matter at hand. Regarding any ensuing obligation and binding effect, community-level participation is definitely comparable and basically involves the same group of citizens. As a result, these two forms can be qualified as average participation, but with community-level participation there is slightly more and broader participation than with the citizens' panel.

The referendum can—in principle and insofar as the evaluation of the decision is involved—be qualified as a 'maximum' participation model, although this is largely determined by the type of referendum involved. It is necessary, however, to take a nuanced approach to the phases of the decision-making process and to non-binding referenda. True maximum participation occurs when a particular group of citizens is authorized to decide for itself on how to spend a community-allocated budget.

Basically, all four forms of participation can be used for the various phases of the policymaking process. Taking into account effectiveness and efficiency, the greatest degree of participation is made possible when opportunities to participate are available from the start of the policymaking process. Opportunities to participate during later phases of the policymaking process are less effective and less efficient. Participation should not only be discussed from a quantitative perspective, but also from a qualitative perspective.

Readers are encouraged to explore and consider alternative views, such as those provided by Lipman and Stokes,[25] who conclude that the opportunity to participate throughout an entire policymaking process is just as important as initial participatory opportunities. For this reason, including arguments from other authors such as Lipman and Stokes would also enhance a text's ability to stimulate thoughts and debate. This is because readers would also consider the views that participation in the later stages of policymaking offers the added advantage of ensuring policies are in accordance with agreements made in the first-instance participatory consultations, linking the importance of good participatory principles with the concepts of accountability and good governance.

6. Conclusions

In a representative democracy, not all government actions are controlled by parliament, the representatives of the people. Generally, the main topics or the general lines of administrative policies are controlled elsewhere. For that reason, there is an additional need for participation by the citizens. It is important that in all the government's activities which have direct consequences for people, the directly affected persons are involved in the decision-making process. However, participation is linked to the legitimacy of the administration in a more substantial way. Direct democracy and representative democracy often strengthen each other.

There are different types of participation. The following forms of public participation have already been described several times: popular initiatives, citizens' panels, referenda, and community-level participation. Some forms are related only to some phases in the process of policy-development, but other forms can be used in all the phases of the policy-process. It means that a choice always has to be made, based both on the issue involved and on the desired degree of participation of citizens. An example concerning the citizens' initiative at the EU level can be found in article 11(4) TFEU.

There is a lack of sufficient methodology on direct democracy and the principle of participation enjoys a great variety of standards throughout Europe. For example, if one compares the use of direct democracy in the United Kingdom to Switzerland, there is a vast contrast. Since the 1850s, Switzerland has held over 500 national referendums. If a petition is signed by one per cent of the electorate and submitted calling for a referendum on an issue under consideration by the government, then a referendum must be held. The signatures of 2 per cent of voters are enough to call a referendum on an issue not under government consideration.[26] In contrast, since 1973, there have been only eleven referenda in the United Kingdom, and none since 1997. They have generally been used over the issue of devolution or other major constitutional issues, such as remaining as part of the EU in 1975. In fact, a report by the House of Lords Select Committee on the Constitution in relation to referendums concluded that there are significant drawbacks to the use of referenda. In particular, we regret the ad hoc

[25] Lipman and Stokes 2008.

[26] McConnachie 2000.

manner in which referendums have been used, often as a tactical device, by the government of the day. Referenda may become a part of the UK's political and constitutional practice, but only in certain areas of decision making.'[27] Finally, we see that several of these types of participation have already been formulated in legislation, but not all. In particular, newer forms of participation often have an informal character.

[27] House of Lords Select Committee on the Constitution, 12th Report of Session 2009–10, 'Referendums in the UK'.

10

The Principle of Effectiveness

1. Introduction

In this and the next chapter, we discuss principles which may be new for many lawyers. In this chapter the principle of effectiveness is discussed and, in the next one, the principle of accountability. This novelty is partly due to the fact that these principles are related not only to law but also to social sciences and economics. Modern textbooks on administrative law are split into two parts: one part on administration and law and another part on law and administration.[1] The first part is, from an administrative law perspective, the most innovative. It is mainly focused on policy, constitutional, and organizing aspects of the administration. The approach is contextual and it draws on different disciplines. It deals with administrative developments, centralized and decentralized administration, the different types of administration, the management aspects of administration, the development of agencies, the different methods of internal and external coordination, and the position of the key players in the field of the administration. The second part concerns the analysis of the principles of judicial review as they have been developed by the courts, the ombudsman, and other controlling institutions. These principles are applied so as to control and structure the administration. It also takes full account of the legislative and political initiatives that are relevant for the development of administrative law, including the role played by the different powers in the state.

In this chapter, we integrate these two parts of 'administration and law' and their corresponding approaches. This reflects the interdisciplinary nature of the development of the principles in general and more specifically in the principle of effectiveness. These principles can also be applied *mutatis mutandis* in other contexts that restrict the perspective of the administration in a narrow sense, like the administrative court and the fourth power institutions.

(a) Law in the books and law in practice

The classical approach of administrative law focuses on the protection of citizens against the government. This is still very important in administrative law because it concerns several civil rights. More recently, there has been more attention for the instrumental side of administrative law, which relates to the different legal instruments employed by the administrative authorities and the actual effect of legislation. Thus, compliance and enforcement of the law have become increasingly important for two reasons. First, in order to examine if a law is effective and second, in order to determine possible changes so that the aims of a law will be realized when it is found ineffective.

The next sub-paragraphs use the terminology 'administration and law' and 'law and administration', in order to give a more complete overview of the two sides of the same

[1] Craig 2006.

coin. The first side is more concerned with the functioning of the administration while the second side is more concerned with the institutions controlling the administration.

(b) Administration and law

Law in the context of public administration and politics means more focus on the operation of the administration,[2] in particular on process, legitimacy, competency, and the aspects of effectiveness and efficiency.

First, we have to realize that important developments have taken place institutionally. Competences and tasks of many administrative institutions have been delegated to separate agencies, sometimes even to private institutions. A second aspect is the development related to more direct democracy by stimulating the principles of transparency and participation. This means that even in indirect ways, representative elements of direct democracy have been introduced. A similar development took place with the accountability principle. We currently have the traditional constitutional accountability of ministers in relation to the parliament but in addition, other forms of accountability are needed alongside this. The third element is related to the organization of public institutions and especially to the coordination inside them. Taking into account the increase of the institutions and their greater diversity, coordination mechanisms are crucial both internally and externally.

(c) Law and administration

In law and administration, the focus is more on the classical legal aspects, law as a general norm, concrete decisions, and cases.[3] Sometimes, however, the modern and the classical approach are integrated.[4] The formal side represents the regulations which relate to procedures at the courts and the ombudsman-type institutions. Not all the controlling institutions have the same position and competences. The starting point in studying these institutions is the question of whether these are competent to investigate the request related to a public activity. In that context, the position and respective powers of the administrative and the controlling institutions are both important, especially in relation to the issue of the discretionary character of the power. The controlling institution has to keep some distance from the administration. Another point in this context is the difference in standards of control like the legal rules, the principles of good administration, and fundamental human rights. These standards apply differently in different countries.

Finally, controlling institutions exist in different forms: the classical and the hybrid ombudsman institutions. In the context of courts of audit, we see quasi-judicial courts of audit, administrative courts of audit, parliamentary courts of audit, and independent courts of audits. When it comes to courts, we distinguish between ordinary courts and specialized courts.

(d) Legal philosophy and effectiveness

In the literature on legal philosophy there are already several publications in which the meaning and conditions of effectiveness have been explored. Such findings are also relevant for the traditional legal context. When we try to understand the meaning of

[2] Ibid. [3] Ibid. [4] Harlow and Rawlings 2009.

the effectiveness of legal norms it shall be limited because of the phenomena of validity and realization.[5] Validity means, in this context, that it is based on truth or reason and is acceptable. Realization is the point when you start to understand a situation or when you are becoming aware of it.

The effectiveness of legal norms can be described as the relationship between their effective result and the social objects which the norm was designed to achieve. Often, different levels or dimensions of the effectiveness of legal norms are distinguished, like legal effectiveness and social effectiveness. Other dimensions can also be addressed, like economic effectiveness. Sometimes, these are described as the only dimensions or the most extreme dimensions. Legal effectiveness is furthermore described as the attitude of the addressees corresponding to the prescriptions of legal norms. Social effectiveness does not only focus on the lawful conduct of the addressee but also the realization of the social object which the regulation was designed to achieve. There are different conditions for the effectiveness of legal norms.[6] These conditions are not only the legal conditions but also the non-legal, social, economic, cultural, ideological, political ones. They are not only related to the norms in the law as such, but also in the application of law and the level of legal consciousness.

In the legal philosophical literature, a link is made between applicability and effectiveness of legal norms. That is relevant because a proper reconstruction of the concept of applicability is of great importance for understanding the concept of effectiveness and for providing insight into the nature of law.[7]

2. Development of the Principle of Effectiveness

The principle of effectiveness has been developed because there was also a need to know whether or not a certain regulation had indeed produced the desired result. Often this was seen as a factual question and not as a legal question. This would suggest that while the principle of effectiveness is in the interest of good governance, it would be difficult to establish an effectiveness norm. At most, there can be an obligation to act in the interests of effectiveness or try to predict what the outcome of the decision will be. In the sense of effectiveness as a principle of good governance, the issue is very relevant from a more modern perspective. Policies must be effective and timely, delivering what is needed based on clear objectives, implementing policy in a proportionate manner, and taking decisions at the most appropriate level. Relevantly, we see that this effectiveness approach has consequences for new regulations as well.[8]

Effectiveness gives rise to different ideas. Some people immediately think about the goals of international regulation and what to do when these goals are not realized. Other people think about the implementation in the national legal system. Finally, some people are still of the opinion that this is not a legal question. Here we clarify the idea of the principle of effectiveness and the importance of this principle as one of the standing principles of good governance, which may be confusing in some discussions.

We start with an explanation of the notion of effectiveness based on a variety of definitions and the position of this norm within the principles of good governance. Subsequently, we explore questions like 'why is effectiveness relevant for law?' and 'which general aspects can be found in the legal fields?' We explore three levels of law where this principle has been more or less developed: international law, EU law, and

[5] Visegrády 2002, 52–6. [6] Ibid, 51. [7] Navarro and Moreso 1997, 201.
[8] Addink 2010c.

national administrative law. In each of these fields, we look for the specific meaning and application of the effectiveness principle.

The meanings and application in a non-legal context are relevant to understanding the development of this legal principle and therefore we have used some dictionaries. When we look at the general definitions of effectiveness in sources like the *Oxford Compact English Dictionary* and other dictionaries, we find in essence the following definitions: (1) producing a desired or intended result; (2) (of law or policy) operative; (3) existing in fact, though not formally acknowledged as such. In these definitions effectiveness also extends to functionality, meaning a functioning administration and system of judicial review. This is the procedural aspect of the principle of effectiveness.

Sometimes a broader definition of effectiveness can be found that includes an efficiency element. The efficiency element means doing things in the most economical way with a good input to output ratio. The word 'effective' here is, in essence, used in a quantitative way: 'being very effective or not'. This does not shed light on the direction (positive or negative) and the comparison to a standard of the given effect. Efficacy, on the other hand, is the ability to produce a desired amount of the desired effect or success in achieving a given goal. Hence, efficacy means getting things done and meeting targets. Contrary to efficiency, the focus of efficacy is on the achievement as such, not on the resources spent in achieving the desired effect. Effectiveness in this context is doing the 'right' things, setting the right targets to achieve an overall goal and including the elements in the process. Therefore, what is effective is not necessarily efficacious, and what is efficacious is not necessarily efficient.

To sum up, the usual way to distinguish between the terms effectiveness, efficacy, and efficiency is as follows:

- *efficacy*: getting things done, meeting agreed targets, only concerned with realizing the outcome as such;
- *efficiency*: doing things in the most economical way, minimizing input and maximizing output;
- *effectiveness*: doing the 'right' things, this means setting the right targets to achieve an overall goal, including the different elements in the process (the effect).

The terms 'effectiveness' has various meanings in different disciplines. It is relevant to have some indications of the content of the word, especially in law, the social sciences, and economics.

The *Oxford Legal Dictionary* gives the following definitions: (1) producing a desired effect: effective revocation of the contract; (2) capable of bringing about an effect; effective assistance of counsel; (3) being in effect; (4) of a rate of interest: equal to the rate of simple interest that yields the same amount when the rate is paid once at the end of the interest period as a quoted rate of interest does when calculated at compounded interest over the same period.[9] In the *Oxford Companion to Law*, one can find another legal definition as stated below:[10]

> An important principle in relation to the jurisdiction of a court. In general, a court can only claim jurisdiction over a person or subject-matter of dispute if it can make any order it pronounces effective, by coercion of the individual seizure of the subject matter, or otherwise. Also more generally a principle followed by courts generally in that they seek to make law actually regulate the relations of parties and their rights and not be merely statements of pious aspirations. Thus the International Court has shown determination to secure a full degree of effectiveness of

[9] Merriam-Webster's Dictionary of Law 2011. [10] Walker 1980, 394.

international law in general and in particular of the obligations undertaken by parties to treaties, declining to have obligations negative by strained interpretation and holding that the maximum of effectiveness should be given to an instrument creating an obligation consistently with the intention of parties.

In both definitions, the focus is on two general meanings of effectiveness: namely the qualities or the ability to produce the desired effects. It can be used either to dictate that the facts adhere to the law (if it operates as a governing principle) or that the new law and legal status adapt the facts (if it operates as an assessment of the factual reality). Both sides of the principle are relevant in the framework of international law, European law, and national administrative law, and are ways of applying in concrete situations the legal concept of the principle of effectiveness.

The effectiveness aspects have been developed in the social science fields as well and from which we can learn the effectiveness of law—if not just 'obedience to a command'—from a variety of mechanisms. Sociology uses various methods of empirical investigation and critical analysis to develop and refine a body of knowledge about human social activity. It is often conducted with the goal of applying such knowledge to the pursuit of social welfare in which the subject matters can range from micro to macro level. For example, in education, sociologists are using effective sociology assessment plans developed by mission statements, learning goals and objectives, and assessment mechanisms.

In economics, the terms 'effectiveness' and 'efficiency' are mostly discussed in the context of the public sector.[11] It is important that the public sector provides the services required in the most effective and efficient way possible, which means the highest quality service at the least possible cost. In public administration, where the term 'effectiveness' is used, the predominant concept in economics is efficiency. With regard to the public sector, this means reaching a policy goal at minimum costs. One major concept of efficiency in economics is the Pareto criterion for allocative efficiency, which defines a situation as efficient when nobody can be made better off without making anybody else worse off. Other concepts, which are not relevant for our study here, are technical efficiency, productive efficiency, and dynamic efficiency, just to mention some.

3. The Concept of Effectiveness

We first explore the general aspects of legal effectiveness and then this principle as a principle of good governance. For a long time, effectiveness was not seen as a legal norm and therefore, at the national level, lawyers were not really interested in the discussion about the contents of the principle of effectiveness. However, in international law and especially in EU law we often speak about the concept of effectiveness or the principle of effectiveness. This principle is also seen in the context of, or as one of, the principles of good governance. Moreover, in EU law there have been strong developments on the good governance principles in different EU institutions. These norms, including the norm of effectiveness, are often seen as parameters for administrative actions, not only at the European level but also at the international level and, due to spill over, also at the national level. These developments will be presented below. There are also examples outside of the EU. For example, within the United States, effectiveness is treated much like accountability. There are many agencies and institutions that audit

[11] Mulreany 1991, 7–36.

the government and its actions. For instance, the Department of Defense evaluates its decisions on national security and the army. They publish their missions as much as safety allows, however, their effectiveness lies in how well they accomplish their jobs.[12]

Another aspect which is relevant for the multilevel legal system is the idea that a distinction can be made between substantive and formal aspects of the principle of effectiveness. This is relevant because it has legal and non-legal consequences for both the activities of the administrative authorities and the decisions of controlling institutions. In July 2001, the Commission's White Paper on European Governance was published. It explained the principles of good governance and the consequences of these principles were elaborated by concrete points of action.[13] However, this was not the start of the discussions on good governance at the European level, since various contributions on the subject had already been made several years earlier.[14] In 1991, the EU Council of Ministers provided a brief description of the contents and the importance of good governance in a resolution on Human Rights, Democracy and Development.[15]

In 1997, the European Ombudsman provided a definition of maladministration in his annual report and the European Ombudsman used the terms 'Principles of Good Administration' or 'Good Administrative Behaviour' frequently in their reports. Since 1998, the ECJ often refers to the 'principles of good administration'.[16]

It is interesting to see that in the July 2001 White Paper, the Commission mentioned and developed five principles of good governance: openness, participation, accountability, effectiveness, and coherence. Earlier, in the White Paper on Administrative Reform that was adopted by the Commission, the same key principles of a European public administration were stressed.[17] Later on, these elements were elaborated in the Commission's Code of Good Administrative Behaviour.

In the White Paper, the Commission gave the following definition of effectiveness as a principle of good governance:

> Effectiveness. Policies must be effective and timely, delivering what is needed on the basis of clear objectives, an evaluation of future impact and, where available, of past experience. Effectiveness also depends on implementing EU policies in a proportionate manner and on taking decisions at the most appropriate level.

It is important to conclude that not only the European judiciary and the European Ombudsman, but also the European Administration use the principles of good governance and are obliged to do so.[18] But there are also problems with this way of defining, as it does not comply with the rule that a definition should avoid circularity. A definition is circular when the definiendum is defined in terms of itself.[19] This is

[12] These missions can be found at <http://www.defense.gov/about/>.

[13] European Commission, *White Paper on European Governance*, July 2001, COM (2001) 428.

[14] Chiti 1995; Schwarze 1995.

[15] European Union Council of Ministers (1991), *Resolution of the Council and of the Member States meeting in the Council on Human Rights, Democracy and Development*, 28 November 1991, [Doc. no. 10107/91], (European Commission, Brussels).

[16] ECJ 19 November 1998, C-252/96 P, *Parliament v Gutierrez de Quijano y Llorens*, ECR I-7421; ECJ 4 March 1999, C-119/97 P, *UFEX and others v Commission*, ECR I-1341; ECJ 9 September 1999, T-127/98, *UPS Europe v Commission*, ECR II-02633; also in the ECJ 13 February 2003, T-333/01, *Meyer v Commission*, ECR II-119 these terms were used; the Court also sometimes speaks of 'Maladministration', see ECJ 10 July 2003, C-472/00, *Commission v Fresh Marine Company*, ECR I-7541.

[17] European Commission, *White Paper on Administrative Reform*, March 2000, COM (2000) 200, volumes I and II.

[18] Decision of the Secretary-General of the Council on a code of good administrative behaviour, 25 June 2001 (2001/C 189/01).

[19] Hurley 1999, 113.

exactly what happened in this definition, because the word 'effective' was used to determine 'effectiveness'. This remark might not have a real value for the text, but the logic of this remark needs to be taken into account.

The European Commission stated that the application of these principles reinforces the principles of proportionality and subsidiarity. In our opinion, there is a broader legal effect which can be illustrated by the example that the effectiveness principle is nowadays seen as one of the general principles of EU law.

The discussion on the notion of good governance is not a discussion unique to EU law; in international law and national law we can find a similar debate, although these discussions are not always recognized as good governance discussions as they do not necessarily use the same terms with the same meaning. There are comparable tendencies in the discussions on good governance in three fields of law: administrative law, EU law, and international law. For this reason, it is very important to clarify the relationships between these discussions in the different legal fields.

The social science research on law is tied quite closely to the study of legal effectiveness. The goal is to understand the conditions under which legislation and judicial decisions effectively guide behaviour or result in anticipated and desired social changes. Legal effectiveness research begins by identifying the goals of legal policy and moves to assess its success or failure by comparing the goals with the results produced. Where, as is almost inevitably the case, the results do not match the goals, attention is given to the factors which might explain the gap between the law in the books and law in action. Sometimes the conclusion offers a reorienting strategy for empirical research on law in action.[20]

The dominating legal view of legal effectiveness in social science research[21] is based on the idea of a gap between what the law states or commands and how the people act.[22] When behaviour is not in accordance with law, the legal system is not considered completely effective. From a sociological and systems theory perspective, an analysis of legal application and legal effectiveness has been made. It is well-known that imported laws function worse than internally developed laws, but explanations differ. This suggests that effectiveness is connected to acceptance, but that is not the idea here. Acceptance is not a principle of good governance but more a part of democracy and legitimacy. The principles can stimulate democracy and legitimacy.

According to the conventional effectiveness concept, the poorly functioning imported law is a paradox. It has been shown that, from a new effectiveness concept, the poor functioning of legal transplants can be explained. In that concept, there is the idea that legal evolution may be accelerated by using laws from economic ideals such as the United States and Germany. Luhmann's system theory suggests that effectiveness should not be understood as a matter of obedience, conformity, or application. Rather another level of analysis can be introduced which recognizes that people can reject not only the content of the legal message, but also the legal type of message. Legal references are a voluntary form of communication. People may refer to them or choose another form for expressing the functionally equivalent effect. When other types of communication are used, the legal system does not affect the choice of behaviour. A legal norm is effective in a population of users if they feel confident regarding their ability to use legal terminology with relevance for the norm, and feel confident that their communication will be accepted as law.[23]

[20] Sarat 1985, 23. [21] Keefer 2004.
[22] Torpman and Jörgensen 2005, 515; Hoekema 1998, 73–108.
[23] Torpman and Jörgensen 2005, 533–4.

There are social science studies of legal criticisms about the central role of the 'gap-theory'. Gap studies reflect an instrumentalist conception of law. This conception collapses the distinction between law and policy and ascribes to legal norms a primary importance in governing and directing social life. An instrumentalist conception of law begins by attacking the distinction between rights and results by suggesting that the language of rights provides a rationalization for legal decisions whose real origin is to be found in the imperatives of some utilitarian calculus, the power of some social interest, or the political preference of the decision-maker. These understandings of the sources of legal norms contrast with the so-called classical understanding of law, which assert the pre-existence of rights and ascribe to them a binding status as guides to legal decision-making. Instrumentalism denies the possibility of an objective or neutral legal logic; every legal act, every legal norm is portrayed as the product of some particular individual's social choice.[24]

According to Austin Sarat, the sociology of law exposes and denigrates the claim that law and legal processes are neutral, autonomous, and impartial. The gap studies, however, call for more effective legal regulation and would subject society to a more penetrating legal order. The sociology of law becomes, at best, an alienated and alienating activity. At worst law becomes an unwitting ally of particular interests in this society.[25] As Sennett[26] writes:

> The dilemma of authority in our time is the peculiar fear it inspires, is that we feel attracted to strong figures we do not believe to be legitimate. What is peculiar to our time is that the formally legitimate powers in dominant institutions inspire a strong sense of illegitimacy among those subject to them. Authority without legitimacy means that society is held together by its very disaffections.

For a more recent overview of the crisis in legal sociology in the literature, an overview of the two reference points has been given, one being the state, the other being the market. The central-sociological question raised in this constellation is about the effectiveness of law.[27]

As mentioned before, attention has been paid to the relation between the applicability and effectiveness of norms.[28] Description of the law in force usually assumes that the legal norms which make up the system are applicable and effective.[29] In a general philosophical analysis, the following general and intuitive definition of effectiveness is related to the observance of norms. A legal norm is effective when it is observed by its addressees. Although observance of norms is often regarded as a paradigm of the effectiveness of legal norms, there are also other criteria (eg enforcement or acceptance of norms) which are frequently employed in legal theory for assessing the effectiveness of law.

Effectiveness and applicability of legal norms are often related in several ways, but it is important to distinguish the two different concepts of applicability. The first one concerns the institutional duties of normative authorities and is called external applicability. The second refers to the spheres of validity of legal norms and is called internal applicability. A reconstruction of the concept of a norm must provide a proper account of the conditions under which certain properties, like effectiveness, can be attributed to legal norms. The notion of applicability can define the range of the concept of effectiveness. Our framework relies on certain conceptual distinctions, a brief sketch of which is necessary. [30]

[24] Sarat 1985, 24. [25] Ibid, 28. [26] Sennett 1980, 125.
[27] Zumbansen 2009. [28] Navarro and Moreso 1997, 201. [29] Raz 2003, 203.
[30] Navarro and Moreso 1997, 211.

Sarat and Kearns have described more concise and easily understandable explanations of this theory.[31] They describe instrumentalism as conceiving law 'as a tool for sustaining or changing aspects or social life' and distinguish between 'effects' and 'effectiveness', believing that instrumentalists are centrally concerned with the effectiveness of the law and not the effects more broadly conceived and additional to the intended effects of the law. In addition, Robert W Gordon has noted how instrumentalists

> divide the word into a social and a legal sphere. Society is the primary realm of social experience (...) the legal system is a distinctly secondary body of phenomena. It is a specialized realm of state and professional activity that is called into being by the primary social world in order to serve that the world needs.[32]

Sarat and Kearns also note that whilst legal scholarship may be focused less on the study of gaps and effectiveness and more on the variety of relations between which law and other normative systems stand, such a focus would be encouraged by adopting the perspective of everyday life as the point of departure for law and society studies.

4. Specification of this Concept

In many legal traditions, the focus of administrative law has been on its safeguard functions. Present-day administrative law is increasingly concerned with good governance principles and specifically the principle of effectiveness.[33] This innovation in administrative law is important since policymakers have often complained that all sorts of legal restraints prevented them from taking the policy measures considered necessary.

In the literature, the balance between policy rationality and the administrative law rationality is seen as a tension, not as an optimum. With the good governance view on administrative law, there is a more integrated approach which brings a better balance between the policy needs and the legal conditions of administrative law.

Some authors give the principle of effectiveness a place in the distinction between the procedural and the substantive principles of law, concluding that it is a procedural principle.[34] The procedural side denotes the existence of some procedural rights the applicant claims to possess because of an underlying legal norm which generates effectiveness. The substantive side refers to the situation in which the applicant seeks a particular benefit or commodity because of the effectiveness of the substantive legal norm. An administrative authority can also claim such a position in the procedure due to the public interest. It is submitted that the procedural side of the principle of effectiveness—effective protection and effective judicial review—is more developed than the substantive side.[35]

To conclude, the instrumental dimension is part of administrative law and the principle of effectiveness is also an element of that dimension. In this context, the focus of the principle of effectiveness is on the aim or the objective of a legal instrument. The principle has both a procedural and a substantive side.

[31] Sarat and Kearns 1993, 23. [32] Sarat 1997, 18. [33] Buijze 2008.
[34] Accetto and Zleptnig 2005, 383. [35] Tridimas 2006.

5. Institutions Involved

All the government institutions are involved in the development of the principle of effectiveness. The legislator is involved because of the codification of the principle of effectiveness in, for example, the Financial Account Acts. Since norms can be found in such acts for the administration in relation to the development of the different types of audits, the effectiveness aspect has a place in the legal regime. In the controlling phase, the Court of Audit looks to the effectiveness aspects, especially in the frame of the policy audits.

This can be seen as the traditional scope of effectiveness. However, there is more in international and European law where different institutions can have a task in relation to the effectiveness approach. We first give a short overview and then come to conclusions in relation to the institutions involved at different levels.

(a) Effectiveness in international law

Effectiveness is a concept often referred to in international law literature. Birnie and Boyle write that effectiveness of different regulatory and enforcement techniques is largely determined by the nature of the problem.[36] Saito is of the opinion that the effectiveness of international law rests on the recognition it receives from the governments of the world.[37] From another perspective, it is said that the validity and effectiveness of international law depends on the continuing consent and support of nation states.[38] The effectiveness of international law largely depends on the flexibility of the international law-making processes, as well as its ability to combine new concepts and techniques.[39] There is a strong relation between the international and local level inferred in the statement that the effectiveness of international law as its capacity to be implemented at the international and national levels is ultimately measured according to its enforcement at the local level.[40]

In the *Encyclopedia of Public International Law* attention is paid to the substantial aspects of effectiveness in international law by Hiroshi Taki.[41] He writes:

> The term 'effectiveness' has been used in international law since the mid-20th century, at times ambiguously, and with various meanings. Primarily, it refers to the efficacy (actual observance) of law as distinguished from the validity (binding force) of law. An example of this use of 'effectiveness' can be seen in the phrase 'The principle that a legal order, as a whole, must be by and large effective in order to be valid is itself a norm,' i.e. 'a norm of positive international law, the principle of effectiveness prevailing within this law'.
>
> The principle of effectiveness is sometimes used to denote a rule for treaty interpretation. Beyond these meanings however, many writers in international law seem to use this principle to express the following state of affairs: a factual situation (reality) has a stronger and more widespread effect on a legal norm than it does in municipal law.

From this quotation, we can conclude the following three meanings of the principle of effectiveness in international law: (1) the efficacy of law as an actual observance; (2) to denote a rule for treaty interpretation; and (3) to express that a factual situation

[36] Birnie and Boyle 2002, 10. [37] Taylor Saito 1998. [38] Shen 2000.
[39] Limpitlaw 2001. [40] Giraud-Kinley 1999.
[41] *Max Planck Encyclopedia of Public International Law* (MPEPIL) online edition, edited by Rüdiger Wolfrum.

has a stronger effect on a legal norm than it does in national law, thus including 'administrative law'.

These three meanings of the principle of effectiveness have to be explained in more detail to get a better understanding of the content of the principle of effectiveness on the international level. This includes effectiveness as an actual observance, as a rule for treaty interpretation, and as a factual effect of legal norms.

(b) Effectiveness as an actual observance

There is a special legal situation in the context of international law which is relevant in relation to the first meaning of the principle of effectiveness. Unlike national administrative law, the international legal order has no central organ that is empowered to apply and enforce law. Such functions are entrusted to the concerned states. Consequently, in the international legal order, the subjects of international law must rely on means of self-enforcement to protect and enforce their own individual rights. In the book *Principles of International Law*, the first meaning of the principle of effectiveness is seen in the framework of the essential function of international law: the determination of the spheres of validity of the national legal orders as to the legal existence of the state by the international legal order.[42]

(c) Effectiveness as a rule for treaty interpretation

The second meaning of the principle of effectiveness has been developed in the context of international courts in relation to specific 'interpretative' articles in the Vienna Convention. Rietiker has recently examined the principle of effectiveness in the jurisprudence of the European Court of Human Rights. He writes of how, in an ever-growing fragmentation of international legal systems, lawyers discuss the same legal question in different fora.[43]

(d) Effectiveness having a strong factual effect on a legal norm

With regard to the third meaning, one must ask: which legal phenomena are to be taken as examples? Opinions vary on this matter, and two extreme lines appear.[44] At one extreme, effectiveness is held to refer to all phenomena in which the factual situation affects the legal norm. Effectiveness, from this perspective, is how some writers refer to the phenomenon whereby superpowers have a decisive impact on the establishment of international law, or to the phenomenon where new rules of international law may be formed rapidly by a sudden change of social reality. In truth, the issues addressed (such as the impact of the power relations among states or actual demands in society, on the establishment of international law) really belong to sociology. At the other extreme, many writers construe effectiveness so narrowly as to confine it only to cases where a factual situation corresponding to legal status and legal rights exists. This makes it clear that at the international level the third meaning of the principle of effectiveness includes an argument of factual existence that both proves legal authority and demands legal recognition.

[42] Kelsen and Tucker 1967, 420–33. [43] Rietiker 2010. [44] Tucker 1953.

(e) International law

Given that the international community has negotiated countless treaties over the last several decades, one would imagine that it would have a clear conception of what constitutes effective international law. But despite its frequent use and the numerous studies that have dealt with the topic, there remains a poor understanding of effectiveness in international law. Just a few of the references to effectiveness in international law demonstrate the wide variety of definitions and understanding of the concept.[45]

Traditionally, under international law, the principle of effectiveness was employed as a precondition for establishing rights.[46] A right was granted if the effectiveness principle could first be proven. The traditional principle of effectiveness focused more on the form and power of treaties rather than on their design or impact.[47] The reality of the effectiveness of treaties is quite contrary; design and impact are critical to a treaty's effectiveness. In the literature, several legal models of effectiveness[48] have been developed, such as: (1) rule-based positivist models; (2) social legal models; (3) other legal models; and (4) international relations model. But there is a need for redefining legal approaches to effectiveness in which the following aspects have been developed: (a) resolving measurement perimeters; (b) compliance still matters; (c) robustness as a determinant of legal effectiveness; (d) a treaty's supporting provisions; (e) external international legal environment; and (f) financing.

The conclusion is that there are various conceptions of the effectiveness of international treaties and that the positivistic notion of legal effectiveness is an overly narrow approach. In the first place, such an approach does not take into account why states behave as they do. This approach also does not take into account modern studies done through legal scholarship that view law as a process instead of a body of neutral rules to be complied with. Studies from the area of social science have taken a broad approach to studying effectiveness, from the standpoint of regimes. Finally, there is a theory that looks to the various components of the treaty itself and argues that there are three critical elements to the measurement of legal effectiveness: (1) performance data compared with its objectives; (2) why states comply with international rules without the enforceability of strong sanctions in the treaty; and (3) review treaties through scientific mechanisms.

In the decisions of international tribunals, the doctrine of restrictive interpretation of treaties, which limits the sovereignty of states, has been no more than just words. The principle of effectiveness has played a prominent and ever-growing part in the administration of international law. The principle of effectiveness in the interpretation of treaties appears in national and international jurisprudence in various forms. In the United States it has been repeatedly invoked and acted upon by the Supreme Court in the form of that Court's theory of liberal interpretation. In English jurisprudence and practice, the term 'liberal interpretation' seems to have been used in a somewhat wider sense as connoting generous rather than pedantic interpretation. International jurisprudence—and particularly that of the Permanent Court of International Justice as well as its successor—has constantly acted upon the principle of effectiveness as the governing canon of interpretation.[49]

[45] Chambers 2004. [46] Döhring 1984. [47] Kelsen 2009.
[48] Chambers 2004. [49] Lauterpacht 1949, 48.

(f) European Union law

The development of the principle of effectiveness is somewhat different from the other general principles of EU law. It is not directly based on the laws of the member states, but derives its distinct character from EU law, by means of the concept of primacy and direct effect. This makes it the development of a real EU-law principle.[50] The proper functioning of the European Union is predicated on the effective and coherent implementation of its rules. Apart from substantive provisions, the national procedural framework is also essential for the effectiveness of EU law. This is because the substantive legal regime greatly depends on the national procedural and institutional framework to develop its full effect.[51] Therefore, rules governing the procedural framework are only minimum standards or obligations for the member states. Through the Aarhus Regulation, the procedural framework is not only developed at the national level, but also at the EU level.

We have to be cautious when it comes to the relation between the principle of effectiveness and other general principles of EU law. There is not always a clear difference between the different types of principles. Sometimes principles partly overlap or have a more or less fundamental or general character. The principle of effectiveness is sometimes seen as a background principle, which plays a role in EU administrative law, especially in the framework of the tools of review and compensation in order to hold the administration to account.[52] The principle of effectiveness underlies a series of developments in the sphere of judicial protection and has been recognized as a general principle of EU law by the ECJ and its predecessor.[53] The origins of the principle of effectiveness lie in the interpretative techniques of the ECJ, which favoured a liberal construction of Treaty provisions so as to ensure the direct effect of directives. Gradually, the Court has placed more emphasis on the affinity of the principle to the fundamental right of judicial protection as guaranteed by articles 6 and 13 ECHR and which is also laid down in article 47 of the EU Charter. In the Charter, we find the right to effective remedy and the right to a fair trial.

A central problem for effective implementation of European legislation is the impact of national administrative traditions, since the formal and practical transformation of the EU law rests mainly at the national level.[54] The implementation of effectiveness depends on the 'institutional scope' of European adaptation pressure, which is effected by European requirements and the embedding of the respective administrative traditions and national capacities for administrative reform. According to the degrees of adaptation pressure, different paths can be distinguished, for which more or less effective implementation is suggested.[55] In cases of high adaptation pressure, implementation is likely to be ineffective since European policies require fundamental institutional changes which cannot be achieved by adaptations following the 'logic of appropriateness'. In cases of low adaptation pressure, it is assumed that effective implementation is a result of the full compatibility of European requirements and existing national arrangements. In cases of moderate adaptation pressure, where European legislation requires adaptations that remain within the national scope of appropriateness, we find that institutional factors provide no sufficient explanation for the varied implementation results observed in the case studies. [56]

[50] Tridimas 2006, Ch 9: The Principle of Effectiveness, 418–76, more specific at 418.
[51] Craig and De Búrca 2007. [52] Craig 2006, 277. [53] Tridimas 2006.
[54] van den Broek 2015. [55] Knill 1998, 1. [56] Ibid, 25.

There is some autonomy left for the member states of the EU. This is, however, not absolute because in order to ensure effective and uniform application of EU law, the ECJ has formulated two requirements which national law must be able to meet in procedures where EU law rights are involved: the principle of equivalence or non-discrimination and the principle of effectiveness or minimum protection.[57] More recently, a third requirement has come into place. National rules of procedure and remedies must comply with fundamental rights as guaranteed by the ECHR.

We can conclude that in international law, effectiveness has its place. In EU law, the principle of effectiveness operates in the implementation and the execution of EU law. An effective procedural framework is a minimum norm. The framework is also seen as a general principle of EU law, which sometimes functions as a background principle and sometimes as underlining other principles. There is also a strong role in the development of the principle by the ECJ, in which the norm of effective judicial review is prominent. The consequence of these developments in international and EU law is that all the institutions on both levels are involved in the development of this principle of effectiveness.

6. Sources of the Principle of Effectiveness

In international law and in EU law, the sources of the principle of effectiveness are international and EU regulations, their implementation at the national level, and the case law on the different levels. At the national level, effectiveness has for a long time not been regarded as a legal norm. Thus, many lawyers have not been particularly interested in the discussion about the concept of effectiveness. At the same time, lawyers were concerned with effectiveness in the context of legislation becoming 'effective' at a certain moment.

However, lawyers are no longer uninterested in the principle of effectiveness. There are three reasons for the need for lawyers, even at the national level, to open their eyes to this principle and treat it as a legal principle. The first reason is internationalization and a growing interdisciplinary approach, both of which have grown enormously over the last ten years. The second reason is the importance of an effective transposition, implementation, and execution of international and European regulations at the national level. The third reason is conceptual: when there is a relationship between legal norms and facts, focusing only on the legal norm is too restrictive a legal perspective. These three aspects of the effectiveness principle in national administrative law will be elaborated upon below.

(a) Internationalization and interdisciplinary approach

The internationalization of national law is growing. The importance of interdisciplinary approaches is growing, not only in the functional fields of law (like economic law, financial law, and environmental law) but also in the general fields of law, like administrative law (and public administration) and criminal law (and criminology). Both developments have increased the importance of the principle of effectiveness in the field of law. More specifically, administrative law has in the last twenty years started

[57] Widdershoven and others 2007, 292 ff.

to focus not only on the protection of citizens but also on the instrumental aspects of administrative law.

(b) Effective transposition, implementation, and execution at the national level

At the national level, EU law has to be implemented, enforced, and complied with. The effectiveness of EU regulations depends on the national legal system and the legislative and administrative measures adopted by member states. Effectiveness also depends on whether the member states are implementing EU law in a proper, timely, and effective manner. This effectiveness underlies the EU legal system as a whole.

In national administrative legal systems, the focus is on these questions: which administrative authority is competent; which legal and non-legal instruments are available; which norms have to be fulfilled; which authority is competent for enforcement; and how is legal protection organized? Based on these questions, the member state designs national legislation that will implement European and international instruments.

These national implementation laws are the basis for executive action by the competent authorities using the instruments they need, fulfilling the norms for applying these instruments. Subsequently, we have the phase of enforcement, when there is a violation of the norms of national implementation regulations. We often distinguish here between the supervision and the sanctioning side.

At the national level, a violation of the effectiveness principle can theoretically occur in three different phases: (1) the phase of the implementation of EU law by making national regulations; (2) the phase of the execution of these national regulations; and (3) the phase of enforcement of these national regulations. However, in practice the principle of effectiveness can also be violated by the fourth power because control—as a phase—can also be inefficient.

(c) Effectiveness: interrelation between legal norms and facts

In the literature, three fundaments of administrative law are often mentioned: the rule of law, democracy, and the instrumental character.[58] In this instrumental fundament, more attention is given to the results and the quality of the administration by choosing different legal and non-legal instruments to realize public aims. The focus is on guidance through law. But this guidance through law for realizing public aims can only be done when conditions of the democratic rule of law have been fulfilled. From that perspective, there should be a balance between these more fundamental legal conditions and the legal instruments to realize the public aims. That is important in the process of making norms, but it is equally important in the compliance and enforcement of these norms. When it comes to compliance and enforcement, there should be a good balance between fundamental norms and instrumental aims.

The instrumental aspects, sometimes qualified as governance aspects, are not only relevant for the quality of administrative work but also for the public interest and hence for the interest of the citizenry. Today, increasing attention is paid to the effectiveness aspects of the law and some notions of legal effectiveness are emerging. The development of the principles of good governance has increased the importance of the

[58] Van Wijk, Konijnenbelt, and Van Male 2005, 46.

principle of effectiveness at the national level, as part of said principles.[59] In this context, the interrelation between legal norms and facts becomes clear.

7. Conclusions

We started this exercise on the principle of effectiveness with some dictionary definitions of 'effectiveness'. We then found that effectiveness is subject to research in non-legal disciplines. In social science, 'effectiveness' refers to the ways of using methods of empirical investigation to develop knowledge about human social activity. In physics, it is the framework intended to explain certain observed effects. In medicine, it is used for a drug that produces a certain effect and, in economics, it means the highest quality at the least possible cost, which is more the definition of efficiency.

It must be noted that the principle of effectiveness is intertwined with the other principles of good governance, which are the tools used to reach the goal that is good governance. However, this goal will not be reached if the principles are not implemented effectively, and therefore we encounter overlaps between the principle of effectiveness and other principles of good governance. It is necessary to stress that principles of good governance do overlap and work together, and therefore effectiveness should not be viewed as a completely separate principle.

In a legal context, two aspects of effectiveness are relevant: that effectiveness is a principle of good governance and that effectiveness has procedural and substantive aspects. In international law, the principle of effectiveness has been developed along the following lines: effectiveness as actual observance, effectiveness as a rule for treaty interpretation, and effectiveness as a strong factual effect on a legal norm.

Effectiveness in EU law means: the effective implementation of EU rules, substantively and procedurally; effectiveness as a principle of EU law, developed by the ECJ; and equivalence and effectiveness in the context of effective judicial review.

Effectiveness in national administrative law is about internationalization and the interdisciplinary approach of administrative law, effective implementation and execution at the national level, and effectiveness in the sense of the interrelation between legal norms and facts.

[59] Addink 2005a, 21–48.

11

The Principle of Accountability

This chapter explains the principle of accountability as part of the principles of good governance. The principle of accountability is already far beyond financial accounting, and it comes closer to the accountability of the minister in their relationship with the parliament and with the civil and criminal responsibility of persons and institutions in general.

1. Development of the Principle of Accountability

The principle of accountability has been developed in five steps, according to the literature.[1] It became more and more clear that accountability was not only needed from a financial perspective but also for a much broader functioning of the public administration.

The first step goes from accounting to accountability, which refers to a transformation of the traditional book-keeping function in public administration into a much broader form of public accountability. It also means, for instance, that auditing is not just about financial auditing but something much more important. The most concise description of public accountability would be 'the obligation of an actor to publicly explain and justify conduct to some significant other'.[2]

The second step is from compliance to performance. The most important transformation is from traditional financial control to what the British have called 'value for money auditing'.[3] An example of how such a concept operates is the audit conducted by the National Audit Office in the United Kingdom. Besides a general responsibility check, this independent parliamentary body carries out a 'value for money' audit. This means that areas of government expenditure are evaluated and a judgement is reached on whether value for money has been achieved.

Value for money auditing is less concerned with the legality and procedural correctness of public spending and more with its efficiency and effectiveness. The numerical, quantifiable criteria of financial accounting are substituted for much more output-oriented, qualitative performance indicators. Thus, good governance is not only measured in terms of compliance with prescribed financial rules and procedures but also in terms of actual performance. Attention has shifted from inputs and throughputs to outputs and, most importantly, outcomes.[4] The introduction of performance auditing has also led to a shift from *ex post* to *ex ante* auditing. The step from compliance to performance auditing therefore also implies a shift from hard to soft standards and it moves auditors beyond the secure grounds of financial auditing into the marshier discipline of policy evaluation.

The third step is from internal to external accountability. In reaction to a deemed lack of trust in public institutions, there is an urge in many western democracies for more

[1] Based on Bovens 2005. [2] Bovens 2004. [3] Harlow 2002, 19.
[4] Pollitt and others 1999, 195.

Good Governance: Concept and Context. Henk Addink. © Henk Addink 2019. Published 2019 by Oxford University Press.

direct and explicit accountability relations between public agencies and civil actors.[5] Agencies or individual public managers should feel obliged to account for their performance to the public at large or, at least, to civil interest groups, charities, and associations of clients.[6] 'Public accountability' thus also stands for a regime of responsiveness and transparency in public agencies. This shift from internal to external accountability is often realized through public panels and public reporting. Accountability is intertwined here with the principles of transparency and participation. In the late 1990s, many public agencies established citizen charters, focus groups, and citizen panels to foster public accountability. In the Netherlands, for example, many agencies have set up small consumer panels or advisory boards with delegations of interest groups, which they can consult about performance or policy changes. Public reporting is another instrument for public accountability that has been adopted from the private sector. Agencies make their annual reports, their assessments, and their benchmarks publicly available, or they publish separate annual reports directed at a general audience.

The fourth step is going from reporting about financial goals and issues to reporting about a broad range of public concerns. This shift is most visible in the private sector. Many large listed companies have begun publishing separate social and environmental annual reports in order to accommodate their critics and to express that they accept corporate social responsibility. These come under different labels: social and environmental reporting, sustainability reporting, and citizens reporting. This form of public accountability is still evolving. There are as yet no generally accepted standards for good governance or sustainability that can be used to assess the social responsibility of private or public organizations.

A fifth step, from vertical to horizontal accountability, has also been mentioned in the literature. This step has less to do with the contents and more to do with the change of the character of relations in organizations. Moreover, this is not a shift which is typical for accountability. It reflects broader developments in society on the role of government. These developments also have consequences for accountability. In the context of the principles of good governance, it is in essence a reason why these principles have been strongly developed during the past years.

This could give the impression that the starting point of the discussion of accountability is the traditional financial auditing. That is not correct, because accountability goes back a lot further than that and was always about substantive performance. Military commanders and other officials were accountable to their sovereigns for more than their expenditure of money.

2. The Concept of Accountability

The literature focuses a lot on the concept of public accountability. Bovens is an author who paid much attention to this issue.[7] Public accountability is a hallmark of modern democratic governance. Democracy remains a paper tiger if those in power cannot be held accountable in public for their acts and omissions, decisions, policies, and expenditures. In addition, it can increase the quality of the administration as part of the development towards good governance and, in doing so, it can prevent government errors.[8]

[5] McCandless 2001. [6] Busuioc 2010. [7] Bovens 2007. [8] Ibid.

Historically, the concept of accountability is closely related to financial accounting. In fact, it literally comes from bookkeeping. In modern times, accountability has moved far beyond its bookkeeping origins and has become a symbol for good governance, both in the public and in the private sector. Here we have to realize that the legal contexts in the public and the private sectors are different and, for that reason, it is better to use different terminology for the principles of corporate governance in the private sector and the principles of good governance in the public sector. The corresponding principles of accountability also need an apt interpretation to both concepts. The aims of both sectors are considerably different. The public sector serves the general interest, while the private sector is concerned with maximizing profit. The actors involved in the accountability process also differ, as citizens are stakeholders in the public sector while a private corporation is mainly concerned with shareholders and a somewhat more limited scope of stakeholders.

(a) A broad concept of accountability

In contemporary political and scholarly discourse, 'accountability'[9] often serves as a conceptual umbrella term that covers various other distinct concepts, such as transparency, equity, democracy, efficiency, responsiveness, responsibility, and integrity.[10] Particularly in American scholarly and political discourse, 'accountability' is often used interchangeably with 'good governance' or virtuous behaviour. For many states, the term 'accountability' is used to refer to 'best practices'. However, in the United States, the Government Accountability Office deals mostly with auditing spending and not regulation of good governance as a whole.

Such quite broad conceptualizations of the concept have made it difficult to establish empirically whether an official or organization is subject to accountability. The reason is that each of the various elements needs extensive operationalization itself. Another reason is that the various elements cannot be measured along the same scale. Some dimensions, such as transparency, are instrumental for accountability but not constitutive to accountability. Others, such as responsiveness, have more evaluative rather than analytical dimensions. Accountability in this very broad sense is basically an evaluative and not an analytical concept. It is used to qualify positively a state of affairs or the performance of an actor. It comes close to 'responsiveness' and 'a sense of responsibility', a willingness to act in a transparent, fair, and equitable way. Accountability in this broad sense is an essentially contested and contestable concept because there is no general consensus about the standards for accountable behaviour and because these are so dependent on circumstances of time, place, and the like.[11]

(b) A narrow concept of accountability

Bovens has not defined the concept in such a broad, evaluative sense, but in a narrower, somewhat sociological sense.[12] 'Accountability' is then not just another political catchword but also refers to concrete practices of being accountable. The most concise description of accountability would be 'the obligation to explain and justify conduct'. This implies a relationship between an actor, the accounter, and a forum, the accountholder or accountee.[13] Bovens has therefore stayed close to its etymological and

[9] Ibid. [10] Mulgan 2000, 555; Behn 2001, 3–6. [11] Fisher 2004.
[12] Bovens 2007, 452. [13] Pollitt 2003, 89.

historical roots and defined accountability as a specific social relation.[14] Accountability is a relationship between an actor and a forum in which the actor has an obligation to explain and to justify his or her conduct. While the forum can ask questions and pass judgement, the actor may face consequences. We use this description of accountability as an analytical instrument and also as a part of the normative framework of the principles of good governance.[15]

3. Specification of the Concept

The concept of accountability has been specified by Bovens in different ways. Here the focus is on the substantive elements of the concept. We distinguish accountability based on the relevant substantive aspects of finance, procedure, and product. In accountability relationships, the actor is obliged to explain and provide justification for his conduct. There are many aspects to this conduct, making it possible to distinguish a number of accountability relationships on the basis of the aspect that is most dominant.[16] The classification is often made according to the type of forum. In the case of legal accountability, the legality of the actor's conduct is obviously a dominant aspect, while professional accountability is centred on the professionalism of the conduct. Political and administrative accountability frequently involve several aspects. An audit by the Chamber of Audit, for example, may be classified as financial accountability if the focus is on the financial propriety of the audit, as legal accountability if the legality of the conduct is at issue, or as administrative if the central concern is the efficiency of the organization's policy. Another distinction found in the literature is one between accountability for the procedure or process and accountability for the product or content.[17]

4. Institutions Involved

It is vital to look at the institutions to whom a certain person is accountable. Based on the nature of the forum, we may distinguish the following types of accountability: political, legal, administrative, professional, and social. Here, we consider from what perspective is account to be rendered. The second aspect is the nature of the actor on which basis we distinguish: corporate, hierarchical, collective, and individual accountability. Here, we question who should render the account and who is the relevant actor to appear before the forum. This is explained below.[18]

(a) Political and legal accountability

Political and legal accountability are both extremely important types of accountability within democracies, as they concern the accountability of the government, civil servants, and politicians to the public, to legislative bodies (such as congress or parliament), and to judicial bodies. In a few cases, recall elections can be used to revoke

[14] Day and Klein 1987, 5; Romzek and Dubnick 1998, 6; Lerner and Tetlock 1999; McCandless 2001, 22; Scott 2000; Pollitt 2003, 89; Mulgan 2000, 7–14.

[15] Bovens 2007, 452.

[16] Day and Klein 1987, 5; Sinclair 1996, 219; Behn 2001, 6–10.

[17] Day and Klein 1987, 27.

[18] Bovens 2007.

the office of an elected official; generally, voters do not have any direct way of holding elected representatives to account during the elected term. Additionally, some officials and legislators may be appointed rather than elected, which could have consequences for the legal accountability of these persons. The word 'accountability' in this context has strong relations with the terms 'responsibility' and 'liability', and for that reason both political and legal accountability will be discussed.

(b) Accountability and responsibility: ministers and parliament

Accountability can be seen as an overall term in which we have to distinguish different elements. Responsibility has a strong constitutional connotation and it has links with the concept that members of the cabinet must have the confidence of the parliament. It means that ministers are responsible to parliament for all their activities, including the activities of the civil servants who are working under them. It means that the minister not only has to give the information to parliament but also has to defend their activities, including in situations they refrain from. If the parliament is not satisfied, they can accept a motion in which they declare that the minister(s) no longer has (have) the support. Then it depends on the interpretation of the minister or the cabinet what interpretation to give to this motion. This is unwritten constitutional law.

In other countries, individual ministerial responsibility is called a constitutional convention. In governments using the Westminster System, the cabinet minister bears the ultimate responsibility for the actions of their ministry or department. Individual ministerial responsibility is not the same as cabinet collective responsibility, which states that members of the cabinet must approve publicly of its collective decisions or resign. This means that a motion for a vote of 'no confidence' is not in order should the actions of a government body fail in the proper discharge of its responsibilities. Where there is ministerial responsibility, the accountable minister is expected to take the blame and ultimately resign, but the majority or coalition within the parliament of which the minister is part is not held to be answerable for that minister's failure.

This means that if waste, corruption, or any other misbehaviour is found to have occurred within a ministry, the minister is responsible even if the minister had no knowledge of the actions. A minister is ultimately responsible for all actions carried out by his ministry because even without his knowledge of crime committed by subordinates, the minister approved the hiring and continued employment of those civil servants. If misdeeds are found to have occurred in a ministry, the minister is expected to resign. It is also possible for a minister to face criminal charges for malfeasance under their watch.

The principle is considered essential as it is seen to guarantee that an elected official is answerable for every single government decision. It is also important to motivate ministers to closely scrutinize the activity within their departments. One rule stemming from this principle is that each cabinet member answers for their own ministry in parliament's question time. The reverse of ministerial responsibility is that civil servants are not supposed to take credit for the successes of their department, allowing the government to claim them.

In recent years, some commentators have argued the notion of ministerial responsibility has been eroded in many Commonwealth countries. While the doctrine is a constitutional convention, there is no formal mechanism for enforcing the rule. Today ministers frequently use ignorance of misbehaviour as an argument for lack of culpability. While opposition parties rarely accept this argument, the electorate is often more accepting. Courts of the United Kingdom have become less likely to find ministers guilty when their individual knowledge of or involvement in a crime cannot be proved. In most other Commonwealth countries such cases are today hardly ever brought to trial.

There are also internal mechanisms for correction and the constitution, or statute, can empower a legislative body to hold their own members, the government, and government bodies to account. This can be through holding an internal or independent inquiry. Inquiries are usually held in response to an allegation of misconduct or corruption. The powers, procedures, and sanctions vary from country to country. The legislature may have the power to impeach the individual, remove them, or suspend them from office for a period of time. The accused person might also decide to resign before trial. Impeachment in the United States has been used both for elected representatives and other civil offices, such as district court judges. In parliamentary systems, the government relies on the support of parliament, which gives parliament power to hold the government to account. For example, some parliaments can pass a vote of no confidence in the government.

(c) Accountability and liability: legal accountability in the courts

In many countries, legal accountability is of increasing importance to public institutions as a result of the growing formalization of social relations. Courts as independent actors have a crucial role here in neutralizing administrative excesses. Such courts can be the 'ordinary' civil courts, as in the United Kingdom, or specialized administrative courts, as in France, Belgium, and the Netherlands. Legal accountability is usually based on specific responsibilities, formally or legally conferred upon authorities.

Legal accountability is the most unambiguous type of accountability, as the legal scrutiny is based on detailed legal standards prescribed by civil, penal, or administrative statutes or precedents. From the civil law and the criminal law perspective, liability also has a specific meaning. Civil liability means the legal responsibility for one's acts or omissions. Failure of a person or entity to meet that responsibility leaves him open to a lawsuit for any resulting damages or subject to a court order to perform. In order to win a lawsuit, the suing party (claimant or plaintiff) must prove the civil liability of the defendant if the claimant's allegations are shown to be true. This requires evidence of the duty to act, the failure to fulfil that duty, and the connection of that failure to some injury or harm to the claimant. Liability also applies to alleged criminal acts in which the defendant may be responsible for acts which constitute a crime, thus making him subject to conviction and punishment.

The civil and criminal liability aspects can also be relevant in the context of the government for ministers and civil servants as well as for public institutions. In this context, the concept of immunity is relevant. Governmental immunity stops people from suing the government, government employees, and government officials in many cases. This is the doctrine from English common law that no governmental body can be sued unless it gives permission. Historically, this was an absolute doctrinal position that held federal, state, and local governments immune from tort liability arising from the activities of government. This policy makes it easier for the government to make decisions since it protects the government from interference from lawsuits. This protection, however, has resulted in terrible injustices since public hospitals, government drivers, and other employees could be negligent and free from judgement. These days, the application of sovereign immunity is much less clear-cut, as different governments have waived liability in differing degrees under differing circumstances. In the United States the Federal Tort Claims Act and state waivers of immunity (with specific claims systems) have negated this rule, which stemmed from the days when kings set prerogatives. Broader government immunity does not prevent all lawsuits against the government. However, even if you can sue, the government may also be immune from types of remedies, such as punitive damages. There are many situations where suing the government is still appropriate.

(d) Parliamentary democracy: parliamentary representatives

Representative democracy is probably one of the most well-known democratic models. In many countries today, this model or a variation of it is used to elect officials and govern the state. Elected representatives or officials are persons who won the office in a free election. Formally, the person represents another or others like a community in a legislative body.

As such, it is important to review this model in full while also comparing it to direct democracy. Essentially, the representative democratic model allows all citizens within a state to elect representatives that will sit at the legislature. This gives them the authority to approve legislation and control the funds of the government. It was first developed during the ages of monarchical rule. Monarchies wanted to impose new taxation regulations upon certain areas of the state, and in order do so, support from a group of prominent people was needed. As time passed, the power that the monarchy had shifted to the representatives. Governing was therefore the responsibility of those elected. Still, only certain individuals could be elected and many citizens did not have the right to vote. In the twentieth century, these rights were gradually expanded so that all individuals could participate in the electoral process.

Today, there are many truly democratic governing systems. Even though there is a variety of different representatives, there are only a few that have considerable amounts of power. The individuals that make the governing decisions are elected members of the executive. The other representatives have limited power. They debate legislation that the executive introduces and either pass or block it. More often than not, representatives are members of a political party. Thus, elections are battles between political parties and those who are elected will usually vote in accordance with their political party's beliefs. An excellent example of the representative democratic model is the parliamentary system. Elected officials are in legislature, which is the parliament. The executive is comprised of the prime minister and his members of the cabinet, who oversee and conduct the governing of the state. The executive is often made up of members of the legislature and must maintain a majority support of the elected representatives to avoid getting removed from office. It is important to note that most democratic nations do not directly identify with the representative democratic model, but instead with a combination of both direct and representative. In a way, the definition of a representative democracy could be summed up by saying it is an 'indirect democracy' because citizens within the state do not make the governing decisions directly. Rather, they just select individuals to make decisions on their behalf via the electoral process. Plebiscitary democracy uses many fundamental elements of this democratic model, but combines these selected features with tools associated with direct democracy to give citizens more power.

Elected representatives or officials are persons who won the office in a free election. Formally, the person represents a community in a legislative body. Mostly, these representatives are members of a political party, a political organization that typically seeks to influence or entirely control government policy, usually by nominating candidates with aligned political views and trying to seat them in political office. Parties participate in electoral campaigns and educational outreach or protest actions. Parties often espouse an ideology or vision, expressed in a party programme, bolstered by a written platform with specific goals, forming a coalition among disparate interests.

(e) Politics: representatives and political parties

When the party is represented by members in the lower house of parliament, the party leader simultaneously serves as the leader of that party's parliamentary group. Depending on a minimum number of seats held, Westminster-based parties typically allow for leaders to form frontbench teams of senior fellow members of the parliamentary group to serve as critics on different aspects of government policy. When a party becomes the largest party not to be represented in a Westminster-style parliament, the party's parliamentary group forms the official opposition, with official opposition frontbench team members often forming the official opposition shadow cabinet. When a party achieves enough seats in an election to form a majority, the party's frontbench becomes the cabinet of government ministers. Parliamentary party members and leaders who are part of neither the government nor official opposition frontbenches are known as backbenchers, and are relegated to sitting behind or perpendicular to designated frontbenchers.

The freedom to form, declare membership in, or campaign for candidates from a political party is considered a measurement of a state's adherence to liberal democracy as a political value. Regulation of parties may run from a crackdown on all opposition parties (a norm for authoritarian governments) to the repression of certain parties which hold or promote ideals that run counter to the general ideology of the state's incumbents (or possess membership by-laws which are legally unenforceable). Furthermore, in the case of far-right, far-left, and regionalist parties in the national parliaments of many EU countries, mainstream political parties may form an informal *cordon sanitaire* that applies a policy of non-cooperation towards those 'outsider parties' present in the legislature viewed as 'anti-system' or otherwise unacceptable for government.

Political parties are funded by contributions from party members, individuals, and organizations that share their political ideas (eg trade union affiliation fees), stand to benefit from the party's activities (eg corporate donations), or from governmental and public funding. Political parties are lobbied vigorously by organizations, businesses, and special interest groups such as trade unions. Money and gifts-in-kind to a party or its leading members may be offered as incentives. Such donations are the traditional source of funding for all right-centre oriented parties. Starting in the late-nineteenth century, these parties were opposed by the newly founded left-centre workers' parties. They started a new party type, the mass membership party. In the United Kingdom, it was alleged that peerages had been awarded to contributors to party funds, the benefactors becoming members of the House of Lords and thus in a position to participate in the legislative process. Famously, Lloyd George was found to have been selling peerages. To prevent such corruption in the future, Parliament passed the Honours (Prevention of Abuses) Act 1925 into law. Thus, the outright sale of peerages and similar honours became a criminal act. However, some benefactors are alleged to have attempted to circumvent this by cloaking their contributions as loans, giving rise to a 'cash for peerages' scandal. Such activities, as well as assumed 'influence peddling', have given rise to demands that the scale of donations should be capped. As the costs of electioneering escalate, so too the demands made on party funds increase. In the United Kingdom, some politicians are advocating that parties should be funded by the state; a proposition that promises to give rise to interesting debate in a country that was the first to regulate campaign expenses in 1883. In many other democracies, such subsidies for party activity (in general or just for campaign purposes) were introduced decades ago. Public financing for parties and/or candidates (during election times and beyond) has several permutations and is increasingly common. Germany, Sweden, Israel, Canada, Australia, Austria, and Spain are cases in point. More recently France, Japan, Mexico, the Netherlands, and Poland, among others, have followed suit.

(f) Voters, election, and representation

Voting is a method by which a group can decide or express an opinion, often following discussions, debates, or election campaigns. Democracies elect holders of high office by voting. In a democracy, a government is chosen by voting in an election. In a representative democracy, voting is the method by which the electorate appoints its representatives in its government. A vote is a formal expression of an individual's choice in voting, for or against some motion (eg a proposed resolution), for a certain candidate, a selection of candidates, or a political party. A secret ballot has become standard practice, to prevent voters from being intimidated and to protect their political privacy. Voting usually takes place at a polling station. It is voluntary in some countries and compulsory in others (such as Argentina, Australia, Belgium, and Brazil).

Different voting systems use different types of votes. A 'plurality voting system' does not require the winner to achieve a vote majority, that is, more than 50 per cent of the total votes cast. In a voting system that uses a single vote per race, when more than two candidates run, the winner may commonly have less than 50 per cent of the vote. A side effect of a single vote per race is vote splitting, which tends to elect candidates that do not support centrism, and tends to produce a two-party system. An alternative to a single-vote system is approval voting.

To understand why a single vote per race tends to favour less centric candidates, consider a simple lab experiment where students in a class vote for their favourite marble. If five marbles are assigned names and are placed 'up for election', and if three of them are green, one is red, and one is blue, then a green marble will rarely win the election. The reason is that the three green marbles will split the votes of those who prefer green. In fact, in this analogy, the only way that a green marble is likely to win is if more than 60 per cent of the voters prefer green. If the same percentage of people prefer green as those who prefer red and blue, that is to say if 33 per cent of the voters prefer green, 33 per cent prefer blue, and 33 per cent prefer red, then each green marble will only get 11 per cent of the vote, while the red and blue marbles will each get 33 per cent, putting the green marbles at a serious disadvantage. If the experiment is repeated with other colours, the colour that is in the majority will still rarely win. In other words, from a purely mathematical perspective, a single-vote system tends to favour a winner that is different from the majority. If the experiment is repeated using approval voting, where voters are encouraged to vote for as many candidates as they approve of, then the winner is much more likely to be any one of the five marbles, because people who prefer green will be able to vote for every one of the green marbles.

(g) Administrative accountability: auditors, inspectors, and controllers

Next to the courts, a wide range of quasi-legal forums exercising independent and external administrative and financial supervision and control has been established in the past decades. Some even speak of an 'audit explosion'. These new administrative forums vary from European, national or local ombudsmen and audit offices, to independent supervisory authorities, inspector generals, anti-fraud offices, and chartered accountants. In Australia, administrative accountability forums build their legitimacy on their independence in order to avoid conflicts of interest. Without their independence, their legitimacy would be undermined and be perceived in the eyes of the public and puppets of the administration who do not serve in the public interest.

(h) Professional accountability: professional peers

Many public managers are, apart from being general managers, professionals in a more technical sense. They have been trained as engineers, doctors, veterinarians, teachers, or police officers. This may imply accountability relationships with professional associations and disciplinary tribunals. Professional bodies lay down codes of standards of acceptable practice, binding for all members. These standards are monitored and enforced by professional supervisory bodies based on peer review. This type of accountability is particularly relevant to public managers who work in professional public organizations, such as hospitals, schools, psychiatric clinics, research institutes, police departments, fire brigades, or for some of the experts in international organizations.

(i) Social accountability: interest groups, charities, and other stakeholders.

Influenced by the debate on corporate social responsibility and corporate governance in business, more attention is being paid to the role of non-governmental organizations, interest groups, and customers or clients as relevant stakeholders, not only in determining policy, but also in rendering account. Agencies or individual public managers should feel obliged to account for their performance to the public at large or, at least, to civil interest groups, charities, and associations of clients. A first step in this direction has been the institution of public reporting and the establishment of public panels. The rise of the internet has given a new dimension to this form of accountability. Increasingly, the results of inspections, assessments, and benchmarks are put on the internet. It remains an empirical question to what extent these groups and panels ensure full accountability mechanisms since the possibility of judgement and sanctioning is often lacking. Also, not all of these accountability relations involve clearly demarcated, coherent, and authoritative forums that the actor reports to and could debate with.

Agencies in the United States, such as are mentioned in the Administrative Procedures Act (APA) and National Environmental Policy Act (NEPA), can be mentioned here. Before the APA or NEPA can instigate regulations, their actions must be justified with informative content and responses to any criticism that might be encountered. Similarly, in the EU, agencies are expected to undergo the same scrutiny and accountability. Highlighting this comparison would set the argument that accountability is a key principle to good governance.

(j) Who is the actor?

The other side of the social relation is the actor. Who is the actor? Here we have the problem of many hands. Accountability forums often face similar problems, but in reverse. They can be confronted with multiple potential actors. Here we pay attention to different types of actors.

(k) Corporate accountability: the organization as actor

Many public organizations are corporate bodies with an independent legal status. They can operate as unitary actors and can be held accountable accordingly. Most western countries accept corporate liabilities in civil, administrative, and even criminal law. Public organizations are usually included in these corporate liabilities, with the exception of criminal liability. Legal and administrative forums often follow this corporate accountability strategy. They can, in this way, circumnavigate the troublesome issues of identification and verification of specific individual actors. In the event of organizational deviance, they can turn directly to the organization and hold it to account for the collective outcome, without worrying too much about which official has met what criteria for responsibility.

(l) Hierarchical accountability: one for all

The idea behind hierarchical strategies of accountability is the organization as a pyramid or as a hierarchy. Processes of 'calling to account' start at the top with the highest rank of official. The rank and the file do not appear before external forums but hide behind the broad shoulders of the minister, the commissioner, or the director of the agency. The head must at least in dealings with the outside world, assume complete responsibility and take the blame. In the case of hierarchical schemes, processes of calling to account thus take place along the strict lines of the 'chain of command' and the middle managers are, in turn, both actor and forum. This is the official venue for accountability in most public organizations and most types of accountability relationships, with the exception of professional accountability. It is particularly dominant in political accountability relations.

(m) Collective accountability: all for one

Public organizations are collectives of individual officials. Theoretically, a forum could therefore also apply a collective strategy of accountability and pick any member of the organization and hold that person personally accountable for the conduct of the organization as a whole, by virtue of the fact that he or she is a member of the organization. In the case of organizational misconduct, every member of the organization can be held accountable. The major difficulty with collective accountability lies with its moral appropriateness. Collective arrangements of personal accountability are barely reconcilable with legal and moral practices and intuitions in current modern democracies. A collective accountability strategy is appropriate and effective in specific circumstances only, for example with small, collegial public bodies, such as cabinets in various countries and, in some instances, the European Commission.

(n) Individual accountability: each for himself

During the judgement phase, which can involve the imposition of sanctions, hierarchical and collective accountability strategies often run up against moral objections because a proportional relation between crime and punishment is by no means always evident. Individual accountability, in which each individual official is held proportionately liable for his personal contribution to the wrongful conduct of the organization, is from a moral standpoint a far more adequate strategy. Under this approach, each individual is judged on the basis of his actual contribution instead of on the basis of his formal position. Individual officials will thus find it impossible to hide behind their organization or minister, while those in charge are not required to shoulder all the blame. This approach is characteristic of professional accountability. In the case of medical errors, individual physicians are called to account by the disciplinary tribunal, which attempts to establish precisely the extent to which the physician's individual performance satisfied professional standards.

5. Sources of the Principle of Accountability

The sources for the principle of accountability are first the classical ones: legislation, decisions, case law, and literature. The principle of accountability is also relevant in legislation, policy rules, case law, and reports of the Ombudsman and the Court of Audit. A specific law must be taken here as an example. The Government's Accounts Act is the basis for the financial audit and the efficiency audits which have to be made by public institutions and which are subject to control by the Court of Audit. Especially in the context of efficiency audits, there is a broader accountability check than on financial aspects. We read in the former Dutch Government's Account Act – which has been updated and came into effect 2018 - the following relevant articles in relation to the principles of accountability in the context of financial audits.

(a) Regularity audit

Part 2. Regularity audit

Section 51

1. The Court of Audit shall scrutinise:
   a. Our Ministers' financial management and the associated annual financial statements;
   b. the financial records kept for the said management and statements.
2. With regard to financial management, the Court of Audit shall examine whether commitments, expenditures and receipts have been made in accordance with budgetary legislation and other statutory provisions and whether in general the requirements of order and control have been met.
3. With regard to the annual financial statements, the Court of Audit shall examine whether they represent financial management accurately and are drawn up in accordance with the relevant requirements.
4. The Court of Audit shall set out its findings and its opinion on the financial management and the associated financial statements in the reports referred to in section 67 (2).

Section 52

With regard to the central government accounts and trial balance referred to in section 66 (2), the Court of Audit shall examine whether these documents are in keeping with the financial statements referred to in section 51 (1), and have been drawn up in accordance with the regulations issued for that purpose.

Section 53

1. In performing its duties, the Court of Audit may, without prejudice to its right to conduct its own audits, use of the results of audits conducted by others.
2. At the Court of Audit's request, Our Ministers shall supply it with the audit programmes of those charged with the audit function and shall give the Court of Audit full information on audit results by handing over reports or in such other manner as the Court of Audit may determine.

Section 54

1. In all sectors of central government, the Court of Audit may, in so far as it regards this as essential to the performance of its duties:
   a. examine the cash accounts for the monies and securities referred to in section 19 (1), in so far as Our Ministers are responsible for the management thereof;
   b. inspect records of stocks of non-monetary assets as referred to in section 19 (3);
   c. inspect books, documents and other information carriers in such manner as it may determine.
2. Our Ministers shall upon request supply the Court of Audit with any information which it regards as necessary for the performance of its duties.
3. In respect of secret budget sections, the provisions of subsections 1 and 2 shall be implemented by, and the information shall be supplied to, the President of the Court of Audit in person. Section 46 (2) and (3) shall not apply.
4. The President of the Court of Audit shall maintain confidentiality in respect of information supplied to him in connection with secret budget sections. He shall inform Our Minister concerned in person of his findings in so far as he considers this necessary.

Section 55

1. If, following an audit as referred to in section 51, the Court of Audit has any objection regarding the financial management or the associated statement, it shall notify Our Minister concerned of this objection.
2. Within one month of receiving such notification, Our Minister concerned shall inform the Court of Audit of the steps that may meet its objection.
3. On expiry of this period, the Court of Audit shall take its final decision and inform Our Minister concerned accordingly. If the Court of Audit maintains its objection, it shall also inform Our Minister of Finance accordingly.

Section 56

1. If, in its final decision, the Court of Audit maintains its objection and the objection relates to commitments, expenditures or receipts not according with budgetary legislation and other statutory provisions, then unless steps satisfactory to the Court of Audit have already been taken, a Bill introducing an Indemnity Act shall be submitted to the Lower House within two months.
2. If the Court of Audit finds that no such submission has occurred on expiry of the period referred to in subsection 1, it shall notify the Lower House accordingly.
3. If, in its final decision, the Court of Audit maintains its objection and the objection is not such as referred to in subsection 1, it shall record this fact in the report referred to in section 67 (2) and may also add a note to the central government financial statement.
4. Our Minister concerned shall make his standpoint concerning the objection referred to in subsection 3 known to the States General in additional explanatory notes to the financial statement.

(b) Efficiency audit

Part 3. Efficiency audit

Section 57

1. The Court of Audit shall devote attention to the efficiency of the management, organisation and policies of central government.
2. Our Ministers shall inform the Court of Audit in good time of efficiency audits instituted by them and of the results thereof.
3. Sections 53 (1) and 54 above shall apply mutatis mutandis.

(c) Other acts

Part 4. Other duties and powers

Section 58

The Court of Audit may institute certain audits at the request of either House of the States General.

6. Conclusions

For our conclusions, we follow Bovens' line of thought in his publications. The step from purely financial accounting to public accountability offers audit offices a chance to emancipate themselves from their somewhat dull bookkeeping background. They can enhance their public legitimacy by taking up new roles, for example, the vigilant public accountant who watches over the efficiency and effectiveness of public programmes. We see such developments at the national level as well as at the EU level.

These new roles require new skills, however. Establishing the effectiveness of policies and programmes often requires a variety of sophisticated evaluation techniques that may also vary within the sector that is being evaluated. Old-fashioned financial accounting or legal scrutiny will not suffice. Audit offices have to establish multidisciplinary teams and interdisciplinary understanding becomes more important.

Some of these new roles may also create new dilemmas. Auditors may find it difficult to combine both the traditional accounting role and the new role, where they have to apply the principle of accountability in the context of the principles of good governance. Establishing the effectiveness and the accountability of public policies and programmes also moves audit offices into the realm of policy evaluation. Nevertheless, it will be important to evaluate based on objective criteria, such as the principles of good governance.

The step from financial accounting to public accountability therefore puts audit offices in the political spotlight. They have to account for themselves as well, for the standards they apply—the principles of good governance—and for the sophistication and independence of their judgement at the risk of decreased government legitimacy.

12

The Principle of Human Rights

The term 'human rights' has different meanings and is used in many academic subjects. It is used by lawyers and politicians, by philosophers and theologians, and, more generally, by the public. The term is used to denote a broad spectrum of very diverse rights, ranging from the right to life to the right to a cultural identity. They involve all elementary preconditions for an existence worthy of human dignity. These rights are ordered and specified in different ways.

Often a distinction is made between civil and political rights on the one hand and economic, social, and cultural rights on the other. Some also add collective rights as a third group. The first group is related to restricting the powers of the state in respect of the individual. The second group often requires governments to intervene actively in order to create good conditions for human development, such as employment, education, and healthcare.

When we speak about the right to good governance, we have to distinguish between the right as such and the underlying norms which are part of the principles of good governance: properness, transparency, participation, effectiveness, and accountability. This means that the underlying norms of the right to good governance are also related to these five principles.[1]

The inclusion of human rights as one of these principles here is to make it more explicit that this is not only a subjective right for the citizens but also an obligation for the government. The right and the obligation are two sides of the same coin.

1. Development of the Principle of Human Rights

Human rights and its corresponding principle have been developed as a result of the common and universal confidence that the dignity of each person must be respected. We find in the preamble of the Universal Declaration of Human Rights: 'Whereas recognition of the inherent dignity and of the equal and inalienable rights of all members of the human family is the foundation of freedom, justice and peace in the world.'

The emergence of the right to good administration, as the right to good governance is called in the European Union, represents the establishment of a new fundamental right. The great role of the EU at this point must be emphasized. In the EU, this concept applies to 'every person' coming into contact with the Union's institutions and bodies.[2] The principle of good administration has been developed by the jurisprudence of the Court of Justice of the European Union and is based on the existence of a community governed by the rule of law.[3]

The European Ombudsman is authorized to receive complaints in cases of maladministration by the institutions of the European Union. In April 2000, the Ombudsman made a recommendation that contained the principles to be included in a code of good

[1] Addink 2008, 305–8; Hirsch Ballin 2000; Wakefield 2007.
[2] Kańska 2004.
[3] Tridimas 2006.

Good Governance: Concept and Context. Henk Addink. © Henk Addink 2019. Published 2019 by Oxford University Press.

administrative conduct, applicable to the civil servants of institutions and bodies of the European Union, in their relations with the public. The Commission has added a code of this type in an appendix to its internal regulations, in the context of the reform of its services and operations. The other institutions and bodies of the Union have also adopted a code of good administrative conduct based on the Ombudsman's recommendations, or are in the process of doing so.[4]

2. The Concept of the Principle of Human Rights

The underlying ideas of human rights have a long history and can be found in ancient Greek philosophy and in various world religions. In the eighteenth century, the concept of human rights emerged as an explicit category and was seen as a basic precondition for an existence worthy of human dignity. The term 'human rights' appeared in the American Declaration of Independence of 1776, which referred to inalienable rights, as well as in the French *Declaration des Droits de l'Homme et du Citoyen* in 1789. The idea of basic rights originated from the need to protect the individual against the arbitrary use of state power. There are different categorizations in relation to human rights. On the international level, a distinction is usually made between civil and political rights on the one hand, and economic, social, and cultural rights on the other. Another distinction is made between classic rights (rights which restrict the powers of the state in respect of the individual) and social rights (rights which often require governments to intervene actively). Finally, some people talk of generations of rights. The first are civil and political rights, the second are economic, social, and cultural rights, and the third-generation rights are called the solidarity rights, like the right to peace and the right to a clean environment.

Human rights can be found in national constitutions and in international treaties. For international human rights, the relationship between international law and national law is relevant. Here the terms monism and dualism are used to describe this relationship. From the perspective of monism, the internal and international legal systems form a unity. Depending on whether a state has a monist or dualist legal system, the influence of international human rights on the national system is more direct or indirect.

The concept of the right to good governance can best be explained by looking at the text of the Charter of Fundamental Rights of the European Union. In it we find the right to good administration in article 41:

1. Every person has the right to have his or her affairs handled impartially, fairly and within a reasonable time by the institutions and bodies of the Union.
2. This right includes:
   - the right of every person to be heard, before any individual measure which would affect him or her adversely is taken;
   - the right of every person to have access to his or her file, while respecting the legitimate interests of confidentiality and of professional and business secrecy;
   - the obligation of the administration to give reasons for its decisions.
3. Every person has the right to have the Community make good any damage caused by its institutions or by its servants in the performance of their duties, in accordance with the general principles common to the laws of the Member States.

[4] Diamandouros 2007.

4. Every person may write to the institutions of the Union in one of the languages of the Treaties and must have an answer in the same language.

3. Specification of the Concept

Many human rights require action on behalf of the government. These activities relate to the duties to respect, protect, and fulfil human rights.[5] There are many rights, like the economic and social rights, which provide the conditions necessary for prosperity and well-being. More generally speaking, many economic, social, and cultural rights are related to the activities of the government and to governance in a broader perspective. It does not mean that everything has to be done by the government itself. The government has the responsibility to create the right framework and a good climate to enable the civil society to fulfil human rights and its aims.

Both groups of norms for the government—human rights norms and good governance norms—can only be realized by each other, so these norms are complementary to each other. Human rights need good governance and good governance needs human rights. This means that there is an interaction between these two types of norms and several of these norms are the same. For example, the principles of transparency and participation, which are principles of good governance, can be found in several international human rights treaties. In the literature,[6] participation (and especially transparency) in the context of access to information is still recognized as a human right. I think the principle of human rights administration is important because, in a way human rights can restrict several principles of good governance. For instance, transparency can be restricted due to national security or right to a private life.

In this context, an interesting development is that several of these principles of good governance, like the participation or the transparency principle, are reflected in human rights. In this case, the principles of good governance are strengthened because of the legally binding nature of the human rights contained in international treaties. This development can be observed for several good governance principles. It is therefore not surprising that the right to good governance in general has emerged. This right to good governance has been included and elaborated in 2000 by the Nice Charter on Fundamental Rights of the European Union. This Charter became binding for all EU member states through the Treaty of Lisbon, which entered into force in 2009 in all EU countries, except for Poland and Great Britain. These countries did not accede to the Charter by signing an additional protocol of the Treaty of Lisbon. Thus, we can conclude that there is a clear interaction between the principles of good governance and the right to good governance.

The principle of good administration has been developed by the jurisprudence of the Court of Justice of the European Union and is based on the existence of a community governed by the rule of law. Paragraph 1 of the article about the right to good administration reaffirms this general right, the essential elements of which are elaborated in paragraph 2. The right to good administration arises from a concern for equal treatment, in accordance with the jurisprudence of the Court, and with

[5] UNHR Office of the High Commissioner for Human Rights, 'What are human rights', see <http://www.ohchr.org/en/issues/Pages/WhatareHumanRights.aspx>.

[6] Hins and Voorhoof 2007.

the right to an effective remedy (article 47 of the Charter) as well as rights which go with it—the right to be heard and the right for each person to access his or her file. This right to an effective remedy is also contained in article 2 of the International Covenant on Civil and Political Rights and article 13 of the European Convention on Human Rights. The institutions' obligations arise from the provisions of general EU treaties.

4. Institutions Involved

Here we will specify several institutions that achieved significant developments in what concerns the concept of human rights. These institutions are the United Nations, the Council of Europe, and the European Union, and we will mention here some important documents produced by these institutions.

(a) United Nations

In the International Covenant on Civil and Political Rights (ICCPR) we read:

Article 2, paragraph 3:
Each State Party to the present Covenant undertakes:

a) To ensure that any person whose rights or freedoms as herein recognized are violated shall have an effective remedy, notwithstanding that the violation has been committed by persons acting in an official capacity;
b) To ensure that any person claiming such a remedy shall have his right thereto determined by competent judicial, administrative or legislative authorities, or by any other competent authority provided for by the legal system of the State, and to develop the possibilities of judicial remedy;
c) To ensure that the competent authorities shall enforce such remedies when granted.

Furthermore, we find norms of good governance at the UN level in the Code of Conduct for Law Enforcement Officials, adopted by the General Assembly on 17 December 1979 (Resolution 34/169), where we read in article 7: 'Law enforcement officials shall not commit any act of corruption. They shall also rigorously oppose and combat all such acts.'

In addition, we also find relevant norms in the Convention Against Transnational Organized Crime, of 15 December 2000 and in the Convention Against Corruption of 31 October 2003. The former UN Commission on Human Rights (the predecessor of the current UN Human Rights Council) adopted Resolution 2000/64 on 'The role of good governance in the promotion of human rights'. In that resolution, the Commission identified the key attributes of good governance: transparency, responsibility, accountability, participation, and responsiveness to the needs of the people. In Resolution 2005/68, the role of good governance in the promotion and protection of human rights has been further elaborated.

(b) Council of Europe

Several articles of the European Convention for the Protection of Human Rights and Fundamental Freedoms are relevant. In this context, a key provision is Article 13, the right to an effective remedy:

Everyone whose rights and freedoms as set forth in this Convention are violated shall have an effective remedy before a national authority notwithstanding that the violation has been committed by persons acting in an official capacity.

The Committee of Ministers of the Council of Europe made the following Recommendations related to Good Governance: Resolution (97) 7 of 1 April 1997 (on local public services and the rights of their users) and Resolution (2000) 10 of 11 May 2000 (on codes of conducts for public officials).

(c) Other general sources

The following articles from international documents are part of the six principles of good governance which have been discussed in this book, and therefore they are also part of the right to good governance:

- Article 2 International Covenant on Civil and Political Rights.
- Article 7 Code of Conduct for Law Enforcement Officials, adopted by General Assembly of 17 December 1979 (Resolution 34/169).
- Article 13 European Convention for the Protection of Human Rights and Fundamental Freedoms.
- Article 41 Charter of Fundamental Rights of the European Union.

The following articles from international declarations and treaties are specifically related to the principle of properness:

- Article 1 Universal Declaration of Human Rights.
- Article 2 International Covenant on Civil and Political Rights.
- Article 3 International Covenant on Economic, Social and Political Rights.
- Article 14 European Convention for the Protection of Human Rights.

The following articles apply specifically to the principle of participation:

- Articles 8 and 11 Universal Declaration of Human Rights.
- Article 14 International Covenant on Civil and Political Rights.
- Articles 6, 13, and 16 European Convention for the Protection of Human Rights.

Some relevant articles in European Union Law

- Article 1 Treaty of the European Union: 'This Treaty marks a new stage in the process of creating an ever closer union among the peoples of Europe, in which decisions are taken as openly as possible and as closely as possible to the citizen.'
- Article 24 (4) TFEU: 'Every citizen of the Union may write to any of the institutions or bodies referred to in this article or in article 13 of the Treaty on European Union in one of the languages mentioned in article 55(1) and have an answer in the same language.'
- Article 253 EC Treaty: 'Regulations, directives and decisions adopted jointly by the European Parliament and the Council, and such acts adopted by the Council or the Commission, shall state the reasons on which they are based and shall refer to any proposals or opinions which were required to be obtained pursuant to this Treaty.'
- Article 288 EC Treaty: 'In the case of non-contractual liability, the Community shall, in accordance with the general principles common to the laws of the Member States, make good any damage caused by its institutions or by its servants in the performance of their duties.'
- Helsinki European Council, 10 and 11 December 1999; Presidency conclusions:

'Effective institutions:

- 21. The European Council recalls its commitment in support of reforming the Commission's administration, especially financial and personnel management, in order to enhance efficiency, transparency and accountability and thus ensure the highest standards of public administration. The Commission will present a comprehensive programme of administrative reforms in early 2000. The European Council calls for rapid implementation of these administrative reforms.'
- White Book of 1 March 2000, concerning the reform of the Commission. COM (2000) 200.
- Recommendation of the European Ombudsman of 11 April 2000, following an own initiative inquiry into the existence and the public accessibility, in the different Community institutions and bodies, of a Code of Conduct on good administrative behaviour of the officials in their relations with the public. At the EU level, several codes of Good Administrative Behaviour have been accepted.

The actions of EU institutions foster respect for the law in the performance of administrative tasks. The non-judicial function mainly concerns the fight against corruption, which constitutes an infringement on equal treatment. The second concern is the establishment of rules of good administrative behaviour. This second point is directly linked to the role of the Ombudsman appointed by the European Parliament, who reviews complaints relating to maladministration by EU institutions and bodies (article 195 EC Treaty), which can be lodged by any citizen of the Union (article 21 EC Treaty) or by any physical or legal person residing or having its registered office in a member state. The right to apply to the Ombudsman of the Union is written down in article 43 of the EU Charter of Fundamental Rights.

(d) European Parliament's resolutions

The European Parliament adopts Annual Resolutions on the Situation of Fundamental Rights in the European Union. In some of these resolutions,[7] the European Parliament recommended that codes similar to the code of good conduct proposed by the European Ombudsman be adopted in the near future by all EU institutions and decentralized bodies. It also recommended that the principle of public service neutrality be included in the codes of good conduct adopted by the member states and European institutions, together with the principles of fairness and impartiality which should guide any administration. Finally, several resolutions[8] drew attention to the major role played by the European Ombudsman in applying the principle of good administration and access to documents.

5. Sources of the Principle of Human Rights

Table 12.1 gives a good overview of the articles from international human rights declarations as well as treaties in which issues of good governance have been reflected:

In most situations, the implementation of human rights can only be realized by way of the principles of good governance. In addition to international regulations on good governance and human rights, international human rights courts have also made important contributions to good governance. An example is the case law of the ECtHR,

[7] Resolution A5-0050/2000 of 16 March 2000 Report Harder (1998–1999); Resolution A5-0223/2001 of 5 July 2001 Report Cornillet (2000).

[8] Resolution A5-0451/2002 of 15 January 2003 Report Swiebel (2001) and Resolution A5-0281/2003 of 4 September 2003 Report Sylla (2002).

Table 12.1 Overview of the articles from international human rights declarations as well as treaties in which issues of good governance have been reflected

Treaty	UDHR	ICCPR	ICESCR	ECHR	ESC
Due care		(13)		6(1) (due care)	
Legal certainty			4, 8(1d), (2)		
Equality	1, 2	3, 14(1)	Preamble par. 2, 2(2), 3, 7bi	14	20, 27
Public participation	6, 8, 14(1), 21(1), (2), 29(1)	6, 9(4), (5), 13, 16, 25		5(4), 6(3b-e), 13, EP3	15, 22
Transparency		8, 40 ff			21, 29
Accountability	30	1, 5, 40 ff		19ff	
Effectiveness	22, 25(1)	2, 3, 17(2), 22(3), 23(4)		5(2), (3), 13, 17	
General			Preamble para 2, 2(3)	1 (shall secure), 2(1) (protected by law)	Part I

which often partly relates to the way in which governmental institutions have reached their decisions. The ECtHR asks if institutions balance all relevant interests in a proper way, if their action is proportional, and the like. This is already reflected in one of the underlying ideas of the European Convention of Human Rights: the rule of law. The case law of the Court makes it clear that the rule of law regulates the relationship between the powers distinguished in the democratic principle of *trias politica*, or separation of powers. From the rule of law, the Court distils requirements for states, such as consistent patterns of decision-making, legitimacy, and legal certainty, and formal protection of legal interests. If we look at the substantive rights, we see that they are structured in such a way that the freedom of the individual always comes first. When the state interferes with this freedom, it always needs to justify its action. This has important consequences for the power of the government to intervene in this freedom and, from the point of view of administrative law and procedural administrative law, for the law of evidence. Another important aspect is that, in the rights contained in the European Convention, the Court has not only recognized negative obligations, but also positive ones. For instance, the Court has interpreted the substantive Convention rights so that they also imply procedural protection. The most essential in this sense is perhaps the obligation to involve a person whose Convention rights are infringed upon in the decision-making process. Intrinsically, the Convention rights place the obligation upon the national authorities to apply a fair balance between the public interest involved and the private interest affected.

(a) Sources: case law of the European Court of Justice

This part contains a selection of the case law of the European Court of Justice in relation to different aspects of the right to good administration. Specifically, the following rights have been developed: the right of every person to have his or her affairs handled impartially, fairly, and within a reasonable time by the institutions and bodies of the Union; the rights of the defence in a preliminary enquiry; the right to a fair trial; the right to remain silent whilst subject to a Commission enquiry; the right of every person to have access to his or her file; the right to state adequate reasons for decisions; and the right to compensation. For each right we will give only a summary of one case as an illustration.

Every person has the right to have his or her affairs handled impartially, fairly, and within a reasonable time by the institutions and bodies of the Union. In the case *Solvay and Cie v Commission of the European Communities*,[9] it was held that the rights of the defence, as a fundamental principle, must be observed not only in administrative procedures which may lead to the imposition of penalties, but also during preliminary inquiry procedures which may be decisive in providing evidence of the unlawful nature of conduct engaged in by undertakings and for which they may be liable.

The right of defence in a preliminary enquiry was in discussion in the case of *Technische Universität München v Hauptzollamt München-Mitte*.[10] In order to be able to fulfil its tasks, the Commission must have a power of appraisal which respects the rights guaranteed by the European legal order in administrative procedures of fundamental importance. It was decided that those guarantees include, in particular, the duty of the competent institution to examine carefully and impartially all the relevant aspects of the individual case and the right of the person concerned to make his views known and to have an adequately reasoned decision.

The broader right to a fair trial was discussed in the case of *Fiskano AB v Commission of the European Communities*.[11] The observance of the right to be heard is, in all proceedings initiated against a person which are liable to culminate in a measure adversely affecting that person, a fundamental principle of European law which must be guaranteed even in the absence of any rules governing the procedure in question.

The right to remain silent whilst subject to a Commission enquiry is an element in the case *Kish Glass and Co Ltd v Commission of the European Commission*.[12] Once the Commission decides to proceed with an investigation of a complaint referred to it, it must, in the absence of a duly substantiated statement of reasons, conduct it with the requisite care, seriousness, and diligence so as to be able to assess with full knowledge of the case the factual and legal particulars submitted for its appraisal by the complainants.

Of importance is also the right of every person to have access to his or her file, which was in discussion is the case *F v Commission of the European Communities*.[13] In the right to have access to one's file, in the instance of a disciplinary procedure, the *audi alteram partem* principle is applicable in proceedings. An example is for those who are before the disciplinary board, it requires that an official accused of misconduct should have knowledge of all the facts on which the opinion of the disciplinary board has been based. That should be done in such a way that there is sufficient time to submit his observations.

The obligation to state adequate reasons for decisions was an element in the case *Stork Amsterdam BV v Commission of the European Communities*.[14] The extent of the

[9] ECJ 18 October 1989 C-27/88, *Solvay/Commission*, ECR 1989, 3355.

[10] ECJ 21 November 1991 C-269/90, *Technische Universität München v Hauptzollamt München-Mitte*, ECR I-05469.

[11] ECJ 29 June 1994 C-135/92, *Fiskano AB v Commission of the European Communities*, ECR I-02885.

[12] ECJ 30 March 2000 T-65/96, *Kish Glass and Co Ltd v Commission of the European Communities*, ECR II-01885.

[13] ECJ 29 January 1985 C-228/83, *F v Commission of the European Communities*, ECR 1985, 00275.

[14] ECJ 17 February 2000 T-241/97, *Stork Amsterdam BV v Commission of the European Communities*, ECR II-00309.

obligation to state reasons depends on the nature of the measure in question and on the context in which it was adopted. The statement of reasons must disclose the reasoning of the institution in a clear and unequivocal fashion and in such a way as to give the persons concerned sufficient information to enable them to ascertain whether the decision is well founded or whether it is vitiated by a defect which may permit its legality to be contested, and to enable the Community judicature to carry out its review of the legality of the measure.

Finally, the right to compensation is part of the case of *Laboratoires pharmaceutiguees Bergaderm SA and Jean-Jacques Goupil v Commission of the European Communities*:[15]

Liability of the Member States: The conditions under which the European Union may incur non-contractual liability for damage caused by its institutions or by its servants in the performance of their duties cannot, in the absence of a particular justification, differ from those governing the liability of the State for damage caused to individuals by a breach of Community law. The protection of the rights which individuals derive from Community law cannot vary depending on whether a national authority or a Community authority is responsible for the damage.

(b) National sources of the fundamental right to good administration

Here follows a selection of national norms and regulations related to the fundamental right to good administration:

Charter of Fundamental Rights and Freedoms of the Czech Republic

Article 36

2) Anybody who claims that his or her rights have been violated by a decision of a public administration organ may turn to a court for a review of the legality of such decision, unless the law provides differently. However, review of decisions affecting the fundamental rights and freedoms listed in the Charter may not be excluded from the jurisdiction of courts.
3) Everybody is entitled to compensation for damage caused to him or her by an unlawful decision of a court, another organ of the State or public administration, or through wrong official procedure.
4) The conditions and detailed provisions in this respect shall be set by law.

Constitution of the Italian Republic

Article 113

It shall always be permitted to bring a legal case against a decision taken by the public administration before an ordinary or administrative court, in order to protect one's own rights under civil or administrative law.

[15] ECJ 4 July 2000 C-352/98 P, *Laboratoires pharmaceutiques Bergaderm SA and Jean-Jacques Goupil v Commission of the European Communities*, ECR I-05291.

Constitution of the Republic of Lithuania

Article 25

The human being shall have the right to have his own convictions and freely express them.

The human being must not be hindered from seeking, obtaining, and imparting information as well as ideas.

Freedom to express convictions, as well as to obtain and impart information, may not be restricted other than by law, if it is necessary to protect the health, honour and dignity, private life, and morals of a human being, or to defend constitutional order.

Freedom to express convictions and impart information shall be incompatible with criminal actions—the instigation of national, racial, religious, or social hatred, violence and discrimination, slander and disinformation.

The citizen shall have the right to obtain any available information which concerns him from State institutions in the manner established by law.

Article 33

Citizens shall have the right to participate in the government of the State both directly and through their democratically elected representatives, as well as the right to enter into the State service of the Republic of Lithuania under equal conditions.

Citizens shall be guaranteed the right to criticise the work of State institutions or their officials, and to appeal against their decisions. Persecution for criticism shall be prohibited.

Citizens shall be guaranteed the right to petition; the procedure for its implementation shall be established by law.

Constitution of the Republic of Hungary

Article 57

'(5) In the Republic of Hungary everyone may seek legal remedy, in accordance with the provisions of the law, to judicial, administrative or other official decisions, which infringe on his rights or justified interests. A law passed by a majority of two-thirds of the votes of the Members of Parliament present may impose restrictions on the right to legal remedy in the interest of, and in proportion with, adjudication of legal disputes within a reasonable period of time.'

Republic of Austria—Federal Constitutional Laws

Article 18(1)

The entire public administration shall be based on law.

Article 23(1)

The Federation, the Laender, the districts, the municipalities and the other bodies and institutions established under public law are liable for the injury which persons acting on their behalf in execution of the laws have by illegal behaviour culpably inflicted on whomsoever.

Constitution of the Republic of Poland

Article 51

1. No one may be obliged, except on the basis of statute, to disclose information concerning his person.

2. Public authorities shall not acquire, collect nor make accessible information on citizens other than that which is necessary in a democratic state ruled by law.
3. Everyone shall have a right of access to official documents and data collections concerning himself. Limitations upon such rights may be established by statute.
4. Everyone shall have the right to demand the correction or deletion of untrue or incomplete information, or information acquired by means contrary to statute.
5. Principles and procedures for collection of and access to information shall be specified by statute.

Article 61

1. A citizen shall have the right to obtain information on the activities of organs of public authority as well as persons discharging public functions. Such right shall also include receipt of information on the activities of self-governing economic or professional organs and other persons or organizational units relating to the field in which they perform the duties of public authorities and manage communal assets or property of the State Treasury.
2. The right to obtain information shall ensure access to documents and entry to sittings of collective organs of public authority formed by universal elections, with the opportunity to make sound and visual recordings.
3. Limitations upon the rights referred to in paras. 1 and 2 above, may be imposed by statute solely to protect freedoms and rights of other persons and economic subjects, public order, security or important economic interests of the State.
4. The procedure for the provision of information, referred to in paras. 1 and 2 above shall be specified by statute, and regarding the Sejm and the Senate by their rules of procedure.

Article 63

Everyone shall have the right to submit petitions, proposals and complaints in the public interest, in his own interest or in the interests of another person—with his consent—to organs of public authority, as well as to organizations and social institutions in connection with the performance of their prescribed duties within the field of public administration. The procedures for considering petitions, proposals and complaints shall be specified by statute.

Article 77

1. Everyone shall have the right to compensation for any harm done to him by any action of an organ of public authority contrary to law.
2. Statutes shall not bar the recourse by any person to the courts in pursuit of claims alleging infringement of freedoms or rights.

Constitution of the Portuguese Republic

Article 22

The State and other public bodies shall be jointly and severally liable under the civil law, with the members of their organs, their officials and their personnel, for acts or omissions in the performance of their functions, or caused by the performance of their functions, which result in contravention of rights, freedoms or guarantees or in damage to another person.

Article 266

1. The Public Service shall work to promote the public interest, while observing the rights and interests of citizens that are protected by law.
2. The organs and officials of the Public Service are subject to this Constitution and the law, and shall perform their functions with full respect for the principles of equality, proportionality, fairness, impartiality and good faith.

Article 268

1. Citizens are entitled to be informed by the Public Service, when they so require, about the progress of proceedings in which they are directly interested and to know the final decisions that are taken with respect to them.
2. Citizens shall also enjoy the right to have access to administrative records and files, subject to the legal provisions with respect to internal and external security, investigation of crime and personal privacy.
3. Administrative action shall be notified to interested parties in the manner prescribed by law; it shall be based on stated and accessible substantial grounds when it affects legally protected rights or interests.
4. Interested parties are guaranteed effective protection of the courts for their legally protected rights or interests, including recognition of these rights or interests, challenging any administrative action, regardless of its form, that affects these, enforcing administrative acts that are legally due and adopting appropriate protective measures.
5. Citizens are also entitled to object against administrative regulations that have external validity and that are damaging to their legally protected rights or interests.
6. For the purposes of paragraphs 1 and 2, the law shall fix the maximum period within which the Public Service must respond.

Article 271

1. Officials and other personnel of the State and other public bodies shall be responsible in civil, criminal or disciplinary proceedings for their acts or omission when performing their functions for actions that result in infringements of the rights or interests of citizens that are legally protected; no action or proceedings in respect of these matters shall be dependent, at any stage, on the prior approval of a superior authority.

6. Conclusions

The right to good governance or good administration has not developed in isolation. Several principles of good governance were already developed in regulations and in codes which can be seen as the building blocks for the development of the right to good governance. There were even more developments since the controlling institutions, such as the European Ombudsman, have also developed these principles of good governance in different ways in their assessments of the activities of the administration. In parallel, specific rights such as the right to transparency and the right to participation are also in development.

PART III

IMPLEMENTATION OF THE PRINCIPLES OF GOOD GOVERNANCE ON THE NATIONAL, EU, AND INTERNATIONAL LEVEL

13

Implementation of the Principles of Good Governance on the National Level

General Discussion

In the study *Good Governance in the EU Member States*,[1] we investigated the interpretations and implementation of good governance and its principles in the EU member states, taking into account the different functions of government bodies. Good governance is of growing importance on a national level in the fulfilment of public tasks by the general public authorities, but also in relation to private institutions, when fulfilling tasks that are in the public interest. Good governance embodies norms which are relevant for the development of a well-functioning civil society in which people pursue not only their own interests but are also aware of common interests, in the context of the municipality, the district, and the state. The common interest is related to a society's underlying public values and it is directly linked to the concept of good governance. Good governance has a dual nature: the factual and the ideal.[2] It claims that good governance comprises both a real or factual dimension and an ideal or critical one. The factual dimension is represented by the realization of good governance as an administrative fact and the ideal dimension in the element of conceptual (moral) correctness. Once conceptual correctness is acknowledged as a necessary element, the picture fundamentally changes: a non-positivist concept of good governance evolves. So, the dual nature includes not only positivism but implies also non-positivism. An example is the situation that the administrative authorities are very careful in the process of collecting technical information about an application for an environmental licence but that is not enough. In the process in relation to this application more is needed—based on the concept of democracy—like the publication of information and the public participation of citizens. Good governance promotes cultural, economic, and social dynamics coherently within a society and in concrete situations. It is about libraries, schools of music, licensing related constructions, the environment, and the quality of schools and hospitals, among many other interests. It also sets out norms for the exercise of power in managing a country's economic and social resources for development and innovation. Good governance is the backbone of any modern European state.

During the preparation of this book, we also made some studies about good governance in states outside the European Union. Of course, there are important differences between and within continents; nevertheless, we can take a similar approach to other states in Africa, America, and Australia. These studies of the non-EU-states were somewhat restricted by the short preparation time, but were deeper and focused. The findings of these individual studies presented here are the results of using several contacts and student research, and we think these studies will make this book more complete.

[1] Addink 2015b. [2] Addink 2013, 243.

One of the new elements is also the attention to the issue of integrity in relation to the concept of good governance.

The literature on good governance often traces the origin of this concept to the international level. In the 1980s, we saw good governance applied by the IMF, the World Bank, and the United Nations in their relations with countries and dealing with the conditions which governmental institutions should have fulfilled. In their definitions of good governance, they incorporated their institutional aims. The consequence is that each international organization now has its own definition of good governance; therefore, it is useful to analyse and find the common elements of good governance on the international level. We will present more clearly the concept of good governance in its concrete sense inside and outside Europe. We found good governance norms specified in legislation, policy documents, and decisions of courts and other controlling institutions like the Ombudsman and the Court of Audit. In Europe, we will see that the EU member states gave an important impetus to the development of the concept of good governance and to its application by international and European institutions. This shows that the elements of good governance are rooted in national law developments. But the application of the concept and the principles can also be found outside Europe. A special point of attention is the link—in both theory and practice—between good governance and integrity.

1. Good Governance: The Need and the Practical Relevance

Before continuing this part, we need to know why we need the practice of good governance on a national level in different countries all over the world. It is acknowledged that the factual situation is not the same in every country, but there are some common arguments for most of the investigated countries. We also make the link between good governance and the quality of the government in countries.

The first argument for good governance in practice is preventing malfunctioning of state institutions, but there are more relevant factors such as:

- the problem of the fragmentation of legal norms, which impedes legal certainty and equality;
- the existing need for good governance regulations for new independent administrative authorities because of the risk of uncontrolled execution of governmental power;
- the complexity of modern society needs a highly qualified administration, with an open view to society;
- the link between the good governance norms applied by review-makers (like the judiciary and ombudsmen) and the norms developed and applied by regulators; and
- the development of good governance to prevent fraud and corruption, and to promote integrity.

As a response to weaknesses in their governance systems (also revealed by the economic crisis), many countries have taken a wide range of measures to strengthen good governance and to achieve sustained convergence, economic growth, and job growth. The key question is to what extent the newly introduced rules and case law have been effective in achieving their objectives, and to what extent they have contributed to progress in ensuring closer coordination of economic policies and sustained convergence of economic performances of states, while at the same time ensuring a high level of transparency, credibility, and democratic accountability.

Good governance is about the quality of the governance by those institutions which act in the public interest. But the question is: where can we find the concrete norms of good governance within the legal framework of states? We find these in the constitution or in the laws as developed by the legislator. An example is section 21 of the Finnish Constitution:

> Provisions concerning the publicity of proceedings, the right to be heard, the right to receive a reasoned decision and the right of appeal, as well as the other guarantees of a fair trial and good governance shall be laid down by an Act.

And section 124, which states that 'by delegating administrative powers to others than public authorities, the guarantees of good governance should not be endangered'. But these norms can also be found in administrative regulations, for example in the Netherlands' Code for Good Public Governance. Another example can be found in the judiciary's case law, like the decision of the International Court of Human Rights: in examining the conformity of a particular situation with the Convention on the Protection of Human Rights, the Court reiterates the particular importance of the principle of good governance.

In these examples, we recognize the two ways in which the principles have been developed; we speak in this context about the 'two sides of the same coin of good governance': the norm of good governance is both a rule for the administration, as well as for protecting the citizens. According to each institution's role and position there will be different specifications of the concept of good governance.

2. Concept and Principles of Good Governance and Integrity

The following three subjects are relevant in understanding the scope of good governance in practice (pertaining to the specification of this concept): the difference between good governance and good administration, the relation between good governance and integrity, and the concept and the specification by principles of good governance.

The administration is in essence only one of the three (or four) powers in the state (the executive power), and its principles of good administration are only those related to the executive powers. In a narrow sense (as used here), good governance is the situation in which one of the three (or four) powers makes a decision in relation to the activities of the administration.

Good governance and integrity have interrelated elements and partly overlap. Integrity has both a legal and a moral component and is focused (among others) on the actions and behaviour of the civil servants, the public authorities, or even the organization of these authorities. As such, integrity includes the following principles of good governance: properness, accountability, transparency, and sometimes human rights. But good governance is much wider, as it includes the principles of citizen participation and scrutiny, and also focuses on the human rights aspects of the conduct of state bodies and employees. In most of the country reports, attention has been given to the implementation of strategies for fighting and preventing corruption, particularly in relation to promoting integrity and good governance. We distinguish between a narrow and a broad view on integrity. In the narrow view, the focus is only on corruption, fraud, and theft. The broad view of integrity is related to the following activities and situations:

1. *Corruption*, including bribing, 'kickbacks', nepotism, cronyism, and patronage (with gain for oneself, family, friends or political party).
2. *Fraud and theft* of resources, including manipulation of information to cover up fraud.
3. *Questionable promises, gifts, or discounts.*
4. *Conflict of interest* through jobs and activities outside the organization (eg 'moonlighting').
5. *Improper use of violence* towards citizens or suspects.
6. *Other improper (investigative) methods of policing* (including improper means for achieving noble causes).
7. *Abuse and manipulation of information* (unauthorized and improper use of police files; leaking confidential information).
8. *Discrimination and (sexual) harassment* (indecent treatment of colleagues/citizens).
9. *The waste and abuse of organizational resources*, including time.
10. *Misconduct at leisure* (domestic violence, drunken driving, use of drugs etc).

Finally, the specification of the concept of good governance is made along the lines of the six most common principles: properness, transparency, participation, effectiveness, accountability, and human rights.[3] These principles are legal principles and can be enforced in different ways. They are articulated as a response to issues of malfunctioning of state institutions. Therefore, new principles can also be developed (such as the principle of integrity).

3. Studies on the Implementation of the Good Governance Principles. Main Elements of the EU Country and the Non-EU Country Studies

For the studies on the implementation of good governance, three elements were relevant: the research questions, the normative framework, and the methodology. We describe here the (structure of the) EU country studies, but their elements were *mutatis mutandis* applied in the studies for the other states.

The central point of the EU country studies was to answer the following question:

What interpretations and applications of good governance exist in the member states, taking into account the different functions of the governmental bodies?

Some related questions were:

1. What differences exist among the member states and how are conflicts between principles of good governance dealt with?
2. How do these supposed differences influence the agenda and attitude of member states as to European politics?
3. What are the problems and opportunities of this for the European Union?

[3] Addink, 2010a, 28; Addink, 2010b, 11–134.

These three questions are divided into six sub-questions:

- What interpretations of good governance exist in the member states and what are the underlying values (suitability, integrity, and transparency)? This sub-question is strongly related to the following sub-question:
- How are the principles of good governance applied in the member states? The findings are linked to the different nature of institutions involved in different activities.
- How are conflicting values balanced? It can often be the case that two principles of good governance conflict with each other. We expect that, when it comes to conflicts, member states will not always follow the same approach, because countries place different emphasis on different values.
- What is the influence of interpretations and applications of good governance in member states on their attitudes on the European level? This sub-question is discussed and will also connect to the following two sub-questions:
- What are the main differences between the various methods of interpretation and application of the principles of good governance?
- How could these be explained and what are the benefits and problems with regard to European politics?

The research questions have been approached from an interdisciplinary perspective.[4] Elaborating upon the sub-questions allows us to give sufficient account of the diverse aspects of good governance from the outset, as well as its meaning and underlying values and the multiple perspectives on good governance.

The research was divided into three steps. In September to November 2014 the twenty-eight country reports—based on individual desk studies—were written and sometimes with help from experts from these countries. The country reports all have the same structure. In December 2014 to February 2015, we asked the contact persons of the European Ombudsman in each of the twenty-eight countries—experts in these countries—to make comments on the written draft versions of the country reports. We received comments and suggestions from twenty contact persons. In February to March 2015, we finalized the country reports and made some general provisional conclusions based on these revised country reports. In April to May 2015, the report was written and finalized in September 2015.

4. Five Regions in Europe and Three Countries in Three Regions outside Europe: Africa (South Africa), America (Canada), and Oceania (Australia)—Three Groups of Values and Practices of Good Governance

The countries within and outside Europe have been investigated individually and, for cultural, social, and internal comparative reasons, were grouped differently.

In Europe we distinguished five regions:

Northern Europe (NE): Denmark, Finland, and Sweden;
Western Europe (WE): Belgium, Germany, France, the Netherlands, Austria, and Luxembourg;
Southern Europe (SE): Greece, Italy, Portugal, Spain, Cyprus, and Malta;
Central Europe (CE): Estonia, Latvia, Lithuania, Poland, Hungary, Slovenia, Croatia, Slovakia, the Czech Republic, Bulgaria, and Romania;
The United Kingdom and Ireland.

[4] Van Kersbergen and Van Waarden 2004, 143–71; Addink 2013.

Outside Europe we have especially studied the following three countries: Australia; Canada; and South Africa. These countries were chosen for practical reason but also because these countries are part of three different continents.

Relevant are the functions and structure of the state in relation to shifts in development of good governance. Good governance is a general concept consisting of three groups of values. The first group is that of rule of law values, the second group is that of democracy values; and the third group is that of modern institutional and constitutional values. These values can be seen as sources for the further development of the concept of good governance. The development of the concept of good governance has taken place along the same three distinct groups shown in Figure 13.1.

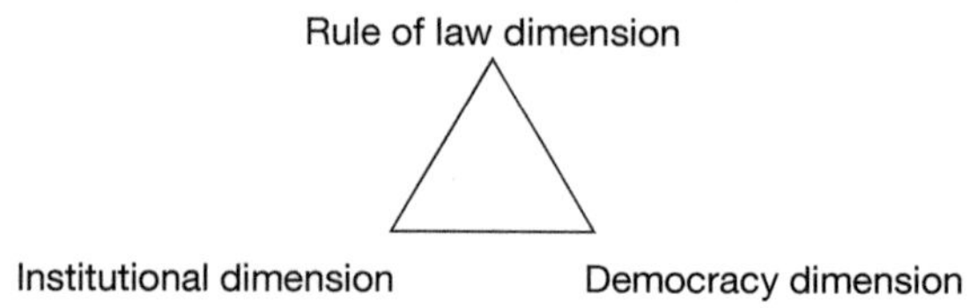

Figure 13.1 Good governance values

The three groups of values were further developed into six principles. The rule of law principles are properness and human rights, the democracy principles are transparency and participation, and the modern value principles are effectiveness and accountability. These principles are interlinked as shown in Figure 13.2.

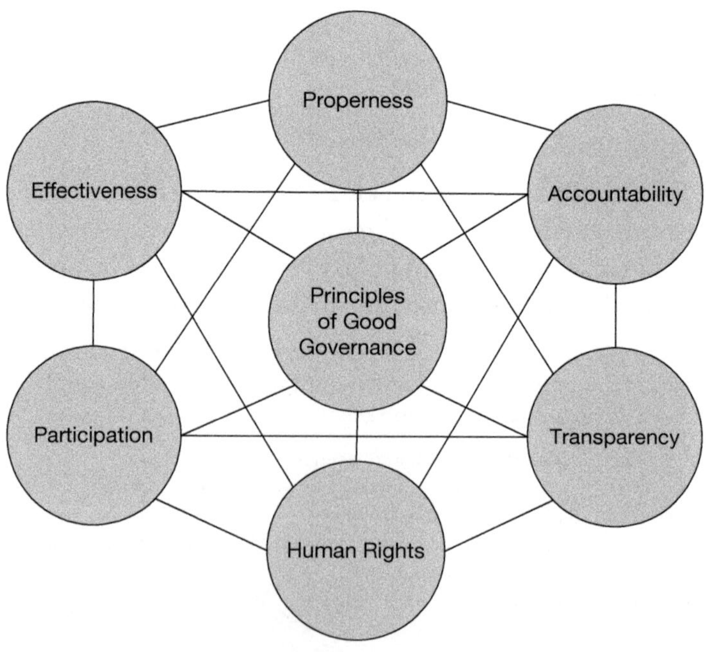

Figure 13.2 The principles of good governance

The principles of good governance have been developed in states by several institutions from different perspectives and each of them developing good governance norms. This development is strongly related to the function and structure of these institutions. The legislator mostly works on the development of generally binding regulations containing norms with an instrumental character and norms protecting citizens. The administration develops instrumental norms in regulations, including policy rules or internal directives which sometimes take the form of regulations or codes. The administration also develops norms in individual cases, for instance by requesting public participation in the decision-making process. The judiciary applies the principles of good governance in concrete cases by using them as norms for review. That is similar to how the Ombudsman works, producing informal solutions or reports. The Court of Audit applies these principles as review norms in relation to more general budget questions.

In a more instrumental way these principles are normative for the administration, but good governance principles are also developed by the controlling institutions as norms for review. The legislation and the administrative regulation (including the policy rules in which principles have been implemented) are more related to the instrumental dimension of good governance; the controlling function of the judiciary and the Ombudsman, and in a certain way also the Court of Audit, use good governance principles as review norms. Put more simply, the first and the second powers are more focused on the instrumental dimension of good governance and the third and the fourth powers are more focused on the controlling dimension of good governance.

These principles of good governance are partly unwritten, but we increasingly find them in a written form. This is done by institutions belonging to all four powers of the state. The legislator and the administration have a more instrumental character, while the judiciary and fourth powers are closer to the position of citizens. But they all produce good governance norms and they interact with each other. The good governance developments on the decentralized level are also very relevant in this context, as well as developments at the level of the European Union and international organizations.

(a) Practices and principles of good governance on a national level

We must look at what means are employed to pursue good governance and how these means are understood against the background of the whole national legal system. It is exactly at this point that underlying domestic values come into play. This is why each country should be studied separately first.

In the country reports based on individual study, each country was the subject of research. In the introduction of the report, attention was given to the geographical and historical development of the country, and the structure and the powers of the state. This information was relevant to finding out if the concept of good governance and its specification can be found in each country's system—and if so, where. The results of the government policies and actions were studied to find out how the principles of good governance are specified and how the instrumental and reviewing approaches of good governance interact. Not only these more general lines of specification of principles, but also concrete cases were described to understand more clearly how these principles were put into practice. These cases pertained to each of the following combination of policy fields: (1) health and/or social policy; (2) economic and/or financial policy; (3) environmental and infrastructure policy; (4) education policy and/or policy on justice. An indication of good governance is formulated based on this information.

A substantial relation is that between the application and the practical effect of good governance, understanding the concept of good governance is in the end the most essential. Therefore, it is necessary to emphasize the bond between values and principles. Good governance is put into practice through the principles of good governance. These principles may differ in character from one country to another, through the different ways in which the principles are included in different means of legislation and judicial interpretation. Principles are usually laid down in policy documents, which are not generally binding, but can have a binding effect when such documents bear a sufficiently formal character. However, policy documents that have no direct legal effect may still be to a certain extent binding through the principles of proper administration. A different situation exists when a Code is meant to be exemplary to other governmental institutions.

We have seen that good governance entails values for public governance, especially related to institutions fulfilling a public task. This concept manifests itself in several principles in different fields of study: legal principles, policy principles, and economic principles. Legal principles are divided into general principles and other principles. General principles refer to fundamental ideas concerning order in society. Yet even when principles are vague, they represent underlying values of the national legal system. As a consequence, these can be looked at when interpreting the law. Some other principles are not really fundamental, but yet invaluable and therefore normative to the legal system.

5. Different Developments in the Practices of Different Countries

For each of the three dimensions—rule of law/democracy/institutional—we made an illustration of two partly overlapping ovals or ellipses for the EU-member state study. Because of the overlap we created three options. In the first option, we have the original and more general concept of the dimension; in the second option is the full specification by principles; and in the third option of overlapping is a mix of general concept and specified principles. The rule of law concept contains properness and human rights, democracy contains transparency and participation, and the institutional concept contains effectiveness and accountability. For example, in relation to the rule of law dimension, in the general development there is a strong focus on legality, and the specific development by the properness and the human rights principles. The intermediate position is a mix of the general and specific development.

The next step was to find out what could be the position of the country: first, second, or third option. For each of the groups of the EU member states we start in alphabetical order. This positioning is based on the information gathered from this research and it is a theoretical position which may be subject to discussion. The idea of presenting the results in this way makes it possible to have a discussion within and between the member states on the developments and the shifts of the principles of good governance.

The theoretical positioning of countries is repeated for each of the five groups of countries, based on a certain level of cultural and social coherence. The discussion in practice will be centred around the following points: the institutions which apply good governance norms in relation to their functions; the developments of the concept by specification of principles of good governance; the form and binding effect of the specified principles (including the integrity principle); and the prevention of malgovernance (including corruption) by promoting good governance.

The next step was to find out, based on the country reports and the remarks from the national specialists—the ombudsman coordinators in each country—what the position of the country is. This positioning was done based on the information we received in the frame of this research and it is a theoretical position which may be subject to discussion. The idea of presenting the results in this way makes it possible to have a discussion within and between the member states on the developments and the shifts of the principles of good governance.

The theoretical positioning of countries is repeated for each of the five groups of countries. That was done because we saw within these groups of countries some level of cultural and social coherence and, based on that idea, we think that such a comparison will stimulate the same discussion in and between countries. The discussion in practice will be centred around the following points: the institutions which apply good governance norms in relation to their functions, the developments of the concept by specification of principles of good governance, the form and binding effect of the specified principles (including the integrity principle), and the prevention of malgovernance (including corruption) by promoting good governance.

In the coverall graphics we distinguish five phases of development of good governance: no concept, concept, concept principles, principles, and full principles. These five phases, shown in Figure 13.3 have been applied to the three dimensions of good governance: rule of law, democracy, and institutional structure.

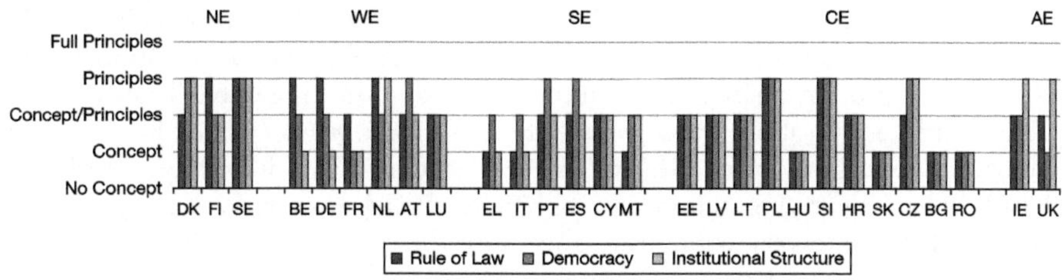

Figure 13.3 Five phases of good governance

6. Cases about the Implementation of Good Governance Principles

In the study, we paid attention to cases in different policy fields in the twenty-eight EU member states: public health, the economy, the environment, and education. This section offers an example from each of these policy fields.

An example of *good governance and public health policy* is found in Austria. The aim of the Austrian Federal Ministry of Health is to create a high level of transparency and solve issues concerning health insurance.[5] The SGI Network—an institution that reports and advises countries internationally on their good governance status in the core policies of the state[6]—has drawn up a report on the good governance status in Austria and concluded that Austrian health policies are some of the best in the world. The Network noted, however, that the healthcare system creates major inequalities for the population who cannot afford additional private health insurance. Another

[5] <http://www.bmg.gv.at/cms/home/thema.html?channel=CH1013>.

[6] <http://www.sgi-network.org>.

problem found is the division of responsibilities between the Federation (regulation on public health care insurance) and the (decentralized) Länder governments (funding hospitals), which created a disadvantage for both public and private hospitals.[7] This complexity causes higher expenditures, for both the state and the population, while the efficiency and effectiveness of the cooperation between the Federation and Länder decreases. The principles of effectiveness and accountability are thus significantly disadvantaged by this conflict.

The next case is about a court decision on *good governance and education policy* in Belgium.[8] Since France put in place numerous clauses for medical students, Belgium had to face an increasing number of students coming to the French part of Belgium to study. The parliament of the French community in Belgium adopted, in 2006, a decree limiting the number of foreign students allowed to stay and study in Belgium, making a distinction between inhabitants and non-inhabitants. French students petitioned the Constitutional court to cancel this decree, and the Constitutional court referred a preliminary question about the interpretation of some provisions to the European Court of Justice—relating to the easy access to education and prohibiting discrimination—of international treaties. The community argues that their students are a burden for the public finances. This is the point of the case law, and substantively the answer of the Court: different treatment can be justified in the light of the goal set for it. So long as discrimination can be justified, it is not an illegality. This establishes the principle of proportionality: human rights are not absolute; they have to be balanced against other considerations. Thus, the European Court of Justice (Grand Chamber) held that the provisions of the EU law conflict with the 2006 decree, unless the Constitutional court considers it as proportionate in relation to the goal of protecting public health.

The third case is about *good governance and environmental policy* in the Deep Geological Repository case.[9] The Czech Radioactive Waste Repository Authority (RAWRA) has been trying to find sites for high level nuclear waste for some years now, but has failed due to very strong resistance from the people in the villages chosen as possible sites. Upon the finding of a suitable site which is deemed safe for storing waste and spent fuel by geological assessment, the acceptance for the solution by the public (the affected villages) will be tested. Local level 'yes or no' referenda (a sub-principle of the good governance principle of participation) took place. All of the villages were heavily against hosting the Deep Geological Repository. This public participation prevents a misuse of power and allows the decision to be made by the communities. The group running the project, SURAO, will incentivize participation by financial contributions. There is also community level participation through the use of 'working groups', consisting of two representatives of the possible site, one representative of an environmental NGO, and two representatives with nationwide activities. These working groups are meant to strengthen transparency of the processes used to search for a site and take into account the interests of the public, which also helps to uphold human rights. These working groups also fulfil legal requirements: general principles for public participation based on the international Aarhus Convention on Access to Information, and rules for providing information on the state of the environment and

[7] <http://www.sgi-network.org/2014/Austria/Social_Policies>.

[8] CJEU (Grand Chamber) case C-73/08 13 April 2010, *Bressol, Chaverot and Others*/Cour constitutionnelle (Belgium).

[9] Nuclear Risk and Public Control, 'Questions of call to nuclear regulation SUJB Aarhus in the Nuclear Field in the Czech Republic', accessed online: <http://www.joint-project.org/experience_aarhus_cz.htm>.

natural resources according to the national and regional legislation. Thus, we can see that this case study implements a method of effective transparency and participation by clearly laying out their process and methodology concerning such a contentious area. This shows a vast cross section of administration and society working together and negotiating to achieve a common aim.

The last example is a case[10] on *good governance and economic policy* in Denmark. For a number of years, exporting companies have purchased large quantities of ground beef from a slaughter house and exported it to Arab countries. Pursuant to Community regulations, the exporter received approximately DKR 100 million by way of refunds. According to the relevant legislation, the amount of funds depended on the proportion of beef included in the composition of the product, namely 60 per cent in the present case. Subsequent investigations revealed that the beef content was in fact only 28 per cent. The Ministry sought to recover the refunds, but the exporters contended that they could not be held liable for the reprehensible conduct of the slaughter house, and it was in fact the responsibility of the Ministry and the customs to check the quality of the goods. The Eastern Regional Court upheld the exporters' point of view. The Ministry decided to refer several questions to the European Court of Justice. The findings of the ECJ were respected and followed by the Danish domestic court. The ECJ found that it would not be proportionate to make the exporter surrender his right to plead his good faith as regards the conformity of the goods with the description that was given in the declaration submitted. The Court upheld its decision that Community law does not preclude grounds for excluding repayment from being taken into account where these are related to the administration's own conduct. Therefore, the negligence of the state authorities with respect to the quality checks should be taken into account and this should preclude the repayment of the funds. Finally, the Court held that Community law does not preclude the national courts from taking into account the period of time that has elapsed since the payment of the aid. The principles of good governance developed in this case are proportionality and legitimate expectation.

These concrete examples illustrate the application and the importance of the principles of good governance for both governments and citizens in different policy fields.

7. Conclusions

Here we will come to some conclusions by answering the general research question and the six specified sub-questions. The sub-questions are drawn from the general research question, and their answers come in the form of conclusions and recommendations. The general research question is: what interpretations and applications of good governance exist in the member states, taking into account different functions of the governmental bodies?

The issue of good governance receives the attention of the EU member states, as supported by the fact that elements of history and culture relating to good governance can be traced back for decades. In the literature, it is said that the cultural dynamics led to several shared philosophical principles and that these principles should be the foundation of a European-wide dialogue on good governance. The results of this study contain the instruments for this dialogue.

[10] Case C-366/95 *Landbrugsministeriet v Steff-Houlberg Export and Others.*

Good governance is part of the modern state not only in Europe, but also in other parts of the world, not only on national and local levels, but also on the regional and international levels. This concept has been developed through its six principles. Good governance has a dual nature, comprising both a real (or factual) dimension, and an ideal (or critical) one and has to be studied based on an interdisciplinary view. There are several reasons to work on good governance: the prevention of maladministration (including corruption), the fragmentation of legal norms, the need for good governance norms for new independent administrative authorities, the needs of a highly qualified administration, the proper control of the administration and legal protection by courts, the good control by fourth power institutions like the Ombudsman and Court of Audit.

The theme of the study was developed through a theoretical framework and research questions. We have looked for interpretations and practices of good governance and underlying values. Attention was also paid to cases where, in applying these norms, different governmental institutions reveal differences in interpretation and application in the countries we examined, and which also influence the countries' attitudes at EU level. We distinguished three dimensions of good governance in the practice of the member states and noted that there are differences between the use of the terms *values* and *principles*, as well as the term *integrity*. It is interesting to notice that there are not only shifts in the different dimensions of good governance but also a shift in thinking about situations of violation of integrity norms.

From a theoretical perspective, two elements are particularly relevant for the concepts and the definitions in this research: the concepts of good governance and the concept of states—the latter being linked to government and (good) governance. We showed the differences in definitions between government and governance, governance and administration, principles of good governance and of proper administration, good governance and integrity.

We have developed an interdisciplinary approach of good governance and distinguished a factual and a normative line of good governance, and discussed the interaction between the two lines. Based on this normative framework we described the good governance situation in the twenty-eight EU member states, which we have divided into five regional groups.

We made a distinction between three dimensions of good governance: rule of law, democracy, and institutions. Within each of the three dimensions we distinguished between the following three developments: the general development, the specification, and the intermediate position. For example, in relation to the rule of law dimension: the general development in which there is a strong focus on legality, and the specific development by the properness and the human rights principles. The intermediate position is a mix of the general and specific development. Within each development we can distinguish between a written development in the constitution, the law or the regulations, and a development of (un)written principles by case law and/or in the literature.

(a) Specification of the conclusions by answering the research sub-questions

The first sub-question was: what interpretations of good governance exist in the member states of the EU and what are the underlying values (suitability, integrity, and transparency)? We can conclude that in all EU member states the concept of good governance is used as a norm for the activities of the administration, by the administration. It is mostly not applied as a norm for the other powers of the state: the legislator or the judiciary. Nevertheless, the two other powers are increasingly using and developing these norms for the administration. For that reason, we can speak about good governance here, but in a strict sense it is about good administration. In countries where corruption is an issue (which in a strict sense can be seen as a violation of the principle of prohibition on misuse of power), a link is also made with the principle of integrity. In the Netherlands, the violation of integrity has a broader application than for corruption situations, and we find there some links with the principles of good governance. In this research, we distinguished ten forms of violation of the integrity principle, which are directly related to the principles of properness, human rights, transparency, and accountability.

Our second sub-question was: how are the principles of good governance applied in the member states? In general, we conclude that in all the countries the concept of good governance by way of its principles is known and applied. In almost all the countries we find the three dimensions of the principles of good governance: rule of law, democracy, and institutions.

- For the rule of law dimension, in the Northern Europe countries there is a strong focus on the principles of properness and human rights (two of the three countries; one country was intermediate). In the Western Europe group, three countries focused on properness and human rights principles, while three were intermediate. In the Southern Europe group, the focus was more on the general line of the rule of law for three counties, while three other countries were intermediate. For the Central Europe group there was a mix in which five countries were intermediate, four countries more focused on the general rule of law line, and two countries more on the specification of properness and human rights. In the Anglo-Saxon Europe group, both countries were in the intermediate bracket.
- For the democracy dimension, in the Northern Europe group we found that two of the three countries had specified transparency and participation, while one country was intermediate. For the Western Europe group, most of the countries (four) were intermediate and one country was more focused on the general development of democracy, while another country was focused on the specification of transparency and participation. For the Southern Europe group, four of them were intermediate and two countries had a specification of transparency and participation. In the Central Europe group, four countries were intermediate, two focused on the general aspects of democracy and three on the specification of transparency and participation. In the Anglo-Saxon Europe group, one country focuses on the general aspects of democracy, while the other is intermediate.
- For the institutional dimension, in the Northern Europe group, one is intermediate, while one focuses on effectiveness and accountability. In the Western Europe group, three countries focus on the general aspects of the institutions and one country on the principles of effectiveness and accountability, while two are intermediate. In the Southern Europe group, most of the countries (four) are intermediate and two focus on the general aspects of the institutions. For Central Europe, we found four countries to be intermediate, four countries focusing on the general aspects of the institutions and three countries on the specific aspects of effectiveness and accountability. In the Anglo-Saxon Europe group, we found that both are focusing on the specification of effectiveness and accountability.

According to the following aspect, we had to answer the question: what differences exist as to the interpretation and application of good governance as to the different functions of government (policy development, implementation, supervision)? In relation to the three dimensions of good governance, we see that general aspects are often worked out in the constitution and general laws and regulations; this means there is an important role for the policy development and implementation components of the government. The specification of the dimensions by the development of principles is mostly initiated by the supervisory and controlling bodies of the government. After some time, we usually find codification of the specified principles in the general laws.

It is interesting to see that there are some differences in relation to each of the three dimensions. We find more often specification of the human rights, transparency, and participation principles; the specification of the properness sub-principles is lagging behind a little. The specification of the accountability and effectiveness principles is behind the properness principles. These differences can be applied *mutatis mutandis* for the five groups of Europe countries.

Another sub-question was: how are conflicting values balanced? It concerns choices in member states, but sometimes it also concerns cooperating countries differently weighing in on these values. Sometimes the legislator has already prevented the conflict in two ways: first by codifying one principle and not the other, or by giving priority to one principle over the other principles; the executive power also achieves that by making political priorities related to principles. So, the question is: how should apparent conflicts of principles be dealt with? Given the fact that there is no hierarchy whatsoever, other factors are decisive in balancing the principles. According to the Dutch legal system, principles could be more important—on a case-by-case basis—depending on their legal status. For example, principles that are laid down in international treaties or formal law need to be applied in several countries. Also, principles can be laid down in policy documents and may therefore be more important than principles that have no formal status. The rule is: the more a principle has a legal basis, the more likely it is that this principle outweighs other principles. Thereby, two other rules stem from case law. The first is that of specialty. In the case law, often a special rule has priority over a general rule, but that can be regulated differently in the law. The second rule is less explicit, but not less important. When a court voids a decision on the basis of so-called principles of procedure, a governmental body may come to the same decision, as long as it follows the correct procedure. This is not the case if the decision was made void on the basis of a principle affecting the merits. Therefore, it may be that the latter may prevail over procedural principles. But this balance is made on a case-by-case basis. Apart from these rules, might certain principles be more successful in certain situations? It should be assessed whether a certain conflict is general or particular in nature and if these conflicts can be solved according to the previously mentioned rules of the legal system. Also, the courts are doing this in two ways: by specifying a principle or by translating the principle in terms of a human right.

We also had to answer the following question: what is the influence of interpretations and applications of good governance in member states on their attitudes at the EU level? It is important whether the countries have a monistic or a dualistic system. In a monistic system, internationally binding norms are also directly enforceable in the national legal system; in a dualistic system, there is always a need for national transformation of international law into national norms before these norms have legal effect on a national level. In countries with a dualistic system, there is a more explicit discussion about the relation between the national and international norms and principles.

We see a growing attention for the national norms from these countries, in their position on a regional or international level.

The last sub-question was: what are the main differences in the interpretation and application of the principles of good governance? How could these be explained and what are the benefits and problems with regard to European politics? We see at the EU level a strong development by the Fundamental Rights Charter, in which we find a fundamental right of good administration. Also, the Court of Justice of the European Union is strongly developing the principles of EU law, of which the principles of good administration are a part. In the literature, there is a strong emphasis on the development of a European administrative act. The EU executive level is very fragmented: the European Parliament is strongly focused on a more integrative approach of the principles of good governance.

14

Implementation of the Principles of Good Governance on the National Level in the EU

We investigated the implementation of good governance in the EU member states (by interpretation and application), taking into account the different functions of government bodies. Good governance as a pivotal public value in each of the member states has fundamental roots in the different phases of European history. In these phases we find aspects of the rule of law, democracy, and the institutional state developing and becoming natural dimensions of good governance, a common public value for European states.

We found good governance norms developed in the member states sometimes in a general, abstract way, such as the concept of the rule of law, the notion of democracy, and the classical framework of constitutional institutions. There is, however, a tendency to specify these general dimensions of the good governance concept through principles, in some countries more than others. We discovered a *principles-based* development of policies in the member states, which is the key to good governance in these states. In different legal forms—constitutions, laws, policy papers, case law, and reports of ombudsmen and audit institutions—are the six specific aspects of the theoretical framework pertaining to Europe. These principles have been developed as legal principles by the (four) powers in the states of Europe, both as norms for the administration, as well as rights for citizens.

1. General Remarks and Results

In Northern Europe, Sweden had a strongly developed specification of the principles, but the other countries were not far behind. In Western Europe, the Netherlands, Germany, and Austria had a strong specification of the principles (though each country specified some principles better than others) and we found similar tendencies in the other countries. In Southern Europe, Spain and Portugal stand out regarding the specified development of the democracy principles. In Central Europe, Poland and Slovenia have developed the principles of good governance strongly, and the Czech Republic is also very close behind, while the other countries are all still on the same level. Finally, in the United Kingdom and Ireland, Ireland has developed these principles just slightly more than the United Kingdom.

The *general conclusion* is that there are differences in the focus of each of the three dimensions (rule of law, democracy, and institutional development) and to the extent to which principles have been developed—more focus on human rights and transparency than on accountability and effectiveness—between countries. But where countries developed these principles, we found coherence in the contents of the principles of good governance in the member states. Good governance in the EU member states is represented by *unity in diversity*.

In the research five phases have been applied to the three dimensions of good governance: rule of law, democracy, and institutional structure. The results are shown here in Figure 14.1.

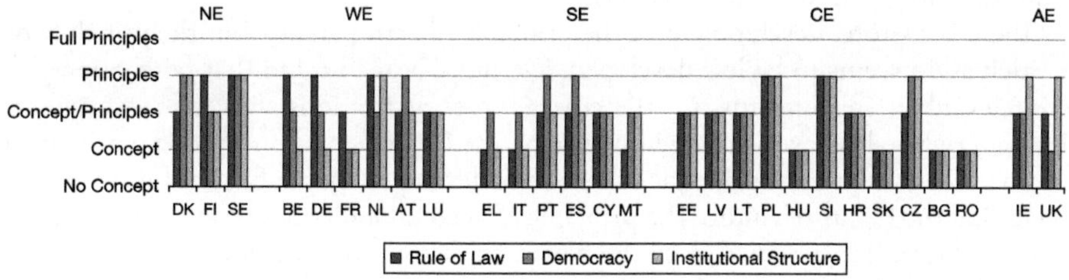

Figure 14.1 Application of the six principles of good governance in different policy fields

We investigated the application of the six principles of good governance in different policy fields. As illustrated in Figure 14.1 there is, *first*, a difference between the *instrumental* function of the principles in the frame of the specific policy fields, and their *protective* function when these are applied by reviewing institutions like the courts and the ombudsmen. Most principles started from the idea of developing protection. A *second* point of attention is that after some time there is a discussion about the extent of codification and harmonization of these in case-law-developed principles. On the one side, codification offers legal certainty and equality, on the other side, (un)written principles may leave room for case-specific interpretation by courts and ombudsmen which give space for flexibility. The *third* point is the relationship between the principles: is there a legal ranking of principles? We see that sometimes the legislator has given priority to one principle over another, while other times the court gives priority to the most specified principle.

The *final conclusion* of the research on principles of good governance is that a *bottom-up discussion* amongst the member states regarding similarities and dissimilarities in good governance norms is necessary. It will create more trust among member states, also enabling the states to shape the discussion on good governance in the context of the European Union. The ReNEUAL Model Rules can serve as a convenient framework for the discourse. The *confidence of all EU citizens and national authorities* in the functioning of good governance is particularly vital for the further economic, social, and cultural development of the member states.

In the following description we have focused more on the individual countries in each of the parts of Europe. So, our focus was not primarily the comparative part of the study, but the primary object of the study was to describe the situation of good governance in the individual countries and the roles of the institutions. And second—based on the individual description—we tried to make general conclusions also but only within each of the parts of Europe.

2. Implementation of Good Governance in Northern Europe

The good governance concept has been strongly implemented—see Figure 14.2—in the three Northern European countries, which are all unitary states.

In Finland we find the concept of good governance in the context of legal protection in the Constitution. In general, some of the six principles of good governance have been explicitly codified in the Constitution or in a General Administrative Procedure

Act, but most of the principles are developed in coordination, between two or more public institutions and probably by way of policy rules or case law in the three countries. There is also a strong influence related to these principles of good governance from the European to the national level.

There is a strong development of the principle of transparency, but the principle of participation seems to be less developed. We must bear in mind that both principles are relevant in creating trust for the citizens in their relations with the government. Human rights also have a strong influence on the implementation of good governance norms. The effectiveness principle is especially developed by the financial institutions, including the Court of Audit. The principle of accountability has been the least developed and least implemented in all the Northern European countries.

For Denmark it is remarkable how trust has been created by an active government taking the initiative and listening to public concerns. For Finland it is remarkable that all the principles are implemented in national regulations. For Sweden it is remarkable how it has proven the effectiveness of all of the principles of good governance.

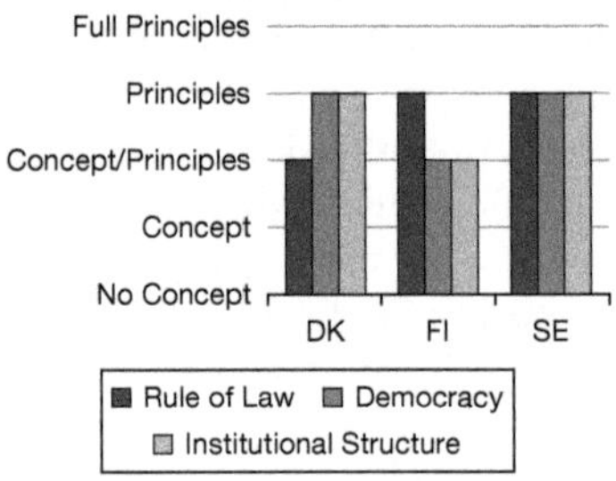

Figure 14.2 Good governance in Finland, Denmark, and Sweden

3. Implementation of Good Governance in Western Europe

The Western European countries are different in two ways. First, there are linguistic differences: Dutch (the Netherlands, Belgium I), French (Belgium II, Luxembourg, and France), and German (Germany and Austria). Second, from the perspective of the structure of the state, three countries have a unitary system (the Netherlands, Luxembourg, and France), and the other three have a federal system.

Looking at the legal basis for the principles of good governance, in some countries we find a rather broad codification (the Netherlands, Germany, and Austria). In Belgium, Luxembourg, and France these are codified in the Constitution or in the Administrative Procedure Acts. There is less codification of the principles because in the last-mentioned countries the judiciary (and ombudsman institutions) are more active in the developing of the principles of good governance. In all the countries, the Court of Audit is active in the development of the principles of accountability and effectiveness. Countries with a federal system show a stronger development of the principles of good governance on the local level, which is more independent from the central level. It seems that in smaller unitary states the central level is more active than in bigger states.

For an overview of the good governance principles in the Western European countries: see Figure 14.3.

In all these countries the principles of human rights are very strongly developed, especially in countries with more than one language (like Belgium). In most countries it seems that not too much attention is paid to the integrity aspects and their links to good governance; on the contrary, in the Netherlands there is a rather broad legal treatment of integrity aspects and the principle of integrity. In France, the principle of good administration is used as an umbrella term, containing several sub-principles; of interest is the special role that the principles of good governance play in relation to independent administrative authorities in France.

In Austria, we find the classical principles, like properness and human rights, in the Constitution, with the democratic principles still under development. The principles of effectiveness and accountability are especially used by the Federal Ombudsman and the Court of Audit.

In Luxembourg, the principles of good governance are also used but not so intensively. Special attention is paid to the principles of equality (as part of properness), participation, and effectiveness. In Belgium, human rights have a special position in the development of good governance principles, in part because of the contribution of the Constitutional Court. A problem is that there are so many bodies within the government that it creates confusion for the citizens.

In Germany, we see that some states (länder) have an ombudsman; it seems that the work of the ombudsman had an inspiring influence on the work of the administration.

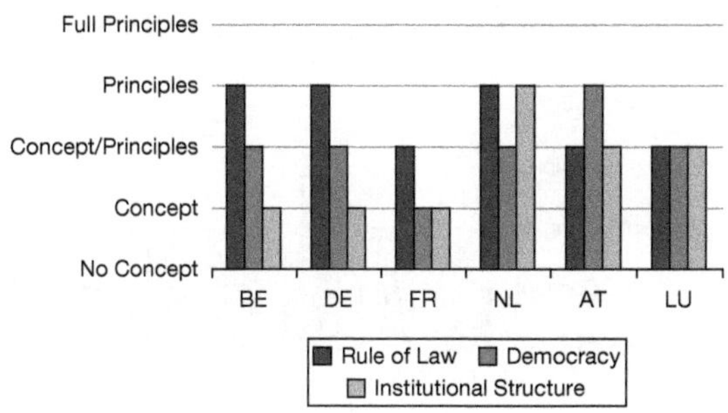

Figure 14.3 Good governance in Western European countries

4. Implementation of Good Governance in Southern Europe

All the Southern European states are unitary states, which means that most of the powers of the state are concentrated on the central level and that the principles of good governance start at the central level and move on to the decentralized level from there. For an overview see Figure 14.4 (Implementation of good governance in Southern Europe). The histories of each country are rather different.

Comparing Spain to Portugal, we notice some important differences. In Spain, we find some principles in the Constitution, but these principles are especially well developed by judicial interpretation. We see in practice that not all principles are respected and that the more democratic principles (such as transparency and participation) are not very well developed in Spain. There is also the problem with corruption. In Portugal, the principles have been strongly developed during recent years, in part due to the influence of international organizations. However, the principle of effectiveness especially should be further developed.

Italy and Malta also have big differences, including geographical ones. In Italy, we see big differences between the public institutions in the application of the principles of good governance. Rather recently, a law on administrative procedures has been drafted in which several of the classic principles have been developed. We see that the executive power and the judiciary are working on the development of these principles, both from a general and from an individual perspective. The literature plays a major role in the development of the principles. In Malta we see, especially with regards to the violation of human rights, a connection drawn with the principles of good governance (which play an important role).

Greece and Cyprus are in different positions from a good governance perspective. In Greece, we find several principles of good governance worked out in the Greek Code of Administrative Procedure, and their interpretation and application are determined by the courts. There is less participation of citizens and a significant amount of corruption, which is also called a lack of integrity. However, more recently, in the Greek Action Plan 2012, we see several initiatives for establishing a new social contract between the state and the citizens, and for developing citizens' initiatives, panels, and referenda. Also, the participation of Greece in the Open Government Partnership shows Greece's efforts to provide a more effective public administration on all levels. Cyprus is a divided country. Its Constitution includes the classical elements of the rule of law. The ombudsman is especially important in developing the principles of good governance, playing an important role particularly in furthering accountability and effectiveness.

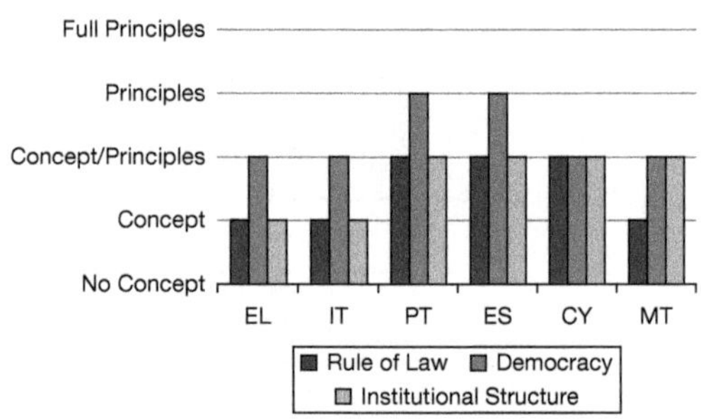

Figure 14.4 Implementation of good governance in Southern Europe

5. Implementation of Good Governance in Central Europe

Looking at the three Baltic states—Estonia, Latvia, and Lithuania—we can conclude there is a development on good governance in the frame of their constitutional systems consisting of a single chamber parliament elected by the people. The three constitutional powers in these unitary states—legislative, executive, and judicial—are strictly separated. A very strong influence from the EU (including in the area of the principles of good governance), but also from other international organizations, is also visible. These countries have a monistic system in relation to international law, meaning it can be applied without the need for transposing domestic legislation. The people themselves do not have much trust in their governments, which also has to do with their history. The implementation of democratic principles of good governance, like transparency and participation, is rather weak. Nevertheless, in some countries these principles have been codified (for instance, in Latvia). In relation to this last point, it is relevant that the Russian minorities do not have by default the nationality of the countries where they reside, and that creates separation within the countries. The principle of properness has been codified in all three countries. The ombudsman plays an important role in the development of the human rights principles.

Poland and Hungary are the countries where we find most of the principles of properness and human rights in the constitution or in the administrative laws. In Poland, where the codification of the human rights in the Constitution is noteworthy, the Constitutional Court plays an important role in the development of good governance elements through constitutional human rights. Hungary has developed legislation in relation to the democracy principles—transparency and participation—and these regulations are enforced by different controlling institutions.

Slovakia recognizes the three classical powers in the state and each of these powers are implementing the principles of good governance. We find many of the principles in the Administrative Code, but not all the institutions have the same interpretation of the principles. The democratic principles are fully developed and effectiveness and accountability are also under development. The human rights protection is on an adequate level. The Czech Republic has had a slow start, due in part to the political change of public management: after each change there is sometimes a loss of institutional memory. The Czech Republic has a lot of catching up to do, but is making good progress in the development of the principles.

Slovenia and Croatia have rather similar constitutional institutions and instruments, but there are two important differences. In Slovenia, there are several Codes of Ethics in addition to the classical regulations, and the constitutional institutions are active in working with the principles of good governance. Croatia still has a long way to go, especially when it comes to implementing the principles of good governance, because the codification and the regulations have been developed, but the application in practice creates a lot of difficulties.

Bulgaria is a unitary state with local self-governance and Romania is a decentralized unitary state. In both countries, we find the classical three powers of the state. In Bulgaria, there was regulation on these principles, but there was no awareness at the level of public institutions. Since 2007, that has changed, also under the influence of the EU. We also find more policy papers in Bulgaria about the implementation of the principles of good governance, but in daily practice there still is a long way to go. In Romania there is already—more than in Bulgaria—a significant application of principles of good governance in practice. Of interest is the conflict between principles like transparency versus the right to privacy. Romania is also very active in the implementation of the new international regulations like the Aarhus Convention.

In Figure 14.5 an overview of the implementation of the good governance principles can be found.

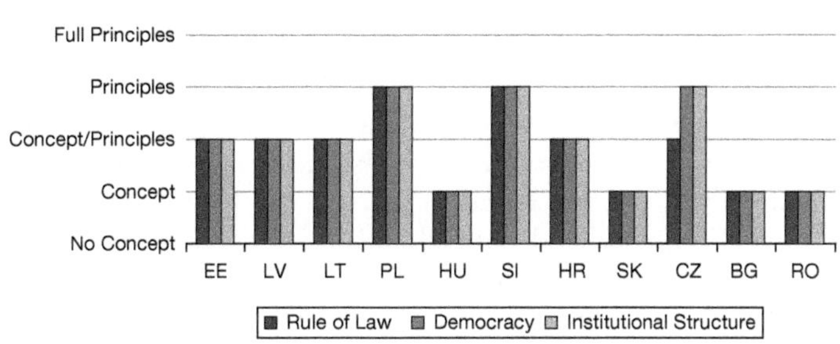

Figure 14.5 Implementation of good governance in Central Europe

6. Implementation of Good Governance in the United Kingdom and Ireland

In Ireland, there is a noticeable fragmentation in the application of good governance, and not in the concept as such or in the regulations specifying the principles of good governance. There is a variation in form and degree in their application by the relevant bodies. Of importance for enforcement are the codes of conduct which are backed by legislation. Especially where there are merely good governance values or guidelines, the situation is weakest. The courts are consequently applying principles of proper administration, but the departments and local authorities exhibit a generally inconsistent approach to the application of the principles. Accountancy and transparency receive inadequate attention. But there are also positive developments which offer more details about the principles, like in the Local Government Reform Act 2014 and the creation of the Referendum Commissions. As a whole, the application of the principle of human rights is adequate.

For the United Kingdom the right to good governance is a step too far. The reason is that Parliament does not want this codification due to a fear of complications or abuse of procedures. Therefore, in general, there is a preference for secondary regulations and soft law, like codes and regulations. We see that various bodies and professional organizations have created their own codes or regulations. So perhaps there are less generally binding norms for the principles of good governance, but in practice each government body or profession tends to follow its code as if it were law. It is complex because of the fragmented approach, but the members of each institution follow the norms. In this way, the British display relative uniformity because each document features almost the same principles, even if differently named or phrased.

For an overview of the implementation of the principles of good governance, see Figure 14.6.

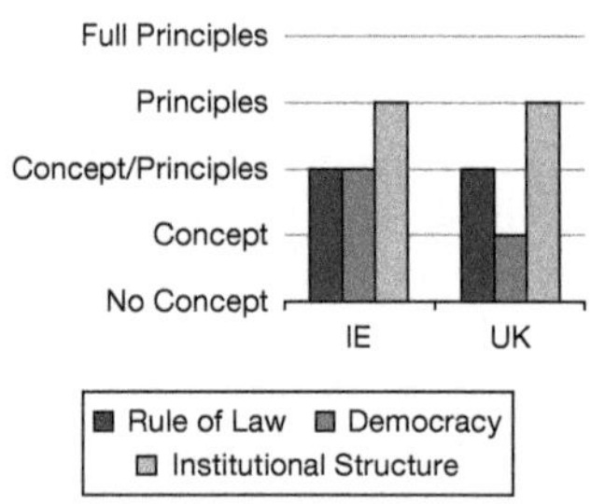

Figure 14.6 Implementation of good governance in the United Kingdom and Ireland

7. Conclusions

The first conclusion is that different countries focus on different aspects of the three dimensions of good governance—rule of law, democracy, and institutional structure—and the structure of the state can influence this process. We conclude that the interpretation of good governance (and good administration) is done through these three dimensions. Sometimes this focuses on the general aspects, sometimes on the specific aspects, and sometimes on a mix of these general and specific aspects. In each of the five groups of countries, we see that some have more general aspects and others more specific aspects. We have to conclude that there is diversity in the application of the good governance concept. It is important to realize that the structure of the state can also have a certain influence on the diversity and development of good governance norms, especially on the decentralized level. In a unitary state, the good governance norms will come more often from the central level than in a federal system, where on state level these norms will be developed almost automatically.

The second conclusion is that the general principles of good governance are sometimes codified in the constitution by general norms, but more often we found specific principles therein, and even when these are not constitutionalized the legislator has developed these principles mostly into general laws. In the first situation, the legislator has to specify these constitutional norms of good governance which will create legal certainty and equality. That is also useful from the perspective of enforcement of these aspects of good governance. It will also create trust in the civil society. We can also have situations where there are no specific constitutional norms of good governance, but the legislator has developed these specific norms by law, resulting in the same situation as with constitutional good governance norms. For practical purposes these will produce the same effect. Finally, the administrative authorities can specify good governance norms in policy rules and internal directives. In that case, there is a more indirect binding effect of the good governance norms, by way of the principles of proper administration. This conclusion can be seen as the instrumental approach of the good governance norms.

A third conclusion is that the courts have also developed principles of good governance, often by interpretation of regulations but also occasionally developing unwritten principles. This conclusion is about the courts developing good governance norms by interpretation. It is important to mention here that the court acts in individual cases, meaning that these norms can be applied only on a case-by-case basis. But when that is done more frequently, we see a line of cases developing a principle. We notice here the protection approach in the development of good governance norms. It is important to realize that these norms create a form of continuity.

A fourth conclusion is that the Ombudsman and the Court of Audit, the fourth power institutions, develop and apply principles of good governance in their advising activities. This is important because when these institutions develop norms of good governance, in general or in specific cases, the outcome is an advice to the public administration. But in practice we see that the good governance norms developed by these institutions are enforced de facto. So, we see that also these fourth power institutions are important sources of good governance norms.

A fifth conclusion is that the institutional principles (effectiveness/accountability) are often applied in the instrumental context, the democracy principles (transparency/participation) are applied for the citizens' protection, and the rule of law principles (properness/human rights) in both situations. In this conclusion we see that the starting point of these principles can be the legislator, the administration, the court, or the fourth power institutions. Often, we see the fourth power institutions or the court developing a principle of good governance.

A sixth conclusion is that it is remarkable that when countries developed principles of good governance, we see a rather similar content to the six principles of good governance: properness, human rights, transparency, participation, effectiveness, and accountability. Differences are found in the concrete application of the principles. This conclusion brings us to a situation where the three types of principles have the same direction and there will not frequently be a conflict between the principles.

Another point we noted was that when there are incidental conflicts between principles, such a conflict has to be solved by the legislator, the administration, the court, or the fourth power institutions. This refers to the situation where principles with a more instrumental function could easily have another direction than the principles with a protection function. Then we have a situation of conflict of principles. If there is discretion, each institution can use its own instruments, using a clear motivation as to why one principle has priority over another principle(s). Thus, each of the institutions can have instruments to give one principle priority over another.

There is a general consensus on all the concepts and dimensions of good governance, but not yet about the specification of the principles. This goes back to the question of whether there is consensus on all the concepts, dimensions, and principles of good governance. Concerning the concept and the general aspects of the three dimensions there is a consensus in the twenty-eight countries. Real differences can be found between the specifications of all the three groups of principles. Perhaps not so many differences exist for the principles of properness and human rights, but more for the principles of transparency and participation, and most for the principles of accountability and effectiveness. There is a more or less broad interpretation of the principles of good governance, due to social or historical reasons, but it can also be a consequence of the legal system.

15

Implementation of the Principles of Good Governance on the National Level outside the EU

In this chapter, the focus is on the implementation of good governance norms in three countries outside Europe: Australia, Canada, and South Africa. As this chapter focuses on the implementation on the national level, there is an important limitation, and as such only a few countries from different continents were selected. This is because we prefer to do a deeper research on a limited amount of countries than a very superficial research on many different countries and this chapter illustrates the good governance situation outside Europe.

While information on the application of the principles of good governance is sometimes difficult to access in these countries, we have tried to obtain as much information as possible.

1. General Remarks on Good Governance outside Europe

It is often said that good governance is a typical western—or, more specifically, European—concept and therefore one will find there is more detailed specification of the principles in Europe than in countries outside Europe. When we look to countries in other continents, it is relevant to find out if this concept is found there and if there is a specification of the concept by way of development of principles. Do we see differences between the countries in these continents? Of course, there is a clear limitation of countries in this chapter. Nevertheless, it is worth finding out if these principles have been developed outside Europe.

2. Implementation of the Good Governance Principles in Australia

Here we will discuss the role of good governance practices in Australia. Whilst these principles gain considerable attention and appreciation in Europe, they are far from solidified and universally known in the further reaches of the world. Thus, Australia has adopted its own personalized version of the principles of good governance to suit the needs of the country. The current practice does not come without its recommendations on future reform to guarantee increased effectiveness and respect for rights.

A widely held belief is that the concepts of the rule of law, democracy, and good governance are the cornerstones of the modern state. Australia indeed maintains a strong rule of law. The style of parliamentary democracy, encouraging the principle of participation, stems from the Westminster system of responsibility and accountability.

Interestingly, there is not a large school of thought focused specifically on principles of good governance, as the term is not yet widespread; rather, these principles can be seen as running in parallel with Australia's desire for and enforcement of good administration.

As a society, there is a strong expectation that government decision-makers will act in a way that is protective of our rights as citizens. It is through this line of thinking that the six principles of good governance—properness, effectiveness, human rights, accountability, transparency, and participation—are slowly being worked into the Australian legal system through the common law system and increasingly creating for themselves a statutory presence through codified judicial review, legislation, and tribunals with extensive jurisdiction.

Within the principles of good governance, attention is especially paid to the relationship between freedom of information, in particular with regards to the principles of transparency and participation. We will provide an outline of the Freedom of Information Act 1982 ('FOI Act'), comparing this legislation with the New South Wales Government Information (Public Access) Act 2009 (GIPA). It will also be argued that the FOI Act has historically failed to enhance transparency and participation in Australia. A case study demonstrating the failure of the FOI Act to rectify the information asymmetry that exists between government and citizens will be advanced, providing evidence for this argument. Nonetheless, it must be noted that the success of the Act does vary between agencies and recent reforms may have improved the situation.

(a) Historical background and good governance approaches

Historically, Australia followed the Diceyan way of thinking in enforcing the rule of law, which ran along the lines of 'a government of laws not men',[1] essentially meaning that the government was disallowed from exercising arbitrary or unfettered power and that instead the boundaries of law must be followed. Dicey also stressed the importance of equality before the law, meaning there was a need to have the same law for both the governors and the governed, to be administered and enforced by an independent judiciary; these are not drastic or extreme ideals to aim for. Dicey showed a clear preference for courts enforcing rights, illustrating his dislike for specialist tribunals. It has been posited by some[2] that, for these reasons, his views hampered the development and modernization of administrative law in Australia.

There are two main approaches in ensuring there is compliance with the norms expected of governmental operation. There is the *regulatory approach*, whereby the focus is on the future and influencing human behaviour and its outcomes through behavioural standards and mechanisms for both monitoring and promoting compliance. Courts, tribunals, and ombudsmen enforce administrative law by providing qualified complainants with various forms of redress for breaches of its rules and principles, thus incentivizing compliance with these requirements in order to avoid unnecessary time in arbitration. From the regulatory perspective, law is one, but not the only, tool for influencing human behaviour.

In contrast, the *legal approach* focuses on the law and legal institutions, considering regulations as only one of the possible purposes and aims. It functions in a retrospective way and focuses on accountability and fixing bad decisions. Its success in

[1] Koven 2008, 37. [2] Jones 2000.

promoting good governance will be seen in the acceptability of the values it expresses and its ability to provide solutions for those adversely affected by unlawful decisions.

(b) Separation of powers

The separation of powers concerns the three main branches of government: the parliament, the executive, and the judiciary. All three groups have specialized roles and work within defined areas of responsibility to ensure that Australia continues to prosper as a nation. Furthermore, it is imperative that the powers are distinct from each other to avoid an oppressive government. This, in effect, ensures that the Australian government remains proper and accountable by creating checks and balances on the use of power. However, Australia has a much milder separation of powers. The three powers of government are clothed by the concept called the Rule of Law. The Oxford Dictionary defines the Rule of Law as the 'restriction of the arbitrary exercise of power by subordinating it to well-defined and established laws'. This notion further reinforces the fact that Australia is built on good governance as it suggests several principles about the behaviours of the three powers: that Australians should be treated equally before the law; that the law should be fair, clear, and stable; that the government and its public authorities are accountable under the law; and that the courts should be easily accessible—to name just a few.[3]

The separation of powers may ensure a more 'effective' form of administrative law, in that it assists courts in retaining their institutional integrity and independence. Enhanced authority in the determination of questions of legality is prevalent and consequently reduces the threat of arbitrary power. Having said this, there are inherent weaknesses in the system and questions regarding the institutional competence on a number of issues. For example, the court is not strong in hearing polycentric issues, such as issues with a number of different factors and areas of possible conflict such as the Fair Work Australia legislation. A common area of weakness arising repetitively in Australia is the intersection of politics and the legal system. Politically loaded and contentious areas are not areas in which the courts have performed strongly; cases such as *Peko-Wallsend* in regard to native title legislation demonstrate this point. Other areas clashing with politics include environmental claims, economic considerations, and international obligations and the so-called 'national interest'. This is where conflict with the principles of good governance arises in the areas of the principles of human rights and accountability to citizens. The following sections will delve into a deeper analysis of these three powers of government and, notably, how the good governance principles are interpreted differently depending on the specific competence of each power of government.

(c) New administrative law reforms

The starting point of the administrative law of Australia shifting to adopt the principles of good governance can be found in the publication of the highly important Kerr Committee Report[4] in 1971. This surged reform in the area leading to the New Administrative Law reforms (NALs). Its main areas of work included the codification of judicial review of administrative action, through the Administrative Decisions

[3] World Justice Project, *What is the Rule of law?*, <http://worldjusticeproject.org/what-rule-law>.

[4] Commonwealth Administrative Review Committee, *Kerr Committee Report*, Parliament of the Commonwealth of Australia, Canberra, 1971.

(Judicial Review) Act 1977, the establishment of the Administrative Appeals Tribunal, countering the previously followed Diceyan model, the enactment of the Freedom of Information Act 1982 (Cth),[5] and the emergence of the Federal Court of Australia as the leading administrative forum. The tribunal has created the jurisdiction to review administrative decisions on a merits basis, and there was increased codification and procedural reform of the system of judicial review—as well as the creation of the Office of the Ombudsman through the Ombudsman Act 1976.

Kirby, a leading High Court judge in the Australian Federal system, is of the view that the Act's overall impact was 'overwhelmingly beneficial'[6] despite some problems. For example, in assessing the effectiveness, strengths, and weaknesses of the Administrative Decisions (Judicial Review) Act 1977 (ADJR), introduced under the NALs, a number of different angles are considered.

Some positives include the high accessibility—and hence public participation—due to simplified procedures and the requirement to give reasons upon request as to why a decision was made,[7] thus encouraging transparency. A positive is also the allowance for increased remedial flexibility, as it is essential in upholding the rule of law to ensure that government decision-makers are acting within the boundaries of their power. Thus, the principle of properness is enforced as judicial review prevents arbitrary and ultra vires decision-making.

Some weaknesses include the fact that the straightforward conceptual nature of the ADJR has been lost in a 'jurisdictional swamp' due to the requirements of the three components—the decision, the administrative, and the enactment—being too strict. There are also issues when distinguishing between what is jurisdictional and what is non-jurisdictional. There is no clear public policy purpose achieved by limiting the jurisdictional formula to decisions made 'under an enactment'. For example, it is not clear why decisions of an administrative character, that affect an individual's rights, interests, or legitimate expectations, involve the expenditure of public funds and/or the provision of government services, should only be reviewable where the decision is specifically provided for in the statute.

Essentially, legitimacy in government decision-making and action is underpinned by a number of characteristics. The most commonplace view is that law defines the boundary; thus, judges must confine themselves to judicial review of points of law. However, confining judges in this way raises a plethora of alternative conceptual problems such as 'what is law' and how do we explain the role of judges in 'creating law'? Institutional competence seeks to define this scope, meaning that judges cease to engage in legitimate judicial review when they go beyond the boundaries of their competence. In practice, in order to ensure effectiveness and properness, judges must exercise some degree of judicial restraint in interpreting legislation which has been enacted by a democratically elected parliament. Decisions made at a cabinet level will generally not be subject to judicial review. The reason for this is that the cabinet is politically accountable to parliament. Thus, it is non-justiciable as a result of collective responsibility.

In a note on the principle of *simples ultra vires*, it can be explained simply that it is a decision going beyond the available jurisdiction. This legal principle stems from the case of *Parisienne Basket Shoes*[8] and *Re Refugee Tribunal*,[9] whereby a jurisdictional

[5] Now known as the Government Information (Public Access) Act 2009.

[6] Kirby 2000, 12.

[7] Administrative Decisions (Judicial Review) Act 1977 (Cth), s 13.

[8] *Parisienne Basket Shoes Pty Ltd v Whyte* [1938] HCA 7.

[9] *Re Refugee Tribunal; Ex Parte Aala* (2000) 204 CLR 82.

error is made where a decision-maker either: exceeds the jurisdiction; flouts a statutory limitation; breaches natural justice; asks the wrong question; or the decision is wrongly constituted. Thus, put simply, as in the case of *Schlieske v Minister of Immigration and Ethnic Affairs*,[10] it establishes that administrative decisions must be designed to achieve a purpose or object authorized by the empowering legislation—the whole concept behind good governance.

Each part of the New Administrative Law package provided an important reform, but the full impact of the package came from its combined effect. It made substantial progress in introducing the general right to reasoned decisions, a single test for standing, codified the grounds for review, allowing for full transparency, and abolished a significant amount of procedural technicalities. For example, the need to distinguish between jurisdictional and non-jurisdictional errors was abolished. The introduction of the Administrative Appeals Tribunal (AAT) provided a right to reasons for decisions, a simplified process of a more favourable merits review, and the right for citizens to receive a new decision. The introduction of the Ombudsman in line with the AAT meant that individual complaints could be investigated and wider investigations into systemic problems in government could be undertaken. As a result of these reforms, two highly important principles of good governance came to the foreground: accountability and transparency. The NALs were considered a 'major leap forward',[11] but criticism has now crept in some years after its initial implementation. Freedom of information legislation is argued to provide 'too many exemptions and loopholes'[12] for governments and a lack of information for the average citizen. The AAT has been attacked for being 'too formal, adversarial and court like'[13] and criticism stretches as far as the ADJR in that its 'codified grounds of review inhibit the growth of new or existing grounds of review'.[14] Whilst progressive at their time of writing, the environment which they now operate in is very different. Nonetheless, the overarching unifying aspect of all of the developments is the importance given to the rule of law and those exercising power operating within and under the law and not above it.

(d) Rule of law

A key aspect of the rule of law is that when a government purports to act or decide anything, it must be able to point to some source of legal authority for what is done, establishing the principle of legality. In building on this concept, not only must there be a source of legal authority but decisions must not be made in breach of an accepted norm.

The norms underpinning judicial review proposed by the Judicial Review Council[15] are along the same lines as the principles of good governance, but have some differences. They include accountability, rationality, efficiency, and the public interests and protection of rights and impartiality.[16] The separation of powers doctrine entails that judicial review should not allow courts to impose ideas of good administration on the executive, as they inherently overlap. This is why parliament has created alternative

[10] [1988] FCA 48. [11] Groves 2014, 308. [12] Jowell 2011, 211.

[13] Osborne 1982, 150; Administrative Review Council, *Better Decisions: Review of the Commonwealth Merits Review Tribunals (Report Number 39)*, Parliament of the Commonwealth of Australia, Canberra, 1995.

[14] Goldring 1981, 102.

[15] Judicial Review Council, *Judicial Review in Australia—Consultation Paper*, Commonwealth of Australia, 2011.

[16] Ibid.

means of accountability mechanisms and protections separately such as Merits Review and the Ombudsman.

Theoretically, individual rights and freedoms can be overridden by an incumbent parliament. However, any statutory or non-statutory powers are granted subject to these rights and statutes will be read subject to fundamental rights, upholding the rule of law. Judicial review works to protect the upholding of these rights as well as international treaties, as where statute is ambiguous, courts will favour a construction in accordance with any obligations under international law. Uniquely, at the Commonwealth level, Australia does not have a Bill of Rights, thus the effect of certain provisions under state law such as the Victorian Charter of Human Rights and Responsibilities Act 2006 (Vic) and Human Rights Equal Opportunity Commission Act 1986 (SA) is to act as a guide for establishing a breach of human rights as an independent ground for review. This results in human rights protection legislation being rather disjointed and lacking in consistency, which compromises its effectiveness.

(e) Position of the fourth power

In recent years, Australia has seen a growth in alternative accountability mechanisms such as the quasi-adjudicative, inquisitorial Ombudsman, the Privacy Commission, Human Rights and Equal Opportunity Commission, and Independent Commission Against Corruption, and in system monitoring, in looking for systemic issues in government handling.

These bodies, including the Administrative Appeals Tribunal represent the fourth 'integrity' arm of government. The rule of law is concerned with safeguarding individual liberty and integrity against government acts. Spigelman supports this notion and proposed that we should 'recognise an integrity branch of government as a fourth branch, equivalent to the legislative, executive and judicial branches'.[17] The constitutional practice has been to classify these accountability or integrity agencies as part of the executive; however, this brings to the surface problems associated with the entanglement of power. The Ombudsman remains accountable to the executive, not the parliament. Some criticize this, as distance would ensure a greater degree of independence from the executive; however, this would mean its source of funding would be non-existent. As the Constitution is written law and firmly entrenched, it is unlikely that a fourth arm of government will ever be recognized at a federal, centralized level.

However, at the more adaptive state (decentralized) level, these integrity agencies are starting to be recognized: for example, the Victorian Constitution recognizes and includes the Ombudsman and the Auditor General,[18] consequently entrenching their role. There is further criticism around this model of the fourth arm, in that the Australian government has a 'multiagency approach to combatting corruption'.[19] Some activists in the area, such as Callinan and Aroney, dislike this approach, arguing that 'an extraordinary multiplicity of agencies and officials give rise to serious questions of complexity and inefficiency'.[20] However, as is discussed below, the Ombudsman is quite successful in its approach to upholding the principles of good governance in Australian society.

[17] Spigelman 2005, 1–16.
[18] Victorian Constitution Act 1975 (Vic), s 13.
[19] Callinan and Aroney, in: Groves 2014, 312.
[20] Ibid, 314.

(f) Ombudsman

The function of the Ombudsman, as defined in section 13 of the Victorian Constitution, is to enquire and investigate into administrative action taken by any government department, public statutory body, and see if the behaviour alleged is incompatible with a human right set out in the Victorian Charter of Human Rights and Responsibilities 2008 (Vic).

The independent legal mechanism for upholding the rule is the judiciary, due to their ability to make conclusive findings on questions of law and their independence and impartiality. The Ombudsman and its specialist offices[21] can only complement and not supplant this judicial role for a number of reasons: (1) it cannot make declarations of invalidity, but rather it must rely on recommendation, persuasion, and publicity to effect change; (2) it cannot command action or award compensation; (3) it cannot investigate ministerial or judicial action or decisions, the conduct of intelligence bodies, or employment action in the public service; and (4) it is subject to budgetary constraints. These weaknesses, however, should not overshadow the substantial, beneficial work of the Ombudsman. Some benefits include: the public can contest an action, not just a decision; it works at both a centralized, federal level and a decentralized, state level; an action need not have been made under an enactment promoting fairness; it has an inquisitorial operation, meaning strong powers are at their disposal for investigation; its informal, independent, and impartial character (the three Is); the effective protection of human rights, capturing arguably the most fundamental human right—the right to complain against and challenge government in an independent forum; its spread into the private sector, for example, telecommunication, banking, and finance, indicating institutional acceptance in an increasingly privatized society.

The role of the Ombudsman is to explain to the general public why certain government action is not maladministration, thus demonstrating the strong value of explaining decisions as part of the rule of law. This has a follow-on beneficial effect in that people are more likely to comply with decisions and recommendations when they are provided with justified reasons, as they feel transparency is upheld. It can provide an alternative forum for legal issues affecting a large number of people as compared to the cost and complexity of commencing a legal proceeding or judicial review. There is a special role in hearing disclosures and investigations in regards to the following matters: 'whistle-blower' and freedom of information legislation; the police and ASIO under anti-terrorism legislation; and compliance of the AFP and the Australia Crimes Commission with legislation authorizing telecommunication interception and controlled operations.

As a result of these strengths, the Ombudsman provides a frequent source of assistance with grievances against government bodies and has reinforced in Australians the important good governance principle that they have the human right to complain against the government. This, as a result, bolsters the notions of individual liberty and upholds integrity of government action. The Ombudsman hears complaints not only against government bodies, but also against private entities that are providing services on behalf of the Commonwealth, under Commonwealth legislation or contract. This shows the Ombudsman's adaptive quality in dealing with problems associated with privatization and supervision of contracted bodies for outsourced functions. It also contrasts bodies such as the AAT, as their jurisdiction is defined by and is at the

[21] For example, the Australian Defence Force, Immigration, Law Enforcement, Australia Post and Tax.

mercy of parliament. The flexibility allows for increased accountability: for example, in 2005, the Ombudsman's jurisdiction was extended[22] to cover non-government entities, which provide goods or services to the public under contract to the government.

The Ombudsman is strong in its investigatory powers, which include entry to premises,[23] obtaining documents with ease,[24] and examining witnesses.[25] Whilst it would have been thought that these powers were too extensive, departments being investigated tolerate these broad powers as the Ombudsman, which at the end of the day cannot make binding determinations, merely reports and makes recommendations.[26] Some argue that this leads to the strength of the Ombudsman being undermined; however, nearly all formal recommendations are accepted and there is a high compliance rate,[27] which is a credit to its resourceful nature in deciding how best to resolve a conflict.[28] The powers to make reports and recommendations to departments if maladministration has occurred are founded in the Ombudsman Act 1976, section 15. The Ombudsman finds some strength in the ability to make reports to the Prime Minister and Parliament under sections 16 and 17 respectively, should the Department's response be inadequate.

(g) Good governance and human rights

Furthermore, good governance is an interdisciplinary concept that denotes a different interpretation for diverse intuitions; however, the following sections will primarily focus on how good governance principles intertwine with the Australian legal system. Despite being a broad and open concept, good governance can be divided into six categories in which we also find the human rights principles.[29] In addition, several sources will be explored to examine whether, and to what extent, these six principles are actually practised within the Australian government.

Human rights are inherent to every human being and all nations should seek to uphold, promote, and maintain the basic rights that every citizen is entitled to. In Australia, in particular Victoria, a specific piece of legislation codifies the rights, freedoms, and responsibilities of all citizens of Victoria and, in effect, guides the relationship between the Australian government and its nationals. This legislation is the Charter of Human Rights and Responsibilities Act 2006 ('the Charter'). The Charter mandates that all public authorities, such as the Victorian government, public servants, local councils, and Victorian Police, act in accordance with the human rights stipulated in the Act and to use the Charter as a template in developing policies, making laws, delivering services, and making decisions. Therefore, the Charter essentially aims to ensure both that the Australian Government considers the civil and political interests as well as shielding and encouraging human rights by means of limiting the control of public authorities.

The Charter contains twenty important human rights, all of which reflect four key principles: freedom, respect, equality, and dignity. Each new law must be checked against the Charter, accompanied with a 'Statement of Compatibility' to show its relevance to human rights. In addition, a 'Declaration of Inconsistent Interpretation' can be issued by the Supreme Court if the law is challenged on the basis that it is not compatible with the fundamental human rights stipulated in the Charter. In essence, human rights correspond to several principles of good governance and in the

[22] Ombudsman Act 1976 (Cth), s 5. [23] Ibid, s 14. [24] Ibid, s 9.
[25] Ibid, s 13. [26] Ibid, s 15. [27] McMillan 2004.
[28] Compensation is the remedy most commonly adopted. [29] Addink 2015a, 25.

Charter in particular, the principles of participation, transparency, and accountability are explored.

(h) Principles of participation, transparency, and accountability

Another principle of good governance is the ability of citizens to take an active and equal part in how a government steers its policies and laws. This is evident in the Charter under section 16 and particularly section 18:

Section 16: Your right to peaceful assembly and freedom of association

People have the right to join groups or unions and to meet peacefully.

Section 18: Your right to taking part in public life

Every person has the right to take part in public life, such as the right to vote or run for public office.

Transparency involves open and clear information that is available to the public. The Charter itself helps to promote transparency because it sets out the fundamental human rights visible in one Treaty and, as a result, makes it a legal obligation for the government and its public authorities to conform to them. This, in effect, allows Victorians to freely access the Charter and challenge laws that are contradictory to their fundamental human rights. In addition, accountability refers to the government being held liable for their citizens, for instance, judicial, political, and financial liability. Here, the Charter promotes the principle of accountability as the government and public authorities must act in accordance with the Charter and, if a new law or process does not, the judiciary is then accountable with regards to issuing a declaration of inconsistent interpretation.

The Charter's purpose is to uphold the fundamental human rights when developing policies and laws within Australia. This principle is highly valued and also effective as the Charter promotes subsequent good governance principles and the fact that a statement of compatibility and a declaration of inconsistent interpretation can be issued also reinforces this idea. On the other hand, it only specifies twenty individual rights, which suggests that Victoria could work on adding more fundamental human rights to ensure each proposed law is scrutinized more thoroughly. In addition, it indirectly, rather than explicitly, promotes subsequent principles, such as transparency and accountability, through the mere existence and purpose of the Charter. This could be problematic as the promotion of these subsequent good governance principles are dependent on interpretation. Nonetheless, the principle of human rights is definitely recognized and promoted in Australia through the Charter.

(i) Principles of good governance and the Freedom of Information Act

The Freedom of Information Act 1982 (Cth) was passed at the Federal Commonwealth Level. Previously, there was no obligation to release information, because the 'traditional Westminster system of governance is fairly closed to public scrutiny'.[30] The act was considered a 'landmark in the development of Australian democracy'[31] and was enacted in response to the idea of open government, meaning citizens having the right to access the documents and proceedings of the government to allow for effective public oversight. This legislation applies to all 'ministers, departments and public authorities',

[30] Stubbs 2008, 667–84. [31] Ibid.

caveat to exceptions, which will be discussed later. The purposes of the enactment link strongly to the following principles of good governance:

- increased public scrutiny and *accountability* of government, with a requirement to explain itself to citizens as to why it was making certain decisions;
- increased level of public *participation* in processes of government, empowering them to be more democratically involved;
- providing individuals with access to personal information held about them and about circumstances concerning them, promoting *transparency*.

Unsurprisingly, this right to access documents is subject to exceptions and exemptions:[32]

- disclosure is not required where it is necessary to protect essential public interest and private and business affairs. There is a lot of ambiguity and debate in this area as to what is essential and what should be considered private;
- refusal allowed where work involved in providing documents would substantially and unreasonably divert the resources of the agency or interfere with work of minister;
- no 'public interest'[33] in releasing the following:
  - cabinet documents
  - harm to national security and international relations
  - any document regarding defence
  - law enforcement and public safety
  - breach of secrecy provisions in other Acts
  - legal professional privilege
  - obtained in confidence
  - trade secrets or commercially valuable information
  - ASIO has a blanket exemption

These exemptions are subject to the public interest test, which means that the onus is on the agency to show that it would be contrary to the public interest to release a document. Whether an item can be classified as a document for freedom of information purposes is assessed with regard to their relation to 'the affairs of an agency or department',[34] leaving many political, administrative, and personal documents out of reach. This weakens the strength of the Act.

Interestingly, here, freedom of information is only for access to documents, which is opposite to the situation in New Zealand, where 'information' is much more broadly defined. Thus, in Australia, problems arise in that the document must be pre-existing and identifiable, and a request for a document must be in writing and contain reasonable information as to the document in order for it to be located.[35] The procedure has also been criticized by journalists as being 'prohibitively costly',[36] arguably aiming to reduce transparency. Apart from the media, the other extensive users of freedom of information legislation are opposition parties, for use in attacks on the ruling party, which is why so many documents are kept out of the public domain.

[32] Freedom of Information Act 1982 (Cth), Part IV. [33] Ibid, s 11B.
[34] Ibid, s 15. [35] Ibid, s 15. [36] Ricketson and Snell, 42.

(j) Freedom of information and the Commonwealth Freedom of Information Act 1982

Freedom of information first became a popular concept in Australia with the election of the Whitlam government, which had taken freedom of information as a key policy to the 1972 election. Their policy was modelled largely on the US system.[37] However, a FOI Act was not passed at the Commonwealth level until 1982. By 1994, every Australian jurisdiction had a statutory scheme guaranteeing the right of public access to information as the states and territories followed suit.[38]

Freedom of information legislation did not realize its object of enhancing transparency and participation in Australia under the Howard government, particularly given the government's High Court defence of 'exclusive certificates'. The government also defended the right to suppress Treasury research that had the potential to undermine government policies.[39] *McKinnon v Secretary, Department of Treasury*[40] is a case illustrative of this problem. Michael McKinnon was the freedom of information editor for *The Australian* and requested two separate sets of documents relating to the first homebuyers' scheme and a bracket creep within the taxation system from the Federal Department of Treasury in 2002. These requests were largely rejected and McKinnon went to the Administrative Appeals Tribunal (AAT) on appeal.

The legislation at the time allowed 'conclusive certificates'. 'Conclusive certificates' enabled responding ministers to conclusively declare documents to be restricted on the basis that disclosure was not in the public interest. External review bodies had no grounds on which to order the release of any document that had been restricted under 'conclusive certificates'. By the time that McKinnon's appeals were listed, the Treasurer had issued conclusive certificates under section 36(3) of the FOI Act on the documents in question. This meant that the AAT, in effect, could no longer undertake a full merit review of the claim that disclosure of a document would be contrary to the public interest.[41] This issue was rectified in 2008 with the Freedom of Information (Removal of Conclusive Certificates and Other Measures) Bill 2008 as part of the Rudd Labour party's election promise: 'Government Information: Restoring trust and integrity'.[42]

There are three key elements to freedom of information in Australia: the right of access to public information in documents held by government agencies; the right to request access and amendments to personal information; and an obligation for government agencies to record and publish or make publicly available information.[43] However, prior to the 2010 amendments, the public often faced practical difficulties when attempting to exercise the right to request access to public information. These included difficulties in framing requests, the high cost of making a request, delay by government agencies in responding to requests, and difficulties in challenging decisions made to refuse access to information.[44]

Delivering on the Labour government's election promise, the Freedom of Information Amendment (Reform) Act 2010 was passed in May 2010 and came into effect from November 2010. These reforms aimed to promote a pro-disclosure culture and included abolishing application fees for freedom of information request and

[37] McColl 2010. [38] Ibid. [39] Mulgan 2008, 238.

[40] (2006) 229 ALR 187. [41] Stubbs 2008, 675.

[42] The Parliament of the Commonwealth of Australia, The Senate, 'Freedom of Information (Removal of Conclusive Certificates and Other Measures): Explanatory Memorandum' (2008) <http://parlinfo.aph.gov.au/parlInfo/search/display/display.w3p;query=Id%3A%22legislation%2Fems%2Fs702_ems_54393c39-10e2-4651-bc6b-9f7fc6072df7%22>; Rudd 2007.

[43] Transparency International 2012. [44] Popple 2012, 401.

applications for internal review. Applicants who seek access to their own personal information do not pay any charges and for all other applications the first five hours of decision-making time is free of charge.[45] The reforms to the FOI Act in Australia shifted the focus from a reactive model of disclosure, where information was provided on request, to a proactive model of publication of public sector information through the Information Publication Scheme (IPS).[46] The IPS requires agencies to publish a broad range of information on their websites, and to make it available for downloading where possible. The reforms also established the Office of the Australian Information Commissioner (OAIC), an independent statutory agency that conducts merits reviews of freedom of information decisions.[47]

(k) New South Wales Government Information (Public Access) Act 2009

The New South Wales reforms were prompted by the Review of the Freedom of Information Act 1989 that was set out in a Special Report to Parliament by the Ombudsman in February 2009. The Report, made by the Ombudsman under his independent statutory reporting power, recommended 'new legislation which is written in plain English in a modern drafting style, which focuses on policy and principle' as the 1989 FOI Act was thought to be too complex.[48] Section 3(1)(c) of the GIPA sets out as one of its objects 'that access to Government information is restricted only where there is an overriding public interest against disclosure'.[49] Section 5 provides for a presumption in favour of disclosure, unless there is an overriding public interest.

Examples of public interest considerations in favour of the disclosure of information include situations where disclosure could reasonably be expected to promote open discussion, enhance government accountability, contribute to positive and informed debate, ensure effective oversight of the expenditure of funds, or reveal that an agency has engaged in misconduct or negligent, improper, or unlawful conduct.[50] The recent freedom of information reforms in Australia have been described as 'the significance of the legal, governmental and cultural change that is occurring'[51] and act to address a past criticism that freedom of information legislation works on the basis of a 'pull' model where information is largely disseminated in response to individual requests.[52]

(l) Freedom of Information Act 1982 and the Government Information (Public Access) Act 2009

The reforms in both the Commonwealth and New South Wales jurisdictions have a number of similarities. The reforms saw both jurisdictions establish an independent information commissioner with a comprehensive oversight and advocacy role.[53] Both reforms see a commitment by the government to strengthen the legal framework for access to information and to address weaknesses in existing freedom of information

[45] Freedom of Information Amendment (Reform) Act 2010 (Cth).
[46] Popple 2011, 256. [47] Ibid. [48] McColl 2010, 21. [49] Ibid, 22.
[50] Office of the Information Commissioner New South Wales, 'Open Access Information: Fact Sheet' (March 2012) <https://www.ipc.nsw.gov.au/sites/default/files/file_manager/Fact%20sheet%20Open%20Access%20Information-ACC.pdf>.
[51] McMillian 2010, 1.
[52] FOI Independent Review Panel, *The Right to Information: Reviewing Queensland's Freedom of Information Act*, 16–17.
[53] McMillian 2010, 1.

legislation.[54] Since the reforms, there has been close cooperation and sharing of ideas between the new Information Commissioners in the Commonwealth, New South Wales, and Queensland.[55] There has also been coordination between freedom of information legislation and privacy legislation, balancing the need to protect both these interests.[56]

However, differences can be seen between the two sets of reform. New South Wales and other states that have also initiated reforms, such as Queensland and Tasmania, have achieved greater reform by disposing of existing laws and legislating from scratch, while the Commonwealth merely made changes to its legislation. Key features of the state laws include the requirement for information to be provided in plain English and the creation of offence and penalty regimes for interference with proper decision-making.[57]

(m) Freedom of Information in enhancing transparency and participation in Australia

In the Freedom of Information Amendment (Reform) Act 2010 it is stated that the object of the law is to increase public participation in government processes, with a view to promoting better-informed decision-making and increasing scrutiny, discussion, comment, and review of the government's activities.[58]

This objective is evident in a number of the reforms that have taken place. For example, factors such as a potential loss of confidence in or embarrassment caused to the government may not be used to justify non-disclosure. Allowing the use of exemptions such as these is not conducive to open and transparent government, therefore the prohibiting of these exemptions is a positive step.[59]

Additionally, freedom of information decision-makers are required to operate on a presumption in favour of access to documents when considering freedom of information requests.[60] As explained, freedom of information can have an important role to play in enhancing transparency and participation. However, there are a number of ways in which Australia's freedom of information system has failed to do this. Despite the objectives of the reform and the government rhetoric promising more open, transparent, and participative governance, there is still doubt as to the actual impact of the reformed legislation. The Commonwealth Information Commissioner, John McMillan, has struggled to secure adequate resources for his office. This negatively impacts on the Office's ability to ensure that independent reviews of freedom of information decisions are conducted expeditiously. Furthermore, the government has largely managed to avoid scrutiny over their handling of immigration freedom of information requests—an important and controversial policy area.[61]

In order to assess the success of the FOI Act in increasing public participation and transparency, administrative compliance with the act must be assessed. Roberts provides three categories of administrative non-compliance in freedom of information.[62] These categories are malicious non-compliance, adversarialism, and administrative non-compliance. Malicious non-compliance is 'a combination of action, always intentional and sometimes illegal, designed to undermine requests for access to records',

[54] Ibid, 4. [55] Ibid, 5. [56] Ibid, 2. [57] Dargaville 2011, 18.

[58] Freedom of Information Amendment (Reform) Act 2010 (Cth), Sch 1, s 3.

[59] Office of the Australian Information Commissioner, 'About freedom of information', <http://www.oaic.gov.au/foi-portal/about_foi.html>.

[60] Faulkner 2009. [61] Parnell 2012. [62] Roberts 1998, 47–50.

for example, the destruction of records, avoiding responding to the request, removing information from files, or the deliberate non-recording of information.[63]

Adversarialism is 'a practice of testing the limits of FOI laws, without engaging in obvious illegalities, in an effort to ensure the interests of governments or departments are adequately protected' including the adoption of broad interpretations of exemptions, deliberate delays, poor giving of reasons, and the rejection of requests for fee waivers.[64] The third category is administrative non-compliance where the right to access information is undermined by inadequate resourcing, poor record-keeping, or other weaknesses in administration.[65]

(n) Compliance differs from entity to entity

The NBN Co Limited, a corporation owned by the Commonwealth and charged with implementing a technology policy of delivering broadband internet to Australians, has shown compliance with its obligations under the FOI Act.

According to Stuart Morris QC, who conducted a review of the NBN's freedom of information performance, 'NBN Co. has not only fulfilled its lawful responsibilities under the FOI Act, but also has achieved a high standard in its administration of the Act'.[66] Although access to documents was refused in three of the thirty-five requests, it was found that NBN had used a careful process to identify exempt documents, provided clear reasons for relying on the exemptions, and did not utilize exemptions extravagantly. Furthermore, the company operated in a timely manner and generally adopted a pro-disclosure attitude.[67]

On the other hand, the Department of Immigration and Citizenship (DIAC) has been criticized for its processing of non-routine (eg complex requests for non-personal information) freedom of information requests. One of the major concerns was the significant delay involved in processing non-routine freedom of information requests. This delay could be classified as an adversarial practice under Roberts' categories of administrative compliance. Although requests should normally be dealt with in a thirty-day period this time limit was not adhered to in any of the twenty-seven cases considered in the review. The quickest decision was made within eighty-three days of receiving the request, the slowest after 507 days.[68] Other areas of concern were the inadequate communication with freedom of information applicants about delays in processing their requests and poor engagement with the OAIC in resolving the complaints.[69] In another review conducted by Robert Cornall, a number of recommendations were made including the instilling of a culture within the agency attuned to effective freedom of information, providing internal training, regular monitoring, and reviews of freedom of information performance and establishing high quality records management.[70]

These two examples demonstrate the difficulty in making a definitive conclusion on the effectiveness of the FOI Act in enhancing participation and transparency in Australia. It can be seen that the FOI Act is being utilized by NBN to proactively disclose information through their IPS and a disclosure log,[71] as well as to provide information where requested. Information appears to be clear and easily accessible,

[63] Ibid, 10–11. [64] Ibid, 11. [65] Ibid. [66] Morris 2012, 3.
[67] Ibid, 9. [68] McMillan 2012a, 4. [69] Ibid. [70] Ibid.
[71] See: NBN Co. 'Disclosure log' <http://www.nbnco.com.au/about-us/freedom-of-information/disclosure-log.html> and 'Proactively released documents' <http://www.nbnco.com.au/about-us/freedom-of-information/proactively-released-documents.html>.

the disclosure log making the majority of previously requested documents available for download. A list of proactively released documents, with links to the actual documents, is also provided.[72]

In contrast, while DIAC also has a disclosure log on their website, this is simply a list of documents available. In order to access the actual documents, members of the media or public are required to contact the department. Immigration is a contentious issue in Australia and a policy area that many individuals and civil society groups wish to participate in. Without timely access to the information sought through freedom of information requests, such as information on conditions of detention and the health and reported deaths of detainees in immigration detention centres, individuals cannot make informed decisions when campaigning or using their democratic vote to further their preferred policy. Therefore, it can be seen that the FOI Act can help to enable participation and transparency in some cases, and fails to do so in others.

(o) Freedom of information and the 'structural imbalance'

One problem with administrative law in Australia is the marked imbalance that exists in the relationship between citizens and the state.[73] Terrill offers a number of factors that contribute to this 'structural imbalance'. Governments have the advantage of institutional memory and in-house specialized expertise. Administrative bodies have a superior knowledge of the workings of the system and are connected with other administrative actors.[74] Individuals may face governments who make strategic decisions to refuse an otherwise unthreatening request for information, review, or benefit, if they judge that success in the area might create an unwelcome precedent.[75] On the other hand, individuals, particularly those from minority groups, possess poor knowledge of the process[76] and are often 'atomized', each applicant beginning the process anew.[77]

Not only do citizens face a structural imbalance, but they are also up against the complex web of Australian departments, agencies, and government programmes.[78] Most citizens, and especially those belonging to marginalized groups, do not have an understanding of the legislation, schemes, or workings of multiple government agencies and programmes that may be needed in order to fully participate in governance activities.[79] McMillan contends that 'a common cause of the complaints that people have against government is that legislative schemes of entitlement and regulation are nowadays detailed, complex, specific and sometimes rigid and harsh'.[80] He argues that the concept of the rule of law is just as concerned with assisting individuals to understand why decisions were made as it is with determining whether a decision was legally proper.[81] Greater transparency in governance, facilitated by freedom of information, could enable individuals to reach this understanding, thereby increasing trust in government.

In theory, freedom of information should act to re-balance this imbalance and remove the power of the state to determine what information citizens receive, thereby controlling the public perception of government. This is a power that existed under traditional monarchical and Westminster systems[82] and to some extent still exists today. Joseph E Stiglitz argues the intention of freedom of information is to remove the traditional imbalance of information possessed by the government, in relation to citizens. On the other hand, Rhys Stubbs argues that the way in which freedom

72 See ibid. 73 Kirby 1989, 6. 74 Terrill 2000, 30. 75 Ibid.
76 Ibid. 77 Snell and Upcher 2002, 37. 78 McMillan 2010, 2. 79 Ibid.
80 McMillan 2004, 6. 81 Ibid. 82 Stubbs 2008, 669.

of information has been introduced in Australia perpetuates traditional information asymmetries between the citizenry and the state; one party continues to hold better and more information against the other.[83] 'The laws have been designed so as to work around the assumption of closed representative government, forming a barricade that distinguishes what the public can and cannot access.' According to Terrill, this 'barricade' sees the public struggling to access information due to deficient legislation and against governments with 'institutional memory, specialized expertise and ... a longer term interest in influencing the evolution of case law'.[84] In this way, the FOI Act is failing to rectify the structural imbalance, or information asymmetry, that exists in Australia. As long as this information asymmetry remains entrenched the principles of transparency and participation cannot flourish.

Many of these critiques of the FOI Act—that it fails to rectify the information asymmetry—were written before the recent round of reforms took place. Post-reform, however, there are still critics. *The Age* has argued that the government is spending thirteen times more money on high-performance shredding machines than they are on training public servants to handle information requests: $10 million, compared to $764 000. 'There is also a growing backlog of FOI decision reviews, a state of affairs that is being exploited by agencies seeking to delay the release of sensitive information.'[85] On the other hand, *The Australian* reported that government is more open as a result of the reforms. Previously harder to access documents, such as ministerial submissions, expense accounts, and audit reports have been made available through government agency logs; there has been an increase in freedom of information requests for policy documents; lower freedom of information cost recovery and faster processing of requests. Proactive disclosure has also greatly increased.[86] It may therefore be concluded that the Freedom of Information Amendment (Reform) Act 2010 has had some success in reducing the information asymmetry but that improvements are needed to place the public on an equal footing with government when it comes to access to information.

Australia's Information Commissioner, John McMillan, has proposed a number of changes, most significantly the introduction of a new fee system to address the inadequacy of resources faced by the Office of the Australian Information Commissioner (OAIC). The fee system would aim to encourage an administrative access scheme, with freedom of information being a second resort. Applicants would be charged a $50 application fee if they failed at first attempt to access the document through informal means. The informal administrative access scheme would be free to use, and would require the agency to respond within thirty days.[87] 'Administrative access' is the release of government-held information, in response to a request, without the need for a formal freedom of information request. For example, administrative access would occur when a person calls or emails an agency requesting a document and a response is received via telephone or email. Customer client contact centres or public affairs units could deal with such requests. At the end of this process, if the individual is not satisfied that their right to access information has been met, they can then use their legally enforceable rights under the Freedom of Information Act 1982.[88] A reform such as this would enable citizens to access information easily, informally, and inexpensively, thereby facilitating transparent governance and enabling public participation.

[83] Ibid, 670. [84] Terrill 2000, 31. [85] Dorling 2012. [86] McMillan 2012a.
[87] McMillan 2012b, 6–7. [88] Ibid, 51.

(p) Administrative Appeals Tribunal (AAT)

The AAT was founded by the Administrative Appeals Tribunals Act 1975, alongside numerous other tribunals which came in with the NALs, due to their low set up and running costs. In order to be heard in the AAT, a specific reference to the decision being reviewed by the AAT is required,[89] which has a limiting factor on what can be heard. Standing is given to any 'persons whose interests are affected by decision'[90] and, further to this, 'decisions', is applied more broadly by the AAT as compared to the ADJR, to include questions of fact, contrasting the ADJR where it must only be 'decisions under enactment'.[91] The AAT operates a 'merits review'[92] of the decision of the original decision-maker[93] and exercises all powers of the original decision-maker with the added advantage of considering contemporaneous evidence. 'Merits review' considers issues of fact and law[94] in arriving at the 'correct and preferable'[95] decision adhering to the *Wednesbury* principles.[96] Under the AAT Act, if you initiate an action for merits review, the government decision-maker must provide all documents upon which it based its decision to the AAT, demonstrating that good governance is starting to creep in through legislative reforms.

It has improved the quality of decision-making for a number of reasons:

- the possibility of merits review inspired those in the public service of the need to train decision-makers in order to improve effectiveness;
- the legislation gave a requirement to give reasons;[97]
- the AAT has elaborated the meaning of statutory provisions that had not previously been authoritatively interpreted by an external reviewer;
- establishing accountability for those in power and thus improving quality and properness in decision-making.

It is up to the AAT to decide what part ministerial policy plays in their policymaking. What is in the best interests of the nation is a highly subjective issue and each decision-maker will vary in their perceptions and the effect of the offending conduct. The prospect of inconsistency in decision-making becomes a real threat to the principle of properness in decision-making. This is particularly relevant in migration and cases such as *Re Minister for Immigration and Multicultural Affairs; Ex Parte Miah* (HCA, 2001), involving deportation from Australia, as the effect is very large on the impacted party. In cases such as this, there is a strong argument in favour of ministers adopting policy as integrity of decision-making can be better assured as it has been subjected to parliamentary scrutiny and must adhere to statute. The AAT is at liberty to adopt whatever policy it chooses[98] in fulfilling its statutory function, however, in most cases, lawful ministerial policy is to be applied by tribunals unless cogent reasons to the contrary

[89] Administrative Appeals Tribunal Act 1975 (Cth), s 25(1): an enactment may provide that applications may be made to the AAT for review of decisions made in the exercise of powers conferred by that enactment.

[90] Ibid, s 27(1).

[91] *Griffith University v Tang* (2005) 213 ALR 724.

[92] Administrative Appeals Tribunal Act 1975 (Cth), s 43.

[93] Ibid, s 43(6).

[94] *Collector of Customs (NSW) v Brian Lawlor Automotive Pty Ltd* (1979) 24 ALR 307.

[95] *Greens v Daniels* (1977) 33 ALR 1.

[96] *Associated Provincial Picture Houses Ltd v Wednesbury Corporation* [1948] 1 KB 224: *Wednesbury Principle:* that the decision was so unreasonable that no reasonable decision-maker could have arrived at that decision.

[97] Administrative Appeals Tribunal Act 1975 (Cth), s 2.

[98] *Drake v Minister for Immigration and Ethnic Affairs* (1979) 24 ALR 577 and *Drake No 2* (1979) 2 ALD 634.

exists. There is much debate in this area. For example, Spigelman believes that there should be no need at all for the AAT to follow policy. This intersection of politics involves the principle of political accountability intersecting with legal accountability, which of course does not come through issues.

Criticism is creeping in on the current role of the AAT and its lower prominence in society. It has been argued by Kellam AO J that it has 'settled into the sedate middle age of a court substitute, dispute resolution and accountability mechanism'.[99] This decreased role has come about due to a number of reasons, including the increased prominence of internal review mechanism, increasing privatization and flaws in the system meaning that the AAT will not be expressly given jurisdiction and the excision of migration decisions.

Privative clauses are a 'mechanism by which the Executive attempts to regain control over a particular decision making process'.[100] For example, in 'high level' areas of policy such as migration law in the late-twentieth century it was found that, as migration is a big political issue, Courts have to respect the implementation of that policy, and as courts should not theoretically be involved in the implementation of policy, it leaves migration issues unaccountable for and unable to be judicially reviewed.

However, especially in the current state of events, there is a strong need for questioning and transparency in the migration law area. As of late, there has been a blatant abandonment of international conventions that Australia is a signatory of and breach of international law such as the Convention on the Rights of the Child 1990 and the International Covenant on Civil and Political Rights 1976, not to mention the 1951 Refugee Convention.[101] It is for these reasons that accountability of the government should be put into question, and urgently. The breach of international law is an illegality, however due to this area of law being exempted from review, one cannot go to court and obtain a remedy against this illegality and be subject to review.

This is even in spite of international organizations such as the United Nations and the United Nations High Commissioner for Refugees expressing 'deep concern of Australia's enhanced screen procedures and their non-compliance with international law'.[102] This raises the very on point idea that every breach of a legal norm needs to be enforceable in a court in order to escape areas becoming 'untouchable'. This also conflicts with the separation of powers, as in the instance of a privative clause, protecting an administrator's decision from judicial review; the reality is that the administrator can conclusively determine what the law is. Plainly put, that confers judicial power on an executive power, violating the separation of powers. Privative clauses also come into conflict with section 75(v) of the Australian Constitution 1901 (Cth) whereby it is stated that the 'HC has original jurisdiction where … remedy … is sought against an officer of the Commonwealth'. It is commonly questioned, to no real avail, how this entrenched law can be disregarded. This is an area where significant substantial issues

[99] National Alternative Dispute Resolution Advisory Council, *Legislating for Alternative Dispute Resolution: A guide for government policy makers and legal drafters*, Parliament of the Commonwealth of Australia, Canberra, 2006.

[100] *Administrative Review Council, The Scope of Judicial Review—Report to the Attorney General*, Parliament of Australia, Canberra, 2006.

[101] ABC News, 'Children in Detention: Is Australia breaching international law?', <http://www.abc.net.au/news/2014-03-31/children-in-detention-is-australia-breaching-international-law/5344022>, 8 April 2014.

[102] UNHCR, 'Returns to Sri Lanka of Individuals intercepted at Sea', Press Release, <http://www.unhcr.org/53baa6ff6.html>, 7 July 2014.

of process and system exist and until they are resolved, no real application of the entire scope of the principles of good governance can be realized.

(q) Findings

The function of the abovementioned integrity institutions and legislation, including judicial review by courts, was to ensure that the community-wide expectation of how governments should operate in practice was realized. This idea of integrity goes beyond matters of simple 'legality'. Integrity encourages being faithful to the purposes for which an institution was created and the application of values which an institution is expected to obey. The important distinction to be made is ensuring that powers are exercised for the purpose for which they were conferred and the manner in which they were intended to be exercised, and the reasonableness or appropriateness of the decisions made in the exercise of such powers. A further possible recommendation in this area would be for a Ministerial Code of Conduct, a concept proposed by Uhr,[103] in which it would be clearly set out, with full transparency, the conduct expected and responsibilities of ministers, thus creating 'agreed benchmarks to which the public can hold ministers'.

The influx of integrity commissions, ombudsmen, and means of judicial and merits review follow the line of thought of prominent and influential political scientist Guillermo O'Donnell. He posits that 'good governance efforts were based on the institutionalisation of a more developed concept of horizontal accountability between institutions'.[104] This, in conclusion, means that the classical institutions of the executive, legislator, and the judiciary, in combination with new 'polyarchies',[105] are working, albeit with some hiccups along the way, to provide a system of checks and balances on government power in order to protect and uphold the rights of every citizen of Australia. It is in this way that the early beginnings of good governance can be seen, but there is indeed more work to do in order to catch up to our European counterparts.

The principles of good governance provide the guidelines for a government to ensure stability and performance for their nation. In Victoria, the good governance principles were explored in the Charter whereby several principles interlinked with each other; however, it was noted that adding more fundamental human rights would enhance the Charter's credibility. Moreover, the Australian Constitution provided the structure and roles of the three arms of powers, but its rigidity and drafting makes it difficult to make any changes to the Constitution and, arguably, harder to determine the principles of good governance. Even so, the Constitution is silent on important roles, such as the prime minister, which should be included to ensure better administration. In addition, the mild separation of powers experienced in Australia demonstrates how the three powers provide checks and balances on each other. Moreover, the Commonwealth Ombudsman and the Australian National Audit Office (ANAO) provide an extra assurance that the Australian Government is functioning and performing to its optimal level. Nonetheless, there are many aspects of the Australian government that could have been explored; however, these four areas demonstrate that Australia does value a government that is just and fair. This does not mean Australians cannot strive for better means of good governance.

Freedom of information systems have the potential to promote the principles of good governance, and the Australian Commonwealth Freedom of Information Act

[103] Uhr 2005. [104] O'Donnell 1999, 29–39. [105] Ibid.

1982 is no different. Freedom of information legislation advances transparency by establishing a governmental obligation to release government information, both proactively and reactively, and to ensure that information is delivered in a timely and accessible manner. Freedom of information can enhance participation by creating informed citizens. Despite this potential, the Freedom of Information Act 1982 has historically failed to achieve these aims due to high costs, lengthy delays, and a governmental culture that promoted secrecy over transparency. The Act served to facilitate an information asymmetry between government and the public. The Freedom of Information Amendment (Reform) Act 2010 has served to address some of these issues, demonstrating a shift from a 'pull' model of information disclosure to a 'push' model. A continuation in the direction of a 'push' model, facilitated by the use of information and communication technology, and the utilization of an administrative access scheme, could realize the potential of the Freedom of Information Act 1982 to enhance public transparency and participation in Australia.

3. Implementation of the Good Governance Principles in Canada

Understanding 'good governance' in Canada is a difficult task. While there is literature to suggest that there is 'good governance' in Canada,[106] it is not specifically defined by the Constitution, in any legislation, in policies, or in case law. There are, however, principles of good governance, as defined by the United Nations (UN), which Canada practices. These principles have various sources throughout Canada. Some principles are newer and less practised, whereas others have been engrained in society since the independence of Canada as a country with the British North America Act 1867. While learning about good governance in Canada, the history behind the practices and principles and how it works in everyday life, it is evident that Canada is largely a country wherein good governance is practised. There are, however, improvements that can be made, as Canada, like any other country, has its flaws.

We begin with an explanation of the concept of good governance in Canada. This is followed by an outline of where the principles of good governance practised within the country can be found. Second, the sources of good governance will be explained. Within this section the 1982 Constitution ('the Constitution') and the Canadian Charter of Rights and Freedoms ('the Charter') are explored, specifically focusing on 'peace, order, and good government', the 'rule of law' in Canada, and the 'equality rights' guaranteed to Canadian citizens. The next part discusses the judiciary, one of the three branches of government within Canada. Specifically, judicial independence and the transparency of the judiciary will be explained. Subsequently, it will be argued that Canada's electoral system represents the principle of participation, as it is representative of Canadian citizens and its provinces and territories. In the following part, a specific Act of Parliament is discussed to further prove the principles of transparency and accountability within the Canadian government. Afterwards, the accountability of administrative officials in Canada is discussed. The last part examines various examples

[106] Graham, Amos, and Plumptre 2003, 1–9; Wilson 2012, 12; Treasury Board of Canada Secretariat, Meeting the Expectations of Canadians: Review of the Governance Framework for Canada's Crown Corporations (Report to Parliament) (Her Majesty the Queen in Right of Canada, 2005), <http://www.tbs-sct.gc.ca> [Meeting the Expectations of Canadians] at 7.

of certain principles of good governance, and specifically how the courts have interpreted these principles, creating binding case law throughout the country.

(a) Good governance concept

Given that Canada's unofficial national motto is 'Peace, Order, and Good Government', it may not come as a surprise that good governance is an area in which Canada has been identified as a country with experience and knowledge.[107]

Good governance has become a fundamental feature of the Canadian identity, and is heavily promoted in Canada's foreign and development policy.[108] That being said, deciphering what 'good governance' means in Canada is not necessarily an easy task. Good governance is not explicitly defined in the Canadian Constitution, or in legislation, overarching government policies, or case law. Indeed, in 2007, during a panel discussion on Canadian good governance at the Centre for International Governance Innovation in Ottawa, a consensus on what 'good' meant could not be reached.[109] Several different organizations, committees, councils, and institutions have formulated lists of principles defining what 'good governance' actually is. However, similar themes and principles can be found throughout the literature, and most seem to be based on the United Nations Development Programme's (UNDP's) set of principles.

Canada does not have a specific set of principles of good governance that the country is governed by, but it does practise good governance as defined by the UN, which Canada has been a member of since its foundation in 1945.[110] The UN states that 'Good governance promotes equity, participation, pluralism, transparency, accountability and the rule of law, in a manner that is effective, efficient and enduring'.[111] This terminology translates into principles of good governance, which are similar to those in the European Council. The sources of good governance in Canada come from the Constitution, the Charter, case law that has interpreted the Constitution and the Charter, the judiciary, Canada's electoral system, Acts of Parliament, and the country's commitment to a transparent and accountable government.

(b) Good government, good governance, and the principle of properness

When discussing good governance in Canada it is important to look at the Constitution and the Charter. The introduction to section 91 of the Constitution reads:

> It shall be lawful for the Queen, by and with the Advice and Consent of the Senate and House of Commons, to make Laws for the Peace, Order, and good Government of Canada, in relation to all Matters not coming within the Classes of Subjects by this Act assigned exclusively to the Legislatures of the Provinces.[112]

This introduction, specifically the words 'peace, order, and good government', essentially enables Parliament to enact laws on matters not conferred upon the provinces. More importantly, it establishes that good government is important in Canada. The history of peace, order, and good government is significant. Prior to 1867, within

[107] Welsh 2007, 279. [108] Thompson 2007. [109] Ibid.

[110] Government of Canada, Canada and the United Nations (2015), online: Permanent Mission of Canada to the United Nations <http://www.canadainternational.gc.ca/>.

[111] United Nations, Governance (2015), online: United Nations <http://www.un.org/>.

[112] Constitution Act 1982, s 91, being Sch B to the Canada Act 1982 (UK), 1982, c 11 [Constitution].

Britain the phrase used was 'peace, welfare and good government'. However, the word 'welfare' was replaced with 'order' in the British North America Act 1867.[113] The former term 'welfare', which was associated with 'commonwealth' or 'common good', 'implied a concern for the well-being of the individual citizen', whereas 'order' is 'concerned with the group or the state'.[114] Peace, order, and good government ensure powers that are not allocated to the provinces rest with the national government, which 'continues the traditional commitment of the Crown to its citizens'.[115] The Constitution, which 'is the supreme law of Canada',[116] sets out the importance of good government within Canada. Although 'good government' is not the same as 'good governance', this introduction shows Canada's commitment to its country, having a government that is fair, transparent, representative, effective, accountable, and that promotes equality.

Further expanding on Canada's commitment to good government, the preamble to the Charter reads: '[w]hereas Canada is founded upon principles that recognize the supremacy of God and the rule of law'.[117] This means that Canada is 'ruled by law, not by those who enforce the law or wield government power. No one in Canada is above the law'.[118] Furthermore, 'everyone is subject to the law', no matter how important that person is.[119] The rule of law is seen and practised outside of the Canadian context as well.

The rule of law is defined by the UN Secretary-General as a principle of governance in which all persons, institutions and entities, public and private, including the state itself, are accountable to laws that are publicly promulgated, equally enforced and independently adjudicated, and which are consistent with international human rights norms and standards. It requires, as well, measures to ensure adherence to the principles of supremacy of law, equality before the law, accountability to the law, fairness in the application of the law, separation of powers, participation in decision-making, legal certainty, avoidance of arbitrariness and procedural and legal transparency.[120] Several principles can be drawn out from this definition, namely: judicial independence, equality, supremacy of law, accountability, fairness, separation of powers, participation, legal certainty, and transparency. Some of these principles of the rule of law overlap with the UN's definition of good governance.

Thus, while abiding by the rule of law, Canada follows international principles of good governance. As previously mentioned, the UN's principles of good governance can be found in the Constitution, the three branches of government, and by practice within Canada. The principle of human rights, or the UN's equity, is found in section 15 of the Charter, which lays out equality rights: 'Every individual is equal before and under the law and has the right to the equal protection and equal benefit of the law without discrimination and, in particular, without discrimination based on race, national or ethnic origin, colour, religion, sex, age or mental or physical disability.'[121] This is enforced and interpreted by the courts through litigation, like the rest of the Constitution. This section has been interpreted many times by the judiciary within Canada, but most importantly by the Supreme Court of Canada (SCC), which is

[113] Wilson 2012, 237. [114] Ibid, 238. [115] Ibid, 237.

[116] Constitution Act 1982, s 52(1).

[117] Canadian Charter of Rights and Freedoms, Part I of the Constitution Act, 1982, being Schedule B to the Canada Act 1982 (UK), 1982, c 11 [Charter].

[118] Canadian Superior Court Judges Association, The Rule of Law (2006), online: CSCJA <http://www.cscja-acjcs.ca/>.

[119] Forsey 2012, 30. [120] Ibid. [121] Canadian Charter, s 15(1).

Canada's highest court and the general court of appeal from all Canadian courts of law.[122] Decisions made by the SCC are binding on all lower courts of Canada.

(c) The principle of human rights

The courts are the protectors of the Charter and are able to interpret it in such a way that if a law is inconsistent with the Charter the court has the ability to strike it down. In Canada, under section 15 of the Charter all persons in the same situation must be accorded the same treatment. To make a claim for equal treatment, an individual or group must demonstrate their 'sameness' to the norm and their differential treatment from that norm.[123]

In *Egan v Canada*,[124] the plaintiffs were a gay couple and upon reaching the age of 65, Mr Egan became eligible to receive old age security from the government under the Old Age Security Act. Mr Egan was refused on the basis that the definition of spouse did not include a member of the same sex. The plaintiffs alleged that the definition of 'spouse' constituted an infringement on their section 15 equality rights under the Charter and that this infringement was discriminatory on the basis of sexual orientation. The Court unanimously held that under section 15 of the Charter sexual orientation is an analogous ground.[125] The definition of 'spouse' as someone of the opposite sex reinforces the stereotype that homosexuals cannot and do not form lasting, caring, mutually supportive relationships with economic interdependence in the same manner as heterosexual couples. This case shows the courts' ability to interpret the Charter and align with current views, adding analogous grounds to our equality rights. The SCC has discussed the 'living tree' theory and said the Constitution was drafted with an eye to the future, capable of growth and development over time. There is a need for a broad perspective, which must meet the realities of the time.[126]

An example of a controversial decision made by the SCC is *Canada (Attorney General) v Bedford*. The plaintiffs argued that three provisions of the Criminal Code of Canada ('the Criminal Code') surrounding bawdyhouses, living on the avails of prostitution, and communicating for the purposes of prostitution were unconstitutional.[127] The SCC declared sections of the Criminal Code inconsistent with the Charter and hence the laws were void. This SCC decision gathered much media attention. However, because of judicial independence, the judges are able to make an impartial decision without fear of retribution.

(d) The principle of transparency

Transparency has been enshrined in Canada by Acts of Parliament. Transparency means 'the public has the right and should have the means to assess whether or not the government is delivering on its policy commitments and whether or not public funds are being managed effectively'.[128]

In 1985, the Canadian Parliament enacted the Access to Information Act, which allows Canadian citizens to request access to government records. The purpose of the Access to Information Act is to: 'extend the present laws of Canada to provide a right

[122] Supreme Court of Canada, The Canadian Judicial System (2008), online at <https://www.scc-csc.ca/court-cour/sys-eng.aspx>.

[123] Macklem and others 2010.

[124] [1995] 2 SCR 513.

[125] *Egan v Canada* [1995] 2 SCR 513.

[126] *Hunter v Southam Inc* [1984] 2 SCR 145.

[127] *Canada (Attorney General) v Bedford*, 2013 SCC 72 at 3–6.

[128] Ibid.

of access to information in records under the control of a government institution in accordance with the principles that government information should be available to the public, that necessary exceptions to the right of access should be limited and specific and that decisions on the disclosure of government information should be reviewed independently of government'.[129]

A Canadian citizen 'has a right to and shall, on request, be given access to any record under the control of a government institution'.[130] Requests to access records must be made in writing to the government institution that has control of the record. Within thirty days after the request is received the head of the government institution must: (a) give written notice of whether or not access or partial access will be granted; or (b) give access to the record.[131]

With respect to the review of information independent of government, section 30 reads: 'the Information Commission shall receive and investigate complaints'.[132] In addition, the Commissioner shall report to Parliament within three months after the termination of each fiscal year. The Commissioner acts as a type of ombudsman to citizens requesting records who have been denied access to the records or receive redacted records. This holds the government institutions accountable for the decisions they make of whether or not to grant access, as well as creates transparency with respect to government records.

In Canada, judicial independence is a fundamental part of the judiciary. If administrative authorities in Canada exercise power they have not been given and thus do not abide by the rule of law, they must answer to the courts,[133] which hold them accountable. Furthermore, the courts interpret the Constitution. Judicial independence allows the judiciary to ensure laws are proper, effective, and equal.

The first component of judicial independence is security of tenure. The English Act of Settlement 1701 states, 'judges, though appointed by the King . . . could be removed only if both houses of Parliament, by a formal address to the Crown, asked for their removal'.[134] Today, section 99 of the Constitution gives superior court justices guarantees with regard to their tenure.[135] This allows justices to be safe in their position, despite the government disliking their decisions, since both the House of Commons and the Senate must both ask for their removal.[136] Section 11(d) of the Charter requires provincial court judges, which do not fall under the heading of 'superior court justice', to be subject to an independent review and determination before removal, and only by causes related to their capacity to perform their judicial functions.[137] Security of tenure allows judges to make controversial or unpopular decisions, or interpret the Constitution in a restrictive or expansive way, in the best interest of the citizens without the fear that they will be fired or reprimanded for their decisions.

The second component is financial security. The Supreme Court of Canada held that section 100 of the Constitution 'requires that the salaries of superior judges be fixed by parliament directly', but section 11(d) of the Charter 'requires that the right

[129] Access to Information Act, RSC, 1985, C A-1, s 2(1) [Access to Information Act].

[130] Ibid, s 4(1). [131] Ibid, ss 6 and 7. [132] Ibid, s 30(1).

[133] Supreme Court of Canada, The Canadian Judicial System, online at <https://www.scc-csc.ca/court-cour/sys-eng.aspx>.

[134] Forsey 2012, 31.

[135] The Canadian Bar Association, Judicial Independence in Canada, (Legislation and Law Reform Department: 2009), online: <http://www.cba.org/> [Judicial Independence in Canada] at 1.

[136] Forsey 2012, 31.

[137] Judicial Independence in Canada, The Canadian Judicial System (2008), online: SCC-CSC <http://www.scccsc.gc.ca/> at 2.

to salary and pension be established by law and not be subject to arbitrary inference by the executive in a manner that could affect the independence of the individual judge'.[138] Judges must be paid sufficiently so they are not in a position of dependence or pressure.[139] This allows judges to make decisions without external pressures or corruption. The SCC, as well as the lower courts, can strike down federal and provincial legislation that infringe Charter rights. Last is administrative independence, which requires judicial control over their matters.[140] This 'means that no one can interfere with how courts manage the litigation process and exercise their judicial functions'.[141] Each jurisdiction within Canada, including the provinces, territories, and federally, has a judicial council that promotes professional standards of conduct. These councils can recommend the removal of a judge if necessary.[142] Therefore, while judges have security of tenure, financial security, and administrative independence, there is still a system in Canada to hold judges accountable for their actions.

In addition to judicial independence, the Canadian judiciary follows the principle of transparency. There is public access to judicial proceedings, 'except where the court has determined that certain proceedings should be closed to the public'.[143] Likewise, all materials filed with the court are public, unless otherwise ordered. Furthermore, hearings are generally open and accessible to the public, unless a court orders the material shall be treated as confidential. An example of restriction to access is 'serious risks to individual privacy and security rights'.[144] Overall, it is apparent that the judiciary operates transparently and allows public access to hearings and decisions. Similarly, the Canadian electoral system and Parliament value the principles of transparency and accountability, as well as participation.

(e) The principle of participation

The electoral system of Canada carries out the principle of participation, as the Members of Parliament represent their specific electoral district in the House of Commons. Within Canada, the legislature is elected democratically, and it is accountable to the executive.

There were 338 electoral districts in the 2015 federal election (thirty more than the previous 308 electoral districts), and the candidate with the highest number of votes in each electoral district is elected as a Member of Parliament and wins a seat in the House of Commons. Moreover, 'the party with the largest number of elected representatives will normally form the Government, and its leader is the Prime Minister. It must be able at all times to maintain the confidence of the House in order to remain in power.' The system within Canada is that of plurality, as one candidate does not have to have the majority of the votes to win, just the most votes.[145]

[138] Ibid.

[139] Government of Canada, Canada's Court System (2015), online: Department of Justice <http://www.justice.gc.ca/>.

[140] Judicial Independence in Canada, The Canadian Judicial System (2008), online: SCC-CSC <http://www.scccsc.gc.ca/> at 2.

[141] Government of Canada, Canada's Court System (2015), online: Department of Justice <http://www.justice.gc.ca/>.

[142] Ibid.

[143] Open Society Justice Initiative, 'Report on Access to Judicial Information' (2009) at 7.

[144] Ibid at 9.

[145] Elections Canada, The Electoral System of Canada (2011), online: Elections Canada <http://www.elections.ca/>.

(f) The principle of accountability

Canada's Parliament values accountability, such as in Crown Corporations, which are corporations owned by the provincial or federal governments.

The Treasury Board of Canada defines accountability as 'a relationship based on the obligation to demonstrate and take responsibility for performance in light of agreed expectations'.[146] Governance, as opposed to government 'is concerned with how other actors, such as civil society organizations, may play a role in taking decisions on matters of public concern'.[147] This can include Crown corporations, which have autonomy over decision-making, but report back to Ministers. These Ministers, who are appointed officials, are accountable to Parliament for their Crown corporations within their departments, for day-to-day operations, but also to show that they are running effectively.[148]

It is important to note the accountability of administrative officials when discussing good governance within Canada. There are various ways to hold an administrative official accountable if he or she exercises power not given to him or her. The first type of recourse is judicial review. This is where the courts oversee the decisions made by public administrative officials to ensure the decisions made are within their conferred powers. Judicial review is specifically for cases of procedural unfairness or when the decision-maker's statutory mandate was exceeded.[149] All legislative and executive actions are subject to review by the judiciary. The relief for judicial review can be: (a) common law remedies, which are historically known as 'prerogative writs'; (b) declaration and injunctions; and (c) damages and costs. A further discussion of the types of relief is beyond the scope of this chapter.

The Charter provides for enforcement of guaranteed rights and freedoms. Section 24(1) reads: '[a]nyone whose rights or freedoms, as guaranteed by this Charter, have been infringed or denied may apply to a court of competent jurisdiction to obtain such remedy as the Court considers appropriate and just in the circumstances.' Furthermore, section 24(2) allows courts to exclude evidence that was obtained in a manner that infringed a Charter right, thus holding the police accountable for their actions. This remedy under the Charter allows courts to give a Canadian citizen a remedy if their rights or freedoms are infringed, holding Parliament accountable for decisions made.

In addition, every province and territory within Canada has an ombudsman, which is a public official appointed by government but is independent and deals with public complaints against government officials. For example, the Ombudsman of Ontario 'investigates public complaints about Ontario government services'. The ombudsman has strong powers of investigation, which are found in the Ombudsman Act, RSO 1990, c O.6 and all provincial government organizations must cooperate with the investigation.[150] The ombudsman recommends solutions and publishes results of major investigations and notable cases in the Annual Report. A glaring omission within Canada

[146] Minister of Public Works and Government Services Canada, Chapter 9: Modernizing Accountability in the Public Sector (Report of the Auditor General of Canada to the House of Commons) (Office of the Auditor General of Canada: Ottawa: 2002), online: OAG-BVG <http://www.oag-bvg.gc.ca>.

[147] Graham, Amos, and Plumptre 2003, 2.

[148] Meeting the Expectations of Canadians, supra note 1 at 7.

[149] Van Harten, Heckman, and Mullan 2010, 26.

[150] Ombudsman Ontario, Frequently Asked Questions (2015), online: Ombudsman Ontario <https://ombudsman.on.ca>.

is that there is no federal ombudsman of a general federal jurisdiction, only specialized ombudsmen dealing with specific areas, such as the Office of the Correctional Investigator[151] or the Federal Ombudsman for Victims of Crime.[152]

(g) Findings

Although Canada does not have a specific source of legislation that explicitly outlines the principles of good governance, it is clear that Canada has put them into practice. There are several sources where good governance can be found throughout Canada, which were discussed.

The Constitution is the supreme law of Canada and guarantees Canadian citizens 'peace, order, and good government'. Although 'good government' is not the same as 'good governance', this constitutional guarantee, from 1867, sets the background for the government's concern with the well-being of the country. Furthermore, the rule of law provides that every person must abide by the law and no one is above the law. Section 15 of the Charter guarantees equality rights to Canadian citizens, showing that the principle of human rights is enshrined in the Constitution. The judiciary is also a source for good governance. Judicial independence allows for effective decision-making by the courts. The transparency of judicial proceedings and cases further enhances Canada's commitment to good governance. Within Canada's electoral system the regional representation in Parliament shows the principle of participation. Additionally, Acts of Parliament, specifically on the release of records, has made the Canadian government more transparent and accountable over the last several decades. Finally, administrative officials are held accountable by judicial review, section 24 of the Charter, and with the provincial, territorial, and specialized federal ombudsman. The last section of this chapter discussed examples of how the judiciary has interpreted the Charter. Their interpretation of equality rights shows an expansion on the enumerated grounds of equality within Canada.

While Canada appears to follow principles of good governance, there is still room for improvement. With respect to participation, only about 20 per cent of the seats in Parliament are held by women.[153] In the 2011 federal election, 9.1 per cent of the Members of Parliament were visible minorities, which is much lower than their proportion of the Canadian population, which is 19.1 per cent.[154] Furthermore, there is no general federal ombudsman holding the federal government accountable. There are specific ombudsmen for various departments, but this leaves gaping holes for departments without an ombudsman. The ombudsman does not play a very important role in Canadian society, and is 'a complaint mechanism of last resort'.[155] Additionally, the Access to Information Act is only thirty years old and transparency is a topic of interest within Canada. Certain new bills, such as Bill C-51, allow the government to make

[151] Government of Canada, Howard Sapers: Correctional Investigator of Canada (2013), online: Office of the Correctional Investigator <http://www.oci-bec.gc.ca/>.

[152] Government of Canada, What we are and what we do (2015), online: Office of the Federal Ombudsman for Victims of Crime <http://www.victimsfirst.gc.ca/>.

[153] The World Bank Group, Proportion of seats held by women in national parliaments (%) (Washington, DC: 2015), online: IBRD-IDA <http://data.worldbank.org/>.

[154] Canadian Parliamentary Review, Racial Diversity in the 2011 Federal Election: Visible Minority Candidates and MPs (Toronto: 2015), online: Rev Parl <http://www.revparl.ca/>.

[155] Alberta Ombudsman, Frequently Asked Questions (2015), online: Alberta Ombudsman <https://www.ombudsman.ab.ca>.

decisions, specifically a no-fly list, which lack transparency. Canada would benefit from having an overall more representative, accountable, and transparent Parliament.

4. Implementation of the Good Governance Principles in South Africa

Good governance in South Africa is regulated and promoted through administrative law, which contains a normative framework for the relation between the administration and the citizens. Maladministration can be defined broadly to cover all cases of economic mismanagement, political inefficiency, and corruption. Maladministration has a demoralizing effect on the citizens of South Africa and produces an apathetic and disinterested electorate. It is true that African states have experienced economic decline since independence due mostly to a mismanagement of resources.[156] We also find in South Africa bid rigging, corruption, maladministration, and political elites serving their own personal interests. Unlike many developing countries in Africa, South African citizens have a fundamental right to just administration. This requires all administrative action to meet the minimum requirements of lawfulness, reasonableness, and procedural fairness. Further, legislative enactments have been undertaken to realize this right and further its development within the governance sector.

(a) Good governance and just administration

It is stated that the concepts of democracy, the rule of law, and good governance are the cornerstones of the modern state, and that governance concerns the state's ability to serve its citizens.[157] This position is justified by the fact that good governance is a citizen's right as well as a governmental norm. This is true for many countries, including South Africa—albeit only within the last twenty years.

While the term 'good governance' is not a term used to describe the oversight of governmental power in South Africa, it translates effectively into what the Constitution of the Republic of South Africa (1996) terms 'just administration'. In *Pharmaceutical Manufacturers Association of South Africa*[158] the Constitutional Court explained that administrative law forms the core of public law in South Africa and overlaps with constitutional law due to the fact that it deals both with organs of state and their relationships with individuals. However, administrative law emphasizes administrative action by the public administration. *President of RSA v SARFU*[159] refines this by stating that the administration is the part of government that is primarily concerned with the implementation of legislation. Thus, in summary, administrative law regulates the activities of bodies that exercise public power or perform public functions. In other words, it regulates the act of governance. It limits the exercise of power by requiring all administrative action to meet the minimum requirements of lawfulness, reasonableness, and procedural fairness as demanded by section 33 of the Constitution of South Africa. We can see how good governance translates effectively to 'just administration' in this context.

[156] Theletsane 2014, 842.   [157] Addink 2015a, 8.

[158] *Pharmaceutical Manufacturers Association of SA and Another: In re ex parte President Republic of South Africa* 2000 (2) SA 674 (CC).

[159] *President of the Republic of South Africa v SARFU* 2000 1 SA1 (CC).

(b) Good governance and administrative law: enforcement by court and ombudsman

Governance in South Africa has had to overcome numerous problems caused by the burden of history.[160] There have been a number of unethical and corruptive constraints as well as a history of government secrecy. In order to overcome these difficulties and to strengthen the rule of law and enhance legitimacy in such a young democracy, an efficient public administration was required. South Africa's Constitutional dispensation has allowed for the creation of a solid foundation for good public administration. In the words of the Constitutional Court, administrative law in South Africa is an incident of the separation of powers through which the courts regulate and control the exercise of public power by the other branches of government.[161]

It is true that the principles of good governance can only become legal norms if they are properly integrated into the legal system. Further, there must be a legal effect flowing from the application of these principles.[162] In South Africa, the right to just administrative action is contained in section 33 of the Constitution of the Republic of South Africa. This is a fundamental right to lawful, reasonable, and procedurally fair administrative action. Section 33(3) goes on to place a positive obligation on the legislature to enact legislation giving effect to these rights. Within that legislation the legislature was to provide for: the review of administrative action by a court or an independent tribunal; impose a duty on the state to give effect to the rights stated above; and promote efficient administration. Since 1994, the judiciary has functioned independently and has been free to render judgements that are in conflict with the policies of the executive. However, a few recent incidents raise questions regarding the current government's dedication towards maintaining the independence of the judiciary.[163]

Not only a court or independent tribunal, but an Ombudsman was also needed. During South Africa's multiparty negotiations preceding the creation of the Constitution, it was agreed that South Africa required an 'Ombudsman'. However, it was later agreed that South Africa's 'Ombudsman' should have a more descriptive name, hence the adoption of the name 'Public Protector'.

(c) Good governance specified by the Promotion of Justice Act 2000

Thus, we can see that in South Africa there is an integration of good governance principles at the highest level, allowing all manner of legal effects to flow therefrom. However, the Constitution is not the only source of administrative law. In order of importance, the sources of administrative law are: the Constitution; legislation (which includes acts of parliament, provincial legislation, by-laws, and regulations); and the common law, which is said to have been subsumed by the Constitution and legislation.[164] Although it is not termed 'good governance', the practical effect that 'just administration' strives for is much the same.

As a result of the positive obligation placed on the legislature by section 33(3) of the Constitution, the Promotion of Administrative Justice Act 3 of 2000 (PAJA) was

[160] Cloete and Auriacombe 2007, 193.
[161] *Pharmaceutical Manufacturers Association of SA and Another: In re ex parte President of the Republic of South Africa* 2000 (2) SA 674 (CC).
[162] Addink 2015a, 17. [163] Theletsane 2014, 840.
[164] *Greys Marine Hout Bay (Pty) Ltd v Minister of Public Works* 2005 (6) SA 313 (SCA).

promulgated. This statute is the cornerstone of administrative law in South Africa and seeks to give effect to the fundamental right to just administrative action. The preamble to PAJA promotes efficient administration and good governance and emphasizes the need for accountability, openness, and transparency in public administration. If a member of the public wishes to invoke their right to just administration they must, due to the principle of subsidiarity, do so through the processes provided for in PAJA. They cannot, for example, directly invoke their Constitutional right.[165] This ensures a proper balancing of interests as well as an opportunity for both sides to appeal the decision to a higher court if necessary.

In section 1, PAJA defines administrative action as any action or decision performed by an organ of state or any exercise of public power other than through executive, legislative, or judicial action. Thus, the definition of administrative action within PAJA correlates with the definition of governance stated above. We can therefore effectively analyse 'good governance' within South Africa by looking at what is termed 'just administrative action'. However, within section 1 of PAJA there are restrictions to its application, in ensuring just administrative action and allowing redress for citizens. In summary, an action will only be termed administrative action (and will therefore be subject to PAJA) if it is a decision by an organ of state (or a natural or juristic person) when exercising a public power or performing a public function in terms of any legislation (or in terms of an empowering provision) that has the capacity to immediately and directly impact on people's rights.[166]

It is important for a decision to fall under this definition if the affected party is to have any legislative remedies regarding the decision. This is criticized as being too restrictive; however, it is also stated that a balance must be struck between ensuring just administrative action and allowing for an efficient, unhindered public service sector. An over-emphasis of the law could result in an overly rigid approach to administration, resulting in a lack of flexibility and efficiency due to the constant fear of prosecution.[167]

Once a decision falls under the definition in PAJA, it will allow the aggrieved party access to remedies contained in section 6 of the Act. Importantly, it allows for a method of enforcing the principles contained in PAJA and ensuring that administrative decisions are made properly, efficiently, and effectively according to the minimum standards of lawfulness, reasonableness, and procedural fairness. Section 6 provides for a process of judicial review whereby the court has discretion to make an order that it determines is just and reasonable under the circumstances. Such an order may vary from damages to the court changing the administrative action in question, depending on the finality and seriousness of the issue.[168]

PAJA does not only facilitate litigation on the basis of administrative action, however, it also calls for the creation of a code for good administration (see section 10). The result is the Code for Good Administrative Conduct. It is stated in the document that good administrative conduct follows the Constitution, the law, and the policies of government that are designed to ensure efficient and effective service delivery. The Code serves to explain the Constitution and PAJA to administrators in order to assist them in the performance of their duties. It therefore provides guidance to ensure that administrators make decisions that are lawful, reasonable, and procedurally fair. Further, it

[165] *Pharmaceutical Manufacturers Association of SA and Another: In re ex parte President of the Republic of South Africa* 2000 (2) SA 674 (CC).

[166] *Greys Marine Hout Bay (Pty) Ltd v Minister of Public Works* 2005 (6) SA 313 (SCA).

[167] Theletsane 2014, 840.

[168] Cloete and Auriacombe 2007, 192–206.

assists them in complying with the requirement that, when requested, written reasons must be given for a decision. The Code does not impose any additional legal obligations on administrators other than those imposed by the Constitution and PAJA.[169]

Section 10 of PAJA also resulted in the creation of the Regulations on Fair Administrative Procedures. This is a legally binding regulation that comes into operation once an administrator decides to hold a public hearing concerning a matter of policy creation or implementation in terms of section 4(1) of PAJA. A Minister may decide to facilitate a public hearing or he or she may be forced to conduct a public hearing depending on the nature of the decision taken and its capacity to directly impact citizens' rights.[170] It is therefore clear that South African law has developed a strategic, purposive, and holistic approach to the topic of good governance, facilitating a unique approach to advance 'just administration', or 'good governance'.

(d) Principles of properness and human rights

Broadly speaking, the principles of good governance apply to all the powers of the state and are very important in the public sector.[171] It should be noted that international investment normally requires for these principles of good governance to be present.[172] Thus, the absence of these principles can destroy a country's economy. The elements of good governance noted below pertain to the South African context and they function effectively in their manifestation of good governance.[173] Rule of law means that the law must be fair and must also be enforced fairly. It strengthens the legal, judicial, and law enforcement systems and ensures their effective application across all spheres throughout the country.[174] The Constitution ensures that government officials are subject to the rule of law and which in essence also include the principle of properness.

Human rights are relevant and it is important to know that South Africa has a liberal Constitution that protects all manner of political, social, and economic rights. *Equity* is a very important topic in South Africa. It is always said that imbalances in society created by Apartheid rule must be corrected in order to gain equity. Thus, equity is at the vanguard of thinking in South Africa.[175] Section 9 of the Constitution contains the 'equality clause', which has horizontal as well as vertical effect. In terms of this clause, 'everyone is equal before the law and has the right to equal protection and benefit of the law'. This illustrates the importance of equality within the South African context. The Constitution also obliges the courts to consider international human rights in their decisions. In *S v Makwanyane*, the Constitutional Court held that both binding and non-binding international law may be used as tools of interpretation.[176] Despite this, the government has struggled to meet demands for social and economic rights and it has failed to address the root cause of the xenophobic violence that has swept the nation. Issues such as unemployment, corruption, and police brutality remain a concern for South Africans.[177] The Constitutional Court plays a crucial role in maintaining an international standard of human rights in South Africa.

[169] Draft: Code of Good Administrative Conduct. Department of Justice RSA (2006).

[170] Regulations on Fair Administrative Procedures. Department of Justice Regulation Gazette no 23674 of 31 July 2002.

[171] Addink, 2015a, 10. [172] Binda 2015, 45. [173] Theletsane 2014, 838.

[174] Ibid, 839. [175] Ibid, 841. [176] *S v Makwanyane* 1995 (6) BCLR 665 (CC).

[177] Horsten 2006.

(e) Principles of transparency and participation

Transparency is related to the availability of information to the public and clarity regarding government rules, regulations, and decisions.[178] The main element of transparency is the public's access to information held by the government.[179] Section 32 of the Constitution gives every South African the right to any information held by the state as well as any information that is held by another person but is required for the protection or exercise of any rights. The Promotion of Access to Information Act 2 of 2000 has been promulgated to qualify and give effect to this right. This facilitation of the right to access information has proved vital in the burgeoning democracy as the country emerges from Apartheid rule where the majority of the population was denied any access to information. However, transparency also has its limits—especially in a developing country—and beyond those limits further transparency may in fact be counter-productive.[180] That being said, further initiatives that have stressed the need for good governance through transparency in Africa, and particularly South Africa, include Transparency International, the Africa Leadership Forum, the World Summit on sustainable Development, and the United Nations Development Programme.[181] Transparency is a principle that is becoming increasingly stressed in South Africa, particularly with regard to financial information.[182] This is due to the large amounts of 'irregular government expenditure' and corrupt tender agreements.

In South Africa, prior to the democratic dispensation, the majority of the population was denied the right to public participation due to Apartheid policy. Black, coloured, and Indian South African citizens were denied the right to vote or to contribute to the policymaking process.[183] However, since 1994 the requirement for public participation can be found in section 19(5) of the Constitution of South Africa. This safeguards constructive public participation regarding matters of governance, policy formulation, and policy implementation. It has been stated that the legislation of South Africa should allow and encourage ordinary members of the public to participate in the policymaking process. Developing a culture of participation helps local people to become aware of their problems, act collectively, and also make them aware of the various alternatives at their disposal.[184] In order to foster this participation, the South African government should make its documents available in all eleven official languages.

(f) Principles of effectiveness and accountability

Effectiveness is also important because South Africa is a country with limited resources and a vast array of social and economic problems. Thus, structures and processes should produce results that meet the needs of the people while ensuring the sustainable use of resources.[185] Certain needs may take preference over others; thus, transparency also plays a role within this element of good governance. Effectiveness therefore relates to the extent to which these structures and processes meet their desired objectives. Efficiency means minimizing the amount of resources used without influencing the quality of the measures used.

Accountability is a key characteristic of any modern democratic government. It is stated that one of the traditional cornerstones of democracy is that each political official and representative is subject to accountability.[186] Section 92(2) of the Constitution

[178] Theletsane 2014, 842. [179] Cloete and Auriacombe 2007, 196. [180] Ibid, 200.
[181] Ibid, 199. [182] Theletsane 2014, 840. [183] Masango 2002, 54.
[184] Ibid. [185] Theletsane 2014, 840. [186] Ibid, 841.

stipulates that cabinet members are collectively and individually accountable to parliament for the exercise of their powers and the performance of their public functions, and that they must provide parliament with full and regular reports concerning matters under their control. There is also a similar level of accountability demanded from Members of the Executive Council (MECs) to provincial legislatures. Further, the Municipal Structures Act 117 of 1998 states that mayors are accountable to municipal councils.[187] These important pieces of legislation show the government's apparent seriousness in holding government officials to account. However, this seriousness has deteriorated over the years, with government officials increasingly avoiding accountability for all manner of things including fake education certificates, lavish spending of taxpayer's money, and corrupt tender schemes. It is to this end that the discussion on the role of the Public Protector within the South African political arena becomes important.

(g) Findings

It is clear from the brief overview provided that South Africa has extensively integrated the principles of good governance into its legal system. Not only is just administration a fundamental right but its infringement also allows for legal consequences to flow therefrom. However, this does not mean that the principles of good governance are protected and promoted to their full potential. South Africa clearly faces many of the same problems that other developing countries in Africa face and it is imperative that these problems are overcome in order for democracy and the rule of law to thrive. Thus, although South Africa has laid a sound legal foundation for the promotion of good governance, lessons can still be learned from other developed nations and regions on how to translate these legal norms into practical application.

5. Conclusions

At the end of each section we have already made some conclusions about each of the countries, Australia, Canada, and South Africa. The general line is that the principles of good governance have not yet been developed as written principles; this has the consequence that there is not deep substantial discussion about the contents of each of the six principles of good governance which have been distinguished in this book.

There is a second more general observation possible from which we can see that the concept of good governance has been accepted in the three countries and that is important because that is the motor for the further development of each of the six principles of good governance. Most explicit is in the Constitution of Canada where the concept of good government has been codified, but this formulation is strongly focused on the government as an institution and not so explicit about the activities of the governmental institutions. In all the three countries the focus is still strongly on the rule of law principles like the principle of human rights and the principle of properness which is strongly related to the principle of natural justice. In each of the countries there is more and more attention paid to the principles which are more related to forms of direct democracy like the principles of transparency and participation. The newer institutional related principles of accountability and effectiveness have not grabbed the

[187] Ibid, 842.

attention of lawyers, nevertheless we see in the social science a strong focus on these principles. Probably there is not yet enough interaction between these two dimensions of the government, but the good governance concept also makes it necessary that such an interdisciplinary approach is needed and will make the implementation of the good governance principles also more complete.

16

Implementation of Good Governance Principles on the European Level

In Chapter 3 we described two important developments in relation to the development of the concept of good governance. The first was related to the focus on good administration on the European level, which was not only developed by the European administrative institutions but also by the legislative and judiciary power on the European level. For that reason, we speak here about the development of good governance on the European level in a narrow sense. In the broader sense, the principles of good governance are also the normative framework for the other powers in the state apart from the administration. The second development was, due to the special legal regime of the European Union and the implementation obligations on the national level, the Europeanization of good governance in which the member states have their own implementation of good governance albeit under the supervision of the European Court of Justice in Luxembourg.

In this chapter, the focus is on the implementation of the principles of good governance, in this context the administrative principles, by the European administrative institutions and the controlling institutions like the European Court of Justice and the European Ombudsman. Nevertheless, the Treaty of Lisbon contains quite a number of rules and obligations in respect of the implementation of the principles of good governance. In that sense, the principle of transparency has found its symbolic expression in the most prominent place of article 1, paragraph 2 TFEU. Equally fundamental is the acknowledgement of the principles of political participation embodied in article 11 TEU. Notably the obligation of the European institutions to hold public hearings with representative associations and to communicate with civil society on a transparent and regular basis are among these principles. The right of access to documents of the Union's institutions has now been recognized as a fundamental rule in article 15 TFEU. Furthermore, according to article 16, paragraph 8 TEU the European Council of ministers has to meet in public when acting as a legislator.

These Treaty rules are complemented by the Charter of Fundamental Rights of the European Union which has entered into force with the final ratification of the Lisbon Treaty. The chapter on citizen's rights contains an impressive declaration of rights, such as the right to vote and to stand as a candidate at elections to the European Parliament and at municipal elections in articles 39 and 40. The right to good administration can be found in article 41 and the right of access to documents is embodied in article 42. This list is completed by the right to refer cases of maladministration to the European Ombudsman in article 43 and by the right to petition guaranteed by article 44. In particular, the right to good administration is worth noting. It gives every person the right to have his or her affairs handled impartially, fairly and within a reasonable time frame by the institutions of the Union. This includes the right of every person to be heard before any individual measure is taken which would entail adverse effects, the right of a person to have access to his or her file while respecting the legitimate interests of confidentiality and of professional and business secrecy and, finally, the obligation of the administration to give reasons for its decisions. In addition, the institutions are under the obligation to compensate for damages caused by their action. Finally, everyone has the right to write to the institutions of the Union in any official language and to receive an answer in the same language.

In search of a better quality of administrative proceedings, a code on good administrative practice, a soft law instrument based on the logic of best practice has ultimately been adopted. Thus, it has to be noted that the code has so far not been able to develop a relevant impact on the administrative decision-making in the European institutions.

1. Implementation of the Good Governance Principles by European Institutions

(a) The European Commission's White Paper (2001) and the Code of Good Administrative Behaviour for Staff of the European Commission

The elements of this policy paper are: the idea to reform European governance; the principles of good governance for this reform; the concrete proposals for change; and the governance in relation to the future of Europe. Why was a reform needed? There are different arguments for this reform: the inability to act effectively; it rarely gets proper credits for its actions; member states do not communicate well about the EU; and many people do not know the difference between the EU institutions. The leading principles of this reform are: openness; participation; accountability effectiveness; and coherence. These five principles reinforce the principles of proportionality and subsidiarity. The following action points were worked out: better involvement; better policies, regulation, and delivery; the EU's contribution to global governance; and refocused policies and institutions.

The White Paper was followed by the 2004 binding Code of Good Administrative Behaviour for Staff of the European Commission. Most of these principles are directly related to the principles of good governance. The principle of lawfulness states that the Commission acts in accordance with the law and applies the rules and procedures laid down in Community legislation. The principle of non-discrimination and equal treatment based on which the Commission in particular, guarantees equal treatment for members of the public irrespective of nationality, gender, racial or ethnic origin, religion or beliefs, disability, age, or sexual orientation. Thus, differences in treatment of similar cases must be specifically warranted by the relevant features of the particular case in hand. The Commission uses the principle of proportionality to ensure that the measures taken are proportional to the aim pursued. In particular, the Commission will ensure that the application of this Code never leads to the imposition of administrative or budgetary burdens out of proportion to the benefit expected. Also, concerning the principle of consistency, the Commission shall be consistent in its administrative behaviour and shall follow its normal practice. Any exceptions to this principle must be duly justified. The principles of objectivity and impartiality, according to which staff shall always act objectively and impartially, are in the Community interest and for the public good. They shall act independently within the framework of the policy fixed by the Commission and their conduct shall never be guided by personal or national interest or political pressure. The principle of transparency applies to information on administrative procedures where a member of the public requires information relating to a Commission administrative procedure. In this case, staff shall ensure that this information is provided within the deadline fixed for the procedure in question, and that interested parties receive information on their rights. Where Community law provides that interested parties should be heard, staff shall ensure that an opportunity is given to them to make their views known. The principle of reasoning means there is a duty to justify decisions and the duty to make arrangements for appeal. Finally, the Commission is committed to answering enquiries in the most appropriate manner and as quickly as possible and to take care for the protection of personal data and confidential information.

2. Implementation of the Good Governance Principles by the EU Court of Justice

In one of his publications, von Danwitz[1] writes about good governance that

> despite a rising number of critics claiming this concept to be without any substance and asking whether it would be new after all,[2] the idea of good governance has flourished ever since and has certainly evolved into a transnational concept of political leadership, a real leitmotiv for a common approach to the way how our global village should be governed.[3] The incredible success story of the striving for good governance is, in my view, due to three cumulative aspects which certainly contributed a great deal to the general agreement that good governance is a concept without proper alternative: Firstly, the concept of good governance is self-evident. It needs nothing else but common sense[4] to be understood: Entrepreneurs will not invest in unstable countries and people, whether entrepreneurs or not, will not wish to live there, if they can afford to go elsewhere.[5] Secondly, the concept of good governance is sufficiently vague to absorb a great variety of political preferences as well as substantive differences. Its flexibility is most certainly the reason why it has met so little resistance and found so much support. And thirdly, it was issued at the right point in time when public opinion was profoundly marked by the experience of the revolutionary force of glasnost and the general inability of corrupt regimes around the world to meet today's challenges.[6]
>
> But beyond all characteristics of our modern understanding of good governance, we should not forget the fundamental insight that the striving for good governance exists as long as mankind is reflecting on ways and means to deal with public matters and notably to govern the polity on local, regional, national and international levels. Therefore the quest for good governance is universal and certainly not specific to our times.

In any case, good governance is a legal concept which also has practical consequences. In this chapter, some documents have been mentioned and discussed which are strongly related to European governance. In 2001, the European Commission issued the White Paper on European Governance in which their principles of good governance have been detailed as steering the process of the further development of the European Union which is a legally developed entity consisting of structure based on the concept of the rule of law and democracy and essentially also good governance. These institutions are based on the same conceptual foundations in which the good governance concept plays an important role. The European Union has been conceived as a community of law and is based on the rule of law and democracy.

[1] In this paragraph, I follow strictly von Danwitz in his publication 'Good Governance in the Hands of the Judiciary: Lessons from the European Example' (2010) Potchefstroom Electronic Law Journal, Vol. 13, No. 1. His remarks about good governance and about the position of judges in the legal system are both so fundamental and convincing that I am citing these parts from his publication.

[2] De Waal 2002, 463. [3] Dolzer 2004, *ZaöRV*, 535. [4] Ibid, 536.

[5] Squires 2004, Cov L J, 45 and 54. [6] Cygan 2002 MLR 229.

The normative consequences of this can be found in the Treaty of Lisbon completed by the Charter of Fundamental Rights. In both documents, we find several aspects of codified good governance. In search of a better quality of administrative proceedings, a code on good administrative practice, a soft law instrument based on the logic of best practice has ultimately been adopted.

(a) The role of the EU Court of Justice

It is quite self-evident that the above-cited provisions of the Treaty of Lisbon and of the Charter of Fundamental Rights have now been able to play a role in judicial findings of the European Court of Justice.[7] In the beginning, the Court has been confronted with a great number of cases dealing with the application of the transparency principle in environmental matters[8] as well as in public procurement cases.[9] In recent years, the right of access to documents has triggered a great deal of litigation before the courts of the European Union.

Ever since the famous *Algera* judgment,[10] delivered in 1957, the Court has taken an active role in the evolution of legal principles which are generally perceived as specific expression of the rule of law. Thanks to the Court's case law on procedural rights, the right to be heard, to have access to files, and the obligation of the administration to give reasons have already been well established before they were finally codified in article 41 of the Charter of Fundamental Rights. Already, since the early 1970s, the right to be heard won recognition in the jurisprudence of the Court through it giving effect to the basic Roman law principle of 'audiatur et altera pars'.[11] The same is true for the

[7] Von Danwitz 2010.

[8] Directive 2003/4/EC of the European Parliament and of the Council of 28 January 2003 on public access to environmental information and repealing Council Directive 90/313/EEC [2003] OJ L41/26; Directive 2003/35/EC of the European Parliament and of the Council of 26 May 2003 providing for public participation in respect of the drawing up of certain plans and programmes relating to the environment and amending with regard to public participation and access to justice Council Directive 85/337/EEC and 96/61/EC—statement of the Commission [2003] OJ L156/17; see Partsch 1998; similar also Wegener 2002, § 1 para 14; Kloepfer 2002, 404; Worm 2001, 10; Partsch 1998, 2559; recital 10 of the preamble to the Aarhus Convention; North Rhine-Westfalia 2001; Turiaux 1995, 129; Proposal for a Directive of the European Parliament and of the Council providing for public participation in respect of the drawing up of certain plans and programmes relating to the environment and amending Council Directives 85/337/EEC and 96/61/EC, COM (2000) 839 final—2000/0331 (COD) [2001] OJ C154 E P. 0123—0128, 2; art 7 of Council Directive 90/220/EEC of 23/04/1990 on the deliberate release into the environment of genetically modified organisms [1990] OJ L 117, 18; Case C-552/07 *Opinion of AG Sharpston delivered on 22/12/2008(Commune de Sausheim v Pierre Azelvandre)* [2009] ECR 00000.

[9] Joined Cases C-285/99 and C-286/99 *Lombardini SpA v ANAS and Mantovani SpA v ANAS* [2001] ECR I-09233 (ECJ); Case C-470/99 *Universale-Bau AG v Entsorgungsbetriebe Simmering GmbH* [2002] ECR I-11617, 11690, para 93 (ECJ); C-315/01 *GAT v ÖSAG* [2003] ECR I-6351, 6409, para 73 (ECJ); T-345/03 *Evropaiki Dynamiki—Proigmena Systemata Tilepikoinion Pliroforikis kai Tilmatikis AE v Commission* (not reported yet) (CFI); C-275/98 *Unitron Scandinavia v Ministeriet for Fødevarer, Landbrug og Fiskeri* [1999] ECR I-08291 (ECJ); C-324/98 *Telaustria Verlags GmbH v Telekom Austria AG* [2000] ECR I-10745, 10794, par 61 (ECJ); Case C-19/00 *SIAC Construction Ltd v County Council of the County of Mayo* [2001] ECR I-7725 (ECJ); Case C-458/03 *Parking Brixen GmbH v Gemeinde Brixen and Stadtwerke Brixen AG* [2005] ECR I-8585, 8630, para 49 (ECJ); Case C-231/03 *Coname v Comune di Cingia de' Botti* [2005] ECR I-7287 (ECJ); Case C-324/07 *Coditel Brabant SA v Communie d'Uccle and Région de Bruxelles-Capitale* (not reported yet) (ECJ); Joined Cases C-226/04 and Case C-228/04 *La Cascina Soc. coop. arl and Others and Ministero della Difesa and Others* [2006] ECR E-1347, 1380, para 32 (ECJ).

[10] Joined Cases 7/56, 3/57 to 7/57 *Algera v Common Assembly* [1957] ECR 39 (ECJ).

[11] Case 41/69 *ACF Chemiefarma NV v Commission* [1970] ECR 00661, 690, para 56/57 (ECJ); Case 17/74 *Transocean Marine Paint Association v Commission* [1974] ECR 1063, 1080, para 15 (ECJ); Case 85/76 *Hoffmann-La-Roche and Co AG v Commission* [1979] ECR 00461, 511, para 9, 11

right of every individual to have access to his or her file as a necessary prerequisite for making effective use of the right of defence.[12] The obligation to give reasons, being explicitly embodied in the Treaty, has in addition been recognized by the Court as a general principle of European Community law, hereby obliging the administrations of the member states to give reasons for all decisions taken in application of Community law. The Court held in particular that the failure to give substantive reasons can result in the annulment of a decision as this duty is seen to be an essential rule of procedure. The statement of reasons must be appropriate to the act at issue and must disclose in a clear and unequivocal fashion the reasoning followed by the institution which adopted the measure in question as to enable the persons concerned to ascertain the reasons for the measure and to allow Community courts to exercise their power of review. The requirements to be satisfied by the statement of reasons depend on the circumstances of each case, in particular the content of the measure in question, the nature of the reasons given and the interest which the addressees of the measure or other parties may have in obtaining explanations.[13] In its landmark decision in the *Kadi* case concerning the protection of fundamental rights, the Court has strongly emphasized the direct link between the obligation to give reasons and the fundamental right to an effective judicial remedy.[14]

In addition to the evolution of these general principles common to all European administrative law systems, the European Court of First Instance already had the chance to associate the right of every person to have his or her affairs handled within a reasonable time by a European institution with the right to sound administration.[15] Later, the same European Tribunal recognized the need to act within a reasonable time in conducting administrative proceedings relating to competition policy as a general principle of Community law whose infringement would justify the annulment of the respective decision insofar as it also constituted an infringement of the rights of defence.[16] The subjective rights of individuals concerned by administrative proceedings are complemented by the liability of the European institutions guaranteed in accordance with the general principles common to the laws of the member states[17] for damages caused by the institutions. In a recent judgment delivered on 16 July 2009, the Court held that an infringement of the obligation to act within a reasonable time is also incumbent on

(ECJ); Joined Cases 46/87 and 227/88 *Hoechst AG v Commission* [1989] ECR 2859, 2932, para 52 (ECJ); Joined Cases T-39/92 and 40/92 *Groupement des Cartes Bancaires 'CB' and Europay International SA v Commission* [1994] ECR II-49, 73, para 48 (CFI); Joined Cases T-44/02 OP, T-54/02 OP, T-56/02 OP, T-60/02 and T-61/02 OP *Dresdner Bank AG and Others v Commission* [2006] ECR II-3567, 3619, para 155 (CFI); Case 17/74 *Opinion of AG Warner (Transocean Marine Paint Association v Commission)* [1974] ECR 1063,1090 (ECJ); Hegels 2001, 80; Nehl 2002, 275; Gornig and Trüe 1993, 884, 886, and 893; Kalbe 2003, underlines the validity in the sector of public services law, which had already been decided by the ECJ: Case 32/62 *Alvis v Council* [1963] ECR 107,123 (ECJ); Case 35/67 *Van Eick v Commission* [1968] ECR 489, 511 (ECJ); Case 25/80 *De Briey v Commission* [1981] ECR 637, 646, para 9 (ECJ).

[12] Case C-51/92 P *Hercules Chemicals NV v Commission* [1999] ECR I-04235, Case C-199/99 P *Corus UK Ltd, formerly British Steel plc v Commission* [2003] ECR I-11177, 11215, para 125 (ECJ).

[13] Case C-367/95 *Commission v Sytraval* [1998] ECR I-1719, 1770, para 63 (ECJ).

[14] Joined Cases C-402/05 P and C-415/05 P *Yassin Abdullah Kadi and Al Barakaat International Foundation v Council* (not reported yet), paras 334 and 351.

[15] Case T-54/99 *max.mobil Telekommunikation Service GmbH v Commission* [2002] ECR II-313, 48 (CFI).

[16] Case T-67/01 *JCB Service v Commission* [2004] ECR II-49, 36, 40 (CFI).

[17] Case C-312/00 P *Commission v Camar Srl and Tico Srl.* [2002] ECR I-11355, 52 (ECJ).

the judiciary and may, if established, justify an action for liability against the European Union, even for immaterial damages.[18]

While strengthening the procedural rights of individuals concerned with administrative proceedings, the Court has not neglected its responsibility for the functioning of the European institutions. But in doing so, the Court never lost sight of its principal objective to guarantee the rationality of all administrative action of the European institutions, which is the utmost objective of the rule of law. Again, this mission is crucial for the supranational action of the European institutions in order to ensure full acceptance of European Union law by the ordinary citizen which remains an indispensable condition for respecting the rule of European law to the same extent as it has become self-evident for the respect of national laws.

(b) The ECJ's jurisprudence on transparency and on the right of access to documents

In recent years, the Court has paid particular attention to ensure respect for the obligation to transparency and notably to the right of access to documents. The importance of this issue is reflecting a general tendency in the recent evolution of administrative law in many countries throughout the world. In the European context, the Nordic countries are particularly attached to the objective of administrative transparency and to a general right of access to documents.[19]

Their strong impetus has led to a far-reaching guarantee of transparency and access to documents in regulation no 1049/2001 which declares in recital 2 that 'openness enables citizens to participate more closely in the decision-making-process and guarantees that the administration enjoys greater legitimacy and is more effective and more accountable to the citizen in a democratic system. Openness contributes to strengthening the principles of democracy and the respect for fundamental rights as laid down in Article 6 of the EU Treaty and the Charter of Fundamental Rights of the European Union.'

Therefore, the regulation describes its purpose in recital 4 as 'to give the fullest possible effect to the right of public access to documents'. Confirming these fundamental findings, the Court has emphasized in its settled case law that exceptions to the right of widest possible access must be interpreted and applied strictly.[20] Accordingly, the right to access covers all documents in possession of the European institutions, even those emanating from member states or from mixed commissions involved in delegated legislation.[21] This general interpretation rule has led to the conclusion that the institutions do not, in quite a number of cases, live up to the full extent of the obligation to ensure public access to documents. Even the legal expertise established by a legal service of one of the European institutions in the course of a legislative procedure is,

[18] Case C-385/07 P *Der grüne Punkt-Duales System Deutschland GmbH v Commission* [2009] ECR 00000, 195 (ECJ).

[19] Classen 2008, 100.

[20] Joined Cases C-174/98 P and C-189/98 P *Kingdom of the Netherlands and Gerard van der Wal v Commission* [2000] ECR I-1, 63, paras 23 and 27 (ECJ); Case C-266/05 P *Sison v Council* [2007] ECR I-1233, 1283, para 63 (ECJ); Case C-64/05 P *Kingdom of Sweden v Commission* (judgment delivered on 18 December 2007) (not reported yet) para 66 (ECJ).

[21] Accordingly, already in relation to Commission Decision 94/90, Case T-188/97 *Rothmans International BV v Commission of the European Communities* [1999] ECR II-2463, 2484, para 60 (CFI).

in principle, covered by the obligation to public access of documents.[22] The particular sensitivity or importance of such a legal expertise might, under given circumstances, justify a refusal of access to documents if an institution is able to demonstrate in a substantive manner that the disclosure would be incompatible with the protection of the legal privilege granted to legal services. Along these lines, the Court has held quite recently that a legal expertise having been produced in the course of an election scrutiny procedure does not have to be disclosed in the following judicial procedure, since this would constitute a breach of the principle of equal defence.[23] Finally, it should be noted that the European Court of First Instance already had the chance to judge the interesting question of how to find a fair balance between conflicting fundamental rights, such as public access to documents in relation to professional and business secrecy or to the right to privacy. Currently, the Court of Justice is considering the appeal in these cases.

Considering the case law of the Court, it is very difficult to judge whether the public right of access to documents has had a considerable impact to improve the legitimacy of the action taken by the institutions of the European Union and the degree of its acceptance by the European citizens. But, however we may evaluate this impact, it is essential to note that the right of public access to documents constitutes a value in itself which proves how much the European integration is attached to democracy and to the rule of law. The right of public access to documents simply ensures that the longstanding prejudice of Brussels bureaucracy being alienated from the ordinary citizen, is proven incompatible with the legal reality of the obligation to implement a transparent administration which is devoted to the interest of the European citizens. The quest for transparency makes it perfectly clear that the citizens of the European Union do not have to consider themselves as mere subordinates to the law and the politics of the European Union, but can proudly perceive themselves as active citizens, as real 'citoyens' who are confronting the European institutions on equal terms. It is therefore evident that the quest for good governance in Europe constitutes an important subject which will not be of minor importance for the enduring success of the European integration.

(c) Good governance and the judiciary

The foregoing remarks were certainly placing the judiciary in the classical role of the ultimate guardian of the right to good governance and more generally speaking of fundamental rights. But who is supervising the supervisors? In the first place, my question points to the obligation of the judiciary to ensure a good administration of justice. Since judges too hold public offices and have to exercise their duties independently and in an unbiased manner, the quality of the administration of justice remains an important element in the quest for good governance. We are well aware that the mere independence of courts and judges is not enough to avoid maladministration of justice. Sometimes it may even be part of the problem. But how do we make sure that the judiciary is fully respecting the objectives of public welfare? Certainly by good law-making based on good law-making principles.[24]

[22] Joined Cases C-39/05 P and C-52/05 P *Kingdom of Sweden and Turco v Council* (not reported), para 68 (ECJ).

[23] Joined Cases C-393/07 and C-9/08 *Italian Republic and Donnici v Parliament* (30 January 2009) (ECJ).

[24] Bartoli 2010, 1–4.

Moreover, we have to be aware that the simple historical evidence that administrative discretion without effective scrutiny has turned into tyranny[25] may well become true one day for the judiciary when its efficient functioning is not maintained. This is why it proved to be necessary in the context of European integration to extend the system of liability for the breach of European Community law to the judiciary[26] and to emphasize that an infringement of the obligation to act within a reasonable time is incumbent as well on the judiciary and may, if established, justify an action for liability against the European Union, even for immaterial damages.[27]

But how can we ensure that the Supreme Courts and Constitutional Courts live up to their respective obligation of good governance? Since constitutions are very difficult to amend, the power of Constitutional Courts is considerable. The same is, *a fortiori*, true for the European Court of Justice since the substance of the Treaties proves to be hardly modifiable in practice. Of course, there is an ongoing evolution in Europe and around the world towards an increasing openness for comparative legal reasoning and discourse. The Constitution of South Africa, 1996, is particularly advanced in that respect.

This growing willingness to enter into a substantial discussion about the own jurisprudence should help a great deal to ensure the quality of a particular judicial solution and, beyond that, even to achieve a certain development towards a common understanding of which elements are fundamental for the rule of law. Naturally, researchers and the legal academia in general form a privileged partner in the debate about the rule of law, pointing at systematic deficiencies or at presumed lacks of coherence. The academic community of legal scholars constitutes furthermore an indispensable forum for discussion in which acceptance, disapproval, and the need for continuous refinement should be expressed.

Finally, it is eminently important for a judge to have a sound attitude towards the right balance of powers. In the end, the office of a judge requires a particular degree of personal humility and of character in order to resist the temptation of always having the last say in a constitutional system, be it national, supranational, or international.

(d) Good governance and the EU Charter: two good governance dimensions of the EU Charter

There are currently two dimensions of principles of good governance within the framework of the EU Charter. In the more classical rule of law approach, good governance is presented as part of the principle of defence, and in the second approach—which was defined in particular in December 2009 with the introduction of the Lisbon Treaty in conjunction with the EU Charter—a separate concept of good governance based on different elements of the EU Charter. Both approaches are discussed here.

[25] Davis 1969, 3.

[26] Case C-224/01 *Köbler v Republik Österreich* [2003] ECR I-10239 (ECR) and Case C-173/03 *Traghetti del Mediterraneo SpA v Italy* [2006] ECR I-1209 (ECR) on the one hand and Case C-385/07 P *Der grüne Punkt-Duales System Deutschland GmbH v Commission* [2009] ECR 00000 (ECR) on the other.

[27] Case C-385/07 P *Der grüne Punkt-Duales System Deutschland GmbH v Commission* [2009] ECR 00000 (ECR), 195.

The principle of good governance as part of the principle of defence

In his book, *The General Principles of EU Law*, Tridimas pays attention to 'the principle of good administration' as part of the principle of defence. He shows that since 1976, but since the 1990s, in a more systematic manner, the case law of the Court of Justice addresses the principle of good governance. His explanation for this is that 'the elevation to a general principle coincides with the growth and increasing diversity of Community administrative actions that led the Community Courts to elaborate standards of good governance and accountability'. Tridimas gives an overview of the principle of good governance in European jurisprudence and distinguishes different components within this principle. He signals that the case law initially spoke of 'proper' and 'sound administration' but that the more recent case law uses the principle of 'good administration'. Then, according to him, it is not a fundamental constitutional legal principle because the EU legislature is not bound by it, but the government of the Union is bound by it. Moreover, in principle, the principle is not primarily developed from the legal systems of the member states. Finally, according to him, the principle has a subsidiary character, breach of which may lead to liability for damage but is less suitable as a ground for destruction.

The right to good governance in the EU Charter of Fundamental Rights

The right to good governance by the EU institutions and bodies is a fundamental right laid down in article 41 of the EU Charter of Fundamental Rights. This article is the codification of EU jurisprudence in which good governance is regarded as a general legal principle. By the entry into force of the Treaty of Lisbon, the Charter has become a treaty. The right to good governance has thus become a subjective right which must be fully tested by the judge when appealed to it and also by judicial review by the court. With that, good governance has become a powerful judging instrument that will not only prove to be a subsidiary character. Moreover, as the Dutch administrative court repeatedly does, the Court of Justice cannot find that these are unclear and precisely defined obligations. This cannot be because those obligations in other judicial decisions have already been applied and, moreover, the obligations as a result of this right to good governance are specified in various Codes of the European Institutions, in particular called the Code of Good Administrative Behaviour of the European Ombudsman. The explanatory memorandum of this Code states that it is intended to explain in detail what the Charter of Good Governance contained in the Charter should mean in practice. In its decision of 1 December 2010, the Administrative Court has ruled that the Charter has become legally binding in our country as well. In view of article 51, paragraph 1 of that charter, it is also addressed to the member states, only when they implement Union law.

The Charter provides the Union and its member states with a list of fundamental rights that are legally binding on its signatories. The Charter makes these rights more visible to all citizens, so that they will be better informed of their rights. In addition, the Charter contains rights that are not protected under the ECHR, which is limited to the protection of civil and political rights. This concerns, in particular, the social rights of employees, the protection of data, and the right to good governance. The Charter contains as fundamental rights of Union citizenship the right to good governance (article 41) and the right to complain of the Union's institutions and bodies on bad governance to the European Ombudsman (article 43).

It should be noted that it is not only article 41 that has given a specification of the right to good administration but also that it is consistent with other provisions of the Charter. Article 43 is important because the European Ombudsman has designed both the Code of Good Governance and assesses whether the complaints submitted to him are bad governance using this Code. But the relationship between articles 41 and 47 concerning hearing from interested parties before making a decision is relevant. This coherence is also the issue of motivating decisions. We see that some specifications of good governance concern both the administrative phase and the judicial phase. However, there may also be different specifications. It is interesting to see that the Court of Human Rights, when it comes to judicial review of the case, speaks of 'good administration of justice'. It is about the 'administrative' treatment by the court that we commit to refer to it as a court of justice. It is apparent that in the judicial process these two types (principles of good, proper governance and principles of good, proper jurisprudence) are not always clearly distinguished. In this context, colleagues sometimes speaks of a confusion of both types of principles. Both types of principles influence each other, which is not strange when one realizes that both have a place in the umbrella term 'principles of good governance'.

(e) Principles of good governance in EU treaty law

The Lisbon Treaty already contains a large number of rules and obligations regarding the concept of good governance and, above all, the principles of good governance. Thus, the principle of transparency is expressed in a very prominent place, namely in article 1, paragraph 2 EU. Equally fundamental is the recognition of the principle of participation in article 11 EU. This also includes the obligation of European institutions to hold public hearings with representatives of relevant organizations as well as the obligation to communicate with civil society on a regular and transparent basis. The right to access documents from Union institutions has been recognized as a fundamental rule of article 15 EU. Furthermore, pursuant to article 16, the European Council of Ministers must act in public when acting as a legislature. In addition, certain principles of good governance, which are to be considered as part of the principles of good governance, are codified in the treaty. An example is the principle of motivation, which is anchored in various places in European law. Thus, article 296 TFEU imposes the requirement for a statement of reasons for making decisions. Finally, I refer to the plans for a comprehensive European governance regime as recently announced at a conference in Brussels, including article 41 of the EU Charter—the right to good governance—and the basis for such a scheme is also mentioned.

(f) Good governance and the distinction between rights and principles in the EU Charter

This concept is based on the idea that good governance is now a fundamental starting point for all states in the European Union and that this requirement of good governance has been given a constitutional status at the constitutional and legislative level in the member states and at Union level. In addition, good governance is a basic principle that has not only been developed as a principle in legislation and regulations but also as a fundamental right. Finally, it is noted that the concept of good governance has developed through the following six lines: decentness, transparency, participation, effectiveness, accountability, and human rights.

It is here that we pay close attention to the fifth and sixth paragraph of article 52 of the EU Charter. Paragraph 5 deals with the distinction between rights and principles as developed in the Charter and in paragraph 6 the link is made with national laws and practices.

Paragraph 5 of article 52 clarifies the distinction between rights and principles as set out in the Charter. According to the explanatory statement, subjective rights should be respected in accordance with this distinction, while principles must be observed (article 51-1). However, I wonder if this is a proper distinction between rights and principles, especially with regard to principles formulated as general binding rules—one can hardly argue that principles must be observed. I would say that such provisions must not only be observed but also be fully followed.

(g) EU case law: principles of good governance in the EU Charter

The concept of good governance can be distinguished between the basic concept and the effect that this concept has acquired in the aforementioned six central principles of good governance. We see in the case law that in addition to the meaning of good governance as a basic concept and the implementation through the six principles, it is sometimes based on a more limited principle of good governance, which is then referred to as a principle of good governance. It is, according to the Court of First Instance, that the unwritten duty that the board has properly acted without having found an effect in written provisions. It is sometimes argued that the Court of First Instance failed to respond to the failure to reply to the plea in law alleging breach of the principle of sound administration for incorrect interpretation and application of the case law relating to the principle of good governance. The Court must provide clarity. It should also be noted that before the binding force of the EU Charter, the Court expressed its views on principles of good governance, such as the principle of transparency in environmental matters, in procurement matters, and in publicity of documents under government. The concept of good public procurement has been further developed in the literature and in practice.[28]

The following deals with case law regarding some specific principles of good governance and interdependence.

The principle of motivation

The principle of motivation is anchored in various places in EU law. We are also opposed to this principle in the EU Charter, which states in article 41-2 that the right to good governance also entails the obligation for the governing body to give reasons for the decision taken. The question concerns the reasoning for the decision to be taken. The relevant decision determines the legal positions of individuals. The reasons given here provide insight into the reasoning and the arguments used. Of course, in this context, third party rights are also relevant to the obligation to state the reasons for that decision. However, giving reasons is not exclusively in the interests of the citizen, it also has the effect of an initial self-control on the part of the board and can thus improve the attitude of government to the citizens. After all, when the reasons are convincing, existing conflicts can be overcome and new legal disputes can be prevented. We thus see that the principle of motivation also improves the quality of governance.

[28] Wibowo 2017, 21.

The Court has ruled that national authorities should in any case give reasons for a decision abolishing the benefit of citizens' right in a concrete case for citizens by Union law. This means that article 41 of the Charter contains not only rules of good governance for the EU institutions but it establishes a more general principle of law that the authorities of the member states should also respect the application of Union law.

The principle of legal certainty

In the judicial proceedings, a misinterpretation of provisions of Union law is often spoken about, and in that regard, the Court of First Instance finds in a given case an infringement of the principles of good governance and of legal certainty. In this way, the Court seems to choose a principle of legal certainty that is in addition to the principles of good governance, the principle of legal certainty as a general principle of justice. In this regard, I note that the principle of legal certainty is applied to different levels of abstraction. In this case, it is the level of the primary regulator and it is acceptable to do so because the principle in this context has a fundamental content. However, the principle of legal certainty is also opposed—but as part of the principles of good governance (which form part of the principles of good governance)—in the context of concrete decisions. These are decisions whose content is not clear or that has been granted retroactively without the need for a legal basis. One must constantly realize which abstraction level of the relevant principle is in the particular case. This ambiguity is not only a matter for administrative decisions but also for judicial decisions. For example, the principle of legal certainty is the subject of a court ruling concerning the obligation of the European institutions to motivate an unfavourable administrative decision for the citizen. It is also a good example of the correlation between principles of good governance and between the principles of legal certainty and motivation.

The principle of motivation, the principle of good governance, and the precautionary principle (hearing)

In the *Evropaiki Dynamiki* case,[29] the parties argued the following three violations of (elements of) the principle of good governance: (a) inadequate reasoning in the ruling; (b) breach of the general right to good governance; and (c) violation of the requirement of proper hearing (carefulness). It is further argued that the arguments put forward have not been discussed so that there is an infringement of the principles of transparency and equal treatment. In conclusion, it is found that the European Commission has violated the rights of good governance and proper hearing as guaranteed by the EU Charter. In addition, it should be noted that, in this context, stakeholders also rely on other regulations and on the general principle of good governance. AG Kokott discusses all these aspects in the report and seems sensitive to the arguments put forward.

In another case, the Court of First Instance deals with the right to good governance and right to a proper hearing and qualifies it as the fundamental rights laid down in articles 41 and 47 of the Charter. The Court finds that it has not been shown how the provisions of the Charter are applicable in the present case, nor does it indicate the aspects of the judgment which constitute an infringement of these provisions. The Court therefore asserts the applicability of these principles of good

[29] *Evropaiki Dynamiki—Proigmena Systemata Tilepikoinion Pliroforikis kai Tilmatikis AE v Commission* (Case C-597/11P Case T-345/03) [2008] ECR II-341.

governance and the requirement that they should be specified. Moreover, it is a settled case law of the Court, which implies that an appeal does not meet the requirements of justification when only an abstract plea is given without being supported by specific information. That specification is also important to determine whether there is a correct interpretation or not.

The precautionary principle: hearing and reasonable time, and the effectiveness principle

An infringement of the right to defence and the right to be heard is often called for. The right to be heard is one of the rights of defence that must be observed during the administrative procedure (in the case of an antitrust case). In secondary EU law, this was codified in article 19-1 of Regulation No 17. Article III-368 does not mean that the European Commission is following the whole process; the Commission can start from the moment it has committed an error in the procedure.

In addition to the right to be heard, it is often called for the right to decide on a matter within a reasonable period of time. It is assumed that this right is recognized in the case law of the Court as a general principle of EU law both in the framework of the administrative procedure and in the context of the judicial procedure and in articles 41 and 47 of the Charter.

Sometimes, a regulation prescribes that an authority should be asked for advice (including international law) and it appears that in a long process this has not happened. It is then said that violations of the regulation have been dealt with but that it also infringes the right to good governance and the right to an effective remedy as set out in articles 41 and 47 of the Charter.

The duration of the procedure is also important in relation to the effectiveness principle. An examination of the duration of the procedure must be conducted to assess whether any violation of such rights has taken place and therefore this course of action is effective. There is a coherence. In addition, the effectiveness principle is not called into question, but here it is the effectiveness in relation to fundamental rights and the violation thereof.

There cannot be recourse to the different nature of administrative and judicial procedures, now that the relevant rights are included in various articles in the Charter. It concerns treatment by an impartial body and the Charter has expressed the same procedural principle in article 41, second paragraph, and article 47, that a person can expect a decision within a reasonable period. The right to make a decision within a reasonable time period cannot be violated if any of the steps in that administrative and judicial procedure are not excessively long. However, as more steps are taken, the more important it is to investigate the duration of the overall length of the procedure.

3. Implementation of the Good Governance Principles by the EU Ombudsman

(a) The European Code of Good Administrative Behaviour (2001)

The Maastricht Treaty established the office of the European Ombudsman to fight maladministration in the activities of Community institutions and bodies. By promoting good administration, the Ombudsman should help enhance relations between the European Union and its citizens. Since the beginning of the Ombudsman's office in September 1995, they have worked to define maladministration, based on the case law of the Court of Justice and the principles of European administrative law and including the national laws on the subject as a valuable source of inspiration. This work has been continued by drafting a Code of Good Administrative Behaviour, later adopted by the European Parliament.

The Code is addressed to European citizens and civil servants. It tells citizens what they have the right to expect from the administration and civil servants what principles to observe in their activities. The expectation was that a full implementation of the Code will enhance citizens' confidence in the European Union and its institutions.

On 6 September 2001, the European Parliament adopted a resolution approving a Code of Good Administrative Behaviour which European Union institutions and bodies, their administrations and their officials should respect in their relations with the public. The European Ombudsman drafted the text, following an own-initiative inquiry, and presented it to the European Parliament as a special report. The Parliament's resolution on the Code is based on the Ombudsman's proposal and was introduced by the Committee on Petitions of the European Parliament.

The Charter of Fundamental Rights of the European Union was proclaimed at the Nice summit in December 2000. It includes as fundamental rights of citizenship the right to good administration and the right to complain to the European Ombudsman against maladministration. The Code is intended to explain in more detail what the Charter's right to good administration should mean in practice.

The Code explains in more detail how the Charter right to good administration works in practice.

The Code has the following three main parts. The first part contains the general articles (articles 1–3) relations with the institutions and their officials; necessary measures (most EU-institutions have special codes; and all relations. The second part concerns the classical basic principles of administrative law (articles 4–12, 16–19, and 22–23) like lawfulness etc. In the third part, we find the articles concerning good administrative functioning (articles 13–15, 20–21, and 24). These articles are about replies to letters, acknowledgement of receipt, transfer to competent service, notification (transparency), data protection, keeping adequate records. In essence, we find in all these three parts different elements of the principles of good administration.

In Part I, the general provision can be found as well as the personal scope of application: all officials and other servants to whom the Staff Regulations and the Conditions of employment of other servants apply, in their relations with the public. In article 3 the material scope can be found, in which it is stated that the Code contains the general principles of good administrative behaviour which apply to all relations of the Institutions and their administrations with the public, unless they are governed by specific provisions.

In Part II, we find the classical principles of public law, starting with the principle of lawfulness; the official shall act according to law and apply the rules and procedures laid down in Community legislation. The official shall in particular ensure that decisions which affect the rights or interests of individuals have a basis in law and that their content complies with the law. In this article the principle equality has been laid down, including the prohibition of discrimination. Article 6 is about the principle of proportionality and article 7 concerns the prohibition of abuse of power. Impartiality, independence, and objectivity are guaranteed in article 8 and article 9. In article 10, the principle of legitimate expectation has been codified and the articles 11 and 12 concern the principles of fairness and courtesy.

Part III is about good administrative functioning: replying to a letter in the correct language (article 13), acknowledgement of receipt, indication of competent official (article 14), and obligation to transfer to the competent service of the institution (article 15). In this part, there are also some codified substantial norms (article 16, right to be heard; article 17, reasonable time limit for decision-making; article 18, duty to state the grounds of decisions). Finally, we find the obligations to indicate the possibilities of appeal (article 19), the notification of the decisions (article 20), and data protection (article 21). Specific norms have been codified concerning requests for information (article 22) and requests for access to documents (article 23). The institution has to keep adequate records (article 24).

(b) Implementation by the European Ombudsman

The European Ombudsman helps citizens as they engage with the EU institutions, bodies, and agencies. The problems that arise range from contractual issues to violations of fundamental rights, to a lack of transparency in decision-making, or refusal of access to documents. In 2016, transparency-related inquiries again accounted for the greatest proportion of cases. In May 2017, the European Ombudsman gave an overview of the key topics on which the European Ombudsman had worked in 2016: transparency in EU decision-making; lobbying transparency; transparency in economic and financial decision-making; access to EU documents; ethical issues; EU agencies and other bodies; and finally EU contracts and grants.

In relation to transparency in EU decision-making, the Ombudsman in July 2016 published proposals to make trilogues—informal negotiations on EU legislative proposals between the European Parliament and Council of the EU in the presence of the Commission—more transparent. These included making available dates of trilogue meetings and summary agendas; the positions of both co-legislators on the Commission's proposal; and the names of the decision-makers present in trilogue meetings. She recommended that documents that track the main stages of the process should be published as soon as possible after the negotiations end. The Ombudsman inspected the trilogue files of two EU laws (Credit Mortgage Directive and Clinical Trials Regulation) and held a public consultation, receiving fifty-one replies including five from national parliaments. In May 2017, the Ombudsman opened a strategic inquiry into how the European Commission carries out conflict of interest assessments for its special advisers. The advisers provide on-demand expert input directly to the Commissioners. The aim of the inquiry, opened following individual complaints, is to ensure that rules are robust enough to avoid inappropriate influence on policymaking. The Ombudsman's case handlers inspected the files concerning special advisers appointed in 2015 and 2016. The inspection report showed significant improvement in certain areas in 2016. The Ombudsman in 2017 continued to focus on possible further improvements in the following areas: how the procedure for appointing special advisers is organized; the Commission's conflict of interest assessment before the appointment; the duty to declare new activities after the appointment; and public access to documents and information. The Ombudsman made a decision on 16 June 2017 in the case nr 01/6/2016/AB and made recommendations on the European Commission's rules and practices for ensuring that its Special Advisers do not have conflicts of interest. One case illustrating the importance of transparent decision-making concerned the process for authorizing pesticides for the European market. Specifically, it concerned the Commission's practice of approving the safe use of an active substance before it gets all of the data necessary to support that decision (known as confirmatory data procedure).

The Ombudsman asked the Commission to report back in 2018 and demonstrate that the procedure is being used restrictively, that there is improved oversight of member states' use of pesticides, and that the remaining assessments of the ten substances highlighted by the complainant have been completed. Another case concerned delays by the Commission in the authorization of twenty applications for genetically modified food and feed. During the inquiry, the Commission dealt with the twenty applications in question. However, the Ombudsman concluded that the delays were not justified and suggested that if the Commission considered the timescale for decision-making in relation to genetically modified food and feed to be inadequate, it should deal with the issue in its review of how such decisions are taken.

The Ombudsman also inquired into the transparency of EU lobbying and related matters. In early 2016, the Ombudsman asked the Commission to take a series of expert group transparency steps, including the publication of comprehensive minutes of their meetings. In May, the Commission replied that it intended to make several changes to the system, including publishing agendas and meaningful minutes; improving conflict of interest management in relation to individuals appointed in a personal capacity; and linking expert group membership to the obligation to be on the EU Transparency Register. Following the urging of the Parliament, the Commission revised the EU Transparency Register in 2016. The Ombudsman provided suggestions for improving the Register by making it a central transparency hub for all EU institutions and agencies. She also called for full funding transparency for all lobbying groups, improved data accuracy, and tightened monitoring. She also called for the final inter-institutional agreement on the Register to mention the right to complain to the Ombudsman. The revised Register is now being negotiated between the Commission, Parliament, and Council.

Decision-making in economic and financial matters is of significant public interest. The Ombudsman's office has dealt with individual complaints in this area and the Ombudsman also sometimes considers it more helpful to point out issues of concern or ask for more information as part of a 'strategic initiative'. She praised the President of the Eurogroup for his proactive measures to make the body more transparent—such as by publishing a detailed agenda and a summing-up letter of its meetings—and asked for further clarifications on his proposals. He responded that since the transparency regime had been introduced, the Eurogroup had made a range of documents available, including material used to prepare the Eurogroup's discussions and the body was committed to furthering the transparency of its political deliberations and that points raised by the Ombudsman would feed into its further reflections. The Ombudsman works on similar issues in her contact with the Supervisory Board of the European Central Bank (ECB) and the Board of Directors of the European Investment Bank (EIB).

Every year, the Ombudsman receives many complaints from individuals or organizations about the EU administration's failure to provide public access to documents. In these cases, the Ombudsman looks to see if the institution is justified in not releasing the document. If the Ombudsman finds it not justified, she seeks release of the requested document. One such case concerned a request for public access to opinions assessing candidates' suitability to be Judges and Advocates-General at the Court of Justice and the General Court of the EU. The Council refused access to the opinions—drawn up by a panel of experts—arguing that EU access to documents rules (Regulation 1049/2001) did not apply in that instance. Following the Ombudsman's intervention, the Council announced that it had decided to apply Regulation 1049/2001. The Ombudsman welcomed the Council's policy change, noting that this case raised the important issue of how to strike the correct balance between the need to protect the personal data of those being assessed for high public office with the need to ensure maximum transparency in the appointment process. She noted that in such cases the balance should generally be in favour of greater openness. In a case concerning the European External Action Service (EEAS), the complainant, a Swedish NGO, wanted access to the Political Dialogue and Cooperation Agreement between the EU and Cuba. The EEAS refused, arguing that the Agreement was still provisional at that stage. The complainant turned to the Ombudsman, who encouraged the Council to deal with any future requests for public access to such documents with this approach in mind. In the European Ombudsman Annual Report 2016, the Ombudsman has noted that the Agreement had already been initialled. In the course of the inquiry, the EEAS released the document after the Commission had adopted the Agreement.

Ethical issues are also investigated by the Ombudsman. The EU administration has comparatively high ethical standards. However, for citizens to have more confidence in the EU, they need to be sure that both EU politicians and staff are working only in the public interest. The rules in place must ensure that Commissioners, both during their term in office and afterwards, do not put this into doubt. Concerns surrounding work undertaken by former Commissioners featured in the Ombudsman's work in 2016. In a decision in June, the Ombudsman found maladministration in that the 2009–14 Commission had failed adequately to deal with a former Commissioner's breach of the Code of Conduct for Commissioners and had not properly investigated the compatibility of the Commissioner's private sector work contract with the EU Treaty obligations, despite concerns raised by the Ethics Committee that deals with these matters. The Ombudsman called for the Code of Conduct to be revised to make its rules more explicit and more easily implementable and to include sanctions for breaches of the Code. The merits of reforming the Code came up for discussion once more when a former Commission President took a position as non-executive Chairman at Goldman Sachs. The Commission stated that he had not breached the Code, which stipulates an eighteen-month cooling-off period, but the Ombudsman noted that under the EU Treaty some posts can continue to be problematic even after the eighteen-month notification period has expired. In a letter to President Juncker, the Ombudsman asked the Commission to refer the matter to the Commission's Ethics Committee and to review the Code of Conduct, but the matter was put to the Ad Hoc Ethical Committee. That Committee concluded that while the former President had not shown 'the considerate judgement one may expect from someone having held the high office he occupied for so many years', there were 'not sufficient grounds to establish a violation of the duty of integrity and discretion, imposed by Article 245 (2) TFEU [Treaty on the Functioning of the European Union]'. Nevertheless, President Juncker did propose to tighten the Code by extending the cooling-off period to two years for ex-Commissioners and three years for ex-Commission Presidents. The Ombudsman welcomed the proposal but repeated the earlier caveat that the extended time will not always be a sufficient guarantee that article 245 has been respected. Robust ethics rules need to apply throughout an institution and not just to its political representatives.

EU agencies and other bodies—which deal with a range of issues from fundamental rights, to the safety and efficacy of medicines, the protection of the environment, health, and environmental risks from chemicals and aviation safety—were the second biggest source, after the European Commission, of inquiries conducted by the Ombudsman in 2016. One major case, opened in 2014, concerned the decision of the European Medicines Agency (EMA) to give only partial public access to clinical trial studies related to the approval of Humira, a drug used to treat Crohn's disease. In June, the Ombudsman closed the inquiry, welcoming increased transparency in this area. However, she expressed concern about four specific pieces of information that the EMA had withheld. The Ombudsman noted that any clinical information of value to doctors, patients, and researchers, should be disclosed in the public interest. The European Chemicals Agency (ECHA) in 2015 agreed to the Ombudsman's proposal concerning how it requires those seeking to register products to show that they have tried to avoid animal testing. This was followed up in 2016 with detailed information about how exactly it was seeking to give effect to the Ombudsman's proposal.

Complaints on EU contracts and grants accounted for 14.5 per cent of the total. The Commission oversees a vast number of projects funded by the EU. It carries out rigorous auditing to ensure that public money is spent as it should be. However, this occasionally gives rise to disputes over how projects are audited or the amount of money that potentially should be reclaimed. In these situations, contractors often turn to the Ombudsman for a solution. In one such case, the complainant, a Polish research institute, had undertaken a number of projects that were co-financed by the EU between 2004 and 2009. After successfully completing the projects, the Commission audited three of them, and decided to recover certain costs. The Ombudsman opened an inquiry and found that the Commission's project officer had agreed in writing (email) to the subcontracting of some services—the costs of which the Commission subsequently decided to recover—and was therefore aware of, and had authorized, the complainant's awarding of the subcontract. The Commission contended that the complainant had not followed the applicable rules of the contract agreement but, in light of the particular circumstances of this case, decided to waive the recovery of more than €86 000. A Croatia-based research institute took part in an EU-funded project under the Seventh Framework Programme for Research and Technological Development. After an audit revealed some irregularities, the Commission sought to recover a substantial amount of funds. The institute lodged a complaint with the Ombudsman, who found that the auditors' findings were based on several uncertainties. Since the most crucial issue at hand was the determination of the actual starting date of the project, the Ombudsman suggested that the Commission should consult an expert to verify the auditors' finding or order a technical audit. The Commission accepted the Ombudsman's proposal.

From this overview, we can conclude that the transparency principle has been developed very strongly in the work of the European Ombudsman. But there are more principles of good governance at stake. When we look at the aspects of the decision-making process, it is not only about the transparency of the process but also the impartiality as part of the properness principle which must be mentioned. The investigation on the lobby groups and the development of a transparency register is only partly relevant, it depends also on which information will be in that register and how and by whom the norms will be enforced. The openness of the work of the financial departments is very important because of the consequences for the civil society. The ethical norms which are directly linked to the principles of good governance are also relevant in this context. Also, the role and functioning of agencies and other bodies are from the perspective of good governance very relevant and not only from the transparency perspective. The discussions about EU subsidies and grants, especially, make it relevant to create a general administrative regulation for all the EU institutions. Harmonization is much needed to create real equality and legal certainty and, by that, good governance.

4. Conclusions

In this chapter, we have explained and discussed the implementation principles by different institutions on the EU level. Attention was given to the EU administration, the EU Commission, and the controlling institutions—the Court of Justice and the Ombudsman both on the EU level.

We started with the EU Commission and noted that this institution has developed two important instruments, normative frameworks, for good governance. The first instrument was the 2001 White Paper in which the Commission developed five important principles of good governance because of its much-needed reform. These principles were openness, participation, accountability, effectiveness, and coherence. These five principles of good administration were seen as mechanisms to reinforce the principles of proportionality and subsidiarity. In the frame of this paper, the following action points were worked out by the Commission: better involvement, better policies, regulation and delivery, the EU's contribution to global governance, and refocused policies and institutions. So, the principles should influence in a preventive way the governance of the Commission by developing good governance. The White Paper was followed by the 2004 binding Code of Good Administrative Behaviour for Staff of the European Commission. This was a normative framework with principles of good administration which should be enforced in relation to activities of staff members of the Commission.

The second institution is the EU Court of Justice. An important framework on the principles of good governance also for the Court are the treaties: the Lisbon Treaty and the Charter on Fundamental Rights. In addition to the further evolution of the general principles common to all European administrative law systems, other principles are also mentioned and further developed: like the right of every person to have his or her affairs handled within a reasonable time by a European institution with the right to sound administration. The need to act within a reasonable time period in conducting administrative proceedings relating to competition policy is a general principle of EU law. The infringement of that principle would justify the annulment of the respective decision. But violating this principle can also be an infringement of the rights of defence, which can be relevant in relation to liability issues. Later, the Court developed jurisprudence on transparency and on the right of access to documents. With article 41 of the Charter, the jurisprudence on the right of good administration, there is potentially the possibility of a new line of thinking in the jurisprudence. Nevertheless, it seems that the Court is working on it step by step, focusing on sub-principles, and only partly on new principles like effectiveness.

The European Ombudsman has developed, based on its own ombudsprudence, a Code of Good Administrative Behaviour. This Code consisted of three parts and each part has principles with a different character. The first part contains the general articles (articles 1–3) relations with the institutions and their officials; necessary measures (most EU-institutions have special codes); all relations. The second part is about the classical basic principles of administrative law (articles 4–12, 16–19, and 22–23) like lawfulness etc. In the third part, we find the articles about good administrative functioning (articles 13–15, 20–21, and 24). These articles are about replies to letters, acknowledgement of receipt, transfer to competent service, notification (transparency), data protection, keeping adequate records. In essence, we find in all these three parts different elements of the principles of good administration.

In practice, the focus of the Ombudsman is, according to its recent annual report: transparency in EU decision-making, lobbying transparency, transparency in economic and financial decision-making, access to EU documents, ethical issues, EU agencies and other bodies, and finally EU contracts and grants. So, in relation to good administration, the focus is especially on transparency and ethical issues.

17

Implementation of the Good Governance Principles on the International Level

During the 1990s, several articles on the principles and the concept of good governance in the context of specific policy topics were published: for instance, the publications of Ginther[1] from 1995 on sustainable development and good governance and Bodansky[2] who wrote in 1999 about the legitimacy of international governance in the context of international environmental law. In 1995, there was the publication by Mutharika[3] on the African perspective on principles of good governance in relation to international law and Pauly[4] wrote in 1999 about good governance and bad policy in the context of international organizations. So, we can conclude that by the end of the twentieth century the concept was applied in specific policy fields like environmental law and in the more general frame of policy by the international organizations. The good governance perspective has also been developed in the context of globalizing administrative law.[5]

1. Good Governance in International Organizations

Wouters and Ryngaert wrote in their article that the twenty-first century could mark a turning point in the development of good governance by international organizations. They explain that the debate on good governance started in the 1980s, when the World Bank and the IMF stated that the growth and equitable development of many developing countries was frustrated by the poorly functioning public sector institutions and weak governments. Then, these financial-economic institutions started to espouse and sometimes absorbed good governance not only for external but also for internal activities and claims as to their own functioning.[6] There are two tensions. The first was the restricted competence of these organizations to financial-economic aspects with respect to the broader scope of the concept of good governance. The second was the minimalistic economic approach of these institutions to good governance which was not accepted by the countries. After a description of good governance was used by other international organizations, it became clear that the concept was actually being used by many international organizations. The OECD found the following principles: respect for the rule of law; openness, transparency, and accountability to democratic institutions; fairness and equity in dealing with citizens; efficient and effective services; clear, transparent, and applicable laws and regulations; consistency and coherence in policy; and high standards of ethical behaviour. These principles have become key in a tentative list of good governance requirements which have later been described by the World Bank, the IMF, and the WTO.

Thus, good governance is increasingly being used by many international organizations. These organizations function in different contexts and settings, and their

[1] Ginther, Denters, and others 1995. [2] Bodansky 1999, 596–624.
[3] Mutharika 1995. [4] Pauly 1999. [5] Esty 2006a, 1490. [6] Shihata 2000.

different uses of good governance developed accordingly with respect to the specific needs of the respective fields. The fields are much broader than the international development aid and international financial institutions. Also, the OECD, WTO, and UN use the concept of good governance, for example, in the fields of social justice, sustainable development, deforestation, different aspects of environment policy, and public health. I want to mention here a recent publication 'International Legal Obligations in Relation to Good Ocean Governance'.[7] We can conclude in most of the international policy fields the concept of good governance is well known and accepted. We also can conclude in the context of international relations, international organizations, and international treaties the concept of good governance has been fully accepted and sometimes qualified as globalizing administrative law or international administrative law.

2. Good Governance in International Case Law

More recently, good governance can be recognized in international case law. This means that the principle does not only function as a norm for national governments or international organizations, but that it is actually being reviewed in judicial procedures. Sometimes it is an international norm of good governance used by the national courts; international courts are sometimes using the principle of good governance as a review norm. Examples of these decisions of international institutions can be found at the International Court of Justice, the East African Court of Justice (EACJ), the European Court of Human Rights, the Inter-American Court of Human Rights, and the WTO Dispute Settlement Body. But national human rights commissions also worked on the further development of good governance in the context of human rights.[8]

The International Court of Justice adheres to the principle of good administration instead of the principle of good governance. In two judgments, the Court gives an interpretation of good administration in the context of good governance. There is a judgment related to the administrative tribunal of the ILO and the fund on international agriculture development. The first judgment is related to the case between the republic of Guinea and the Democratic Republic of Congo. The second judgment concerns a conflict between the administrative tribunal of the ILO and the fund on international agriculture development.[9]

In article 6(d) of the Treaty establishing the East African Community (EAC Treaty) we find fundamental principles intended to guide the institution described as follows: 'good governance including adherence to the principles of democracy, the rule of law, accountability, transparency, social justice, equal opportunities, gender equality, as well as the recognition, promotion and protection of human and peoples' rights in accordance with the provisions of the African Charter on Human and Peoples' Rights'. In 2010, the EACJ further decided that the failure to extend the jurisdiction of the court pursuant to article 27 violated the applicant's legitimate expectations that the matter be expedited and contravened the principles of good governance stipulated in article 6 of the Treaty.[10] In another case, the EACJ decided that it has jurisdiction

[7] Chiang Jang 2010, 589–605.

[8] Horsten 2006, 179 Potchefstroom Electronic Law Journal.

[9] International Court of Justice, 30 November 2010; International Court of Justice, 1 February 2012.

[10] *Sebalu v The Attorney General of the Republic of Uganda*, Ref No 1 of 2010, Judgment (EACJ, 30 June 2011).

to interpret and apply the provisions of the EAC Treaty, including articles 6(d), 7(2), and 8(1)(c) of that Treaty and decided that the failure by the appropriate authorities to charge the person with specific offences for his arrest and detention, as well as to inform him, his family, or his lawyers of the time of his arrest/detention—for a period of five months, during which time he was held incommunicado—was fundamentally inconsistent with Rwanda's express undertakings under articles 6(d), 7(2), and 8(1) of the Treaty: to observe the principles of good governance, including in particular, the principles of adherence to the Rule of Law, and the promotion and protection of human rights. These failures, singly and collectively, constituted an infringement of the said provisions of the Treaty.[11]

3. Good Governance in Case Law: The European Court of Human Rights

We find different lines on the concept of good governance in the case law of the European Court of Human Rights (ECtHR). A rather recent case[12] concerns article 8 of the European Convention on Human Rights (ECHR) and article 1 of the First Protocol. The court has developed the principle of good governance in the context of the violation of the right to property and the right to privacy. The court decided that there is a need for a timely and consistent action and, if not, there would be reason for an obligation to compensate. In that judgment, the Court comes to the conclusion that there is a breach of article 1 of the First Protocol because contrary to the principle of good governance, there was no reasonable and proportional relationship between the means used and the violation of a person's property.[13] In the first paragraph of article 1 of the First Protocol the principle of the peaceful enjoyment of possessions is set down, then in the second sentence of the paragraph (for expropriation) and in the following paragraph (to regulate) the conditions for impairment of that principle. These conditions relate to the expropriation of the requirement of a legal basis, the general interest, and general principles of international law. In this statement they are, according to the Court, fleshed cumulative requirements and the principle of proportionality set out in respect of the third condition. In determining whether the latter principle is violated when determining the means and purpose of the infringement, the Court used the principle of good governance. It is interesting for several reasons to determine which instances of government action by the Court of this principle in this context is used, and which aspects are brought by the Court. Regarding the cases, the following decisions have to be distinguished: (a) the decision to refuse to recognize property rights; (b) the decision on review of ownership because an error was made in the granting of that right; (c) the decision to cancel the property because the applicable law in respect of the property has changed. The process of making these decisions must meet the requirement of the principle of good governance. That means, according to the Court, that there must be timeliness as well as an appropriate and most consistent way of government action. It is then added to the limitation that this general rule

[11] The Attorney General of the Republic of Rwanda, Appeal no 1 of 2012 (EACJ, Appellate Division, June 2012).

[12] 16 May 2013, nr 49317/07 (Villiger (President), Nußberger, Zupančič, Power-Forde, Jäderblom, Pejchal, Antonovych).

[13] There is a very detailed and broad case law about the concept of property which has been discussed in the literature.

(that of the principle of good governance) prevents government mistakes (whether in negligence or otherwise) are corrected. When revoked because erroneous ownership of the principle of good governance of the board should not only correcting raft of his mistake, but it may necessitate the payment of adequate compensation in money or by another appropriate way as can be expected by someone who acts in good faith. The principle of good governance is used here in the context of the review of administrative action and then it may be even more precise to say, at least so it seems, in the key of proportionality. It seems that the court creates a balance between the promotion of the public interest (in this case of article 8 ECHR, derived right of residence) and the special importance of the individual fundamental right of the person concerned (in this case of article 1 of the First Protocol, ownership), in short, a balance between different fundamental rights. With this consideration in mind, the principle of good governance according to the ECtHR is of particular significance and provides the court with sufficient guidelines. It makes demands on the timeliness of government action and the method by which that government action should take place. Here, we have the development of a new test principle from the unwritten law, which is used to give different rights weight and that is a new line in applying the principles of good governance.

We can also discern shifts in the case law of the ECtHR with respect to the principle of good governance. About twenty years ago, in some cases that involved the Netherlands, in particular, the terminology of 'general principles of good governance' or 'general principle of good governance' was used.[14] It appears that, in this context, there continues to be one or some of the famous eight principles of good governance. A more extensive approach of good governance was found in the judgment of *Maritime v Finland*,[15] where the Finnish Constitution speaks of 'Guarantees of a fair trial and good governance': that a broader approach, but citing provisions of the Convention of the Council of Europe, and that good governance is used as a fundamental concept which must be met.[16] Yet, recently, good governance was actively employed by the Court. The first example is the *Rysovsky* judgment.[17] In that case, the principle of good governance was used to assess whether management actions are in compliance with the treaty to which article 1 of the First Protocol provides the legal input. The requirement is made to the board that action is 'in good time and in an appropriateness and above all consistent manner'. The following elements are added in statements: transparency, minimizing the risk of error, utmost care.

4. Conclusions

At present, the implementation of good governance has a much broader meaning than it did twenty years ago. The concept is clearly in development and transition. Elements such as propriety, transparency, participation, accountability, accountability and human rights have been added to the concept. All these elements have been incorporated into several documents over the course. Within the framework of the Council of Europe, the third line shows that the ECtHR develops its own

[14] Examples thereof are: *Nsona v Netherlands* (ECHR No 23366/94, 28 November 1996); *Ahmut v Netherlands* (ECHR No. 21702/9328, 28 November 1996); *Squat v Netherlands* (ECHR No 16034/90, 19 April 1994); *Gasus Gmbh v Netherlands* (ECHR No 15375/89, 23 February 1995).

[15] ECHR No 19235/03, 21 April 2009.

[16] *Guja v Moldova*, ECHR No 14277/04, 12 February 2008.

[17] *Rysovsky v Ukraine* ECHR No. 29979/04, 20 October 2011.

interpretation of the principle of good governance in the review of government action. That interpretation is twofold and makes demands on the speed at which an incorrect decision has to be corrected and may require the administration to provide adequate compensation to pay or offer. Another suitable form of recovery with the dual interpretation of the principle of good governance has been highlighted in this judicial review. Something that deserves more attention than it has received so far. We see that the principles of international law have been applied by the WTO Dispute Settlement Body in the interpretation of the WTO agreements and the customary international law as expressed in the articles 31 and 32 of the Vienna Convention on the Law of Treaties. The interpretation is still not limited to what is expressed in the Vienna Convention, as different principles of international law, like the principle of effectiveness and the principle of legitimate expectation, are employed. This principle of effectiveness and the principle of legitimate expectations are also elements of the principles of good governance. The consequences of these developments are that there are not only new principles in the frame of concept of good governance, but there are also innovations of already existing principles of international law because of the influence of the concept of good governance. This can be found in the decisions of the WTO Dispute Settlement Body.[18]

When comparing the courts in their use of good governance, it is clear that in spite of difference in terminology there is yet to be a common idea of good governance. The International Court of Justice incidentally uses the term in the context of good administration, but, for example, the ECtHR employs the terminology principle of good governance. The Inter-American Court of Human Rights is referring to different elements of the international human rights treaties which can be qualified as principles of good governance. The WTO Dispute Settlement Body is referring to the principle of effectiveness or the principle of legitimate expectations which are both principles of good governance.

We can conclude that the principle of good governance can be found in a more horizontal way in a lot of policy fields of international law. The (specification of the) concept can be found in many treaties in these fields. It is important to note that it can be found in many international treaties on human rights. And it has been qualified as a right for the people.

The implementation of the concept and principle of good governance has grown into the system of international law as a consequence of developments in both international law and national legal systems. At the grassroots of international law, good governance has been accepted as a principle of law, in national legal systems, and from there in regional institutions. Important to mention too is that the concept is not related to only a few policy fields, but is neither implemented in all policy fields. Sometimes this concept is worked out in a general regulation but mostly only some aspects of good governance are worked out in the law and the only principles are developed in practice by the administration and the court. So, it functions as a norm for the administration and the court uses elements of the principle in his review. The concept is applied as such and in the different policy fields.

The concept is made concrete in different types of norms. In policy papers this notion can be found, but in different types of directives and regulations the concept is worked out on an EU-level. Other regional (economic) organizations are frequently working with this concept. Notably, on an EU-level a right to good administration

[18] Cameron and Gray 2001, 248–98.

has been elaborated upon and concretely applied in judicial procedures. And on an EU-level, it is not only about one or two policy fields, it has been used in several policy fields by administration and court.

The international level has accepted and specified the concept of good governance in different treaties related to the economic and environmental issues. And courts and dispute settlement institutions have applied the principle of good governance.

The question, then, is related to the two approaches—narrow and broader—of principles of international law. From the narrow scope, four conditions are made concerning the general principles of international law: (a) general principles; (b) principles as norms (they are neither a rule nor a general practice accepted as law), (c) chronologically already recognized; (d) by civilized nations.

In describing these conditions related to the principles of good governance, the following aspects are relevant. We speak about general principles of good governance because these principles are not restrictive to one or two policy fields; these principles are applied in the broader framework of the administration and the judiciary. These principles are norms, legal norms in the sense that sometimes elements have been codified in the law, in other situations these are still unwritten principles. These principles are recognized in a broad sense, so that this condition has been fulfilled. Finally, these principles are accepted by civilized nations. From the broader perspective, and looking to the different functions of principles, the principles of good governance should be recognized as principles of international law.

We see that the principles of international law have been applied by the WTO Dispute Settlement Body in the interpretation of the WTO agreements and the customary international law. The interpretation is still not limited to what is expressed in the Vienna Convention, as different principles of international law (like the principle of effectiveness and the principle of legitimate expectation) are employed, and they are also principles of good governance. We found that there are not only new principles of good governance, but there are also innovations of existing principles of international law because of the influence of the concept of good governance.

When comparing the courts in their use of good governance, despite the differences in terminology there is a common idea of good governance. The International Court of Justice incidentally uses the term in the context of good administration, but, for example, the ECtHR employs the terminology 'principle of good governance'. The Inter-American Court of Human Rights is referring to different elements of the international human rights treaties which can be qualified as principles of good governance. The WTO Dispute Settlement Body is referring to the principles of effectiveness and legitimate expectations which are both good governance principles. We concluded that the principle of good governance can be found in a more horizontal way in a large number of policy fields of international law.

At the grassroots of international law, good governance has been accepted as a principle of law. From there on it made its way to national legal systems, and from there to regional institutions. It is important to mention is that the concept is not related to a few policy fields only, but is neither implemented in all policy fields. Sometimes this concept is worked out in a general regulation, but mostly only some aspects of good governance are worked out in the law, while others are developed in practice by the administration and the court. So, it functions as a norm for the administration and the court uses some of these principles in its review. The concept is applied as such in different policy fields. The international level has accepted and specified the concept of good governance in different treaties related to the economic and environmental issues. And courts and dispute settlement institutions have applied the principles of good governance. From the narrow approach of principles of international law four conditions are made related to the general principles of international law: a. general; b. principle which is a norm, but neither a rule nor a general practice accepted as law; c. chronologically already recognized; d. by civilized nations. In describing the conditions for principles of international law we can conclude that the principles of good governance are principles of international law.

18

Conclusions on Good Governance

Concept and Context

In this book, *Good Governance: Concept and Context*, we have developed what can be considered the third cornerstone of a modern state (alongside the rule of law and democracy): good governance. Part I deals with the conceptual aspects of good governance. Part II discusses the specifications in the different legal norms of principles of good governance. Finally, Part III deals with the implementation of the principles of good governance. Good governance has been further developed by those institutions acting in the public interest: both in what concerns their internal operation, as well as in their external roles of governance.

1. Part I: The Development of the Concept of Good Governance

In Part I, we described the concept of good governance in relation to three phases in the development of a modern state. In the first phase, the rule of law concept was developed, while in the second phase the concept has been deepened in relation to the concept of democracy. The third phase shows a deepening of the concepts of the rule of law and democracy in relation to the concept of good governance and the further development of the institutional dimension of that concept. Good governance is the third cornerstone of the modern democratic state and is needed to prevent and redress situations of maladministration and corruption.

Principles of good governance can only be legal principles when they have been somehow codified and they have legal effect. Such legal effect is seen in three phases of the legal process: in the process of making regulation, the process of implementing regulation, and in the process of controlling and enforcing regulation by the controlling institutions. In each of these phases, we see the legal consequences of the principles of good governance. These principles are used as guidelines by the legislator, the administration, and the controlling institutions like the judiciary and the ombudsman. The principles sometimes function as norms for the administration and in other situations as protecting norms for the citizens. The good governance principles as norms for the administration can be found in constitutions and in several national pieces of general legislation on administrative law. The protection of good governance principles has been in place for some time in the context of human rights. They were mostly not recognized as principles of good governance but as the implementation of social, cultural, and political rights of citizens. These principles operate by means of regulations and case law.

We have made good governance more concrete by enumerating six groups of principles (properness, transparency, participation, effectiveness, accountability, and human rights). Their content has been tailored for each of the four branches of the state. The development of the balance of powers may be interpreted and applied differently in different constitutional systems and the fourth power is of increasing importance in strengthening the system of checks and balances.

The principles can be found in many documents of national, regional, and international context. The principles are formulated as fundamental legal principles, concrete legal norms, and policy guidelines. Good governance is a multilevel concept that includes the national, regional, European, and international levels. In constitutions, laws, regulations, and policy rules we find these principles already specified. The regional, European level also exerts a strong influence on the national level when it comes to the development of the principles of good governance. We concluded with the importance of the recommendations of the Council of Europe and the specification of principles of good governance on an EU level. Finally, the international level is also an important source of good governance principles. International organizations have developed these norms in their relations with countries, but the use of different definitions and tailored implementation create a somewhat diffuse picture. They have also started to apply comparable norms within their own organizations, which is applauded and supported by many NGOs and by many countries. In the literature, we find the argument that good governance is a principle of international law.

Further, the legal theory approach on good governance has been developed, discussing the character of these principles. From the interpretative approach of Dworkin, there is more room for the development of new good governance principles. Hart would accept such principles if they are laid down in positive law. There are different conceptions around common fundamental values like democracy. These different conceptions are, to a large extent, expressed in the principles connected with the interpretive legal concept. But we also have to see that it is important for legal certainty and equality that these principles have to be codified as much as possible in positive law. Having the principles of good governance as solely unwritten principles is not enough. The idea that these principles are important has led to the codification of the principles in positive law and have been further developed on national, regional, and international levels. There is a continuous line from one level to another in which these concepts become increasingly specified. Good governance is related to positive law and to its underlying principles. These principles are linked to the underlying values.

From a legal perspective, the discussion between principles and rights in the context of good governance is also relevant. We see a difference in the abstract character of the legal norm. The principle is an abstract legal norm and the right is a concrete legal norm. Alexy and Dworkin both have an open eye for the principles and the rules, but on the topic of principles they do not have the same opinion. Alexy gives legal weight to principles whereas Dworkin seems to be of the opinion that the legal effect will be achieved by the rules which codify the principle. The theory of principles is so important because of the ideal of legal weight of principles. That is clear in relation to the principle of proportionality as a substantial principle, but the idea of legal weight is also important—from a different legal scope—for a more formal principle like carefulness. It is interesting to see that in relation to fundamental rights Alexy works with the concept of optimization requirements in relation to these rights. This is also a norm which presents the principles of good governance in context.

Furthermore, principles are differently 'valued', so their role in any particular case may differ depending on how much weight they bear in that case. Values are often regarded as the basis for principles. Different concepts have been developed in relation to this relationship. Most importantly, the principles are requirements of a nature, while values are what we ultimately consider to be good. We can also distinguish this from the comparison between the notion that something has value and something is a value. We conclude by looking at good governance as a principle and good governance as a value. The difference between principles and values is reduced to just one point. This is reflected in the discussion about norms. Norms are distinguished in axiological norms and deontological norms. The first refers to an evaluative criterion or value, the second concerns the existence of a rule or principle. What, under a system of values, is prima facie the best, is under a system of principles what prima facie ought to be; and what under a system of values is definitively the best, is under a system of principles what definitively ought to be. That is relevant in the context of the principles of good governance.

The rule of law is one of the cornerstones of a modern state, but we find in the literature several variations on the vast theme that is the rule of law. In the narrow approach, only principles of procedural fairness are accepted. In the broader approach, there is a more substantive specification of the elements of the *rechtsstaat*. These elements are legality, division of powers, independent judicial control, and protection of human rights. Three generations of human rights have been developed: civil rights, social and economic rights, and finally complex composited rights like the right to development and the right to a clean environment. In this context, there are important differences between the common law and the continental law tradition. In the common law tradition, the focus of the law is to limit the power of the government. In the continental tradition, the law also gives the basis for empowerment of the government. The basis of the different approaches of the rule of law and the *rechtsstaat* is the differing concept of the state. Originally, we had the two different legal systems, but countries are increasingly moving towards a mixed legal system. In such a mixed legal system, the rule of law and the *rechtsstaat* concepts are getting closer to each other. It becomes increasingly important to distinguish the formal and the substantial aspects of these concepts. There are some difficulties in the traditional concept of the rule of law, but there are important developments of the rule of law on two levels. The first level is the objective legal structuring of the state by law, and the second is the subjective individual legal position. Finally, we see that the developments on these two levels make clear that there is a need for a further development of the concept of the rule of law. In this process of broadening the scope of good governance, a new dimension can be added. The good governance concept specifies the two levels of the rule of law, and this combination gives more adequate answers to the normative side of the functioning of the public sector nowadays.

Democracy is a political form of government which can be worked out in different ways. For that reason, we speak about different forms of government. We discussed some aspects that are strongly related to democracy. These aspects are representation after the elections, the relevance of the majority rule, the relationship between direct and representative democracy, and the topics of transparency and participation. We saw the importance of representative democracy, but also the tyranny of the majority. Care for minorities in a democracy is crucial. It is also relevant to consider the different ways of thinking about popular sovereignty and how it is related to the idea of separation of powers. We also noted the importance of the link between the powers in the state and the citizens. There are different types of direct democracy, some existing within representative democracies. This is because in a representative democracy not all the matters in a state can be dealt with by the representatives. There are different opinions about the role of parliament in a representative democracy. Direct democracy can be realized in different ways. Often it depends on the topic, but citizens' initiatives and referenda are good examples. The objectives of participation can be different: it can be from the perspective of the citizen, but it can also be done for management reasons. For legitimizing the aims of the government, different forms of participation can be very relevant.

On the issue of transparency, we distinguished between the narrow and the broad notions, which can be summarized as a more or less open functioning of the institutions of the state. This topic of transparency is often related to the activities of the government, like meetings, the forms of access to information, and the different types of government action. The existing restrictions become significant when dealing with issues of privacy.

2. Part II: The Specification of the Principles of Good Governance

In Part II, we specified the six principles of good governance. We started with the principle of properness, which has also been developed under the name of the principle of natural justice. It is a principle which has originally been developed and specified by the judiciary as an unwritten principle. The second, the principle of transparency, is related to the concept of democracy. Transparency is connected to the principle of participation which has its roots in the concept of democracy. The principles of effectiveness and accountability both have a relationship to the institutional structure and functioning. The last principle is the human rights principle which is linked to the rule of law but also to democracy.

The principle of proper administration and the specification in subprinciples are seen as the starting points for the principles of good governance and can be found in legislation, case law, policy rules, and in ombudsman reports. In this study, eight subprinciples of proper administration are distinguished:

1. The prohibition on *misuse of power*, with its four distinguished specifications: against the purpose of power, striving for an incorrect goal, inappropriate use, and inconsistent use.
2. The prohibition on *arbitrariness*, with four forms of manifestation: arbitrariness grasped as evident unreasonableness, visible unreasonableness in which there is a balance of interest but it is not acceptable, that cannot be done reasonably (marginal judicial review), and is not unfair.
3. The principle of *legal certainty* in which we distinguished two aspects: formal legal certainty in the sense of recognizable rights and duties, and substantive legal certainty in the sense of durability of rules, orders that must be complied with, protection of rights, and the prohibition of retroactive effect.
4. The principle of *confidence (or legitimate expectations)* as worked out in general by policy rules, directives, or circulars. In concrete cases, the following specification criteria for creating confidence apply: who, in what context, how, and by which disposition.
5. The principle of *equality*, which is split into equality for the law and equality of administration and encompassing: no predisposition, no negative discrimination, no positive discrimination, and equal spread of costs made in the general interest.
6. The principle of *proportionality* in general is focused on a right balance between means and aims, and more specifically it applies to administrative sanctions.
7. The principle of *carefulness*, where we note the difference between the substantive and formal components. Substantive carefulness means a careful balance of interest. In formal carefulness, steps in procedure of ordering are specified: (a) treatment, (b) research, (c) consultation, and (d) publication.

8. Finally, within the principle of *reasoning*, there is also a distinction between substantive (bearing reason in relation to: facts, interest, and rules) and formal (recognizable reason by giving or publication of the administrative motives).

The history of administrative judicial review is mainly linked to growing competences at the cost of review powers of higher administrative bodies. The courts mainly developed the principles of proper administration—sometimes they followed the ombudsman interpretations and vice versa. Both did so to counterbalance the increase of discretionary powers of the administration. For this purpose, the courts generated discretionary powers for themselves, in creating and applying the different general principles of proper administration. In many cases they could choose between a restricted and a comprehensive review of an administrative order. At the moment, the courts do not always extensively justify this choice. Ironically, this sometimes leads to legal uncertainty as to judicial review. In the Netherlands, the introduction of the General Administrative Law Act (GALA) has two facets. It is a codification of (sub)principles of a hundred years of judicial review on administrative decisions and creating unity. It is also a modification of the status quo reached in 1994. This modification implies a severe formalization of judicial review in Dutch administrative law, especially when courts refer to their competences as restricted to subjective law enforcement. This may be perfectly alright for citizens and organizations that are used to taking care of themselves with regards to judicial matters. For people who are not used to that, the system has become harder. Given that unity, differences that could not be seen before have become visible due to the codification in the GALA. Most importantly, this effort to create unity and coherence has provided for much more legal certainty and standardization in administrative law.

The traditional relevance of the principle of transparency, such as access to public information, has often been developed into a Freedom of Information Act (FOIA). Regulations have also been developed related to the other two subprinciples: the transparency of meetings and the transparency of administrative acts. But less known is the information developed and published in the framework of public inquiries by specific committees, or the effects this information could have for those who have been investigated. Often, this can include the possible criminal effect of publications and the violation of fundamental rights by these publications. These interests ought to be balanced out in drafting legally correct legislation.

In a representative democracy, not all government actions, especially because of the growth of framework legislation and public contracts,[1] are controlled by parliaments as the representatives of the people. Generally, only the main topics or the general lines of administrative policies are controlled. For that reason, there is an additional need for participation by the citizens. It is important that in all the government's activities which have direct consequences for people, at least the directly affected persons—natural and legal—are involved in the decision-making process. However, participation is also linked to the legitimacy of the administration in a more substantial way, and the form of deliberative democracy promotes that. Direct democracy and representative democracy often strengthen each other. There are different types of participation. The following forms of public participation have already been described several times: popular initiative, citizens' panel, referendum, and community-level participation. Some forms are related only to some phases in the process of policy development, but other forms can be used in all the phases of the policy process. It means that a

[1] Zigirinshuti 2013.

choice always has to be made, based both on the issue involved and on the desired degree of participation by the citizens. An example of the citizens' initiative at EU level can be found in article 11(4)of the TFEU. There is a lack of sufficient methodology on direct democracy and the principle of participation enjoys a great variety of standards throughout Europe. For example, if one compares the use of direct democracy in the United Kingdom to Switzerland, there is a vast contrast. Since the 1850s, Switzerland has held over 500 national referendums. If a petition is signed by one per cent of the electorate and submitted calling for a referendum on an issue under consideration by the government, then a referendum must be held. The signatures of 2 per cent of voters are enough to call a referendum on an issue not under government consideration. By contrast there have been only eleven referenda in the United Kingdom. They have generally been used over the issue of devolution or other major constitutional issues, such as remaining part of the EU in 1975. In fact, there are significant drawbacks to the use of referenda and the ad hoc manner in which referenda have sometimes been used can be regrettable, often as a tactical device by the government of the day. We see that several of these types of participation have already been formulated in legislation, but not all: newer forms of participation often have an informal character. Finally, a ladder of citizen participation has been developed, based on the degree (from minimum to maximum) of participation: manipulation, therapy, informing, consultation, placation, partnership, delegated power, and citizen control.

We started the discussion on the principle of effectiveness with some dictionary definitions of 'effectiveness' and found that effectiveness is subject to research in non-legal disciplines and it is rather new in the legal discipline. In social science, 'effectiveness' refers to the ways of using methods of empirical investigation to develop knowledge about human social activity. In physics, it is the framework intended to explain certain observed effects. And, in economics, it means the highest quality at the least possible cost. It must be noted that the principle of effectiveness is intertwined with the other principles of good governance, which are the tools used to reach the goal that is good governance. An example is the combination of the principle of participation and the principle of effectiveness for which the CLEAR-method has been developed. However, the goal of public participation will not be reached if the principle is not implemented effectively, and therefore we encounter overlaps between the principle of effectiveness and other principles of good governance. It is necessary to stress that principles of good governance do overlap and work together, and therefore effectiveness should not be viewed as an isolated principle. In a legal context, two aspects of effectiveness are relevant: that effectiveness is a principle of good governance and that effectiveness has procedural and substantive aspects. In international law, the principle of effectiveness has been developed along the following lines: effectiveness as actual observance, effectiveness as a rule for treaty interpretation, and effectiveness as a strong factual effect on a legal norm. Effectiveness in European Union law means the effective implementation of EU rules, substantively and procedurally; effectiveness as a principle of EU law, developed by the ECJ; and equivalence and effectiveness in the context of effective judicial review. Effectiveness in national administrative law is about internationalization and the interdisciplinary approach of administrative law, effective implementation and execution at the national level, and effectiveness in the sense of the interrelation between legal norms and facts.

For the principle of accountability, we specified several steps. The step from purely financial accounting to public accountability offers audit offices a chance to emancipate themselves from their somewhat dull bookkeeping background. They can enhance their public legitimacy by taking up new roles: for example, the vigilant public accountant who watches over the efficiency and effectiveness of public programmes. We see such developments at the national level as well as at the EU level. Establishing the effectiveness of policies and programmes often requires a variety of sophisticated evaluation techniques that may also vary within the sector that is being evaluated. Old-fashioned financial accounting or legal scrutiny will not suffice. Audit offices have to establish multidisciplinary teams and interdisciplinary understanding becomes more important. Some of these new roles may also create new dilemmas. Auditors may find it difficult to combine both the traditional accounting role and this new role, in which they have to apply the principle of accountability in the context of good governance.

The right to good administration has not developed in isolation. The right to good administration is also the right to good governance in a narrow sense because it is used as a norm by the different powers in the state in relation to the qualification of the administration. Several principles of good governance were already developed in regulations and in codes which are the building blocks for the development of the right to good governance. There were even more developments since the controlling institutions, such as the European Ombudsman, have also developed these principles of good governance in different ways in their assessments of the activities of the administration. In parallel, specific rights such as the right to transparency and the right to participation have been developed.

3. Part III: The Implementation of the Principles of Good Governance

In Part III, we described the implementation of the principles of good governance on the national, regional (EU), and international level. The description of the main implementation elements of individual countries and the comparison between countries is based on a study on good governance in the EU member states; several countries outside Europe have also been investigated. After that, the regional level was discussed—the European Union and the Council of Europe were chosen as models as far as it was comparable. The last chapter was about the implementation on the international level.

Good governance is part of the modern state not only in Europe, but also in other parts of the world, on both the national and local level. Good governance has a dual nature, comprising both a real (or factual) dimension, and an ideal (or critical) one. In the case studies, a distinction was made between three links of good governance: rule of law, democracy, and institutional. Within each of the three links we distinguished between the following three developments: the general development, the specification, and the intermediate position. For example, in relation to the rule of law dimension: in general development there is a strong focus on legality, and in specific development by the properness and the human rights principles. The intermediate position is a mix of the general and specific development. Within each development we can distinguish between a written development in the constitution, the law, or the regulations, and a development of (un)written principles by case law and/or in the literature. The twenty-eight EU member states were divided into five groups of countries, in which each country separated was studied, in Northern, Western, Southern, and Central Europe, and the United Kingdom and Ireland.

Regarding the interpretations of good governance in the member states of the EU and the underlying values (suitability, integrity, and transparency), we concluded that in all EU member states the concept of good governance is used as a norm for the activities of the administration, by the administration. It is mostly not applied as a norm for the other powers of the state: the legislator or the judiciary. Nevertheless, the two other powers are increasingly using and developing these norms for the administration. For that reason, we can speak about good governance here, but in a strict sense because it is only about good administration and not about good legislation or good judiciary. In countries where corruption is an issue (which in a strict sense is a violation of the prohibition on misuse of power), a link is also made with the principle of integrity. In the Netherlands, the violation of integrity has a broader application than only for corruption situations, and we found links with the principles of good governance. We distinguished ten forms of violation of the integrity principle, which are directly related to the principles of properness, human rights, transparency, and accountability. The application of the principles of good governance was based on the concept of good governance by way of its principles and in which the three dimensions—rule of law, democracy, and institutional—are known and applied.

For the rule of law link, in the Northern Europe countries there is a strong focus on the principles of properness and human rights (two of the three countries; one country was intermediate). In the Western Europe group, three countries focused on properness and human rights principles, while three were intermediate. In the Southern Europe group, the focus was more on the general line of the rule of law for three counties, while three other countries were intermediate. For the Central Europe group, there was a mix in which five countries were intermediate, four countries more focused on the general rule of law line, and two countries more on the specification of properness and human rights. The fifth group (the United Kingdom and Ireland) had both countries in the intermediate bracket.

In relation to the democracy link, in the Northern Europe group of countries we found that two of the three countries had specified transparency and participation, while one country was intermediate. For the Western Europe group, most of the countries (four) were intermediate and one country was more focused on the general development of democracy, while another country was focused on the specification of transparency and participation. For the Southern Europe group, four of them were intermediate and two countries had a specification of transparency and participation. In the Central Europe group, four countries were intermediate, two focused on the general aspects of democracy and three on the specification of transparency and participation. In the fifth group (the United Kingdom and Ireland), one country focuses on the general aspects of democracy, while the other is intermediate.

Regarding the institutional link, in the Northern Europe group, one is intermediate, while one focuses on effectiveness and accountability. In the Western Europe group, three countries focus on the general aspects of the institutions and one country on the principles of effectiveness and accountability, while two are intermediate. In the Southern Europe group, most of the countries (four) are intermediate and two focus on the general aspects of the institutions. For Central Europe, we found four countries to be intermediate, four countries focusing on the general aspects of the institutions and three countries on the specific aspects of effectiveness and accountability. In the fifth group (the United Kingdom and Ireland), we found that both are focusing on the specification of effectiveness and accountability.

In the five groups of countries we found differences as to the interpretation and application of good governance because of the different functions of government (policy development, implementation, supervision). We also see that general aspects are often worked out in the constitution and general laws and regulations; this means there is an important role for the policy development and implementation components of the government. The specification of the dimensions by the development of principles is mostly initiated by the supervisory and controlling bodies of the government. After some time, we usually found codification of the specified principles in the general laws. It is interesting to see that there are some differences in relation to each of the three dimensions. We found, more often than not, specification of the human rights, transparency, and participation principles; the specification of the properness subprinciples is lagging a little behind. The specification of the accountability and effectiveness principles is behind the properness principles.

It is also relevant to see how the conflicting values were balanced. It concerns choices within member states, but sometimes it also has to do with cooperating countries weighting these values differently. Sometimes, the legislator has already prevented the conflict in two ways: first by codifying one principle and not the other, or by giving priority to one principle over the other principles; the executive power also achieves that by making political priorities related to principles. So, the question is: how should apparent conflicts of principles be dealt with? If there is no legal hierarchy, other factors are decisive in balancing the principles.

Then followed some conclusions about countries outside the European Union: Australia, Canada, and South Africa. The general line is that the principles of good governance have not yet been developed as written principles, which has the consequence that there is no deep and substantial discussion about the contents of each of the six principles of good governance which have been distinguished in this book. There is a second more general observation from which we can see that the concept of good governance has been accepted in the three countries and that is important because that is the motor for the further development of each of the six principles of good governance. Most explicit is the Constitution of Canada where the concept of good government has been codified, but this formulation is strongly focused on the internal institutional dimension of the government and not so explicit about the external activities of the governmental institutions. In all the three countries, the focus is strongly on the rule of law principles like the principle of human rights and the principle of properness respectively the principle of natural justice. Gradually, there is more attention paid to the principles of transparency and participation. The newer institutional related principles of accountability and effectiveness receive no attention from lawyers; however, there is a strong focus on these principles in the social sciences.

Then, some remarks about the regional EU implementation of the principles followed. Attention was paid to the EU administration, the EU Commission, and the EU controlling institutions (the Court of Justice and the Ombudsman). The first instrument was the 2001 White Paper in which the Commission developed five important principles of good governance: openness, participation, accountability, effectiveness, and coherence. These five principles of good administration were implemented by the Commission. The White Paper was followed by the 2004 binding Code of Good Administrative Behaviour for Staff of the European Commission. This was a normative framework with principles of good administration which should be enforced in relation to activities of staff members of the Commission. For the EU Court of Justice, the most important framework on the principles of good governance are the treaties: the Lisbon Treaty and the Charter on Fundamental Rights. In addition to the further evolution of the general principles common to all European administrative law systems, other principles are also mentioned and further developed. One example is the right of every person to have his or her affairs handled within a reasonable time by a European institution as part of the right to sound administration. Another is the need to act within a reasonable time in conducting administrative proceedings relating to competition policy as a general principle of EU law whose infringement would justify the annulment of the respective decision insofar as it also constituted an infringement of the rights of defence and makes the link with the civil liability issue. Later, the Court developed the broader jurisprudence on transparency and on the right of access to documents. When it comes to article 41 of the Charter, the jurisprudence on the right of good administration is relevant. Nevertheless, it seems that the Court is working on it a step-by-step and on a subprinciple level—and only partly on new principles like effectiveness.

The European Ombudsman has developed a code of good administrative behaviour. This code consisted of three parts, each part containing principles of a different character. The first part contains the general articles relating to institutions and their officials. The second part is about the classical basic principles of administrative law, like lawfulness. In the third part, we find the articles about good administrative functioning. These articles are about replying to letters, acknowledgement of receipt, transfer to the competent service, notification (transparency), data protection, and keeping adequate records. In essence, we find in all these three parts different elements of the principles of good administration. In practice, the focus of the ombudsman is according to its recent annual report: transparency in EU decision-making, lobbying transparency, transparency in economic and financial decision-making, access to EU documents, ethical issues, EU agencies and other bodies, and finally EU contracts and grants. So, in relation to good administration, the focus is especially on transparency and ethical issues.

We see at the regional, EU level a strong development by means of the Fundamental Rights Charter, in which we find a fundamental right of good administration. Also, the Court of Justice of the European Union is strongly developing the principles of EU law, of which the principles of good administration are a part. In the literature—the RENEUAL report—there is a strong emphasis on the development of a European administrative act. The EU executive level is fragmented: the European Parliament is strongly focused on a more integrative approach of the principles of good governance.

At present, the implementation of good governance has a much broader meaning than it did twenty years ago. The concept is clearly in development and transition. Elements such as propriety, transparency, participation, accountability, and human rights have been added to the concept. All these elements have been incorporated into several documents as time went on. Within the framework of the Council of Europe, the third line shows that the ECtHR develops its own interpretation of the principle of good governance in the review of government action. That interpretation is twofold and makes demands on the speed at which an incorrect decision has to be corrected and may require the administration to provide adequate compensation. Another suitable form of recovery with the dual interpretation of the principle of good governance has been highlighted in this judicial review.

We see that the principles of international law have been applied by the WTO Dispute Settlement Body in the interpretation of the WTO agreements and the customary international law. The interpretation is still not limited to what is expressed in the Vienna Convention, as different principles of international law (like the principle of effectiveness and the principle of legitimate expectation) are employed, and they are also principles of good governance. We found that there are not only new principles of good governance, but there are also innovations of existing principles of international law because of the influence of the concept of good governance.

When comparing the courts in their use of good governance, despite the differences in terminology there is a common idea of good governance. The International Court of Justice incidentally uses the term in the context of good administration, but for example the European Court of Human Rights employs the terminology 'principle of good governance'. The Inter-American Court of Human Rights is referring to different elements of the international human rights treaties which can be qualified as principles of good governance. The WTO Dispute Settlement Body is referring to the principles of effectiveness and legitimate expectations which are both good governance principles. We concluded that the principle of good governance can be found in a more horizontal way in a large number of policy fields of international law.

At the grassroots of international law, good governance has been accepted as a principle of law. From there on it made its way into national legal systems, and from there into regional institutions. It is important to mention that the concept is not related to a few policy fields only, but is neither implemented in all policy fields. Sometimes this concept is worked out in a general regulation, but mostly only some aspects of good governance are worked out in the law, while others are developed in practice by the administration and the court. So, it functions as a norm for the administration and the court uses some of these principles in its review. The concept is applied as such in different policy fields. The international level has accepted and specified the concept of good governance in different treaties related to the economic and environmental issues. And courts and dispute settlement institutions have applied the principles of good governance. From the narrow approach of principles of international law four conditions are made related to the general principles of international law: (a) general; (b) principle which is a norm, but neither a rule nor a general practice accepted as law; (c) chronologically already recognized; (d) by civilized nations. In describing the conditions for principles of international law we can conclude that the principles of good governance are principles of international law.

Bibliography

Accetto and Zleptnig 2005

M Accetto and S Zleptnig, 'The Principle of Effectiveness: Rethinking its Role in Community Law' (2005) European Public Law, Vol 11, No 3, 375–403.

Addink 1999

GH Addink, *Algemene beginselen van behoorlijk bestuur* (Kluwer 1999).

Addink and others 2000

GH Addink, JBJM ten Berge, PAMJ Graat, and PM Langbroek, *Kwaliteit van overheidsbestuur* (WEJ Tjeenk Willink 2000).

Addink 2005a

GH Addink, 'Principles of Good Governance: Lessons from Administrative Law' in DM Curtin and RA Wessel (eds), *Good Governance and the European Union*, Ius Commune Europaeum Vol 49 (Intersentia 2005).

Addink 2005b

GH Addink, 'The Ombudsman as the fourth power. On the Foundations of Ombudsman Law from a Comparative Perspective' in ECHJ van der Linden and FAM Stroink (eds), *Judicial Lawmaking and Administrative Law*, Ius Commune Europaeum Vol 52 (Intersentia 2005).

Addink 2008

GH Addink, 'Goed bestuur: een norm voor het bestuur of een recht van de burger?' ('Good Governance: A Norm for the Administration or a Citizen's Right?') in GH Addink and others (eds), *Grensverleggend bestuursrecht* (Kluwer 2008).

Addink 2009

GH Addink, *Local and Regional Level Participation in Europe* (Utrecht University 2009), at <http://citeseerx.ist.psu.edu/viewdoc/download?doi=10.1.1.611.1299&rep=rep1&type=pdf>.

Addink 2010a

GH Addink, *Goed Bestuur* (Kluwer 2010).

Addink 2010b

GH Addink, 'Good Governance: Overview and Principles of Properness' in *Human Rights and Good Governance*, SIM special 34 (Utrecht University 2010).

Addink 2010c

GH Addink, 'The Principle of Effectiveness' in ECOLEF, *First Delivery to the European Union: Methodology, Questionnaire and Network Contacts* (Utrecht University 2010).

Addink 2012a

GH Addink, 'De toepassing van het concept van goed bestuur in het EU-handvest van de Grondrechten' in HRBM Kummeling ea (eds), *De samengestelde Besselink: Bruggen bouwen tussen nationaal, Europees en internationaal recht* (Wolf Legal Publishers 2012).

Addink 2012b

GH Addink, 'Integriteit, rechtmatigheid en goed bestuur' in JHJ van den Heuvel, LWJC Huberts, and ER Muller (eds), *Integriteit: Integriteit en integriteitbeleid in Nederland* (Kluwer 2012).

Addink 2013

GH Addink, 'Governance and Norms: An Interdisciplinary Approach of Good Governance' in ALB Colombi Ciacchi and others (eds), *Law and Governance. Beyond the Public-Private Law Divide* (The Hague: BJU Publishers 2013).

Addink 2014

GH Addink, 'Europees bestuursrecht in ontwikkeling: op weg naar een Europese Awb' in *Nederlands Tijdschrift voor Bestuursrecht* (NTB 2014) 7, 197–206.

Addink 2015a

GH Addink, *Coursebook Principles of Good Governance* (Utrecht University 2015).

Addink 2015b

GH Addink, *Good Governance in the EU Member States* (Utrecht University 2015).

Addink 2015c

GH Addink, 'Good Governance: A Principle of International Law' in C Ryngaert, E Molenaar, and S Nouwen (eds), *What's Wrong with International Law?* (Leiden/Boston 2015).

Addink 2017

GH Addink, 'Good Governance: Importance in Practice, Theories and Definitions' (2017) *Halu Oleo Law Review (HOLREV, Indonesia)*, Vol 1 No 1, March 2017, 1–32.

Addink and Ten Berge 2006

GH Addink and JBJM Ten Berge, 'Study on Innovation of Legal Means for Eliminating Corruption in the Public Service in the Netherlands' in JHM van Erp and LPW van Vliet (eds), *Netherlands Reports to the Seventeenth International Congress of Comparative Law* (Intersentia 2006).

ADF 2014

African Development Foundation, Participatory Development Handout Definitions (Washington DC, 2014).

Akerboom 2018

S Akerboom, *Between Public Participation and Energy Transition: The Case of Wind Farms*, PhD thesis Amsterdam University (Amsterdam 2018).

Alexy 2002

R Alexy, *Theory of Constitutional Rights* (Oxford University Press 2002).

Alexy 2014

R Alexy, *Constitutional Rights and Proportionality* (Revus 2014).

Alexy 2016

R Alexy, 'Constitutional Rights and Constitutional Review' in K Himma and B Spaic (eds), *Fundamental Rights Justification and Interpretation* (Eleven International Publishing, Den Haag 2016) 63–74.

Allan 2003

T Allan, *Constitutional Justice: A Liberal Theory of the Rule of Law* (Oxford University Press 2003).

Amsterdam Report 2005

Amsterdam Report 2005, Definitions of corruption p. 4 report; the following authors gave their own definition of corruption: BJS Hoetjes, *Corruptie bij de overheid. Een bestuurlijk en politiek probleem, sociaal wetenschappelijk beschouwd* (Gravenhage 1982);M Johnston, 'The Search for Definitions: The Validity of Politics and the Issue of Corruption' (1996) *International Social Science Journal* Vol 149, 321–35;LWJC Huberts, 'Bestuurlijke criminaliteit: Een inleiding' in LWJC Huberts (ed), *Bestuurlijke corruptie en fraude in Nederland* (Gouda Quint 1992); A Heywood, *Politics* (McMillan 1997);GE Caiden, OP Dwivedi, and JG Jabbra, *Where Corruption Lives* (Kumarian Press 2001);AJ Heidenheimer and JM Johnston, *Political Corruption, Concept & Context* (Transaction Publishers 2001).

Arnstein 1969

SR Arnstein, 'A Ladder of Citizen Participation' (1969) *Journal of the American Planning Association*, Vol 35, No 4, 216–24.

Arrowsmith 1998

S Arrowsmith, 'Towards a Multilateral Agreement on Transparency in Government Procurement' (1998) *International and Comparative Law Quarterly*, Vol 47, 793–816.

Arrowsmith 2003

S Arrowsmith. *Government Procurement in the WTO* (Kluwer Law International 2003).

Auby and Cluzel-Metayer 2007

JB Auby and L Cluzel-Metayer, 'Administrative Law in France' in RJGH Seerden (ed), *Administrative Law of the European Union, its Member States and the United States* (Intersentia 2007).

Austin 1995

J Austin, *The Province of Jurisprudence Determined* (first published in 1832 and edited by W Rumble Cambridge University Press 1995).

Austin 2007

J Austin, *J. Austin Lectures on Jurisprudence: or The Philosophy of Positive Law, two volumes* (first published in 1874 and edited by R Campbell, Kessinger publishing LLC 2007).

Banisar 2004

D Banisar, 'The freedominfo.org Global Survey Freedom of Information and Access to Government Record Laws Around the World, May 2004, <http://www.freedominfo.org/documents/global_survey2004.pdf>.

Van Banning and Van Genugten 1993

Th RG van Banning and WJM van Genugten, *Human Rights Reference Handbook* (The Netherlands Ministry of Foreign Affairs 1993).

Van Banning and Van Genugten 1999

Th RG van Banning and WJM van Genugten, *Human Rights Reference Handbook* (The Netherlands Ministry of Foreign Affairs 1999).

Bannister and Connolly 2011

F Bannister and R Connolly, 'The Trouble with Transparency: A Critical Review of Openness in e-Government' (2011) *Policy & Internet*, Vol 3, No 1, 1–30.

Bartole 2010, 1–4.

S Bartole, *Good Law-Making Principles*, report for the European Commission for Democracy through law (Venice Commission), Strasbourg 2010.

Behn 2001

RD Behn, *Rethinking Democratic Accountability* (Brookings Institution Press 2001).

Bernitz and Nergelius 2000

U Bernitz and J Nergelius (eds), *General Principles of European Community Law* (Kluwer Law International 2000).

Bessette 1980

JM Bessette, 'Deliberative Democracy: The Majority Principle in Republican Government' in RA Goldwin and WA Schambra (eds), *How Democratic is the Constitution?* (American Enterprise Institute for Public Policy Research 1980).

Bestuurskunde 2011

Special edition of *Bestuurskunde*, 2011, nr 2.

Binda 2015

M Binda, *Good Governance and Foreign Direct Investment*, PhD thesis Utrecht University (Utrecht University Repository 2015).

Birkinshaw 2005

PJ Birkinshaw, *Government and Information: The Law Relating to Access, Disclosure and Their Regulation* (Tottel Publishing 2005).

Birkinshaw 2006

PJ Birkinshaw, 'Freedom of Information and Openness: Fundamental Human Rights?' (2006) *Administrative Law Review*, Vol 58, No 1, 177–218.

Birnie and Boyle 2002

PW Birnie and AE Boyle, *International Law and the Environment* (Oxford University Press 2002).

Blaau 1990

LC Blaau, 'The Rechtsstaat Idea Compared with the Rule of Law as a Paradigm for Protecting Rights' (1990) South African Law Journal, Vol 107, No 1, 76–96.

Bodansky 1999

D Bodansky, 'The Legitimacy of International Governance: A Coming Challenge for International Environmental Law?' (July 1999) American Journal of International Law, Vol 93, No 3, 596–624.

Bodin 1576

J Bodin, *Les Six Livres de la Republique* (Jacques du Puys 1576).

Botchway 2000

FN Botchway, 'Good Governance: The Old, the New, the Principle and the Elements' (2000) *Florida Journal of International Law*, Vol 13, No 1, 159–210.

Boustra 2010

R Boustra, *Essai sur la notion de bonne administration en droit public* (L'Harmattan Paris 2010).

Bovens 2000

MAP Bovens, *De vierde macht revisited* (Utrecht University 2000).

Bovens 2004

MAP Bovens, 'Public Accountability' in E Ferlie, L Lynne, and C Pollitt (eds), *The Oxford Handbook of Public Management* (Oxford University Press 2004).

Bovens 2005

MAP Bovens, 'From Financial Accounting to Public Accountability' in H Hill (ed), *Bestandsaufnahme und Perspektiven des Haushalts- und Finanzmanagements* (Nomos 2005).

Bovens 2007

MAP Bovens, 'Analysing and Assessing Accountability: A Conceptual Framework' (2007) *European Law Journal*, Vol 13, No 4, 447–68.

Brenninkmeijer 2009

A Brenninkmeijer, *A Study about the Basic Principles of Proper Citizen's Participation* (The Netherlands National Ombudsman 2009).

van den Broek 2015

M van den Broek, *Preventing Money Laundering. A Legal Study on the Effectiveness of Supervision in the European Union*, PhD thesis Utrecht University (Eleven International Publishing 2015).

Brophy 2002

M Brophy, 'Administrative Accountability in the Community: The Role of the Ombudsman' in *The European Ombudsman*, Liaison Letter, No 7, Strasbourg, The European Ombudsman, January 2002.

Buijze 2008

AWJG Buijze, *On the Justification and Necessity of Legal Effectiveness Norm* (Utrecht University 2008).

Buijze 2013

AWJG Buijze, *The Principle of Transparency in EU Law*, PhD thesis Utrecht University (Boxpress 2013).

Burkens and others 2001

MC Burkens and others, *Beginselen van de democratische rechtsstaat* (Kluwer 2001).

Burkens and others 2006

MC Burkens and others, *Beginselen van de democratische rechtsstaat* (Kluwer 2006).

Burkens and others 2017

MC Burkens and others, *Beginselen van de democratische rechtsstaat* (Kluwer 2017).

Busuioc 2010

M Busuioc, *The Accountability of European Agencies*, PhD thesis Utrecht University (Eburon 2010).

Callinan and Aroney, in Groves 2014

Callinan and Aroney, cited in M Groves, *Modern Administrative Law Australia: Concepts and Context* (Cambridge University Press 2014), 312.

Cameron and Gray 2001

J Cameron and KR Gray, 'Principles of International Law in the WTO Dispute Settlement Body' (April 2001) International and Comparative Law Quarterly, Vol 50, 248–98.

Cane 2002

P Cane, *Responsibility in Law and Morality* (Hart Publishing 2002).

Chambers 2004

CW Chambers, 'Towards an Improved Understanding of Legal Effectiveness of International Environmental Treaties' (2004) Georgetown International Environmental Law Review, Vol 16, No 3, 501–32.

Chiang Jang 2010

Y Chiang Jang, 'International Legal Obligations in Relation to Good Ocean Governance' (2010) Chinese Journal of International Law, Vol 9, No 3, 589–605.

Chiti 1995

MP Chiti, 'Are there Universal Principles of Good Governance?' (1995) European Public Law, Vol 1, No 2, 241–58.

Classen 2008

K Classen, *Gute Verwaltung im Recht der Europäischen Grundrechtecharta* (Duncker & Humblot 2008).

Cloete and Auriacombe 2007

F Cloete and CJ Auriacombe, 'Governance and Transparency in South Africa' (2007) Politeia, Vol 26, 192–206.

Connor 1988

DM Connor, 'A New Ladder of Citizen Participation' (1988) National Civic Review, Vol 77, No 3, 249–57.

Craig 1990

PP Craig, *Public Law and Democracy in the United Kingdom and the United States of America* (Oxford University Press 1990).

Craig 1997

P Craig, 'Formal and Substantive Conceptions of the Rule of Law: An Analytical Framework' (1997) Public Law, 467–87.

Craig 2000

P Craig, 'Public Law, Political Theory and Legal Theory' (2000) Public Law, 211–31.

Craig 2006

P Craig, *EU Administrative Law* (Oxford University Press 2006).

Craig 2008

P Craig, *Administrative Law* (Sweet & Maxwell 2008).

Craig 2012

P Craig, *EU Administrative Law* (Oxford University Press 2012).

Craig 2013

P Craig, 'A General Law on Administrative Procedure, Legislative Competence and Judicial Competence' (2013) EPL, 503–24.

Craig 2015

P Craig, *UK, EU and Global Administrative Law: Foundations and Challenges* (Cambridge University Press 2015).

Craig 2016

P Craig, *Administrative Law* (8th edn, Sweet & Maxwell 2016).

Craig and De Búrca 2007

P Craig and G de Búrca, *EU Law, Text, Cases and Materials* (Oxford University Press 2007).

Crince Le Roy 1969

R Crince Le Roy, *De vierde macht: de ambtelijke bureaucratie als machtsfactor in de staat* (VUGA 1969).

Crince Le Roy 1976

R Crince Le Roy, *De vierde macht. Een hernieuwde kennismaking* (VUGA 1976).

Curtin and Dekker 2002

DM Curtin and IF Dekker, 'Governance as a Legal Concept within the EU: Purposes and Principles' (2002) International Law Forum du droit international, Vol 4, No 3, 134–49.

Curtin and Dekker 2005

DM Curtin and IF Dekker, 'Good Governance: The Concept and its Application by the European Union' in DM Curtin and RA Wessel (eds), *Good Governance and the European Union: Reflections on Concepts, Institutions and Substance* (Intersentia 2005).

Curtin and Senden 2011

DM Curtin and LAJ Senden, 'Public Accountability of Transnational Private Regulation: Chimera of Reality?' (2011) Journal of Law and Society, Vol 38, No 1, 163–88.

Cygan 2002

A Cygan, 'The White Paper on European Governance—Have Glasnost and Perestroika Finally Arrived to the European Union' (2002) Modern Law Review 229.

Damen 2009

LJA Damen, *Bestuursrecht I* (BJu 2009).

Von Danwitz 2010

Th von Danwitz, 'Good Governance in the Hands of the Judiciary: Lessons from the European Example' (2010) Potchefstroom Electronic Law Journal, Vol 13, No 1.

Dargaville 2011

J Dargaville, 'The New Right-to-know Landscape', *Government News* (February/March 2011) <http://www.governmentnews.com.au/files/GN%20FEB%20pg17-18%20new.pdf>, 17–18.

Davis 1969

K Davis, *Discretionary Justice. A Preliminary Inquiry* (Greenwood Press Westport 1969).

Day and Klein 1987

P Day and R Klein, *Accountabilities: Five Public Services* (Tavistock 1987).

Degenhart 1998

C Degenhart, *Staatrecht* (CF Muller Verlag 1998).

Diamandouros 2007

P Nikiforos Diamandouros, 'The Principle of Good Administration in the Recommendations of the European Ombudsman', Speech at the EUNOMIA Project Capacity-Building Seminar on 'Ombudsman's Intervention: Between the Principles of Legality and Good Administration', Sofia, Bulgaria, 17 September 2007.

Dicey 1959

AV Dicey, *An Introduction to the Study of the Law of the Constitution* (first published in 1885 and reprinted Macmillan 1959).

Döhring 1984

K Döhring, 'Effectiveness' (1984) Max Planck Encyclopedia of Public International Law, Vol 7, 70–4.

Dolzer 2004

R Dolzer, 'Good Governance: Neues transnationales Leitbild der Staatlichkeit?' (2004) Zeitschrift für ausländisches öffentliches Recht und Völkerrecht 535.

Dorling 2012

Ph Dorling, 'Reform on FOI bogs down', *The Age* (9 April 2012) <http://www.theage.com.au/opinion/political-news/reform-on-foi-bogs-down-20120408-1wjof.html>.

Dowell 2011

J Dowell, 'Principles of Judicial Review' in J Dowell (ed), *The Changing Constitution* (Oxford University Press 2011).

Dworkin 1977

R Dworkin, *Taking Rights Seriously* (Harvard University Press 1977).

Dworkin 1985

R Dworkin, *A Matter of Principle* (Harvard University Press 1985).

Dworkin 1986

R Dworkin, *Law's Empire* (Duckworth 1986).

Edlin 2007

DE Edlin (ed), *Common Law Theory* (Cambridge University Press 2007).

Ellerbrok 2016

T Ellerbrok, 'Der ReNEUAL-Musterentwurf für ein Europäisches Verwaltungsverfahrensrecht in der Diskussion', *Die Verwaltung* (2016), 105–17.

Elliott and Feldman 2015

M Elliott and D Feldman (eds), *Public Law* (Cambridge University Press 2015).

Endicott 2009

T Endicott, *Administrative Law* (Oxford University Press 2009).

Endicott 2015

T Endicott, *Administrative Law* (3rd edn, Oxford University Press 2015).

Esty 2006a

DC Esty, 'Good Governance at the Supranational Scale: Globalizing Administrative Law' (2006) Yale Law Journal, Vol 115, 1490.

Esty 2006b

DC Esty, 'Good Governance at the Supranational Scale: Globalizing Administrative Law' (2006) *Faculty Scholarship Series*, paper 428, <http://digitalcommons.law.yale.edu/fss_papers/428>.

Esty 2007

DC Esty: 'Good Governance at the WTO: Building a Foundation of Administrative Law' (2007) Journal of International Economic Law, Vol 10, No 3, 509–27.

Faulkner 2009

J Faulkner, 'Letter to Departmental Secretaries and Agency Heads', Cabinet Secretary (30 April 2009) <http://www.ag.gov.au/Freedomofinformation/Pages/FOI-Reforms.aspx>.

Fennel 2002

K Fennel, 'The European Ombudsman's Code of Good Administrative Behaviour. Milestone on the Way to a codified European Administrative Law?', paper (Utrecht University 2002).

Fennel 2003

K Fennel, 'The European Ombudsman's Code of Good Administrative Behaviour' in GH Addink (ed), *Principles of Good Governance Coursebook* (Utrecht University 2003), 5.31–5.87.

Fennel 2004

K Fennel, 'The Principles of Proper Administration in Dutch and German Law', Master thesis Utrecht University (Utrecht 2004).

Fisher 2004

E Fisher, 'The European Union in the Age of Accountability' (2004) Oxford Journal of Legal Studies, Vol 24, No 1, 495–510.

Foqué 1998

R Foqué, 'Global Governance and the Rule of Law. Human Rights and General Principles of Good Global Governance' in K Wellens (ed), *International Law: Theory and Practice. Essays in Honour of Eric Suy* (Kluwer Law International 1998).

Foqué 1999

R Foqué, 'Evenwicht van machten en rechtsstatelijke vernieuwing' in A Alen and LJ Wintgens (eds), *De Trias Politica ruimer bekeken, Staatsrechtconferenctie* 1999 (Brussel Larcier 2000).

Forsey 2012

EA Forsey, Minister of Public Works and Government Services Canada, *How Canadians Govern Themselves* (8th edn, Ottawa 2012).

Fuller 1964

L Fuller, *The Morality of Law* (Yale University Press 1964).

Gerards 2009

JH Gerards, 'Proportionality Review in European Law' (2009) *IVR Encyclopaedia of Jurisprudence, Legal Theory and Philosophy of Law* <http://ivr-enc.info/index.php?title=Proportionality_review_in_European_law>.

Gerards 2010

JH Gerards, 'Pluralism, Deference and the Margin of Appreciation Doctrine' (2010) European Law Journal, Vol 17, No 1, 80–120.

Ginther, Denters, and others 1995

K Ginther, E Denters, and others, *Sustainable Development and Good Governance* (Kluwer Academic 1995).

Giraud-Kinley 1999

C Giraud-Kinley, 'The Effectiveness of International Law: Sustainable Development in the South pacific Region' (1999) Georgetown International Law Environmental Law Review, Vol 12, No 1, 125–70.

Giussani 2008

E Giussani, *Constitutional and Administrative Law* (Sweet & Maxwell 2008)

Goldring 1981

J Goldring, 'The Foundations of the New Administrative Law in Australia' (1981) Australian Journal of Public Administration, Vol 40, No 79, 102.

Gornig and Trüe 1993

G Gornig and C Trüe, 'Die Rechtsprechung des EuGH zum europäischen allgemeinen Verwaltungsrecht' (1993) Juristenzeitung 884.

De Graaf 2007

L de Graaf, 'Stakeholder Support in Urban Governance' in J Franzke (ed), *Tensions between Local Governance and Local Democracy* (Reed Business 2007).

De Graaf and others 2011

G de Graaf, A Reijnders, Z van der Wal, and V van Doeveren, 'Good Governance as a Management of Tensions between Different Public Values' ('Goed bestuur als Management van spanningen tussen verschillende publieke waarden') (2011) Bestuurskunde, Vol 20, No 2, 8.

Graham, Amos, and Plumptre 2003

J Graham, B Amos, and T Plumptre, 'Principles for Good Governance in the 21st Century', Policy Brief no 15 2003, 15 Institute on Good Governance, 1–9.

Groves 2014

M Groves, *Modern Administrative Law Australia: Concepts and Context* (Cambridge University Press 2014).

Groussot 2006

X Groussot, *General Principles of Community Law* (Europa Law Publishing 2006).

Harlow 1988

C Harlow, 'European Administrative Law and the Global Challenge', European University Institute, Working Paper RSC No 98/23, 1988.

Harlow 1996

C Harlow, 'Codification of EC Administrative Procedures? Fitting the Foot to the Shoe or the Shoe to the Foot' (1996) European Law Journal, Vol 2. No 1, 3–25.

Harlow 2002

C Harlow, *Accountability in the European Union* (Oxford University Press 2002).

Harlow 2006

C Harlow, 'Global Administrative Law: The Quest, Principles and Values' (2006) The European Law Journal, Vol 17, No 1, 187–214.

Harlow and Rawlings 2009

C Harlow and R Rawlings, *Law and Administration* (Cambridge University Press 2009).

Hart 1961

HLA Hart, *The Concept of Law* (Clarendon Press 1961).

Hart 1997

HLA Hart, *The Concept of Law* (2nd edn, Oxford University Press 1997).

Van Harten, Heckman, and Mullan 2010

G Van Harten, G Heckman, and DJ Mullan, *Administrative Law, Cases, Text, and Materials* (6th edn, Toronto 2010).

Hayek 1960

FA Hayek, *The Constitution of Liberty* (The University of Chicago Press 1960).

Hegels 2001

S Hegels, *EG-Eigenverwaltungsrecht und Gemeinschaftsverwaltungsrecht* (Nomos Verlagsgesellschaft Baden-Baden 2001)

Van der Heijden 2001

GMA van der Heijden, *Een filosofie van behoorlijk bestuur* (Kluwer 2001).

Helder 1989

E Helder, *Ombudsman en administratieve rechtsbescherming* (Twente University 1989).

Herling and Lyon 2004

D Herling and A Lyon, *Briefcase on Constitutional and Administrative Law* (Routledge Cavendish 2004).

Van den Heuvel, Huberts, and Muller 2012

JHJ van den Heuvel, LWJC Huberts, and ER Muller (eds), *Integrity. Integrity and Integrity Policy in the Netherlands (Integriteit. Integriteit en integriteitsbeleid in Nederland)* (Deventer 2012).

Hins and Voorhoof 2007

W Hins and D Voorhoof, 'Access to State-Held Information as a Fundamental Right under the European Convention on Human Rights' (2007) European Constitutional Law Review, Vol 3, No 1, 114–26.

Hirsch Ballin 2000

EMH Hirsch Ballin, 'Een grondrecht op behoorlijk bestuur' (2000) Nederlands Tijdschrift voor BestuursrechtNo 10, 305–8.

Hobbes 1642

T Hobbes, *Elementorum philosophiæ sectio tertia de cive* (1642).

Hoekema 1998

AJ Hoekema, *Integraal Bestuur. De behoorlijkheid, effectiviteit en legitimiteit* (Amsterdam University Press 1998).

Hofmann 2007

H Hofmann, 'Good Administration in EU Law—A Fundamental Right?' (2007) Bulletin des Droits de l'Homme, Vol 13, 44–52.

Hofmann and Türk 2006

H Hofmann and A Türk, 'Policy Implementation' in HCH Hofmann and AH Türk (eds), *EU Administrative Governance* (Edward Elgar 2006).

Hofmann and Mihaescu 2013

H Hofmann and B Mihaescu, 'The Relation between the Charter's Fundamental Rights and the Unwritten General Principles of Law: Good Administration as the Test-Case' (2013) European Constitutional Law Review, Vol 9, No 1, 73–101.

Hofmann, Rowe, and Türk 2011

H Hofmann, G Rowe, and A Türk (eds), *Administrative Law and Policy of the European Union* (Oxford University Press 2011), 1–965.

Hofmann and others 2014

HCH Hofmann, J-P Schneider, and J Ziller, 'The Research Network on European Administrative Law's Project on EU Administrative Procedure—Its Concepts, Approaches and Results' (2014) REALaw, Vol 2, 45–64.

Horsten 2006

D Horsten, 'The Role played by the South African Human Rights Commission's Economic and Social Rights Reports in Good Governance in South Africa' (2006) Potchefstroom Electronic Law Journal (PER) 179 Potchefstroom Electronic Law Journal.

Howe 1999

G Howe, The Management of Public Inquiries (1999) The Political Quarterly, Vol 70, No 3, 294–304.

Huberts 2001

LWJC Huberts, *Corruption and Anti-Corruption Policies in the Netherlands, an Evaluation* (Transparency International, Berlin 2001).

Huberts 2012

LWJC Huberts, 'Visies op integriteit' in JHJ van den Heuvel, LWJC Huberts, and ER Muller (eds), *Integriteit: Integriteit en integriteitsbeleid in Nederland* (Kluwer 2012).

Huberts 2014

LWJC Huberts, *The Integrity of Governance, What is, What We Know, What is Done and Where to Go?* (Palgrave Macmillan 2014).

Hurley 1999

PJ Hurley, *A Concise Introduction to Logic* (Wadsworth 1999).

IMF 2018

IMF Factsheet, 'The IMF and Good Governance', 8 March 2018 at <https://www.imf.org/en/About/Factsheets/The-IMF-and-Good-Governance>.

Janssen 2016

O Janssen, *Administrative Law and its Territory* (Maastricht 2016).

Jones 2000

T Jones, 'Judicial Review and Codification' (2000) Legal Studies, Vol 20, No 517.

Jowell 2007

J Jowell, 'The Rule of Law and its Underlying Values' in J Jowell and D Oliver (eds), *The Changing Constitution* (Oxford University Press 2007).

Jowell 2011

J Jowell, *The Changing Constitution* (Oxford University Press 2011).

Kalbe 2003

P Kalbe in: von der Groeben and Schwarze (eds) 2003 Kommentar zum EU-EG-Vertrag, Band 4, 6th ed Art. 283 EG

Kańska 2004

K Kańska, 'Towards Administrative Human Rights in the EU. Impact of the Charter of Fundamental Rights' (2004) European Law Journal, Vol 10, No 3, 296–326.

Keefer 2004

Ph Keefer, 'A Review of the Political Economy of Governance: From Poverty Rights to Voice', World Bank Policy Research Working Paper 3315, May 2004.

Kelsen 1997

H Kelsen, *Introduction to the Problems of Legal Theory* (Clarendon Press 1997).

Kelsen 2009

H Kelsen, *General Theory of Law and State* (The Lawbook Exchange 2009).

Kelsen and Tucker 1967

H Kelsen and RW Tucker, *Principles of International Law* (2nd edn, Holt, Rinehart & Winston 1967).

Van Kersbergen and Van Waarden 2004

K van Kersbergen and F van Waarden, 'Governance as a Bridge between Disciplines: Cross-Disciplinary Inspiration Regarding Shifts in Governance and Problems of Governability, Accountability and Legitimacy' (2004) European Journal of Political Research, Vol 43, No 2, 143–71.

Kingsbury, Krisch, and Stewart 2005

B Kingsbury, N Krisch, and RB Stewart, 'The Emergence of Global Administrative Law' (2005) *Law and Contemporary Problems*, Vol 68, No 3–4, 15–62.

Kirby 1989

M Kirby, 'Effective Review of Administrative Acts—Hallmark of a Free and Fair Society', presented to 'Law in a Changing Society,' Legal Resources Centre of South Africa, Conference, Johannesburg (12–13 April 1989), 1–49.

Kirby 2000

M Kirby quoted in J Pope, *Confronting Corruption: The Elements of a National Integrity System* (Transparency International 2000).

Kloepfer 2002

M Kloepfer, *Informationsrecht* (Beck Juristischer Verlag Munich 2002).

Knill 1998

C Knill, *European Policies: The Impact of National Administrative Traditions* (Cambridge University Press 1998).

Konijnenbelt and Van Male 2014

W Konijnenbelt and RM van Male, *'Hoofdstukken van bestuursrecht'* (Deventer 2014).

Koopmans 2000

T Koopmans, 'General Principles of Law in European and International Systems of Law' in U Bernitz and J Nergelius (eds), *General Principles of European Community Law* (Kluwer 2000).

Koven 2008

S Koven, *Responsible Governance: A Case Study Approach* (ME Sharpe Publishers, Sydney 2008), 37.

Kumm 2007

M Kumm, 'Political Liberalism and the Structures of Rights' in G Pavlakos, *Law, Rights, Discourse: The Legal Philosophy of Robert Alexy* (Hart Publishing 2007).

Kummeling and Minderman 2002

HRBM Kummeling and GD Minderman, 'De Staten-Generaal als zelfstandige begrotingsautoriteit' (2002) Kamerstukken I, 2000/01, nr 312.

Kuusikko 2001

K Kuusikko, 'Good Administration and Legitimate Expectations: Some Comparative Aspects' (2001) European Public Law, Vol 7, No 3, 455–72.

Lauterpacht 1949

H Lauterpacht, 'Restrictive Interpretation and the Principle of Effectiveness in the Interpretation of Treaties' (1949) *British Yearbook of International Law*, Vol 26, 48–85.

Laws 1995, 1996

Sir John Laws, 'Land and Democracy' [1995] PL 72; 'The Constitution: Moral and Rights' [1996] PL 662.

De Leeuw 2011

M de Leeuw, 'The European Ombudsman's Role as a Developer of Norms of Good Administration' (2011) European Public Law, Vol 17, 349–68.

Lerner and Tetlock 1999

JS Lerner and Ph E Tetlock, 'Accounting for the Effects of Accountability' (1999) Psychological Bulletin, Vol 125, No2, 255–75.

Lessig 2009

L Lessig, 'Against Transparency. The Perils of Openness in Government', *The New Republic* (9 October 2009) <http://www.tnr.com/article/books-and-arts/against-transparency>.

Limpitlaw 2001

EM Limpitlaw, 'Is International Law Waterproof? The Impact of Technology on Oceans as Commons' (2001) Syracuse Journal of International Law and Commerce, Vol 29, No 1, 185–206.

Lipman and Stokes 2008

Z Lipman and R Stokes, 'The Technocrat is Back: Environmental Land-use Planning Reform in New South Wales' (2008) Environmental and Planning Law Journal, Vol 25, No 5, 305–23.

Loughlin 1992

M Loughlin, *Public Law and Political Theory* (Oxford University Press 1992).

Lowndes and others 2001

V Lowndes and others, 'Trends in Public participation: Part 2—Citizens' Perspectives' (2001) Public Administration, Vol 79, No 2, 445–55.

Lust 2007

S Lust, 'Administrative Law in Belgium' in RJGH Seerden (ed), *Administrative Law of the European Union, its Member States and the United States* (Intersentia 2007).

Macklem and others 2010

P Macklem and others, *Canadian Constitutional Law* (4th edn, Toronto 2010).

Madison 1787

J Madison, 'The Utility of the Union as a Safeguard Against Domestic Faction and Insurrection' (1787) The Federalist, No. 10.

McCandless 2001

HE McCandless, *A Citizen's Guide to Public Accountability: Changing the Relationship Between Citizens and Authorities* (Trafford 2001).

McColl 2010

R McColl, 'Freedom of Information—A New Paradigm', The 2010 Whitmore Lecture (15 September 2010) <http://www.lawlink.nsw.gov.au/lawlink/supreme_court/ll_sc.nsf/vwFiles/mccoll150910.pdf/$file/mccoll150910.pdf>, 1–30.

McConnachie 2000

A McConnachie, 'Direct Democracy: Government of the People, by the People, for the People' (March 2000) <http://www.sovereignty.org.uk/features/articles/dirdemoc.html>.

McMillan 2004

J McMillan, 'Ombudsman and the Rule of Law', address to the 'Public Law Weekend', Canberra (5–6 November 2004) <http://www.ombudsman.gov.au/files/5-6_November_2004_The_Ombudsman_and_the_rule_of_law.pdf>, 1–18.

McMillan 2010

J McMillian, 'Freedom of Information Reforms and Cultural Change', Paper presented at a UNESCO Conference to mark World Press Freedom Day, Brisbane (2 May 2010), 1–5.

McMillan 2012a

J McMillan, 'Processing of non-routine FOI requests by the Department of Immigration and Citizenship: Report of an own motion investigation', Office of the Australian Information Commissioner (26 September 2012) <http://www.oaic.gov.au/publications/reports/DIAC_FOI_own_motion_report_FINAL.pdf>, 1–25.

McMillan 2012b

J McMillan, 'Review of charges under the *Freedom of Information Act 1982:* Report to the Attorney-General', Office of the Australian Information Commissioner (February 2012), 1–98.

Marwan 2018

A Marwan, *Good Governance and Ethnic Minorities in Indonesia. A Comparative Law Perspective* (Utrecht 2018).

Masango 2002

R Masango, 'Public Participation: A Critical Ingredient of Good Governance' (2002) Politeia, Vol 21, 54.

Mendes 2009

J Mendes, 'Good Administration in EU Law and the European Code of Good Administrative Behaviour' (2009) EUI Working Papers Law, Vol 9, 1–13.

Mendes 2011

J Mendes, '*Participation in EU Rule-Making: A Rights-Based Approach* (Oxford University Press 2011).

Mihaescu Evans 2015

BC Mihaescu Evans, *The Right to Good Administration at the Crossroads of the Various Sources of Fundamental Rights in the EU Integrated Administrative System* (NOMOS 2015).

Mill 1859

John Stuart Mill, *On Liberty* (first published in 1859, reprinted in Harvard Classics, Vol 25, PF Collier & Son 1909).

Millet 2002

P Millet, 'The Right to Good Administration in European Law' (2002) Public Law, Vol 47, 309–22.

Minister Interior and Kingdom Relations 2013

See the letter of the Minister of the Interior and Kingdom Relations of 8 November 2013 with the research report of Tilburg University, and the discussions on the articles written for the Annual Conference of the Association of Constitutional Lawyers, Amsterdam, 13 December 2013, *Integriteit in politiek en bestuur.*

Minns 2007

O Minns, 'Hart's Rule of Recognition in Canada?' (2007) <http://minns.ca/owen/image/portfolio/rule-of-recognition-in-canada-20070507r2.pdf>.

Von Mohl 1866

R von Mohl, *Die deutsche Polizeiwissenschaft nach den Grundsatzen des Rectsstaats* (H Laupp Tuebingen 1866).

Mohnhaupt 1993

H Mohnhaupt, 1993/94, Acta Facultaties Politico-Iuridicae Universitatis Scientiarum Budapestinensis de Rolando Eotvos Nominatae, 45.

Montesquieu 1748

Ch L de Secondat Montesquieu, *L' Esprit des Lois* (first published in 1748, and reprinted Prometheus Books 2002).

Mori 2007

W Mori, 'The Role of Civil Society in the WTO-transparency, Participation and Efficiency' (2007) Murdoch University e-Law Journal, Vol 14, No 2, 252–64.

Morris 2012

S Morris, 'Review of the operation of the *Freedom of Information Act 1982* insofar as it applies to documents held by NBN Co. Ltd', Report to the Attorney-General (29 June 2012), 1–47.

Mulgan 2000

R Mulgan, 'Accountability: An Ever Expanding Concept?' (2000) Public Administration, Vol 78, No 3, 555–73.

Mulgan 2008

R Mulgan, 'Book Review: Transparency: The Key to Better Governance?' <http://www.davidheald.com/coverage/AJPA%20Mulgan%202008.pdf>, 237–39.

Mulreany 1991

M Mulreany, 'Economy, Efficiency and Effectiveness in the Public Sector: Key Issues' in TO Hardiman and M Mulreany, *Efficiency & Effectiveness in the Public Domain* (Institute of Public Administration 1991).

Munro 2001

CR Munro, *Studies in Constitutional Law* (Butterworths 2001).

Mutharika 1995

P Mutharika, *One Africa, One Destiny: Towards Democracy, Good Governance and Development*, Regional cooperation series (HSRC Press 1995).

Navarro and Moreso 1997

PE Navarro and JJ Moreso, 'Applicability and Effectiveness of Legal Norms' (1997) Law and Philosophy, Vol 16, No 2, 201–19.

Nehl 1999

HP Nehl, *Principles of Administrative Procedure in EC Law* (Hart Publishing 1999).

Nehl 2002

HP Nehl, *Europäisches Verwaltungsverfahren und Gemeinschaftsverfassung* (Duncker & Humblot GmbH Berlin 2002).

Nergelius 2000

J Nergelius, 'General Principles of Community Law in the Future: Some Remarks on their Scope, Applicability and Legitimacy' in U Bernitz and J Nergelius (eds), *General Principles of European Community Law* (The Hague 2000).

Neumann 2002

M Neumann, *The Rule of Law* (Ashgate Publishing Limited 2002).

Nicolai 1990

P Nicolai, *Beginselen van behoorlijk bestuur* (Kluwer 1990).

North Rhine-Westfalia 2001

Home Office of the State North Rhine-Westfalia (ed), *Leitfaden zum NWIFG* (2001).

O'Donnell 1999

G O'Donnell, 'Horizontal Accountability in New Democracies' in A Schedler, L Diamond, and M Plattner, *The Self-Restraining State: Power and Accountability in New Democracies* (Lynne Rienner London 1999).

O'Donnell 2004

G O'Donnell, 'The Quality of Democracy: Why the Rule of Law Matters' (2004) Journal of Democracy, Vol 15, No 4, 32–46.

OECD 1995

OECD, Participatory Development and Good Governance (Paris CEDEX 16 1995) <https://www.oecd.org/dac/accountable-effective-institutions/31857685.pdf>.

OECD 2001

OECD, *Governance in the 21st Century, Future Studies* (2001) <https://www.oecd.org/futures/17394484.pdf>.

Van Oenen 1994

G van Oenen, *Conventie en rechtsintrige; een visie op de rechtstheorie van Ronald Dworkin* (Tjeenk Willink 1994).

Oldenziel 2003

M Oldenziel, *Principles of Good Governance in Community Law. A Comparative Research on the Content of Principles of Good Governance in Case-law of the European Court of Justice, the Court of First Instance and the European Ombudsman and their Codification in Codes of Good Administrative Behaviour*, PhD thesis Utrecht University (Utrecht 2003).

Van Ommeren and Wolswinkel 2014

FJ van Ommeren and CJ Wolswinkel, 'Naar een Algemene wet bestuursrecht voor de EU' (NTB 2014), 7, 189–96

Orellana 2009

MA Orellana, 'WTO and Civil Society' in D Bethlehem et al (eds), *Oxford Handbook of International Trade Law* (Oxford University Press 2009), 671–94.

Osborne 1982

G Osborne, 'Inquisitorial Procedure in the Administrative Appeals Tribunal—A Comparative Perspective' (1982) Federal Law Review, Vol 13, 150.

Papadopoulou 1996

RE Papadopoulou, *Principes Généraux du droit en droit communautaire. Origines et concrétisation* (Sakkoulas and Bruylant 1996).

Parnell 2012

S Parnell, 'Both sides of politics must commit to improve FOI laws- unless they have something to hide', *The Australian* (27 September 2012) <http://www.theaustralian.com.au/news/foi/both-sides-of-politics-must-commit-to-improve-foi-laws-unless-they-have-something-to-hide/story-fn8r0e18-1226482131885>.

Partsch 1998

C Partsch, 'Brandenburgs Akteneinsichts- und Informationszugangsgesetz (AIG)—Vorbild für Deutschland?' (1998) Neue Juristische Wochenschrift, 2559.

Pauly 1999

LW Pauly, 'Good Governance and Bad Policy: The Perils of International Organizational Overextension' (1999) Review of International Political Economy, Vol 6, No 4.

Pfeffer 2006

K Pfeffer, *Das Recht auf eine gute Verwaltung* (Nomos 2006).

Pollitt and others 1999

C Pollitt and others, *Performance or Compliance?: Performance Audit and Public Management in Five Countries* (Oxford University Press 1999).

Pollitt 2003

C Pollitt, *The Essential Public Manager* (Open University Press/McGraw-Hill 2003).

Popelier 2000

P Popelier, 'Legal Certainty and Principles of Proper Law Making' (2000) European Journal of Law Reform, Vol 2, No 3, 312–42.

Popple 2011

J Popple, 'Freedom of Information: A Government Perspective' (2011) Australian Law Librarian, Vol 19, No 4, 256–64.

Popple 2012

J Popple, 'A Commonwealth Pro-Disclosure Culture—Implications and Opportunities' (August 2012) Keeping Good Companies, Vol 64, No 7, 401–4.

Prakke, De Reede, and Van Wissen 2001

L Prakke, JL de Reede, and GJM van Wissen, *Handboek Staatsrecht* (Kluwer 2001).

Préchal and De Leeuw 2007

S Préchal and M de Leeuw, 'Dimensions of Transparency: The Building Blocks for a New Legal Principle?' (2007) Review of European Administrative Law, Vol 1, No 1, 51–61.

Préchal and Widdershoven 2017

S Préchal and RJGM Widdershoven (eds), *Inleiding tot het Europees bestuursrecht*(4th edn, Ars Aequi 2017).

Ragnemalm 2000

H Ragnemalm, 'Leading by Example or Learning on Supremacy? Some Reflections on the Union, the Individual and the Protection of Fundamental Rights' in U Bernitz and J Nergelius (eds), *General Principles of European Community Law* (The Hague 2000).

Rawls 1999

J Rawls, *A Theory of Justice* (first published 1971 revised edn, Cambridge Harvard 1999).

Raz 1977

J Raz, 'The Rule of Law and its Virtue' (1977) The Law Quarterly Review, Vol 93, 195–202.

Raz 2003

J Raz, *The Concept of a Legal System. An Introduction to the Theory of Legal System* (Oxford University Press 2003).

Raz 2009

J Raz, *Between Authority and Interpretation* (Oxford University Press 2009).

Rhodes 1996

RAW Rhodes, 'The New Governance: Governing Without Government' (1996) Political Studies, Vol 44, No 4, 652–67.

Ricketson and Snell 2002

M Ricketson and R Snell 'Journalism: Investigation and Research', in S Tanner, *Journalism: Investigation and Research* (Sydney 2002).

Rietiker 2010

D Rietiker, 'The Principle of "Effectiveness" in the Recent Jurisprudence of the European Court of Human Rights: Its Different Dimensions and Its Consistency with Public International Law' (2010) Nordic Journal of International Law, Vol 79, No 2, 245–77.

Roberts 1998

A Roberts, 'Limited Access: Assessing the Health of Canada's Freedom of Information Laws', Freedom of Information Research Project, School of Policy Studies, Queen's University (April 1998) <http://faculty.maxwell.syr.edu/asroberts/>, 1–85.

Roberts 2006

A Roberts, 'The Glass Case', in *Blacked Out: Government Secrecy in the Information Age* (Cambridge University Press 2006).

Rocha 1997

EM Rocha, 'A Ladder of Empowerment' (1997) Journal of Planning Education and Research, Vol 17, No 1, 31–44.

Romzek and Dubnick 1998

BS Romzek and MJ Dubnick, 'Accountability' in JM Shafritz (ed), *International Encyclopaedia of Public Policy and Administration*, Vol 1: A–C (Westview Press 1998).

Rudd 2007

K Rudd, 'Government information: restoring trust and integrity', Election 2007 Policy Document <http://parlinfo.aph.gov.au/parlInfo/search/display/display.w3p;query=Id%3A%22library%2Fpartypol%2FEFRO6%22>.

Ruffert 2016

M Ruffert, *The Model Rules on EU Administrative Procedures: Adjudication* (Groningen: Europa Law Publishing 2016).

Sarat 1985

A Sarat, 'Legal Effectiveness and Social Studies of Law: On the Unfortunate Persistence of a Research Tradition' (1985) Legal Studies Forum, Vol 9, No 1, 23–32.

Sarat 1997

A Sarat, *Race, Law, and Culture—Reflections on Brown v Board of Education* (Oxford University Press 1997).

Sarat and Kearns 1993

A Sarat and TR Kearns, *Law in Everyday Life* (University of Michigan 1995).

Scheltema 2005

M Scheltema, *Het recht van de toekomst: de gevolgen van de internationalisering van het recht* (Deventer 2005)

Schimmelfennig and Sedelmeier 2004

F Schimmelfennig and U Sedelmeier, 'Governance by Conditionality: EU Rule Transfer to the Candidate Countries of Central and Eastern Europe' (2004) Journal of European Public Policy, Vol 11, No 4, 669–87.

Schlössels and Zijlstra 2017

RJN Schlössels and SE Zijlstra, *Bestuursrecht in de Sociale Rechtsstaat, band 1* (Deventer 2017).

Schmidt-Assmann 2003

E Schmidt-Assmann, 'Der Rechtsstaat' in J Isensee and HC Kirchhof (eds), *Handbuch des Staatsrechts*, Band II, III (CF Müller 2003).

Schmidt-Assmann 2006

E Schmidt-Assmann, *Das allgemeine Verwaltungsact als Ordnungsidee* (Springer 2006).

Schmidt-Assmann 2008

E Schmidt-Assmann, 'The Internationalization of Administrative Relations as a Challenge for Administrative Law Scholarship' (2008) German Law Journal, Vol 9, No 11, 2061–79.

Schmitt 1996

C Schmitt, *The Concept of the Political, translated and with an introduction by George Schwab* (The University of Chicago Press 1996).

Schneider und Marsch 2016

JP Schneider and N Marsch (eds), *ReNEUAL-Musterentwurf für ein EU-Verwaltungsverfahrensrecht* (Beck 2016).

Schröder 2007

M Schröder, 'Administrative Law in Germany' in *Administrative Law of the European Union, its Member States and the United States* (Intersentia 2007).

Schwarze 1992

J Schwarze, *European Administrative Law* (Sweet and Maxwell 1992).

Schwarze 1995

J Schwarze, 'Towards a Common European Public Law' (1995) European Public Law, Vol 1, No 2, 227–39.

Scott 2000

C Scott, 'Accountability in the Regulatory State' (2000) Journal of Law and Society, Vol 27, No 1, 38–60.

Seerden (ed) 2012

RJGH Seerden (ed), *Administrative Law of the European Union, its Member States and the United States*(2nd edn, Intersentia 2012).

Seerden (ed) 2018

RJGH Seerden (ed), *Administrative Law of the European Union, its Members and the United States Comparative Administrative Law* (Intersentia 2018).

Sennett 1980

R Sennett, *Authority* (Random House 1980).

Sepulveda and others 2004

M Sepulveda and others, *Human Rights Reference Handbook* (3rd edn, Costa Rica 2004).

Shen 2000

J Shen, 'National Sovereignty and Human Rights in a Positive Law Context' (2000) Brooklyn Journal of International Law, Vol 26, No 2, 417–46.

Shihata 2000

IFI Shihata, *The World Bank Legal Papers* (Martinus Nijhoff Publishers 2000).

Sinclair 1996

A Sinclair, 'The Chameleon of Accountability: Forms and Discourses' (1996) Accounting, Organisations and Society, Vol 20, No 2–3, 219–37.

Snell and Upcher 2002

R Snell and J Upcher, 'Freedom of Information and Parliament: A Limited Accountability Tool for a Key Constituency?' (2002) FOI Review Vol. 100, 35–41.

Sobota 1997

K Sobota, *Das Prinzip Rechtsstaat: Verfassungs- und verwaltungsrechtliche Aspekte, Jus Publicum*, Band 22 (Mohr Siebeck 1997).

Södermann 1997

J Södermann, *The Role of the European Ombudsman*, Speech at the 6th meeting of European National Ombudsmen (Israel September 1997).

Södermann 1998

JSödermann, *The Citizen, the Administration and Community Law*, general report prepared for the 1998 FIDE Congress (Sweden June 1998).

Södermann 2001

J Södermann, What is good administration? The European Ombudsman's Code of Good Administrative Behaviour, International Seminar *'The Ombudsmen and the European Union Law'* (Bucharest, Romania April 2001).

Soeteman 1992a

A Soeteman, 'R. Dworkin' in PB Cliteur and MA Loth (eds), *Rechtsfilosofen van de twintigste eeuw* (Gouda Quint 1992).

Soeteman 1992b

A Soeteman, 'Recht als interpretatief verschijnsel' (which is a section in his description of the work of Ronald Dworkin), in PB Cliteur and MA Loth (eds), *Rechtsfilosofen van de twintigste eeuw* (Gouda Quint 1992).

Spigelman 2005

Honourable JJ Spigelman, 'The Integrity Branch of Government—The Second Lecture in the 2004 National Lecture Series for the Australian Institute of Administrative Law', Sydney, February 2006, quoted in J McMillan, 'The Ombudsman and the Rule of Law' (2005) AIAL Forum, No 44, 1–16.

Squires 2004 Cov L J

N Squires, 'The Commission for Africa: The Poor are Rich?' (2004) Coventry Law Journal, Vol 45.

Stacey 1978

F Stacey, *Ombudsmen Compared* (Clarendon Press 1978).

Steur and Van der Groot 2006

B Steur and A van der Goot, 'De diagnose van burgerparticipatie op lokaal niveau' in D Huitema and others (eds), *De boel bij elkaar houden* (Vereniging voor Bestuurskunde 2006).

Stolk (ed) 2005

PJ Stolk (ed), *Transparency in Europe II* (The Netherlands Ministry of the Interior and Kingdom Relations 2005).

PJ Stolk and others, *Transparency in Europe 11: Public Access to Documents in the EU and its Member States* (Ministry of the Interior and Kingdom Relations, The Hague 2005).

Stouten 2012

M Stouten, *De witwasmeldplicht*, PhD thesis Utrecht University (The Hague 2012).

Stroink 1995

F Stroink, 'Judicial Control of the Administration's Discretionary Powers' in R Bakker, AW Heringa, and F Stroink (eds), *Judicial Control, Comparative Essays on Judicial Review*, Ius Commune, Band 16 (Maklu 1995).

Stubbs 2008

R Stubbs, 'Freedom of Information and Democracy in Australia and Beyond' (2008) Australian Journal of Political Science, Vol 43, No 4, 667–84.

Stuiveling 2003

S Stuiveling, *The Role of the Court of Audit in Promoting Good Governance* (The Hague, Netherlands Court of Audit 2003).

Taylor Saito 1998

N Taylor Saito, 'Justice Held Hostage: U.S. Disregard for International Law in the World War II Internment of Japanese Peruvians—A Case Study' (1998) Boston College Third World Law Review, Vol 19, No 1, 275–348.

Terrill 2000

G Terrill, 'Individualism and FOI Legislation' (2000) FOI Review No 87, 30–2.

Teubner 1984

G Teubner, 'Autopoiesis in Law and Society: A Rejoinder to Blankenburg' (1984) Law and Society Review, Vol 18, No 2, 291–301.

Teubner 1993

G Teubner, *Law as an Autopoietic System* (Blackwell 1993).

Theletsane 2014

KI Theletsane, 'Drawbacks in South Africa's Pursuit of Democratic Rule and Good Governance' (2014) Journal of Public Administration, Vol 49, No 3, 836–46.

Thompson 2007

AS Thompson, *Exporting Good Governance the Canadian Way*, A Report of the CIC Meeting on Canadian Development Aid and Good Governance Programming, Canadian International Council, 2007 <https://www.cigionline.org/sites/default/files/exporting_good_govemance the_canadian_way. Pdf>.

Timmermans 2014

C Timmermans, 'Developing Administrative Law in Europe: Natural Convergence or Imposed Uniformity—Some Concluding Observations' (2014) REALaw, Vol 2, 35–44.

Tomuschat 2003

C Tomuschat, *Human Rights. Between Idealism and Realism* (Oxford University Press 2003).

Torpman and Jörgensen 2005

J Torpman and F Jorgensen, 'Legal Effectiveness: Theoretical Developments on Legal Transplants' (2005) Archiv für Rechts- und Sozialphilosophie (ARSP), Vol 91, No 4, 515–34.

Transparency International 2012

Transparency International, 'Overview of Freedom of Information in Australia', 2012 <http://transparency.org.au/wp-content/uploads/2012/06/FOI_Summary_Information_06_10.pdf>.

Tridimas 2006

T Tridimas, *The General Principles of EU Law* (Oxford University Press 2006).

Tucker 1953

RW Tucker, 'The Principle of Effectiveness in International Law' in GA Lipsky, *Law and Politics in the World Community* (University of California Press 1953).

Turiaux 1995

A Turiaux, *Umweltinformationsgesetz* (CH Beck München 1995).

Tyler and Huo 2002

TR Tyler and YJ Huo, *Trust in the Law. Encouraging Public Cooperation with the Police and Courts* (Russell-Sage Foundation 2002).

Uhr 2005

J Uhr, *Ministerial Responsibility in Australia: 2005*, presented at the 2005 Constitutional Law Conference at the University of New South Wales (Sydney 2005).

UNDP 1994

UNDP, *Good Governance and Sustainable Human Development, Initiative for Change*, A UNDP policy document (New York 1994).

UNHCHR 2007

UNHCHR, *Good Governance Practices for the Protection of Human Rights* (United Nations, New York and Geneva 2007) <https://www.ohchr.org/Documents/Publications/GoodGovernance.pdf>.

Urbina 2002

S Urbina, *Legal Method and the Rule of Law* (Kluwer Law International 2002).

Van der Jagt 2006

JAE van der Jagt, *Milieuconvenanten gehandhaafd* (Den Haag 2006 Boom Juridische uitgevers).

Van der Vlies 1984

IC van der Vlies, *Het Wetsbegrip en Beginselen van Behoorlijke Regelgeving* (VUGA 1984).

Visegrády 2002

A Visegrády, 'Zur Effektivität des Rechts' in M Troper and A Verza (eds), *Legal Philosophy: General Aspect, Concepts, Rights and Doctrines: Proceedings of the 19th World Congress of the International Association for Philosophy (IVR), New York, 24–30 June 1999* (Steiner 2002).

Vucsán 1995

RL Vucsán, *Bestuursregelgeving en inspraak: een onderzoek naar de wenselijkheid van een algemeen recht op inspraak in de uitoefening van regelgevende bevoegdheden door bestuursorganen van de centrale overheid* (Kluwer 1995).

De Waal 1995

A de Waal, 'A Comparative Analysis of the Provisions of German Origin in the Interim Bill of Rights' (1995) South African Journal on Human Rights, Vol 11, No 1, 1–29.

De Waal 2002

A de Waal, 'What's in the "New Partnership for Africa's Development"?' (2002) International Affairs, Vol 78, No 3, 463–76.

De Waard 1987

BWN de Waard, *Beginselen van behoorlijke rechtspleging* (Tjeenk Willink 1987).

Wacks 2008

R Wacks, *The Philosophy of Law: A Very Short Introduction* (Oxford University Press 2008).

Wade and Forsyth 2009

HWR Wade and CF Forsyth, *Administrative Law* (Oxford University Press 2009).

Wakefield 2007

J Wakefield, *The Right to Good Administration* (Kluwer 2007).

Walker 1971

M Walker, *German Home Towns. Community, State, and General Estate, 1648–1871* (Cornell University Press 1971).

Walker 1980

DW Walker, *The Oxford Companion to Law* (Oxford University Press 1980).

Wegener 2002

B Wegener in T Schomerus, C Schrader, and B Wegener (eds), *Umweltinformationsgesetz* (2nd edn, Nomos Verlagsgesellschaft mbH & Co. KG Baden-Baden 2002).

Welsh 2007

J Welsh, *'Conclusion: Challenges and New Directions for Canada," Exporting Good Governance: Temptations and Challenges in Canada 's Aid Program, Waterloo* (Ontario, WLU Press 2007).

Werner 2002

WG Werner, 'State Sovereignty as an interpretive concept', Paper for the Round Table on Governance and International Legal Theory (Utrecht University 2002).

Weyers and Hertogh 2007

H Weyers and M Hertogh, *Legitimiteit betwist. Verkennend onderzoek naar de ervaren legitimiteit van het justitieoptreden* (WODC 2007).

Wiarda 1952

GJ Wiarda, *Algemene Beginselen van Behoorlijk Bestuur, preadvies Vereniging voor Administratief Recht* (Haarlem 1952).

Wibowo 2017

RA Wibowo, *Preventing Maladministration in Indonesian Public Procurement Law*, PhD thesis Utrecht University (Ridderprint 2017).

Widdershoven 2007

RJGM Widdershoven, 'European Administrative Law' in RJGH Seerden and F Stroink (eds), *Administrative Law of the European Union, its Member States and the United States* (Intersentia 2007).

Widdershoven 2014

RJGM Widdershoven, 'Developing Administrative Law in Europe: Natural Convergence or Imposed Uniformity?' (2014) REALaw, Vol 2, 5–17.

Widdershoven and others 2007

RJGM Widdershoven and others, *De Europese agenda van de Awb* (WODC 2007).

Wiedemann and Femers 1993

PM Wiedemann and S Femers, 'Public Participation in Waste Management Decision Making: Analysis and Management of Conflicts' (1993) Journal of Hazardous Materials, Vol 33, No 3, 355–68.

Van Wijk, Konijnenbelt, and Van Male 2005

HD Van Wijk, W Konijnenbelt, and RM Van Male, *Hoofdstukken van Bestuursrecht* (Elsevier Juridisch 2005).

Wilson 2012

IE Wilson, 'Peace, Order and Good Government: Archives in Society' (2012) Archives in Society, Vol 12, 235.

Witteveen 1991

W Witteveen, *Evenwicht van machten* (Tjeenk Willink 1991,).

Wolfe 2003

R Wolfe, 'Regulatory Transparency, Developing Countries, and the Fate of the WTO' (2003) World Trade Review, Vol 2, No 2, 157–82.

Woods 2000

N Woods, 'Good Governance in International Organizations' (2000) Global Governance, Vol 5, No 1, 39–61.

World Bank 1994

World Bank, Governance—the World Bank's experience. Development in practice (Washington DC, The World Bank 1994) <http://documents.worldbank.org/curated/en/711471468765285964/Governance-the-World-Banks-experience>.

World Bank 1997

World Bank, World Development report 1997, The State in a changing World (1997) <https://openknowledge.worldbank.org/handle/10986/5>.

Worm 2001

H Worm, Die Umsetzung der Umweltinformationsrichtlinie vom 13.6.1990 in Großbritannien und Deutschland sowie Umweltinformationsansprüche in der Schweiz (Universität Bonn Berlin 2001).

Wouters and Ryngaert 2005

JC Wouters and C Ryngaert, 'Good Governance: Lessons from International Organizations' in DM Curtin and RA Wessel (eds), *Good Governance in the EU* (Intersentia 2005).

Young 2017

AL Young, *Democratic Dialogue and the Constitution* (Oxford University Press 2017).

Zigirinshuti 2013

F Zigirinshuti, *Good Governance and Public Contracts*, PhD thesis Utrecht University (Boxpress 2013).

Zoellner 2006

CS Zoellner, 'Transparency: An Analysis of an Evolving Fundamental Principle in International Economic Law' (2006) Michigan Journal of International Law, Vol 27, No 2, 579–627.

Zum, Nollkaemper, and Peerenboom 2014

M Zum, A Nollkaemper, and R Peerenboom, *Rule of Law Dynamics. In an Era of International and Transnational Governance* (Cambridge University Press 201).

Zumbansen 2009

P Zumbansen, 'Law's Knowledge and Law's Effectiveness: Reflections from Legal Sociology and Legal Theory' (2009) CLPE research paper No 11/2009 <http://ssrn.com/abstract=1415565> or <http://dx.doi.org/10.2139/ssrn.1415565>.

Zywicki 2003

TJ Zywicki, 'The Rule of Law, Freedom, and Prosperity', Law and economics working papers (George Mason University School of Law 2003) <http://www.law.gmu.edu/assets/files/publications/working_papers/02-20.pdf>.

Index